New Techniques for Brand Management in the Healthcare Sector

Ana Pinto Borges
European Business School and Research Group, ISAG (NIDISAG), Portugal

Paula Rodrigues
Lusíada University of Porto, Portugal

A volume in the Advances in Marketing, Customer Relationship Management, and E-Services (AMCRMES) Book Series

IGI Global
PUBLISHER of TIMELY KNOWLEDGE

Published in the United States of America by
IGI Global
Business Science Reference (an imprint of IGI Global)
701 E. Chocolate Avenue
Hershey PA, USA 17033
Tel: 717-533-8845
Fax: 717-533-8661
E-mail: cust@igi-global.com
Web site: http://www.igi-global.com

Library of Congress Cataloging-in-Publication Data

Names: Borges, Ana Pinto, 1980- editor.
Title: New techniques for brand management in the healthcare sector / Ana Pinto Borges and Paula Rodrigues, editors.
Description: Hershey, PA : Business Science Reference, [2020] | Includes bibliographical references and index. | Summary: "This book explores the diffusion of new marketing knowledge, tendencies, and qualitative and quantitative methods for brand management in the private, public, and social health sectors and examines the movement from healthcare as a priceless commodity to one that can be, and is, commodified"-- Provided by publisher.
Identifiers: LCCN 2019047044 (print) | LCCN 2019047045 (ebook) | ISBN 9781799830344 (hardcover) | ISBN 9781799830351 (paperback) | ISBN 9781799830368 (ebook)
Subjects: LCSH: Medical care--Marketing. | Branding (Marketing) | Medical tourism--Marketing.
Classification: LCC RA410.56 .N49 2020 (print) | LCC RA410.56 (ebook) | DDC 362.1068/8--dc23
LC record available at https://lccn.loc.gov/2019047044
LC ebook record available at https://lccn.loc.gov/2019047045

This book is published in the IGI Global book series Advances in Marketing, Customer Relationship Management, and E-Services (AMCRMES) (ISSN: 2327-5502; eISSN: 2327-5529)

British Cataloguing in Publication Data
A Cataloguing in Publication record for this book is available from the British Library.

For electronic access to this publication, please contact: eresources@igi-global.com.

Advances in Marketing, Customer Relationship Management, and E-Services (AMCRMES) Book Series

Eldon Y. Li
National Chengchi University, Taiwan & California Polytechnic State University, USA

ISSN:2327-5502
EISSN:2327-5529

MISSION

Business processes, services, and communications are important factors in the management of good customer relationship, which is the foundation of any well organized business. Technology continues to play a vital role in the organization and automation of business processes for marketing, sales, and customer service. These features aid in the attraction of new clients and maintaining existing relationships.

The Advances in Marketing, Customer Relationship Management, and E-Services (AMCRMES) Book Series addresses success factors for customer relationship management, marketing, and electronic services and its performance outcomes. This collection of reference source covers aspects of consumer behavior and marketing business strategies aiming towards researchers, scholars, and practitioners in the fields of marketing management.

COVERAGE

- E-Service Innovation
- B2B marketing
- Online Community Management and Behavior
- Social Networking and Marketing
- Web Mining and Marketing
- Relationship Marketing
- Data mining and marketing
- CRM and customer trust
- Customer Retention
- Mobile Services

IGI Global is currently accepting manuscripts for publication within this series. To submit a proposal for a volume in this series, please contact our Acquisition Editors at Acquisitions@igi-global.com or visit: http://www.igi-global.com/publish/.

The Advances in Marketing, Customer Relationship Management, and E-Services (AMCRMES) Book Series (ISSN 2327-5502) is published by IGI Global, 701 E. Chocolate Avenue, Hershey, PA 17033-1240, USA, www.igi-global.com. This series is composed of titles available for purchase individually; each title is edited to be contextually exclusive from any other title within the series. For pricing and ordering information please visit http://www.igi-global.com/book-series/advances-marketing-customer-relationship-management/37150. Postmaster: Send all address changes to above address.

Titles in this Series

For a list of additional titles in this series, please visit: www.igi-global.com/book-series

Impact of ICTs on Event Management and Marketing
Kemal Birdir (Mersin University, Turkey) Sevda Birdir (Mersin University, Turkey) Ali Dalgic (Isparta University of Applied Sciences, Turkey) and Derya Toksoz (Mersin University, Turkey)
Business Science Reference • © 2021 • 357pp • H/C (ISBN: 9781799849544) • US $195.00

Building Consumer-Brand Relationship in Luxury Brand Management
Paula Rodrigues (Lusíada University of Porto, Portugal) and Ana Pinto Borges (Instituto Superior de Administração e Gestão, Portugal)
Business Science Reference • © 2021 • 318pp • H/C (ISBN: 9781799843696) • US $225.00

Innovations in Digital Branding and Content Marketing
Subhankar Das (Duy Tan University, Vietnam) and Subhra Rani Mondal (Duy Tan University, Vietnam)
Business Science Reference • © 2021 • 311pp • H/C (ISBN: 9781799844204) • US $195.00

Handbook of Research on Applied AI for International Business and Marketing Applications
Bryan Christiansen (Global Training Group, Ltd, UK) and Tihana Škrinjarić (University of Zagreb, Croatia)
Business Science Reference • © 2021 • 702pp • H/C (ISBN: 9781799850779) • US $295.00

Handbook of Research on Technology Applications for Effective Customer Engagement
Norazah Mohd Suki (Universiti Utara Malaysia, Malaysia)
Business Science Reference • © 2021 • 391pp • H/C (ISBN: 9781799847724) • US $295.00

Leveraging Consumer Behavior and Psychology in the Digital Economy
Norazah Mohd Suki (Universiti Malaysia Sabah, Malaysia) and Norbayah Mohd Suki (Universiti Utara Malaysia, Malaysia)
Business Science Reference • © 2020 • 299pp • H/C (ISBN: 9781799830429) • US $195.00

Analyzing the Strategic Role of Neuromarketing and Consumer Neuroscience
Dincer Atli (Uskudar University, Turkey)
Business Science Reference • © 2020 • 304pp • H/C (ISBN: 9781799831266) • US $225.00

Managing Customer Experiences in an Omnichannel World
Taşkın Dirsehan (Marmara University, Turkey)
Business Science Reference • © 2020 • 300pp • H/C (ISBN: 9781799850069) • US $195.00

IGI Global
PUBLISHER of TIMELY KNOWLEDGE

701 East Chocolate Avenue, Hershey, PA 17033, USA
Tel: 717-533-8845 x100 • Fax: 717-533-8661
E-Mail: cust@igi-global.com • www.igi-global.com

Table of Contents

Detailed Table of Contents

The fierce competition in the healthcare sector has forced the hospitals to go for branding. The hospitals have various options like print, radio, TV, and digital media for conducting their brand management exercise. The analysis showed that the best hospitals around the globe have focused more on social media marketing for their brand-building exercise. This study conducted a rigorous structured literature review to understand the best practices for healthcare branding using social media tools. The study also conducted a benchmark analysis of social media marketing efforts of the leading global hospitals. It also analyzed the popular online healthcare communities to find the best social media marketing practices adopted for hospital brand building. The practical suggestions for how to leverage the various social media channels for better hospital brand building have also been highlighted.

Reputations of hospitals were traditionally built on the successful treatment of patients, but today advertising and promotions are used by hospitals as they brand themselves. Patients have become customers, and they are enticed by packaged rates and freebies. Hospitals are operating like airlines, advertising their special offers, package rates, and comfortable services. This approach begs the question: Is a hospital a brand like Gucci, which few can afford, or does it have a larger purpose in society? This chapter argues for hospitals to serve society. Their real branding must come from how they serve patients and not from advertising. The chapter draws on the success of the Aravind Eye Hospital and Narayana Hrudayalaya in India, which have adopted a Walmart approach to reduce costs of complex medical procedures, serving the larger society. Such hospitals represent highly successful branding that draws from an ethical rather than a marketing approach that arises from a genuine desire to fulfill human needs rather than frills and fancies that marketing practitioners are familiar with.

The brand NHS (SNS Serviço Nacional de Saúde) is a registered brand. In 2015, a new legal regime on health advertising practices was introduced. This regime set a more rigid penalty framework, including pecuniary and ancillary sanctions, applied to the undue use of the brand NHS by private providers and disloyal advertising, protecting the brand's reputation and increasing patients' trust. The objective of this chapter was to discuss the undue use of the brand NHS, in Portugal, by private providers, and its impact on brand reputation. The main conclusions are the cases of health advertising and undue use of the brand NHS have been reduced under the new regime; the sanctions applied after 2015 varied from 500 euros to 1,500 euros, which reveals a small financial impact for providers; this reduction could be justified by the negative impact on the image of the healthcare provider under an administrative offense process.

Brand researchers and practitioners acknowledge that brands have the power to create emotional relationships between customers and enterprises. Moreover, it is known that brands can sometimes reflect the strategic vision of a firm. The aim of this chapter is to capture the creation of an identity for a new brand and to create a framework to better manage customer brand engagement in social media. To the best of this author's knowledge, this research creates a new framework that allows managers better handling their social media strategy regarding engagement. This study contributes to the lack of studies regarding brand management in SMEs, found by Krake, Wong and Merrilees, and Merrilees, and more particularly, it addresses Ojasalo et al.'s gap regarding the few literature research about brand management in SMEs. Moreover, it provides some understanding of customer brand engagement evidenced through social media, which, according to Wallace et al., continues to present challenges.

The purpose of this study is to understand the main determinants that influence consumer decision-making processes applied to the purchase of the brand Aspirin. For this, a set of explanatory variables was considered that not only translated the general health habits of the population but also two variables that measure the establishment of a strong emotional relationship with the brand: self-brand engagement and brand love. The authors used a survey to collect the data, and in their treatment, they applied a factorial analysis and a logistic regression to explain consumer behavior. Emotional factors (self-brand engagement

Foreword

As a response to the threat to reduced margins and business growth rates, companies and other organizations in all industries (including healthcare organizations) have, gradually, invested in creating new points of difference: their brands. The academic and professional literature on branding reveals that brands have evolved from a one-dimensional perspective to currently be recognized as a complex, multidimensional and evolutionary entity. It also conceptualizes its nature as a mechanism to achieve a competitive advantage, an interface between the company and consumers, and a system of meaning. Successful brands evolute from mere trademarks to become valuable intangible business or organizational assets. In its recent report “Best global brands 2020”, Interbrand (2020) stressed that “…consumers are beginning to see their consumption choices as votes of confidence.”, and identified three critical priorities for brands in the future: brand leadership, engagement and relevance.

Furthermore, brands are built and activated within specific contexts. The ongoing digital revolution will certainly accelerate and intensify its impacts on the way brands are managed, involving new computing technologies and other disruptive technologies. The current pandemic crisis has also been one of the biggest global challenges for all types of brands and is affecting the brand’s role and it has caused many significant mutations, including the healthcare industry. When this pandemic eventually recedes, they will have to continue to accommodate new opportunities, needs, attitudes and behaviours. Brand leaders must take immediate action to meet higher consumer expectations in the postcrisis era.

Broadly, brand management can be defined as an all-encompassing term to describe marketing techniques and approaches for boosting the overall value and reputation of a brand and its products over time. Modern brand management must be understood as a holistic, iterative and interactive process, of an essentially creative, incremental and differentiating nature, consisting in the challenge of creating, in a consistent way, added value in the minds of consumers, which translate into unique experiences for consumers. Keller and Swaminathan (2020, p. 52), argue that “brand management may be more difficult than ever” in this Digital Era, and identify the new complex challenges faced by brand managers, namely: availability of new technologies, downward pressures on prices, ubiquitous connectivity, sharing information, unexpected sources of competition, disintermediation and reintermediation, alternative sources of information about product quality, winner-takes-all markets, media transformation, and relevance of customer-centricity. Furthermore, those responsible for the healthcare sector brands should focus their attention on the following new key areas: co-creation of brands, brand engagement, digital communications, social media paid channels, mobile marketing, influencer marketing, and content marketing.

According to a recent study by Deloitte (2020), the healthcare industry is also facing other specific strategic challenges: rising costs, changing patient demographics, new consumer expectations and market entrants, complex health and technology ecosystems, innovative care delivery models, data interoperability, and new employment models to build a smart health ecosystem, among others. That study identified technologies such as cloud computing, 5G, Artificial Intelligence, Natural Language Processing, and Internet of Medical Things, that can help streamline health care delivery, align it with changing consumer preferences, and may contribute to a more effective brand performance.

It turns out that the research on branding in healthcare entities has captured a limited attention in the academic and professional literature, despite its economic size, relevance and growth dynamics. The healthcare industry includes businesses that provide medical services, manufacture medical equipment or drugs, provide medical insurance, or otherwise facilitate the provision of healthcare to patients (Investopedia, 2020), and all these entities compete in the most competitive industry and in an environment of enormous complexity (Fortenberry, 2010). Consequently, in an intense and ever-increasing rivalry context, branding becomes a critical mechanism for achieving success, through a sustainable competitive advantage. Healthcare statistics show that it's one of the largest and the fastest-growing industries in the world, it takes more than 10% of the GDP of most developed countries, it was worth $8.45 trillion in 2018, and that global healthcare spending could reach over $10 trillion by 2022 (Policyadvice, 2020).

In the academic literature, conceptually, healthcare branding is mainly been embedded in the service branding context. Essentially, the research on healthcare brands shows that they contribute to transmit an unique meaning and personal experience to consumers, and create an emotional connection and relationship between the consumer and the brand (Kemp et al., 2014). According to Evans et al. (2015, p. 24), "health branding applies marketing principles to promote and produce behavior change as a public good by specifying how brand associations and beliefs can in turn influence behavior".

These are the fundamental reasons for considering this book to be very timely and indispensable to read. It addresses the relevant topic of brand management in the healthcare industry and provides important theoretical contributions to the branding literature related to this strategic sector, with applied case studies. It presents a series of 11 chapters, and covers a fairly broad, relevant and updated topics, including the role of social media in hospital management, hospitals as social brands, branding and marketing in the pharmaceutical industry, medical tourism, happiness and well-being experience in health, rebranding in medical tourism and health wellness, the undue use of the brand NHS, customer brand engagement, and consumer decision-making from a beloved brand. The findings of the selected papers provide relevant insights for healthcare administrators, clinicians, brand managers, students, and other stakeholders, that may gain an understanding of the relevant challenges and key issues of branding, in the context of Digital Era and the pandemic crisis.

A few final words for the editors of this book, Paula Rodrigues and Ana Pinto Borges, who are to be congratulated for the excellent choice of its object of study, which will certainly influence and inspire all those who read it.

Victor Tavares
European Business School and Research Center in Business Sciences and Tourism (CICET-FCVC), ISAG, Portugal

REFERENCES

Deloitte. (2020). *2020 Global Health Care Outlook, Laying a foundation for the future*. Deloitte.

Evans, D., Blitstein, J., Vallone, D., Post, S., & Nielsen, W. (2015). Systematic review of health branding: Growth of a promising practice. *Translational Behavioral Medicine*, *5*(1), 24–36. doi:10.100713142-014-0272-1 PMID:25729450

Fortenberry, J. L. (2010). *Healthcare marketing: tools and techniques* (3rd ed.). Jones and Bartlett Publishers.

Interbrand. (2020). *Best Global Brands 2020*. Available at: Interbrand_Best_Global_Brands 2020.pdf

Investopedia. (2020). *Healthcare Sector*. Author.

Keller, L. K., & Swaminathlan, V. (2020). *Strategic Brand Management* (5th ed.). Pearson.

Kemp, E., Jillapalli, R., & Becerra, E. (2014). Healthcare branding: Developing emotionally based consumer brand relationships. *Journal of Services Marketing*, *28*(2), 126–137. doi:10.1108/JSM-08-2012-0157

Policyadvice. (2020). *The State of Health Care Industry*. Author.

Preface

At the international level, the health systems assume different types of structures, considering that the Government assumes the guarantee of health care as a citizen's right or delegate to the private or social sector the provision of health care. Challenges are ambitious, because the health care providers act in a context of high political, economic, social and technological pressure.

Irrespective of the legal sphere and type of care (primary, secondary or continuous), providers must ensure that users benefit from quality healthcare through the efficient use of resources. In the case of good health, the pressure also increases in relation to the patients' equal treatment, responsiveness and affordability.

Management and marketing have been playing an important role in this sector. More specifically, the importance of branding is growing in the health care market. The chance for branding in health care is determined by the challenge of increasing and improving the consumer's choice. That's something to which providers and health systems, in general, have not been familiarized.

The health sector is continuously changing. The key factors driving the change include innovation (new medicines and technologies), ageing population, the evolution of online information in different platforms and lifestyle changes. We observed an increasingly informed and more demanding patient. In this context, brands' reputation matters more than ever before.

Essentially, health care providers face a high level of competition and brand management tools are essential for their survival. Why is brand management so essential? In fact, successful businesses are the ones that have the capacity of successfully market their brand.

In strategic marketing, brand management is a set of techniques applied to improve the perceived value of a product or service. Effective brand management creates loyal customers/patients through positive brand association and has a positive impact on finance results. It is clear that this demand for market performance is more evident in the private health market, but the public sector must necessarily begin to be bolder in strategies and less dependent on governments.

Being more futuristic, all brand management strategies should be applied across the board to all providers, regardless of their legal sphere. Each and every provider must have a clear regarding the i) vision, mission and objectives, ii) their target market and iii) the brand itself. These three criteria are fundamental to start the development of a brand management strategy. It is important not to forget that we are dealing with a product (a good) that is essential in people's lives - health. In this particular case, the needs are often unfulfilled. Brand management will deal with tangible factors such as the product, image, price, packaging, and so on. But intangible factors play an important role, namely the brand experience. The strategy implies having customers/patients and employees (physicians, nurses, and other health professionals) building emotional attachments and translate them into strong loyalties. This type of good / product carries a high emotional burden that can make this market complex, but at the same time very interesting to be studied.

This book intends to address the brand management in the health sector – whether in the private, public or social sectors – and search to cover the full range of health care services. The book aims to contribute to the field of brand management in the health sector by providing a high-quality vehicle for the diffusion of new marketing knowledge, trends and qualitative and quantitative methods.

The book comprises 11 chapters covering different topics within brand management in the health sector.

Chapter 1 intends to understand the best practices for healthcare branding using social media tools. It also presents the common online healthcare communities to find out the best social media marketing practices implemented for hospital brand building.

Chapter 2 evaluates the hospitals as social brands. This chapter shows the possibility of building brands by serving society. The study draws on the triumph of the Aravind Eye Hospital and Narayana Hrudayalaya in India, which have implemented a Wal-Mart method to cut costs related to complex medical procedures, supplying the larger society.

Chapter 3 highlights the tendencies in which Pharmaceutical branding has progressed over the years into something very different in today's world, through the presentation of the branding activities that are carried out by the four types of pharmaceutical products which include the Patented products, Generics, Branded Generics, and the over-the-counter market.

Chapter 4 addresses the pharmaceutical promotion. The chapter reviews all the important promotional instruments, such as "free drug samples", "gifts", "CME sponsor", "journal advertising" and "honorarium".

Chapter 5 studies a niche market – senior citizens. This chapter identifies the main dimensions of overall experiences in senior medical tourism. The results will help the managers and marketing researchers to define strategies, describing the services in the senior market and identifying which services' quality most significantly influence customers' recommendations.

Chapter 6 conceptualises medical tourism as a sub-segment of health tourism. The authors present an empirical study related to the production of a snapshot of medical tourism in the countries that first started to capitalise on it.

Chapter 7 describes the value of happiness and well-being in unique health experiences and the effect on satisfaction and loyalty in consumer's health through a qualitative methodology.

Chapter 8 studies the importance of brand management (rebranding) in specific contexts of medical tourism, health and wellness. This study aims at discussing brand management in healthcare management and medical tourism contexts.

Chapter 9 evaluates, for the first time, the Brand National Health Service. This chapter discusses the undue use of this brand, in Portugal, by private providers, and its impact on brand reputation.

Chapter 10 evaluates the creation of an identity for a new brand and the creation of a framework to improve customer brand engagement in social media. This chapter creates a new tool that allows managers a better handling as far as their social media strategy regarding engagement is concerned.

Chapter 11 shows the main determinants that influence consumer decision-making processes applied to the purchase of the brand Aspirin. It is highlighted that the self-brand engagement and brand love are the most important factors in the consumer decision-making process.

Ana Pinto Borges
European Business School and Research Group, ISAG (NIDISAG), Portugal

Paula Rodrigues
Lusíada University of Porto, Portugal

Acknowledgment

All the chapters were double-blind review. The editors would like to acknowledge the help of all the people involved in this project and, more specifically, to the authors and reviewers that took part in the review process. Without their support, this book would not have become a reality.

First, the editors would like to thank each one of the authors for their contributions. Our sincere gratitude goes to the chapter's authors who contributed their time and expertise to this book.

Second, the editors wish to acknowledge the valuable contributions of the reviewers regarding the improvement of quality, coherence, and content presentation of chapters. Most of the authors also served as referees; we highly appreciate their double task.

Finally, a special acknowledgement to Isabel Cristina Barbosa, a student of a Master scholarship in Management, of COMEGI (Research Centre in Organizations, Markets and Industrial Management) and Universidade Lusíada – Norte.

Ana Pinto Borges
European Business School and Research Group, ISAG (NIDISAG), Portugal

Paula Rodrigues
Lusíada University of Porto, Portugal

Chapter 1
Role of Social Media in Hospital Branding:
Insights for Marketing Practitioners

Preeti Nayal
National Institute of Industrial Engineering (NITIE), India

Neeraj Pandey
https://orcid.org/0000-0002-6238-6397
National Institute of Industrial Engineering (NITIE), India

ABSTRACT

The fierce competition in the healthcare sector has forced the hospitals to go for branding. The hospitals have various options like print, radio, TV, and digital media for conducting their brand management exercise. The analysis showed that the best hospitals around the globe have focused more on social media marketing for their brand-building exercise. This study conducted a rigorous structured literature review to understand the best practices for healthcare branding using social media tools. The study also conducted a benchmark analysis of social media marketing efforts of the leading global hospitals. It also analyzed the popular online healthcare communities to find the best social media marketing practices adopted for hospital brand building. The practical suggestions for how to leverage the various social media channels for better hospital brand building have also been highlighted.

INTRODUCTION

The high internet penetration has enabled quick dissemination of information about various service options to the customers including hospital services (Ahadzadeh, Sharif & Ong, 2018; Patwardhan, Pandey & Dhume, 2017). The advent of web 2.0 gave popularity to social media in healthcare industry (Wang, Huang, & Gan, 2016). 73% of people in the USA are active in at least one social media platform (Patel, 2015). Social media refers to a set of online interactive communication channels through which users can create online communities to create and share information and content quickly, efficiently and in

DOI: 10.4018/978-1-7998-3034-4.ch001

real-time. This resulted in interesting consumer insights for the hospitals and inputs for enhancing their branding by improving healthcare services. Microblogs, social networking sites, online forums, wikis, virtual reality, and media-sharing sites are the various types of social media.

Generally, social media is used for commercial businesses to create brand awareness, shaping attitudes, engaging customers and knowing customer views and opinions (Pandey and Shinde 2019; Pandey and Singh, 2012; Smith, Blazovich, and Smith, 2015). The increasing use of social media use in healthcare has led to nomenclature of terms like "Health 2.0" and "Medicine 2.0" (Eysenbach, 2008). Literature has categorized social media in two groups for the patients: - (a) online health communities and (b) web base social networks (Kordzadeh, 2016). Online health communities' are formed to discuss health-related issues online such as WebMD, Practo, etc. Web-based social networks are general-purpose social networking sites such as Facebook, Youtube, Instagram, etc (De Maetino et al., 2017). Social media has changed the traditional healthcare system by discussing health-related information on online platforms (Li and Wang, 2017). Myers, Kudsi & Ghaaferi, (2017) reported that in surgery learning from other's experience is quite helpful. The social media such as Facebook, Twitter, etc. provides a platform to the surgeons to get connected. Such platforms help them to enhance their practice and to improve patient health. For example, International Hernia Collaboration, a Facebook group provides a platform to share experiences and ideas on a particular medical condition or practice (Myers et al., 2017). The increased use of smartphones and tablets has further accelerated the use of social media for healthcare information as a consumer now spending more time online (Pentescu, Cetină, & Orzan, 2015). Smartphones are easy to carry anywhere and anytime, hence user can access health-related information in real-time besides participating actively in health-related discussions (Benetoli, Chen, & Aslani, 2017). The hospital system is becoming more patient-oriented where social media and digital technologies have started playing a major role (Househ and Kushniruk, 2014).

Healthcare professionals use social media to analyse user opinion about healthcare issues (Frost, Okun, Vaughan, Heywood & Wicks, 2011; Ngai, Tao, Moon, 2015). This also enables hospitals to resolve the patient doubt and allow them to follow a discussion on a particular topic. Thus, the social media helps patient by saving their time and provides timely information about various healthcare options available in the vicinity (Li, Wang, Lin & Hajli, 2018). Few physicians are even using social media to be in directly touch with their patients to get feedback about their health and for giving them further health advice (Patwardhan, Pandey and Dhume, 2014; Ventola, 2014).

Pentescu et al., (2015) argued that although social media is vastly used in other sectors, it's in the embryonic stage in hospital industry. Furthermore, Li and Wang (2017) also said that despite various advantages of social media, there are some challenges and risks associated with this. One reason could be that healthcare data is more sensitive, so it's become more difficult to identify patterns, performing data analysis and using these to enhance healthcare services (Abirami and Askarunisa, 2017). The other reasons are the availability of poor data, risk to damage professional image, privacy risk to patient medical condition, legal issues (Ventola, 2014), user consent to share health-related information (McGowan et al.,2012; Li et al., 2018) and influence on patient-physician relationship (Benetoli et al., 2017). Smailhodzic, Hooijsma, Boonstra, & Langley, (2016) said that biased articles or discussion forums to promote a particular brand could be another potential risk.

Literature has shown that the potential of social media has not been utilized in hospitals to its fullest extent (Li et al., 2018). Previous research has reported that its implementation has faced several issues (Househ and Kushniruk, 2014; Lim, 2016). However, it has been noted that even though hospital industry is gradually adopting social media, academic research is still at an embryonic stage. Therefore, more number of studies are required to unearth potential social media impact in healthcare 2.0. Against this background, the present study aims to answer the following questions:

How much research has been done so far on adoption of social media in hospital industry and what are the possible future directions?

In addition to systematic literature review, it follows a case-based approach by analysing social media adoption among various hospitals and also popular online communities related to healthcare.

The structure of the study is as follows: first section explains the methodology, second section conducts the review and draw themes based on review. Third section has taken cases of hospital and online healthcare communities and analysed their social media activities. Lastly, discussion and conclusion have been proposed followed by recommending healthcare policies for social media-based hospital brand and future research directions.

METHODOLOGY

This study has adopted two methods to analyse social media impact in hospital industry viz. systematic literature review (SLR), and case-based approach for hospitals and online healthcare communities.

The present study follows SLR process with three steps as proposed by Tranfield et al. (2003): (a) plan for review, (b) conducting review, and (c) dissemination of the results. We identified the need for the review after finding a void in the social media usage in the hospital industry. Literature suggested that the filed is still at embryonic stage and requires further research. Inclusion and exclusion criteria were also decided in the first phase. Those articles were selected which meet the criteria such as published in a peer-reviewed journal, full-text availability to the author, social media effects are clearly analysed, written in English, and articles either qualitative or quantitative in nature. The articles which had not conducted any qualitative and quantitative studies were excluded from the review process.

This research used the definition of social media provided by Kaplan and Haenlein (2010) as "a group of Internet-based applications that build on the ideological and technological foundations of Web 2.0, and that allow the creation and exchange of User Generated Content". "Users of social media in hospital industry" refers to healthcare professionals, patients, pharmacists, medical students and those people who participate in sharing the health-related information in these social media sites. Hospital industry can benefit from social media in multiple ways: by providing an effective way to improve patient health, and by enhancing knowledge of medical professionals (Smailhodzic et al., 2016). In the hospital industry, social media may be used by patients, healthcare professionals and researchers for sharing latest updates and opinions in the medical domain in an efficient way (Pinho-Costa et al., 2016). Social media platform enables seamless information dissemination among multiple users about best practices and success stories in the hospital industry. This helps users to learn from the experiences of the real word with same health conditions and able to make an informed decision about their problems (Leek, Canning, and Houghton, 2016).

In the second phase, databases like EBSCO, Proquest, ABI Inform, Science Direct, Emerald Insight, and Google Scholar were searched for downloading the articles. To identify the articles, the following keywords were searched:(a)"social media" or "social networking sites" or "digital marketing" or "online community" or "Facebook" or "Twitter" (b) "patient" or "hospital"(c) "healthcare" or "doctor" or "health". Furthermore, we focused on articles published till 2020. Books, monographs, and conference papers were excluded from the analysis. 95 relevant papers were short-listed by this inclusion and exclusion criteria. These papers were categorized by keyword searches and themes, and the abstracts of each article were assessed for further categorization. Finally, after this exercise and also going through the full text of the papers, a total of 21 articles were selected for further investigation.

Second, a case-based approach was followed for social media branding of 12 hospitals and social media activities of 5 popular online communities. The twelve hospitals were analysed for their presence in various social media platforms such as Facebook, Twitter, YouTube, LinkedIn, Pinterest, Instagram, Snapchat, and Blogs. Secondly, five most popular online communities such as PatientsLikeMe have been analysed on the basis of how these communities were helping toward enhancing better healthcare services, better patient-professional healthcare relationships, and information sharing. The thematic areas and future research directions were also reported by analysing these twenty articles and cases.

Critical Analysis and Review of Literature

The review of the literature in healthcare social media critically evaluated the methods and context of research along with the findings. The key themes identified were:

Education and Learning Platform: The evolution of social media had offered a new way for medical education as it provides online visuals to the users. Hanzel et al. (2018) stated that social media such as Twitter should be used to share the advancements in medical research. It also offers useful medical information on emerging issues. Furthermore, the study added that the blogs and videos shared online helps young medical professional to educate on a particular topic. Yakar (2019) said that Instagram could be used for an educational purposes to train those who are studying neurosurgery. From the surgeon's point of view, social media is a great platform to consult and collaborate, share new technologies in healthcare, spreading awareness about campaigns (Steele et al., 2015).

Emotional Support: Emotional support refers to support gained through the feeling of concern which helps to uplift the mood of patient. Online support groups such as PatientsLikeMe offers users to express their feelings openly. Literature suggests that various psychological emotional models were proposed to identify these emotions from online communities (De Silva et al., 2018). Gomez-Zúñiga, Fernandez-Luque, Pousada,, Hernández-Encuentra & Armayones, (2012) stated that patient started using social media to share their feelings because of the reasons such as: (a)started blogging to come out with the feeling of loneliness (b) started sharing videos on YouTube to help others to understand the hardships (c) to share the mistakes done by the patient so that someone else can learn from their mistakes (d) finding others with similar symptoms can help patients to manage themselves better as they feel less alone. For example, one quote by patient *"I personally feel supported by my community with similar ailment"*.

Chiu & Hsieh (2013) conducted a qualitative study on cancer patients and found that personal blogs of the cancer patient described their life story about the struggle with cancer and they want to be remembered after their death. The story about the cancer patient changes the perception of those cancer patients who read their story and that influence was even greater than influence of the medical professionals.

Privacy Concerns and Negative Feedback: Yakar et al. (2019) stated that in neurosurgical community, privacy issue is a major concern to use social media. They suggested that posting through social media about patient, there should not be name of the patient and one should ask the written permission before using the patient data for further professional use. Gomez-Zúñiga et al., (2012) said that the main drawback of sharing the video of their medical issue is their loss of privacy. Furthermore, the study added that getting negative feedback on videos shared by them is heart-breaking for the patients. Patient shares their experiences to help other patients but rude comments made them feel like as if they were lying about their situation.

Patient- medical professional relationship: Social media allows multiple users to share and access the data online (Ngai et al., 2015). Pour and Jafari (2019) stated that such data is helpful for patients and healthcare service providers as it can be time-saving activity for patients and healthcare providers and can improve their healthcare services. Ventola (2014) claimed that even today some doctors used social media to directly contact their patients. Li et al. (2018) conducted the study and found that 49% of the patient got answers from their respective doctor within a few hours and 60% of the doctors reported that social media helped to improve the healthcare quality for the patient. Donnally et al., (2018) conducted a study of patient experience with spine surgeons through three websites. The online content was analyzed. It emphasized that the online content such as comments, ratings, patient wait time and visibility of doctors on social media would help in improving the hospital policy for future patients.

Credibility Issues: Social media allows to write and share information by anyone. It, at times, raises question about the authenticity of the information shared. For example, an online support group like PatientsLikeMe has a credibility issue as there is no professional authentication of the data shared by users. Generally, lack of authentication of healthcare information on social media sites leads to misinformation and misinterpretation of information (Smaldone, Ippolito, and Ruberto, 2019). Twitter also has not authentication process on the tweet posted on its platform. Twitter depends on medical professionals who try their best to improve the content of the site. In such cases, it is very easy for non-professionals to express their opinions as true knowledge on a particular topic (Choo et al., 2015). This creates a problem in identifying which source to trust and which not to trust (Pershad, Hangge, Albadawi, & Oklu, 2018).

Promotions: Social media provides a good platform to promote healthcare services through various means such as online reviews, number of followers (Pandey, Jha and Singh, 2019) and visibility across social networking sites. Gomez-Zúñiga B et al. (2012) stated that the patient who posts videos on YouTube can be targeted for the company's product promotion. Furthermore, Hanzel et al., (2018) said that medical professionals use Twitter to promote their brand and about them.

Case Based Approach

We chose twelve hospitals and five online commutes to analyse their social media activities. Table 1 shows the social media presence and activities of various hospitals. We have selected seven hospitals from developed countries and five hospitals for developing countries. We have taken Twitter, Facebook, Linkedin, Pinterest, Instagram and Blog to analyse the social media presence of these hospitals. The number of followers in each social networking sites was taken as an indicator to measure the influence of hospitals among social networking users. The number of users was also one of the important indicators about the brand value of each hospital. For example, Mayo Clinic was one of the top hospitals with maximum number of followers on each social media platform. The last column mentions the key social media activity of the respective hospital. These activities help hospitals to engage the user and in building the brand.

The online healthcare communities were analysed using their cross-links with other social networking sites. The major activities undertaken by each online community have been highlighted. In the last column, we have analysed critically their advantages and disadvantages (Table 2).

DISCUSSION

The structured literature review (SLR) gave six key theoretical themes (Table 3). The social learning, emotional support, credibility, and patient-healthcare relationships were the key areas where research had focused over past years. The case of twelve hospitals as shown in Table1 highlighted that almost every hospital of developed country has a presence in all major social networking sites. This provides insights to healthcare providers about the most followed social media channel by the users so that they can optimize the reach of the posts and information among the users which will further help them for branding. For example, from Table 1, we can infer that Twitter and Facebook have the maximum number of followers. Even the hospital of developing countries (Hinduja Hospital) has a good number of followers on Facebook. Therefore, healthcare providers should try to maximize opportunity on these social media channels.

Mayo Clinic, Cleveland Clinic, John Hopkins Hospital, Singapore General Hospital, and Massachusetts General Hospital were very active in posting the symptoms of diseases, most recent advancements in healthcare, healthy lifestyle tips and achievements of their staff. On the other hand, hospitals such as Henry Ford Health System, Netcare Greenacres Hospital, Barzilai Medical Center, Fortis and Lilavati hospital did not share the relevant information related to healthcare. These hospitals were not so much active in sharing posts related to symptoms of disease but posts generally were about mundane hospital activities. However, interestingly Hinduja hospital is quite active about posting on Facebook about recent healthcare-related news and upcoming technologies in healthcare. The number of posts and sharing information through these sites also engages the users which promote the brand of the hospitals. For example, some hospitals were sharing news related to artificial intelligence use in their hospitals. This type of information helps in building brand equity of the hospital. Blog and microblogs have remained an important platform for hospitals to share stories related to various critical diseases. Mayo Clinic is one of the pioneers in publishing healthcare-related blogs and therefore, a leading brand in hospitals across the world.

***Social Media Policies or Practical Implications*:** Based on SLR and case analysis, this study proposes following policies for hospital branding to the practioners: (a) the first thing is setting the clear objective of social media such as learning platform or connecting professionals or promote the corporate social responsibility (CSR) activities of the hospital. This study recommends that listening to the user's discussion is important in social media as it will give the hospital administrators and the management an idea about how to revisit the social media objectives and realign the promotion campaign; (b) Professionalism is one of the important aspects to optimize the social media usage correctly. Healthcare providers should share useful healthcare tips, misinformation should be avoided and other's opinions should be respected. Mayo Clinic sets an example by setting social media guideline as "Don't Lie, Don't Pry, Can't Delete, Don't Cheat; Don't Steal; Don't' Reveal". (c) There are privacy policies in each social networking sites such as Facebook, LinkedIn, and Twitter, therefore each hospital staff should aware of how to use these privacy settings to control the information. (d) It is not advisable to create two profiles on social networking sites such as Facebook. The healthcare professionals can use social networking sites such as Facebook, LinkedIn, and Twitter for personal networking and professional networking. Facebook can be used to connect with close friends and family and Twitter can be used to post important information regarding healthcare for benefit of the readers and followers. (e) Online technologies were evolving continuously, therefore it may be possible that popular technologies may become obsolete and new ways would emerge.

Table 1. Breadth and Depth of Social Media Presence

Hospital	Twitter	Total Tweets	Facebook	Youtube	Linkedin	Pinterest	Instagram	Blog	Type of Activities
Mayo Clinic(USA)	1.92 m	47.6k	1.12m	283.5k	406k	40.8k	178k	Yes	Tips for healthy food, recent studies done by doctors, advice for symptoms in the body related to some issue like eyestrain, sharing experience of therapies and treatment, technology related updated like role of AI in medical sciences
Cleveland Clinic(USA)	2.01m	53.9k	1.97m	112.7k	265.8k	13.9k	88.7k	Yes	Patient stories, guide to find the doctors through online review, introduction of doctor through some video, tips of healthy life, symptoms of diseases
The Johns Hopkins Hospital(USA)	538k	22.9k	601.5k	116k	56.7k	2.1k	86.5k	Yes	Doctor details, information related to healthy lifestyle, health related news, sharing of news related to advancements in treatments
Singapore General Hospital (Singapore)	38k	1.2k	47.3k	1.4k	14.7k	No	1.7k	No	Health related information sharing, events related activities, comparatively less posting on Twitter
Massachusetts General Hospital(USA)	45k	9.7k	86.8k	7.3k	79.2k	0.9k	16.4k	Yes	Information related to chronic diseases, healthy tips for good food and lifestyle, achievements of surgeons
Henry Ford Health System(USA)	12.9k	11.6k	60.3k	7.1k	40k	1.9k	7.52k	Yes	Yoga classes, healthy lifestyle tips, events related to community discussion, symptoms of illness
Toronto General Hospital	2.7k	4.47k	5.4k	8.9k	NA	NA	2.1k	Yes	New milestones achieved by surgeons with the help of advanced technologies. Healthcare recent disruption related news and information about healthcare summits.
Netcare Greenacres Hospital(South Africa)	No	No	4.2k	0.4k	No	No	No	No	Post about new staff, events news, celebration of specific occasions
Barzilai Medical Center(Israel)	No	No	1.4k	0.09k	271	No	Yes, but no info on followers	No	Advancements of medical treatments in hospital
Fortis (India)	97.4k	17.2k	1.1m	34.8k	Yes-52,748	No	2.3k	Yes	Sharing of the news not related to healthcare too, congratulations messages on specific occasions, health camps related news, hospital event videos
Lilavati hospital(India)	0.4k	1.8k	8.9k	.004k	473	No	1.3k	No	Tips for healthy lifestyle, wishes on events, medical facilities offered
Hinduja Hospital	3.6k	11.7k	203,111	1.78k	19.7k	10	2.0k	Yes	News about healthcare services, Symptoms and information about various diseases and fitness information

Table 2. Social Media Brand Building by Online Healthcare Communities

Online Communities	About the Company	Cross Links	Major Activities	Critical Analysis
WebMD	WebMD is an American based online community. They publish news related to health, well-being and drug.	Facebook (1,826,598), Twitter(3.1 million), Pinterest (103,328), Quite active on these sites	Health care topics, symptom checklist, drug information, pharmacy information and blogs of physicians with specific topics, and also offers a place to save your personal medical information	The good point is medical professionals review the posts of this site. By sharing your experience, you help other emotionally. Have tie-ups with pharma company so there are chances that they promote certain type of drugs although they claim to get you medicine at lowest price
PatientsLikeMe	PatientsLikeMe is an online community where you can find similar patient sharing their experiences of treatment journey. Community claims that this way they offer a good platform to improve the health outcome	Facebook (361,821), Twitter(31,600),LinkedIn (5232), Youtube (1473), Instagram (4975)- Not very much active on these sites	Offers patients to track and share relevant information such as symptoms,medical data and treatment	There is a problem with the credibility of information provided by users as patients are not well known with medical terminology. Therefore, it is necessary that the information shared should be authenticated by medical professional.
Practo	Practo helps users to resolve health issues by finding the right doctors, consulting in medicines, and booking diagnostic tests.	Facebook (368,432), Twitter (20,700), Instagram(5544), Not very active on these sites	Practo Ray app enable users for things such as medical appointments, digitally prescribe laboratory tests, health records, consultation, Practo blog helps doctor about new technology, also provides online medicine delivery insurance solution such as Practo Trinity.	The benefit of Practo is that you get the right doctor after reviewing the feedback online and one can book appointment online. Its good platform to save the time as one gets medical service conveniently. However, the reach of Practo is not to all age bracket users.
Sermo	Sermo is a social tool which allows medical professionals to interact on critical cases and share their experiences with diagnoses	Facebook (4985), Twitter (7282), LinkedIn (4280), not good frequency of posting	Discussion about patient cases with images and videos, discussion about emerging technology in healthcare, humorous posts related to doctors	It is great initiative to help doctors to discuss the complicated cases remotely. Further, it helps to advance the knowledge of the doctors by gaining experience from their peers.
Doximity	It is one of the largest community of medical professionals which consist of nurses, physician assistants and pharmacists too. It helps patients by their strong connected network of healthcare professionals	Facebook (27320), Twitter (8089), LinkedIn (8263) Average number of posts on these sites	85% of the doctors are connected through iPhones and 70% of their activity happened on mobile. Patient cases move faster as connected to all type of professionals in healthcare on one platform. Blogs by professionals	Having a strong presence in mobile media is their core strength due to rapid growth in smartphone usage. It has made accessing information easy. They have strong security features to hide the real identity wherever required

Therefore, the users should be flexible to use these new ways as per the changing needs of the society; (f) The medical professionals should use a separate platforms to connect with their patients. They may use blogs or microblogs to connect with patients. The clinic profile page may also be used for this purpose if the hospital IT management provides these options on the hospital webpage. (g) The quality of healthcare services among hospitals may be improved by strong network among users. For example, Doxmity has a strong network among nurses, physician assistants, and pharmacists. This helps in processing the case of the patient effectively and efficiently which also helps to improve the brand of the hospital (h) There are various online forums, communities, blogs, microblogs, etc. regarding hospital facilities. There may be a posting of any biased/damaging information against the particular hospital by an individual. This might affect the brand of the hospital. Furthermore, healthcare information is very critical, any misinformation may have a long-lasting impact on the brand equity of the hospital. Therefore, it is recommended that there should be a governing body within each hospital to regulate social media posts, information, videos, images, and blogs to the outside world from the official hospital channels. (i) The dark side of social media should also be taken care of by practioners. It is mandatory to understand that although social media is a powerful tool for information dissemination but at the same time misinformation and fake new also get spread. This creates a negative image of the healthcare professionals and degrades the brand equity. Therefore, it is advisable to the policymakers to make stringent healthcare policies (j) Lastly, it is advised that hospitals need to provide seamless hospitals services at every touch point during the medical examination and should be aware that the positive e-wom (electronic word of mouth) can enhance their branding.

Proposed Future Directions

The future researchers may look into following hospital branding related aspects for better patient services and higher profitability of the organization:

***Advanced models to derive insights from chat logs*:** Content of chat logs is an important source to extract the interest of participants. Traditional analytical models such as latent semantic indexing (LSI), latent Dirichlet allocation (LDA) and probabilistic LSI (pLSI) are not sufficient to extract the complex sentiments of recent chat conversation (Leek et al., 2016). For example, a similar message by various users may have a different meaning in such cases traditional models are incapable to draw inferences appropriately. Wang et al., (2016) proposed a new probabilistic model as an extension of LDA to capture the user's interest and topics more accurately from chat logs. Due to the rapid growth of digitalization and smartphone usage, the amount of data generation in social networking sites has been increasing by a huge percentage which also increases the complexity to extract the meaning out of it. Therefore, future researchers should model more advanced techniques to extract meaningful insights from such a huge and complex set of data.

***Leveraging Maturity models*:** Wang et al. (2017) stated that the organization's social media capability should be dynamic. This capability helps organization to deploy their social media applications to gain a competitive advantage (Pandey, Nayal and Rathore, 2020). The organization social media capability can be measured through maturity models. Previous literature has not paid much attention to developing a maturity model for the hospital industry, thus more attention is required in this area. Furthermore, Pour and Jafari (2019) stated that researchers have not paid attention to business capabilities of social media.

Table 3. Key Research Contributions

No	Authors	Journal Name	Objective	Methodology	Findings
1	Hajli et al. (2013)	European Journal of Training andDevelopment	To find out social media importance ine-learning environment in healthcare industry	Qualitative (29 Interviews)	This study concluded that social media users learn by sharing their experiences in sites such as Twitter, Facebook, Youtube, etc.
2	Sinapuelas and Nin Ho (2017)	Journal of Consumer Marketing	To find out the relationship between trust, social connections and information exchange in social networking for healthcare	Quantitative (survey from 1151 people)	The findings suggest that higher trust and social connections encourages information sharing
3	Wanga et al. (2016)	Journal of Biomedical Informatics	This aim of this study is to use online healthcare chat logs to automatically identify user interest and topics	Quantitative (233,452 chat word tokens contributed by 118 users)	The topics and user interests may help healthcare providers to understand the specific concerns related to patient health over time.
4	Hu et al. (2019)	International Journal ofEnvironmental Research and public health	To identify sentiment polarity and social media content relevant to healthcare services in China	Qualitative (content analysis, 29 million records from WeChat and Qzon)	Results showed that patient safety was the top priority followed by information technology and service efficiency in the healthcare
5	Abirami and Askarunisa (2017)	Online Information Review	To develop a systematic method to retrieve patient feelings and experiences about the hospital services from online sites	Qualitative (online reviews-content analysis)	Online reviews are crucial to recognize user's feeling and experiences. MCDM technique is a way to systemize the treatment plan in a better way.
6	Pershad et al.(2018)	Journal of Clinical Medicine	To examine the importance of Twitter in medicine and to share heath related issues in order to improve healthcare services.	Qualitative (Posts from Twitter analyzed)	Twitter has advantages to improve healthcare services as it provides a platform to share the information. However, the potential risks could be there such as misinformation, credibility of source, information overload and wastage of physician time.
7	Pour and Jafari(2018)	Online Information Review	To develop a roadmap to implement social media strategy in healthcare.	Quantitative and Qualitative(Sample size of 474, and Six for focus group discussions)	Develops health 2.0 maturity model consisting of six key dimensions as a roadmap.
8	Long et al. (2019)	BMC Surgery	To explore patient and colorectal surgeon (CRS) use of social media sites for healthcare information.	Quantitative (Survey of 63 patient)	The study found that both patient and CRS found health related information on internet, but social media sites were not good source of information.
9	De Silva et al. (2018)	PLOS ONE	To examine text generated through online support groups in order to enhance healthcare services and policy guidelines.	Qualitative (collected dataset contains 609,960 conversations from 22,233 patients)	The study confirms that in order to improve healthcare services, industry should listen to patient concerns raised through these online support groups
10	Hanzel et al. (2018)	Hospital Topics: Research and Perspectives on Healthcare	To examine healthcare professional's engagement in social media to connect with their peers and related communities.	Qualitative (total of 3,378,285 tweets analysed for content)	Medical professionals use Twitter to share their experiences related to particular disease and surgery, they educate others and also use it to promote themselves and their employer.
11	Chester et al. (2017)	BMC Medical Ethics	To address a gap in data and knowledge related to patient-targeted Googling (PTG) and to examine use of social networking sites among medical students.	Quantitative and Qualitative (survey of 54 users and focus group discussion)	PTG is useful for educating healthcare professionals but at the same time PTG should be used carefully for the safety of patient.

continues on following page

Table 3. Continued

No	Authors	Journal Name	Objective	Methodology	Findings
12	Geletta (2017)	International Journal of HealthCare Quality Assurance	To examine the social media content to measure the patient satisfaction.	Quantitative (a total of 3,520 reviewrecords provided by 3,207 individuals to 866 uniquely identifiable health service businesses)	Healthcare professionals enjoy favourable rating given online by patient. Further, it showed that dentists and physical therapists get more ratings as compared to caregivers.
13	Nemec (2018)	Journal of Health Organization and Management	To examine the credibility of online platforms in identifying patient's dissatisfaction with non-medical issues.	Qualitative (42 forums' topics have been reviewed)	Online platforms are proved to be the crucial source to measure patient dissatisfaction.
14	Smith (2017)	Services Marketing Quarterly	To examine social media usage in different types of hospitals which are of different sizes and provide different services.	Quantitative (100 hospitals for social media usage)	Results showed that social media usage differed as per the size and type of services offered by the hospitals.
15	Yakar et al. (2019)	Interdisciplinary Neurosurgery	To examine the influence of Instagram on Neurosurgery	Qualitative (terms "#neurosurgery" and "#neurosurgeon" were searched on Instagram and content was analyzed)	Twitter proved to be a good platform for the information sharing between medical professionals and patients. It also supports education to neurosurgical students.
16	Schneider et al. (2014)	Journal of theAmerican MedicalInformatics Association	To examine the use of Twitter in the process of weight loss.	QualitativeandQuantitative (survey, 100 participant trying to lose weight)	Twitter proved to be a good platform in the weight loss process for sharing experiences in such cases when patients lack social support from their peers and relatives.
17	Bauer et al. (2013)	Nordic Journal ofPsychiatry	To examine the role of online self-help forums among patients, their family and medical professionals.	Qualitative and quantitative (A total of 2400 postings in two online forums were analysed)	Online forums are platforms for the patients to share their daily life experiences and struggles with the diseases.
18	Chiu & Hsieh.(2013)	Journal of HealthPsychology	To examine the role of writing and reading online in helping cancer patients in their survival through illness.	Qualitative (Focus-group interviews were conducted, with 34 cancer patients)	Writing and reading about fellow patient experiences gives emotional support to the patient and sometimes it better than the emotional support given by any other.
19	Gomez-Zúñiga B et al. (2012)	Journal of MedicalInternet research	To examine the challenges and motivations of sharing videos related to patient experiences on Youtube.	Qualitative (analysis of the videos created by 4 patients about their motivations and challenges they face as YouTube users)	Sharing on YouTube about the patient experiences may create loss of privacy. However, on positive side it also helps to express their feeling which give support to other patients.
20	Wicks et al. (2011)	Journal of MedicalInternet research	To examine the benefits of online community like PatientsLikeMe in terms of sharing patient related information	Quantitative (cross-sectional online survey)	Members of the community reported that they benefited in several ways by this online sharing platforms in improving their health.
21	Smaldone et al., (2020)	European Management Journal	To examine the negative influence of social media in healthcare	Qualitative and Quantitative (web interview and survey)	There is a risk of misinterpretation of online healthcare information among users.
22	Farber and Nitzburg, (2015)	Counselling Psychology Quarterly	To examine the difference between offline (psychotherapy) and online (Facebook) channels for personal disclosure among young adults	Quantitative (Survey)	Facebook discussion was related to positive emotions while therapy disclosure was related to negative emotions. Disclosure in two platforms serves different needs.

***Measuring dissatisfaction of patient experience with healthcare service provider*:** In hospital industry, the patient involvement is higher with medical professionals. Measuring patient satisfaction has been considered as an appropriate way to improve the service quality of hospitals (Gill and White, 2009). However, few studies report a contrary view stating that the above process has its own set of limitations (Gill and White, 2009). Some of the possible reasons are poor quality of survey forms (limited and predefined set of questions and lack of space to express the qualitative opinions). Therefore, researchers suggested that measuring dissatisfaction is more beneficial through qualitative methods like in-depth interviews (Crow et al., 2002). The wide reach of social media platforms today makes them a perfect medium to quickly share the user experiences about the healthcare services leading to more user awareness and more accountability from the service providers. Besides, online platforms provide an effective way to health service providers for serving their customers better by understanding the user experiences and expectations closely. Nemec et al. (2018) found that online communities were an important source to measure patient dissatisfaction and it provides various useful insights to improve healthcare services. Therefore, future researchers may conduct more number of research related to dissatisfaction related to hospital services to improve healthcare policies.

Privacy Risks: Privacy risk emerges as one of the main concern due to technological advancements and the rise of smartphones (Pandey and Gudipudi, 2019). In the healthcare industry, risk of breaching patient confidentiality over social media platforms such as Instagram, Whatsapp, etc is a major concern (Kaliyadan et al. 2016). The images which are privately stored in smartphones can be exchanged through WhatsApp or other apps which may lead to a breach of patient confidentiality (Mobasheri et al., 2015). For example, theft of smartphones may lead to unauthorized access of patient images. For such cases, organization should have strict rules and policies to govern these issues. Future researchers should conduct more number of studies about patient confidentiality and how to make communication more secure over social media platforms.

Relationship between patient and healthcare professionals: The freedom to express on social media leads to patient empowerment. This makes the patient to be more informed and to get more involved in healthcare-related decisions (Colineau et al., 2010). New technologies provide greater power to patients as now accessing the information is more convenient and faster. The current balance of power is higher for patients as compared to healthcare professionals. Many times the patient comes with preoccupied information and resists the healthcare professional's advice (Broom, 2005). However, patient empowerment has its own benefits for healthcare industry as hospitals become more patient-oriented which leads to better decision making for patient health. Future researchers may conduct studies to balance the relationship between healthcare professionals and patient.

CONCLUSION

The aim of this research was to answer the following question: How much research has been done so far on adoption of social media in hospital industry and what are the possible future research avenues? To achieve this aim of the study systematic literature review was conducted on articles related to social media usage for healthcare industry. Six themes were identified after the review process. Furthermore, the cases of hospitals and online communities were analysed. Various policies have been suggested based on cases and review for healthcare professionals. Conclusively, it can be stated that there is a dearth of research in social media usage for hospital industry and social media has not been used from a strategic point of view. The social media research had majorly covered information sharing, emotional support, and social support while privacy concerns, credibility issues, and balancing the patient-healthcare professional lacks research. The case research revealed the usage of social media among hospitals and revealed the influence of each site and the major activities of hospitals in social media. The advanced techniques were required to draw insights from the online discussions. Furthermore, privacy risk, roadmap for social media usage and dissatisfaction measurement were aspects that required further investigation. Although social media is helpful for fast information dissemination but the dark side of social media cannot be ignored especially as healthcare information is too sensitive to handle. Therefore, policymakers should be well aware of this sensitiveness while designing the policies for healthcare social media and should design stringent policies to reduce the misinformation and fake news. The study is not without limitations. Future studies may conduct meta-analysis along with systematic literature review. Furthermore, future researchers may conduct expert interviews from healthcare domain which will help to find new gaps in the area.

REFERENCES

Abirami, A. M., & Askarunisa, A. (2017). Sentiment analysis model to emphasize the impact of online reviews in healthcare industry. *Online Information Review*, *41*(4), 471–486. doi:10.1108/OIR-08-2015-0289

Ahadzadeh, A. S., Pahlevan Sharif, S., & Sim Ong, F. (2018). Online health information seeking among women: The moderating role of health consciousness. *Online Information Review*, *42*(1), 58–72. doi:10.1108/OIR-02-2016-0066

Benetoli, A., Chen, T. F., & Aslani, P. (2017). Consumer health-related activities on social media: Exploratory study. *Journal of Medical Internet Research*, *19*(10), e352. doi:10.2196/jmir.7656

Büyüközkan, G., & Çifçi, G. (2012). A combined fuzzy AHP and fuzzy TOPSIS based strategic analysis of electronic service quality in healthcare industry. *Expert Systems with Applications*, *39*(3), 2341–2354. doi:10.1016/j.eswa.2011.08.061

Chiu, Y. C., & Hsieh, Y. L. (2013). Communication online with fellow cancer patients: Writing to be remembered, gain strength, and find survivors. *Journal of Health Psychology*, *18*(12), 1572–1581. doi:10.1177/1359105312465915

Choo, E. K., Ranney, M. L., Chan, T. M., Trueger, N. S., Walsh, A. E., Tegtmeyer, K., McNamara, S. O., Choi, R. Y., & Carroll, C. L. (2015). Twitter as a tool for communication and knowledge exchange in academic medicine: A guide for skeptics and novices. *Medical Teacher*, *37*(5), 411–416. doi:10.3109/0142159X.2014.993371

Crow, H., Gage, H., Hampson, S., Hart, J., Kimber, A., Storey, L., & Thomas, H. (2002). Measurement of satisfaction with health care: Implications for practice from a systematic review of the literature. *Health Technology Assessment*, *6*(32). Advance online publication. doi:10.3310/hta6320

De Martino, I., D'Apolito, R., McLawhorn, A. S., Fehring, K. A., Sculco, P. K., & Gasparini, G. (2017). Social media for patients: Benefits and drawbacks. *Current Reviews in Musculoskeletal Medicine*, *10*(1), 141–145. doi:10.100712178-017-9394-7

De Silva, D., Ranasinghe, W., Bandaragoda, T., Adikari, A., Mills, N., Iddamalgoda, L., ... Gray, R. (2018). Machine learning to support social media empowered patients in cancer care and cancer treatment decisions. *PLoS One*, *13*(10), e0205855. doi:10.1371/journal.pone.0205855

Donnally, C. J. III, Li, D. J., Maguire, J. A. Jr, Roth, E. S., Barker, G. P., McCormick, J. R., Rush, A. J. III, & Lebwohl, N. H. (2018). How social media, training, and demographics influence online reviews across three leading review websites for spine surgeons. *The Spine Journal*, *18*(11), 2081–2090. doi:10.1016/j.spinee.2018.04.023

Eysenbach, G. (2008). Medicine 2.0: Social networking, collaboration, participation, apomediation, and openness. *Journal of Medical Internet Research*, *10*(3), e22. doi:10.2196/jmir.1030

Farber, B. A., & Nitzburg, G. C. (2016). Young adult self-disclosures in psychotherapy and on Facebook. *Counselling Psychology Quarterly*, *29*(1), 76–89. doi:10.1080/09515070.2015.1078286

Frost, J., Okun, S., Vaughan, T., Heywood, J., & Wicks, P. (2011). Patient-reported outcomes as a source of evidence in off-label prescribing: Analysis of data from PatientsLikeMe. *Journal of Medical Internet Research*, *13*(1), e6. doi:10.2196/jmir.1643

Gill, L., & White, L. (2009). A critical review of patient satisfaction. *Leadership in Health Services*, *22*(1), 8–19. doi:10.1108/17511870910927994

Gómez-Zúñiga, B., Fernandez-Luque, L., Pousada, M., Hernández-Encuentra, E., & Armayones, M. (2012). ePatients on YouTube: analysis of four experiences from the patients' perspective. Medicine 2.0, 1(1).

Hanzel, T., Richards, J., Schwitters, P., Smith, K., Wendland, K., Martin, J., & Keltgen, J. (2018). # DocsOnTwitter: How Physicians use Social Media to Build Social Capital. *Hospital Topics*, *96*(1), 9–17. doi:10.1080/00185868.2017.1354558

Househ, M., Borycki, E., & Kushniruk, A. (2014). Empowering patients through social media: The benefits and challenges. *Health Informatics Journal*, *20*(1), 50–58. doi:10.1177/1460458213476969

Jami Pour, M., & Jafari, S. M. (2019). Toward a maturity model for the application of social media in healthcare: The health 2.0 roadmap. *Online Information Review*, *43*(3), 404–425. doi:10.1108/OIR-02-2018-0038

Kaplan, A. M., & Haenlein, M. (2010). Users of the world, unite! The challenges and opportunities of Social Media. *Business Horizons*, *53*(1), 59–68. doi:10.1016/j.bushor.2009.09.003

Kordzadeh, N. (2016). Social media in health care. In *Contemporary Consumer Health Informatics* (pp. 101–123). Springer., . doi:10.1007/978-3-319-25973-4_6

Leek, S., Canning, L., & Houghton, D. (2016). Revisiting the Task Media Fit Model in the era of Web 2.0: Twitter use and interaction in the healthcare sector. *Industrial Marketing Management*, *54*, 25–32. doi:10.1016/j.indmarman.2015.12.007

Li, Y., & Wang, X. (2017). Online social networking sites continuance intention: A model comparison approach. *Journal of Computer Information Systems*, *57*(2), 160–168. doi:10.1080/08874417.2016.1183448

Li, Y., Wang, X., Lin, X., & Hajli, M. (2018). Seeking and sharing health information on social media: A net valence model and cross-cultural comparison. *Technological Forecasting and Social Change, 126*, 28–40. doi:10.1016/j.techfore.2016.07.021

Lim, W. M. (2016). Social media in medical and health care: Opportunities and challenges. *Marketing Intelligence & Planning, 34*(7), 964–976. doi:10.1108/MIP-06-2015-0120

McHattie, L. S., Cumming, G., & French, T. (2014). Transforming patient experience: health web science meets medicine 2.0. Medicine 2.0, 3(1).

Myers, C., Kudsi, Y., & Ghaaferi, A. (2017). Surgeons Are Using Social Media to Share and Learn New Skills. Retrieved from https://hbr.org/2017/10/surgeons-are-using-social-media-to-share-and-learn-new-skills

Nemec, M., Kolar, T., & Rusjan, B. (2018). Online communities as a new source of exploring patient dissatisfaction. *Journal of Health Organization and Management, 32*(8), 962–979. doi:10.1108/JHOM-03-2018-0104

Ngai, E. W., Tao, S. S., & Moon, K. K. (2015). Social media research: Theories, constructs, and conceptual frameworks. *International Journal of Information Management, 35*(1), 33–44. doi:10.1016/j.ijinfomgt.2014.09.004

Pandey, N., & Gudipudi, B. (2019). Understanding 'what is privacy' for millennials on Facebook in India. *Journal of Data Protection & Privacy, 2*(3), 224–233.

Pandey, N., Jha, S., & Singh, G. (2019). (in press). Promotion of green products on Facebook: Insights from Millennials. *International Journal of Management Practice.*

Pandey, N., Nayal, P., & Rathore, A. S. (2020). Digital marketing for B2B organizations: Structured literature review and future research directions. *Journal of Business and Industrial Marketing, 35*(7), 1191–1204. Advance online publication. doi:10.1108/JBIM-06-2019-0283

Pandey, N., & Shinde, S. (2019). V-Xpress: B2B marketing in the logistics industry. *Emerald Emerging Markets Case Studies, 9*(1), 1–23. doi:10.1108/EEMCS-05-2018-0079

Pandey, N., & Singh, G. (2012). *Marketing issues in SMEs: cases from India*. Pearson Education India.

Patel, S. (2015). How businesses should be using social media in 2015. Forbes/Entrepreneurs. Retrieved from http://www.forbes.com/sites/sujanpatel/2015/06/24/how-businesses-should- be-using-social-media-in-2015/#577081854a5b

Patwardhan, A. A., Pandey, N., & Dhume, S. M. (2014). Analysis of physicians technology acceptance literature in changing indian pharmaceutical marketing context: A markus and robeys causal structure approach. *International Journal of Marketing & Business Communication, 3*(2), 33–45.

Patwardhan, A. A., Pandey, N., & Dhume, S. M. (2017). Integrated model for understanding Indian physicians' internet usage pattern: An empirical approach. *International Journal of Healthcare Management, 10*(1), 19–33. doi:10.1080/20479700.2016.1270385

Pentescu, A., Cetină, I., & Orzan, G. (2015). Social media's impact on healthcare services. *Procedia Economics and Finance*, *27*, 646–651. doi:10.1016/S2212-5671(15)01044-8

Pershad, Y., Hangge, P., Albadawi, H., & Oklu, R. (2018). Social medicine: Twitter in healthcare. *Journal of Clinical Medicine*, *7*(6), 121. doi:10.3390/jcm7060121

Pinho-Costa, L., Yakubu, K., Hoedebecke, K., Laranjo, L., Reichel, C. P., Colon-Gonzalez, M. D. C., Neves, A. L., & Errami, H. (2016). Healthcare hashtag index development: Identifying global impact in social media. *Journal of Biomedical Informatics*, *63*, 390–399. doi:10.1016/j.jbi.2016.09.010

Smailhodzic, E., Hooijsma, W., Boonstra, A., & Langley, D. J. (2016). Social media use in healthcare: A systematic review of effects on patients and on their relationship with healthcare professionals. *BMC Health Services Research*, *16*(1), 442. doi:10.118612913-016-1691-0

Smaldone, F., Ippolito, A., & Ruberto, M. (2019). The shadows know me: Exploring the dark side of social media in the healthcare field. *European Management Journal*.

Smith, K. T., Blazovich, J., & Smith, L. M. (2015). Social media adoption by corporations: An examination by platform, industry, size, and financial performance. *Academy of Marketing Studies Journal*, *19*(2), 127–143.

Steele, S. R., Arshad, S., Bush, R., Dasani, S., Cologne, K., Bleier, J. I., Raphaeli, T., & Kelz, R. R. (2015). Social media is a necessary component of surgery practice. *Surgery*, *158*(3), 857–862. doi:10.1016/j.surg.2015.06.002

Tranfield, D., Denyer, D., & Smart, P. (2003). Towards a methodology for developing evidence-informed management knowledge by means of systematic review. *British Journal of Management*, *14*(3), 207–222. doi:10.1111/1467-8551.00375

Ukoha, C., & Stranieri, A. (2019). Criteria to Measure Social Media Value in Health Care Settings: Narrative Literature Review. *Journal of Medical Internet Research*, *21*(12), e14684. doi:10.2196/14684

Ventola, C. L. (2014). Social media and health care professionals: Benefits, risks, and best practices. *P&T*, *39*(7), 491.

Wang, T., Huang, Z., & Gan, C. (2016). On mining latent topics from healthcare chat logs. *Journal of Biomedical Informatics*, *61*, 247–259. doi:10.1016/j.jbi.2016.04.008

Wang, Y., Rod, M., Ji, S., & Deng, Q. (2017). Social media capability in B2B marketing: Toward a definition and a research model. *Journal of Business and Industrial Marketing*, *32*(8), 1125–1135. doi:10.1108/JBIM-10-2016-0250

Yakar, F., Jacobs, R., & Agarwal, N. (2019). The current usage of Instagram in neurosurgery. *Interdisciplinary Neurosurgery: Advanced Techniques and Case Management, 19*, 100553. doi:10.1016/j.inat.2019.100553

Chapter 2
Hospitals as Social Brands:
Building Brands by Serving Society

Dinesh Kumar
https://orcid.org/0000-0003-3698-8770
Jagran Lakecity University, India

Punam Gupta
Career College, India

ABSTRACT

Reputations of hospitals were traditionally built on the successful treatment of patients, but today advertising and promotions are used by hospitals as they brand themselves. Patients have become customers, and they are enticed by packaged rates and freebies. Hospitals are operating like airlines, advertising their special offers, package rates, and comfortable services. This approach begs the question: Is a hospital a brand like Gucci, which few can afford, or does it have a larger purpose in society? This chapter argues for hospitals to serve society. Their real branding must come from how they serve patients and not from advertising. The chapter draws on the success of the Aravind Eye Hospital and Narayana Hrudayalaya in India, which have adopted a Walmart approach to reduce costs of complex medical procedures, serving the larger society. Such hospitals represent highly successful branding that draws from an ethical rather than a marketing approach that arises from a genuine desire to fulfill human needs rather than frills and fancies that marketing practitioners are familiar with.

INTRODUCTION

The reputation of hospitals is traditionally built on the services they provide. Doctors and staff, equipment and quality of care are important determinants of reputation of healthcare providers. However, today hospitals see themselves as brands and invest time and money in creating a brand image for themselves using high-powered marketing techniques.

DOI: 10.4018/978-1-7998-3034-4.ch002

This paper looks at the way that brands are built and the marketing principles underlying it. While service and care remain the backbone of hospital reputations, today hospitals are sought to be sold like any consumer products or services. Showing beautiful and happy people, pictures of advanced machines or celebrity doctors, hospital advertising and brand-building depends on things like imagery and emotions as part of the brand building process.

While marketing tools do succeed in reaching customers and creating brands, the reputations of hospitals are best built by providing services to society. There is a growing realisation that medical services including hospitals are caught in a vicious circle of high medical costs fuelled by insurance revenues. This leaves out the very large portion of the population which cannot afford the high costs or is not in the insurance system, which begs the question: "Is the purpose of a hospital to provide care only to those who can afford it?" Indeed, the very basic purpose of business is being re-examined today. Many businesses are becoming 'social businesses' – businesses that use their profits for community support. Hospitals are ideal candidates of becoming social businesses and therefore need to rise above profit motives and serve society as well.

The chapter describes cases of some hospitals that have built formidable brands by serving the needs of society. They have succeeded in providing high quality medical services at a fraction of the cost traditionally charged and thereby serve a very large number of customers. The hospitals are profitable but innovate to serve the poor as well. By building strong reputations by serving a large number of people, these hospitals show how hospital brands can be built.

OBJECTIVE

The objective of this chapter is to explore the ethical issues in applying branding and marketing in the case of hospitals. Many hospitals across the world use high-powered advertising and marketing to create their brands, and build elitist hospitals that can be accessed by the rich only. This chapter argues that a better way to build hospital brands is through a more sustainable way by providing high quality medical care facilities at affordable cost in order to serve all segments of society. This approach is highlighted and explained with the help of examples of hospitals that have actually achieved this.

NOVELTY OF THE CHAPTER

Branding is a construct in marketing that relies on creating a space in the minds of customers through advertising and communication. The novelty of this chapter is that it describes an alternative approach that considers hospitals as service. The best hospital branding takes place when satisfied patients and their attendants generate word-of-mouth publicity about the services they received. Indeed, hospitals must serve a larger population rather than pricing their services only rich patients or insured patients who can afford their high prices. Some hospitals are indeed doing this: management principles are used by these hospitals not for image making but for reducing costs of medical services. By expanding services to those who cannot otherwise afford the high cost of medical services, they create much more sustainable brands than those that depend on image building.

BACKGROUND

Branding is a well-known construct that is commonly studied in marketing. Much of the effort in branding goes into creating names and logos and making them widely visible so that consumers can distinguish one from the others. The focus is on high-powered communication to make names recognisable. The methods of services marketing are mistakenly applied to hospital branding, which seems logical, as hospitals come under the services category. Thus hospital ads talk about their ambience, smiling models posing as doctors, the latest machines, and more happy models posing as patients.

Marketing books talk about building brands with powerful identities, employing imagery and logos. Hospitals have learnt to use the elements described by Keller (1998) in what is known as Customer-Based Brand Equity (CBBE) Model. This consists of defining a brand's salience or identity, brand meaning consisting of performance and imagery, consumer response through judgements and feelings, and brand relationships.

One well-accepted way to build brand relationships is to infuse emotions into the communications. Kemp, Jillapalli, and Becerra (2014) examine how healthcare brands use emotional connection to impart meaning and build relationship with the consumer. Hospitals attempt to branding themselves by infusing their communications with emotions linked to patient recovery. Hence, hospitals invest time and money to design the imagery that would appeal to their customers. Schmitt and Simonson (1997) had showed how a brand's look and feel, or aesthetics, impact brand building and an edge over the competition. Hospital advertisements are therefore usually designed to show neat aesthetics and happy people, just like advertisements for consumer goods.

Branding creates recognition, attracts customers, assures them of quality, builds loyalty and above all, earns free word-of-mouth recommendations. Brands are profitable and ensure long term survival of companies. Several brand building approaches are used in the field of marketing.

BRAND BUILDING APPROACHES

Traditionally, brands are created by following one of several approaches. These approaches have evolved with marketing theory over the years. The approaches are summed up in Table 1.

Table 1. Brand Building Approaches

Brand Building Approach	Description
Economic Value:	Consumers buy brands based on the benefit they derive compared to economic price. They try to get the maximum value for their dollar.
Brand Identity:	Based on differentiation, brands develop their unique identity that appeals to consumers.
Consumer based:	Brands are created based on the image created in the consumers' minds and the brand associations they develop over time.
Brand Personality:	Brands are imparted a personality by giving them human or animal qualities, and appeal to consumers on a psychological level.
Relational:	Companies make efforts to develop relationships with consumers
Community approach:	Consumers imparted a sense of community through brandfests, common activities, social media.
Cultural:	Brands associate with popular culture or certain causes; celebrity advertising and brand icons

In the case of hospitals, though some consumers may look for economic value they derive, branding is mostly based on building reputations. Usually brand building is done by using a combination of these approaches, in multiple ways.

In the first instance, differentiation and identity is achieved when hospitals specialise in certain specialisations. Thus hospitals brand themselves as 'children's hospital,' 'cancer hospital,' 'maternity homes' and so on. They are able to segment the market and attract a certain kind of patient.

Consumer-based branding is most powerful as it depends on experiences shared by people. Patients are able to develop pleasant associations with hospitals if they have been cared for well by doctors or staff. Since word-of-mouth publicity is free advertising, hospital brands are built by stories and recommendations that are shared by patients. Further, hospitals acquire personality when pictures of certain specialist doctors or satisfied patients are used in their publicity material. Certain hospitals follow this approach through pleasing advertisements. Personality and trust is also acquired if a celebrity is treated at a hospital.

The relational approach is built over the years when people begin to trust hospitals. When members of a family, for instance, get successful treatment, they develop a psychological relationship with the hospital. Hospitals participate in community activities by organising support groups, common checkup camps, or meetings with past patients. Finally, celebrity advertising is a short-cut approach to develop brands.

While the above sums up the marketing approach to building brands, hospital branding depends on a number of variables. These contribute to building a hospital's reputation. An analysis of the variables in hospital reputation shows how the core purpose plays an important role in their branding.

VARIABLES IN HOSPITAL REPUTATION

An analysis of the variables that contribute to hospital reputation shows that their branding depends on a large number of variables. Services provided by hospitals can be described as providing medical treatments to the sick or injured. In many countries, hospitals run by the government or by not-for-profit agencies have been doing that, at least theoretically providing care to the rich and poor alike.

However, while many companies have used mass media to build brands, it has been suggested that alternative approaches are required in the "post-mass-media age." Joachimsthaler and Aaker (1997) had suggested that brands are best built around their core identity. Since the core identity of hospitals is to provide medical care, the best brand building must be centred around it.

Marketing and branding techniques have historically not been applied to hospital care services since people usually depended on word-of-mouth recommendations from satisfied patients and their relatives. Health-care services were not sold like consumer goods because a sick person would take help from a nearby clinic or hospital rather than look for a "brand." It was also considered morally repugnant to "sell" services to a sick or injured person. One can say that hospitals exerted a pull influence on the basis of their trust and reputation.

Embedded in this thinking was that the hospital should provide the best treatments to all in the society and thereby earn the trust of patients.

This has been changing in recent years. Modern hospitals require huge investments in buildings, equipment and personnel. Investors look for a return on investment, which is dependent on the revenue generated from their patients. In the new dispensation, the patient becomes a customer who must be sold various services in order to generate maximum revenue. Thus, modern hospitals have begun using marketing, branding and selling techniques in their operations.

The reputation of hospitals or their branding is a function of several factors, and can be represented as:

R = f(*So, Dr, WOM, Pe, Ae, Rr, Am, Cl, Tw, Pr*)

Where *So* represents services offered, *Dr* is doctors reputation, *WOM* is word of mouth generated, *Pe* represents patient experience, *Ae* is attendant experience, *Rr* is rate of recovery, *Am* is ambience, *Cl* is cleanliness, *Tw* represents time of wait to see a specialist and *Pr* is pricing of services.

Marketing and advertising play little role in building reputations but are deployed for the branding of hospitals. In doing this they follow well established principles of high powered marketing communications.

CURRENT HEALTHCARE SCENARIO

When marketing and branding techniques are applied to hospitals, the above function is skewed towards things like imagery and emotions that are used as part of the brand building process, but which have very little to do with their core purpose. Hospitals are projected as highly specialised and technologically equipped destinations where one gets packaged medical services. Surgeries such as knee or hip replacement, heart bypass procedures, childbirth, etc are presented as packages that include not only medical but cosmetic services as well. In an effort to improve profitability, hospitals are now branded as integrated services providers. Health insurance further skews the choice of patients, who prefer those hospitals that provide seamless connectivity with their health plans. There is no incentive for cost reduction or widening the reach of hospital services for poor patients. Treating patients as "profit centres," few modern hospitals have gone beyond the marketing applications, devised ways of solving problems of the large sections of society or to create distinct services that actually drive differentiation.

In this process, branding in hospitals is aimed at providing upmarket services that cater to the rich or those who have insurance. As a consequence, the poor or those who cannot afford insurance are left out of the medical system. This is an unfortunate outcome of the application of marketing and branding to hospitals. They operate in a vicious cycle of heavy investments and costs, charging high fees and getting paid by insurance companies. The patient is reduced to becoming an agent that connects hospitals with insurance companies.

Since the patient is just a cog in the machine for payments, it has led to some very unfortunate outcomes. For instance, hospitals are incentivised to perform needless tests and procedures on patients, knowing well that they will be paid by insurance companies. Over-billing is common.

However, when we introduce a revenue or profit element in healthcare, there is a tendency to prescribe tests and procedures that are unnecessary, and sell services such as luxury rooms to people who basically come to recover and be cured of their ailments. Hospitals tend to cross-sell and upsell services in an attempt to improve profitability. As a consequence, hospitals overcharge their patients. This is a global phenomenon, as is evident from reports from various countries. *Bangkok Post* (2019) reported that most private hospitals overcharge, and the "the overcharge rate ranges from 30% to 300% above actual production costs." In India, reports of overcharging are common; one report published in *DNA India* (2018) shows that "private hospitals overcharged items up to a whopping 1737% to patients."

Judging by similar reports from across the world, the trend of overcharging patients by hospitals appears to be a global epidemic. But this is a fragile way of building brands because when reports of wrongdoings become public, they do no good for any hospital's brand or reputation. They may also attract court cases and government regulation. The strategy of trying to recover the maximum revenue from patients could thus backfire in a big way, destroying brands rather than creating them.

Even in the short term, the system is hardly sustainable or fair. Customers must pay insurance premiums that are increased every year, in a system that progressively becomes more expensive both for customers as well as for hospitals.

Another consequence of such branding is that hospitals become places for the elite, like a hotel or a resort, leading to exclusion of large sections of the population. Such a system that denies medical care to the poor and the disadvantaged is hardly moral and begs the question: is healthcare branding only for the rich and the well-to-do? If so, it is a very limited application of marketing, which professes to satisfy human needs, and not simply the needs of the rich. Governments have addressed this problem by providing public sector health care services with varying degrees of success. In India, the government provides low cost health insurance and directs private hospitals not to turn away poor patients. But the long-term solution is to device a system that offers inclusive health care services.

In that sense hospitals are not like other businesses that operate on the principle of maximising profits. Since even traditional businesses are changing and trying to shed their profiteering tag, hospitals must also re-discover their larger purpose in society. Today it is expected that businesses must serve society by solving its problems. As early as 1999 Porter and Kramer had written, "... the most effective way to address many of the world's most pressing problems is to mobilize the corporate sector where both companies and society can benefit."

In other words, hospitals are ideal candidates for being described as "social businesses," which meet the opposing objectives of profit-making and community support. It is debatable whether such a system is sustainable or whether it serves the need of the society as a whole and leads us to the question: "Is the purpose of hospitals to make money from rich patients or to serve patients and society?"

REDEFINING BUSINESS

It is increasingly being recognised that hospitals need to break the vicious cycle of escalating costs and to deliver what its customers need. Speziale (2015) writes that now hospitals need to develop a strategy consisting of "maximizing value for patients by obtaining the best outcomes at lowest cost."

This is in line with the rethinking of business and capitalism that we are witnessing today. Business leaders have realised that the pursuit of profits must be tempered with social benefits. Businesses must be re-oriented to become social enterprises, which is essential for the future of business itself. This calls for long term thinking and taking into account all stakeholders rather than focus single-mindedly on profits and quarterly results is under threat. This is highly unsustainable; Reich (2016) explains, "we are lurching toward a capitalism so top-heavy it cannot be sustained." Hence business must be redefined with a new purpose. Bower, Leonard and Paine (2011) explain that the new role of business is to be "both as innovator and activist – developing corporate strategies that effect change at the community, national, and international levels." This is very well relatable to the modern health-care system.

There is realisation today that the prevailing market capitalism system must be modified so that business must lead as an innovator and as an activist, mobilizing resources to spread the innovations.

Indeed, *The Economist* (2019) reports that companies have "overturned three decades of orthodoxy to pledge that their firms' purpose was no longer to serve their owners alone, but customers, staff, suppliers and communities, too."

The increasing corporatisation of hospitals brings this debate right to their doorstep. The use of marketing techniques such as projecting names, logos and slogans do serve the purpose of creating an image but for hospitals the value delivered to patients must be firmly kept in focus at all times. The challenge is to use such techniques but also to build upon traditional ways that contribute to hospital reputation – by providing service at affordable cost and creating formidable word-of-mouth recommendations. This can only happen when the services can be broad-based.

The coronavirus disaster that the world saw in 2020 highlighted the skewed nature of hospital care in developed countries. The virus was not a disease that could be controlled by corporate hospitals thriving on medical insurance. The poor needed as much testing and care as rich patients but in much of Europe, USA and other countries, medical capacity was limited as hospitals operated as high-cost, insurance funded institutions. Scientists have warned that the world will see more pandemics – and these pandemics cannot be controlled by high-cost hospitals but by a broad-based health care system.

Our contention is that hospital branding is better served when they stick with their core purpose and use traditional elements such as patient care and affordability to build their reputations. This will result in reducing costs and building much more robust brands. Hospitals can also discover ways to differentiate themselves and provide broad-based care so as to serve the larger society. They must operate like ethical and social businesses rather than profit-making machines that merely exploit patients. This would be a much more ethical approach than the marketing approach.

ETHICAL AND SOCIAL CONSIDERATIONS

The ethical and social considerations of high powered communication usually escape practitioners of marketing. For instance, an oil company may pollute our oceans and lands but undertake some well publicized activities in landscaping and thereby project itself as an environmentally conscious company. Or a company whose products come packaged in single-use plastics like bottles and wrappers may project itself as close to nature as it sources its water from Himalayan springs!

Similarly, hospitals may well show themselves as having the best treatments in the world but they are so expensive that they cater to less than 1% of the population. Caught in a system of marketing and fuelled by insurance, many hospitals have become luxury brands that are out of reach for the majority of population. While it cannot be denied that creating modern healthcare facilities call for huge investments and thereby must be priced at high levels, the very purpose of marketing – that of fulfilling human needs – is often ignored. Can the role of marketing of hospitals be expanded to providing affordable solutions apart from creating and distributing communication? Can hospitals lower prices while also make profits?

Hospital branding would be better served by a large word-of-mouth communication about services rather than being popular with only a few well-heeled customers. Hospitals are not luxury brands; they have a social purpose as well.

TOWARDS SOCIAL BUSINESS

Kapferer (2008) writes that brands "must adopt ethical principles and demonstrate that consumption is not a synonym for inefficient waste, pollution and exploitation – themes to which society is becoming increasingly sensitive." In that sense, hospitals must be seen as "social businesses."

Businesses across the world are slowly turning towards entrepreneurial solutions that help poor populations as well. Innovative but simple solutions go a long way in solving long standing problems. Across the world, businesses are trying to serve the larger society and making products and services available to those who cannot afford them. Innovations that serve society call for approaches that solve seemingly impossible problems.

Many businesses are therefore becoming "social businesses," implementing business models for social inclusion. In light of long term sustainability, it is imperative that the very nature of doing business should change and that business becomes more focused towards community improvement rather than mere profit making. Can the best minds – who manage the largest corporations of the world – devote time towards more mundane problems and make the world a better place? Can we modify the very nature of capitalism so that it leads to investing in businesses that do good instead of pursuing profits?

Kumar and Gupta (2017) write about several instances of businesses that had adopted unique and innovative ways to serve the poor and the disadvantaged. Grameen Bank in Bangladesh is a very powerful example of a social business; it inverted traditional banking on its head by giving small loans to poor people who were otherwise un-bankable. They were excluded from the banking system as they had nothing to use as collateral or guarantees. Later, it introduced mobile phones in villages by working out innovative and affordable solutions. Its joint venture with Danone provides an affordable milk preparation to meet the nutritional needs of poor children. Essilor worked out a business model in which reading glasses could be provided to people at low cost in rural areas – people who lacked the means to either get their eyes tested or who could not afford the glasses. On a similar note, Warby Parker gives a pair of glasses to a needy person for every pair of glasses that it sells. Its website says, "five million pairs of glasses have been distributed through our Buy a Pair, Give a Pair program."

Café Feminino in Peru ensures that women coffee producers get a fair price for their produce. The organisation even offers loans that people can use for improving their lives. In France, Renault promises to repair cars of poor customers at nominal cost in its "solidarity garages." Its *Mobilize Social Entrepreneurship* program invests in projects with high social impact and provides "socially responsible mobility solutions with an innovative entrepreneurial approach."

In China, Alibaba broad based its production by creating hubs called *taobao* village clusters. These clusters have contributed to creating jobs and growth in remote areas. In India, Amul organised milk farmers into cooperatives so that they became part-owners of the business, thereby avoiding their exploitation at the hands of middlemen. The effort resulted in a "white revolution" through which India became self reliant in milk and related products. In all these cases, companies have succeeded in using social entrepreneurship to solve local problems and to build business models that incorporate social innovation with commercial profits.

We see from the initiatives of these companies that social innovation consists of the idea that mere selling of goods is not enough, but companies have to rise to solve local problems. Anderson and Markides (2007) explain that is not about creating new product features but adapting existing products to customers who have fewer resources or a different cultural background. It is about establishing basic market ingredients such as distribution channels and customer demand from the ground up.

HEALTHCARE BRANDING THROUGH LOW COST INNOVATION

Similar thinking has resulted in innovations in healthcare as well. Some hospitals in India have applied the "Wal-mart" approach to make services available at lower prices. Govindarajan and Ramamurti (2013) write that an "Uber of health care" is needed in a world in which health insurance premiums keep increasing year on year.

Hospital branding cannot thus be treated as branding in any other industry. It is a consumer driven process, so that customers – who are patients – must be served irrespective of their economic status. Rather than exploit them for revenues, hospitals must focus on service delivery enhancement. This can be done in several ways, from having experienced doctors to modern equipment to specialised services. An alternative approach is that of building hospital brands is to modify the operating model in delivery, cost or processes so that they either become efficient or are able to reduce costs.

One of the most challenging problems is that of providing healthcare in Bottom of the Pyramid (BoP) markets. A majority of the population has low income: data from 110 countries show that the BoP makes up 72% of the population, with an overwhelming majority in Africa, Asia, Eastern Europe, and Latin America and the Caribbean. Though healthcare has attracted investments, delivery remains abysmal. A report in *The Economic Times* (2018), shows that "lack of penetration, inflated billing, opaqueness in diagnosis and poor quality of service have ensured that most Indians get treated below the standards prescribed by the World Health Organisation."

A branding strategy that does not violate the medical code of conduct and sticks to ethics and social responsibility would be much better than treating patients as profit centres. In the next section we describe hospitals in India that have built brands by providing tangible benefits such as affordable healthcare services for people who could not afford them. This has required a radical change in approach and has shown how medical care can become broad-based.

A RADICAL APPROACH TO HEALTHCARE

Increasing population increases demand for health care but facilities and doctors are inadequate in developing countries. Access to medical care is reflected in number of hospital beds per 1000 people, and this figure for India stands at 0.7. There is a big variation in services – from government hospitals to state-of-the-art private hospitals. While the poor lack medical care facilities, modern hospitals provide highly priced services to those who can afford them. Health infrastructure in many under-developed countries, including India, is abysmally poor. In India, a large section of the population has little access to high quality medical services, but ironically, the country also offers many high-class hospitals that attract well-paying patients from abroad in what is termed as 'medical tourism'.

Such an abysmal medical care system calls for radical innovation, because the method of one doctor seeing one patient at a time would require an impossible number of doctors, writes *The Economist* (2012). For example, on average around 2.5 million people require heart surgeries in India the country has a capacity of only 80,000 to 90,000 surgeries annually. Many people suffering from heart disease thus are denied services.

How could the gap be bridged? The solution lay in social innovation. Dr Devi Shetty of Narayana Hrudayalaya Institute of Cardiac Sciences, Bangalore, decided to do expand the services by thinking of ways to lower costs and to increase capacity. Dr Shetty was earlier the personal physician to Mother

Teresa, and he was influenced by her work to invent quality health care that was widely accessible and affordable. His mission has been "to deliver high quality, affordable healthcare services to the broader population in India." His solution was to apply principles of assembly line production to heart surgeries, thereby increasing capacity and reducing prices. At the same time, he ensured that both the poor and the rich could get high-quality healthcare.

According to its website, Narayana Hrudayalaya (NH) is "the lowest-cost, high-quality healthcare service provider in the world." This was achieved by using "process innovation" to reduce costs of heart surgery. One component of cost in surgeries is the time spent by surgeons. To reduce surgeon time and therefore prices, surgeons are required to do complex procedures while other tasks are left to other trained workers. The result is that the cost of surgeries has reduced considerably: they cost less than $2,000 each, about one-fifteenth as much as a similar procedure in America. This is an example of using innovation to solve long standing problems.

Dr Shetty applied the principles of supply chain, called "the Walmart approach" to medical care. Using it in the complex field of heart surgery has been a unique innovation. Process redesign helped reduce costs while costs were further sought to be reduced by negotiating partnership deals with suppliers. Govindarajan and Ramamurti (2013) explain that Dr Shetty kept a firm focus on frugality. The hospital frees up its resources through a unique method: it trains family members to provide post-operative care so that hospital personnel are freed for other tasks. It has also developed a hub-and-spoke model of medical delivery in which the spokes are equipped to provide diagnosis and routine care so that patients can be treated where they are, avoiding crowding at the hospital. The spokes serve as filtering out patients who require advanced specialised care who are then transported to the hospital hub, which is equipped with sophisticated equipments and highly trained doctors.

Today NH has the largest cancer hospital in India and has diversified into an orthopaedic hospital, an eye hospital, research facilities and training rooms. The hospital aims to do reduce costs so that a heart operation can be brought down to US$800 from point of admission to point of discharge. This is only a fraction of the cost of heart surgeries in the United States which can cost up to US$50,000. India has traditionally low prices but still the cost of a heart surgery is between US$5,000-US$7,000, but NH has succeeded in reducing the cost of even complex surgeries to about US$3,000. To help bottom-of-the-pyramid patients, the hospital provides a micro-insurance plan for health care called Yeshasvini that reimburses part of the cost. Yeshasvini was launched in 2002 and is run by an independent trust in association with the state government.

Further cost reductions were attempted using mass production techniques. As NH was providing heart surgeries to a very large population, it could achieve further economies of scale. One major area was negotiating with suppliers for lower bulk prices. This was achieved for basic consumable supplies to medical equipment. For example, the hospital can save about 40% by importing surgical gloves in container loads. By using digital X-ray technology, the cost of film is saved. CT scanners, MRI and other machines are used for 14 hours a day, which reduces per unit costs. Another way of cost reductions is through partnerships: NH negotiated with suppliers to provide expensive equipment for blood gas analysis and catheterization laboratory without buying them. Companies operate the equipment and earn from it. In this way, the hospital saves on the capital cost of the machines and offers lower costs.

NH in Bangalore performs about 30 heart surgeries a day, the highest by any hospital in India. Increased volumes have helped lower costs: staff costs are spread over a large number of customers. Yet, there was no compromise on quality: its maintains a mortality rate of about 2% and hospital-acquired infection rate of 2.8 per 1000 ICU days. These figures are comparable with the best hospitals across the world. An article in *Forbes* (2010) says that the mortality rate in NH is "much lower than in New York State for similar kinds of heart disease."

Another lever for cost reduction was the use of technology. Patients living in distant villages are served through rural clinics and telemedicine facilities, thereby saving cost. Reports are submitted online and doctors can study them and advise medicines without necessitating any travel either from the doctor or from the patient.

In keeping with its principles, Narayana Hrudayalaya does not deny treatment to anyone because of lack of funds. A hybrid pricing model is used, by which rich patients can choose private rooms at a higher cost than poor ones. That is, the revenue streams are maintained even while the poor get affordable medical care. A firm control of the profit and loss statement helps arrive at concessions that can be offered to poor patients on a daily basis. Thus NH can fulfil a great social need without compromising on profitability.

NH has built a formidable reputation by establishing a new health care model not only for India but also for the world. Patients come to its Bangalore facility from more than 50 countries. This reputation contributes to its branding. But the branding has been achieved not by marketing efforts but by concentrating on societal benefit.

The method is used by others as well. India's LifeSpring hospitals slash the price of childbirth by supplementing doctors with less expensive midwives, thereby reducing cost to about one-sixth of that in a private clinic. LV Prasad Eye Institute has a mission "to provide equitable and quality eye care to all sections of society" and operates as a not-for-profit institution.

A similar technique was developed by the Aravind Eye Care System in India. It follows mass eye surgeries to about 350,000 patients a year. In a unique innovation, its operating rooms have two beds, so that surgeons can perform two operations at the same time, thereby reducing cost. Production line techniques are thus used in the field of eye surgeries.

Aravind was founded by Dr V, which is short for Govindappa Venkataswamy, an ophthalmic surgeon. Dr. V started Aravind after his retirement, asking his family members to join in. His sister, G. Natchiar, and her husband, Dr. Nam, both Harvard-educated eye surgeons, joined him in his cause. Initial capital was raised by mortgaging their homes, by which an 11-bed eye clinic was set up in a rented house. With a commitment to the social cause, Dr. V started a service-cum-business model. This model set Aravind apart: while private hospitals work with an eye on revenue maximisation, Aravind practises "honest medicine", keeping a balance between clinical practice and community work.

Today, Aravind operates five hospitals and has diversified into a research institute, an intraocular lens factory, eye bank, research centre and training institute. Since its founding in 1976 it has treated 29 million patients and performed 3.6 million eye surgeries and laser procedures, making it the world's largest and most productive eye-care service group.

Aravind is also a social business and an example of social innovation at its best. Its doctors perform 2,000 surgeries a year, which is five times the national average of 400. Apart from its scale, Aravind provides treatment that is either free or heavily subsidized for the poor. The pull of the brand is evident from the fact that people come from the remotest villages for treatment. It fulfils a great social need as some 4 million Indians develop cataracts in India and need treatment.

Aravind too uses a hybrid pricing model, earning from rich patients and subsidizing costs for the poor. While prices charged vary, the quality of treatment is the same for every patient. Non-paying patients are given a basic hard lens and recover in a common room with other patients. Instead of a hospital bed, patients are provided a mat on the floor. Patients who can afford higher prices can select a soft lens of their choice and also pay for higher categories of rooms. Quality is ensured for all categories of patients by rotating doctors for different sets of patients.

High volumes as Aravind require a steady supply of trained ophthalmic assistants. It has set up its own training institute, offering a two-year postgraduate specialization in ophthalmology.

Interestingly, it also has a program in which young village women are trained to become assistants. These assistants, with two years of training, do the routine tasks, freeing time of the eye surgeon. Doctors hence are able to focus on diagnosis and procedures. Using other lessons of just-in-time inventory management, the hospitals are able to perform surgery with one doctor and two assistants, instead of two doctors used traditionally. This keeps the services affordable.

Aravind represents another example of social entrepreneurship. Apart from its hospitals, it operates primary eye clinics called vision centres in villages, extending its reach. These vision centres are operated by vision technicians who check patients and if need be, arranges doctor consultations via videoconference. This saves travel time. For patients requiring surgery, Aravind transports them to its hospital and treated there.

Further cost reductions are achieved by more innovative methods such as backward innovation. Instead of buying lenses, it set up its own manufacturing unit and today makes lenses with a price range of $2 to $10, while imported lenses cost a whopping $150. Its manufacturing unit is called Aurolab and makes 2 million lenses a year. The unit exports lenses to 120 countries, and has gained a 7% share of the global market for intraocular lenses. Later, it has started making its own suture needles, microsurgical blades, lasers and eye drops.

Aravind has a target to perform 1 million surgeries annually. Its expertise is sought by other hospitals and it has helped some 300 hospitals in India, Bangladesh, Africa and Latin America by providing consultancy services. It has helped about 30 developing countries to set up a training centre like its own. Investment is made in research for prevention of eye diseases. In 2008 it won the Gates Award for Global Health and the 2010 Conrad N. Hilton Humanitarian Prize. Aravind has created a formidable brand not by using marketing techniques but by providing services to a large population, fulfilling a long felt need. This approach, called ethical branding, argues that brands must have ethics built in their DNA rather than project to be so.

ETHICAL BRANDING

Kumar and Gupta (2019) argue that brands are created not just by creating an image, but through actions which speak the sincerity of the brand. This is a much more sustainable way of creating brands. By keeping a focus on serving society, the hospitals described in this chapter have built formidable reputations. By reducing costs of treatment for the poor, these hospitals have taken the path of social inclusion and social service rather merely than trying to create an image. They have tackled the profit making objective not by over-charging their customers but by doing the opposite - innovating service design, reducing cost for patients and making their services broad-based. Reputation or branding has resulted from the word-of-mouth transmittal of a very large number of satisfied patients.

Hospitals should not be treated like brands because when they do that, they deviate from their basic purpose – to provide services to the society. Branding elements – such as applying imagery, themes and emotions to hospitals are at best cosmetic elements. However, when hospitals are treated like any other product or service, then the pressure to earn profits increase. When doctors are given revenue targets, for instance, there will be a tendency to prescribe unnecessary tests and procedures and also to over-charge patients. This is a sad outcome of applying too much marketing and branding elements to hospitals.

Ethical branding implies that social objectives be built in the DNA of any business. That is to say, the hospital must be guided by the principle of doing good in society, rather than primarily on making profit. Our examples of hospitals show that if the company or hospital has socially wired DNA, it will continuously and automatically look at ways of lowering cost and of providing affordable services to a large population rather than to a small elite.

CONCLUSION

In traditional marketing, brands are built by employing advertising and communications that create goodwill among customers. The world's famous brands have been built by using media effectively. The same principles are applied to building of hospital brands. In many countries hospitals position themselves on the basis of celebrity doctors and packaged five-star services. But when we question whether hospitals are akin to consumer brands, we find that building hospital brands in this fashion limits their social reach as they become affordable only to the rich or those who have adequate insurance.

Hospitals have been seduced by marketing to brand themselves just like consumer goods companies. Such hospitals often over-charge for treatments that are paid for by insurance companies. Thus, they get sucked into a vortex of high costs and are unable to serve the large population that is either not rich or not covered by insurance. Such branding falls apart at the first challenge such as a virus outbreak or media highlighting overcharging malpractices.

Arguing that hospitals are social businesses, the chapter builds the case that medical costs must be reduced through innovation. By doing so, hospitals are able to serve a large section of society that is excluded because of high costs. By serving bottom-of-the-pyramid consumers, hospitals can generate greater goodwill than they can by advertising and branding.

By changing their approach from a profit-making objective to becoming social businesses, hospitals can contribute greatly to society. Ethical branding is, after all, being known for doing good and having the social cause built in a brand's DNA. Hospitals are not after all, luxury brands like Gucchi or Calvin Klein.

REFERENCES

Anderson, J., & Markides, C. (2007). Strategic Innovation at the Base of the Pyramid. MIT Sloan Management Review. Retrieved from: https://sloanreview.mit.edu/article/strategic-innovation-at-the-base-of-the-pyramid/

Aravind Eye Care's Vision for India. (n.d.). Forbes. Retrieved from: https://www.forbes.com/global/2010/0315/companies-india-madurai-blindness-nam-familys-vision.html

Aravind. (n.d.). https://aravind.org

Bower, J. L., Leonard, H. B., & Paine, L. S. (2011). *Capitalism at Risk: Rethinking the Role of Business*. Harvard Business Review Press.

Five paradoxes of Indian Healthcare. (2018, July 27). The Economic Times.

Govindarajan & Ramamurti. (2013, November). Delivering World-Class Health Care, Affordably. *Harvard Business Review.*

Joachimsthaler, E., & Aaker, D. A. (1997, January). Building brands without mass media. *Harvard Business Review.*

Kapferer, J.-N. (2008). *The New Strategic Brand Management: Creating and sustaining brand equity long term.* Kogan Page.

Keller, K. L. (1998). *Strategic Brand Management.* Prentice-Hall.

Kemp, E., Jillapalli, R., & Becerra, E. (2014). Healthcare branding: Developing emotionally based consumer brand relationships. *Journal of Services Marketing, 28*(2), 126–137. doi:10.1108/JSM-08-2012-0157

Knowledge@Wharton. (n.d.). Narayana Hrudayalaya: A Model for Accessible, Affordable Health Care? Retrieved from: https://knowledge.wharton.upenn.edu/article/narayana-hrudayalaya-a-model-for-accessible-affordable-health-care/

Kumar, D., & Gupta, P. (2017). Rural Marketing. *Sage (Atlanta, Ga.).*

Kumar, D., & Gupta, P. (2019). Ethical Branding Best Practices. In Ethical Branding: Best Practice Cases and Lessons from the World's Most Ethical and Unethical Companies. Routledge (Taylor & Francis). doi:10.4324/9780429442520-8

Most private hospitals overcharging. (2019, Apr. 6). Bangkok Post. Retrieved from: https://www.bangkokpost.com/business/1657444/most-private-hospitals-overcharging

Narayana Health. (n.d.). https://www.narayanahealth.org/

Porter, M. E., & Kramer, M. R. (1999, November). Philanthropy's New Agenda: Creating Value. *Harvard Business Review.*

Private hospitals fleece patients, overcharge up to 1737%. (2018, Feb. 21). DNA India. Retrieved from: https://www.dnaindia.com/delhi/report-private-hospitals-fleece-patients-overcharge-up-to-1737-2586945

Reich, R. B. (2016). *Saving Capitalism: For the Many, Not the Few.* Icon Books.

Schmitt, B., & Simonson, A. (1997). *Marketing aesthetics: the strategic management of brands, identity, and image.* The Free Press.

Speziale, G. (2015). Strategic management of a healthcare organization: engagement, behavioural indicators, and clinical performance. European Heart Journal Supplements, 17(A). doi:10.1093/eurheartjuv003

The future of medicine. (2012, June 2). The Economist.

What Companies are for. (2019, Aug. 22). The Economist.

KEY TERMS AND DEFINITIONS

Bottom of the Pyramid (BoP) Markets: Markets consisting of a very large but the poorest section of population, living on less than $2.50 a day.

Branding: The creation of a unique identity of a product by marketing efforts consisting of an image that is recognizable and distinct from others.

Customer-Based Brand Equity (CBBE) Model: A branding model proposed by Keller which consists of defining a brand's salience or identity, brand meaning consisting of performance and imagery, consumer response through judgements and feelings, and brand relationships.

Ethical Branding: Branding that matches with the core purpose of the brand, that is, they are created not just by creating an image, but through actions which speak the sincerity of the brand.

Social Business: A social business is defined as a business that has social objectives as its primary purpose. The profits made by social businesses are reinvested for the benefits to society and the environment.

Walmart Approach: The simplifying of processes and deploying technology, along with scaling up of businesses so as to reduce costs of goods and services.

Chapter 3
Branding and Marketing in the Pharmaceutical Industry

Nafisa Fatima Maria Vaz
Goa Institute of Management, India

Ajit Parulekar
Goa Institute of Management, India

ABSTRACT

The pharmaceutical industry is at a phase where the need to embrace marketing and branding strategies on a larger scale has increased as compared to the past. In this chapter, the authors address the trends in which pharmaceutical branding has evolved over the years into something very different in today's world. The pharmaceutical products can be broken down into four types, which include the patented products, generics, branded generics, and the OTC market. This chapter looks at the branding activities that are carried out by each of these. The chapter highlights the learnings from the consumer marketing industry, the complexities involved in building a brand strategy, global challenges faced in branding in the pharma domain, some of the successful strategies that have been implemented in the pharmaceutical industry (success stories), and the future trends in this area.

INTRODUCTION

The pharmaceutical industry has been very successful since the late 1980s, achieving remarkable annual revenue growth levels of over 10% a year and enjoying the resulting rise in profits. This success was mainly based on strong research and development (R&D), aggressive patent defense and the use of a dominant promotional tool, a powerful sales force. The pharmaceutical industry is undergoing drastic changes globally. It is high time that the Pharma companies focus on utilizing marketing and branding strategies on a larger scale. The pharmaceutical industry has been more product and R&D driven and has never been much brand driven. Some observe that Brand building activities taken up in the initial phase of the drug can help extend the commercial life of the product once the patent ends and competitors can

DOI: 10.4018/978-1-7998-3034-4.ch003

enter (Moss, Moss, & Bouleaux, 2007). A powerful branding strategy would make it tougher for new entrants. Prescription drugs with a strong stable brand can seamlessly transition into the over-the-counter (OTC) arena. Implementing effective branding strategies is of utmost importance to the pharmaceutical marketing departments because of the limited time and high costs involved. Being one of the largest Industry in the world, drug companies must be vigilant about marketing strategies to successfully market their products. The time and energy it takes to research and sell, to create a product formulation, to incorporate operating systems, to perform clinical trials and to concentrate on branding is enormous, and each stage has its own issues to tackle. It is therefore essential to have a successful pharmaceutical marketing plan in place (G. Moss & Schuiling, 2004)

With the rise in competition in the Pharmaceutical Industry, the importance of branding has changed over the years. With the importance of branding being seen as a valuable strategic asset in almost all the industries, it is surprising to see very little usage of branding in the pharmaceutical industry. This perhaps is because of the characteristics of the industry, which differs from the others considering the product life cycle. Another deterrent could be that the prescription-only medicine (Rx) sector being highly regulated, making it difficult to apply the usual strategies (Value & Prescribing, n.d.).

EVOLUTION OF BRANDING IN THE PHARMACEUTICAL INDUSTRY

In the 1980s and 1990s, the pharmaceutical industry achieved significant success with a steady economic growth. There was no obvious need to change the way the companies branded their products.(Sciences, 2020). Manufacturers of Pharma products always depended on great R&D, an aggressive defense of patents and a powerful sales force for success (Evolution, 2010). The industry has not changed its approach too much ever since. The R&D costs also include the expenses incurred for combinations that never reached the market. With high R&D costs it is of utmost importance to recover the costs by extending the life beyond the patent phase. Branding is a way in which it can enhance such success. When customers see value related just to the brand name, it stays a long way even after the patent ends and creates a longer lasting mark and relationship in the minds of the consumer.(Executive & Vol, 1999)

Brand is a pathway to create barriers for new entrants into the market. A powerful brand cannot easily be sidelined. They act to bring out the differences between their products and a competitor. Brands result in loyal customers, which helps in long-term success for either the product or the company or both. Often Branded products are higher priced and customers prefer that to be a better quality. For consumers, brands can represent a relationship of trust and loyalty. It is an unspoken understanding that the quality of the brand will remain constant as per the brand promise. Brands also somehow give consumers a feeling of protection against certain risks such as safety risks. Several industries have adopted a brand logic. The FMCG category has been leveraging brands for many years but now, services, durable goods and other industrial companies are also leveraging brands as a key competitive advantage. As an example, Intel has successfully been using a brand logic(Moss et al., 2007). Before 1991, the brand was not known at all by end consumers; since then, however, Intel has reached an acute awareness and created a quality image. They now rank it is now as the fifth strongest worldwide brand in terms of value, being worth more than US$30bn, far ahead of more traditional very well-known brands such as McDonald's or Marlboro. This was achieved by creating a brand identity and communicating it to end-users via a campaign integrating the 'Intel inside' logo in most computer manufacturers' advertising.

Similarly, there is no reason these benefits could not apply to the pharmaceutical industry. With the competition increasing in the Pharma Industry, the need for products to be differentiated rises. Loyalty from the indirect customers is of utmost importance too, even more now with the increased competition. Customers too need and are constantly looking for an assurance of quality and safety that a brand can bring to its users, especially in something related to their health. They wouldn't want any compromise. Successful brands build's trust, which is an important factor for pharmaceutical products that have an indirect impact on the doctor's success too.

In the last few years, the problem of spurious drugs has come up as an issue because of the large number of fake drugs in the market, thus raising red flags regarding quality issues to key stakeholders such as the health ministry, the government and the public has become important. Thus more than the quality of the product is the assurance that a powerful brand carries with itself. Hence, it's important to build a quality product and build the quality of the brand. A positive brand association acts as a promise made by the brand owner to the customer or stakeholder, and in this case a Pharma company to the patient or doctor. Organization's with successful brands are clear of the benefits of their brand. It has been for years now that the brands strategy of pharmaceutical companies was to create a brand and product that was needed, introduce it to Doctors through the routine methods via the sales force and then monitor the results. With several rules and regulations being enforced it causes changes in the pharmaceutical industry how medications are marketed, it has become critical for these companies to brand their products, to create a mark in the mind of the customers(Babu et al., 2018). This is particularly important because more and more drugs are progressively sold over the counter. With the competitive environment becoming more intense in the pharmaceutical industry, branding can represent a new competitive handle that can be used to project a firm in the marketplace. With retail brands now competing with generic drugs, alternative and complementary treatments, pharmaceutical companies cannot overlook or downplay the importance of power branding.

DIFFERENCE BETWEEN BRANDING CONSUMER PRODUCTS AND PHARMACEUTICAL PRODUCTS

The pharmaceutical industry unlike the FMCG Industry is a highly regulated industry that is closely monitored and often under an attack from many regulatory bodies and interested parties trying to reduce the size of the drugs bill (Panigyrakis, 1999). The brand name cannot be transferred to another product post patent expiry, which means the product has a very short lifespan. While if you look at the FMCG products, the product life can continue for as long as possible(Schuiling & Moss, 2004). Pharma companies have to focus not only on the efficacy, safety and side effects of a product brand but also on the management of the brand identity and its resultant brand image with customers. The fact is that the pharmaceutical brand model does not fit in easily with the established consumer brand theory that has developed over the last three decades(Moss et al., 2007). There are several theories regarding consumer product branding, but Pharma product branding needs to be handled differently. One notable difference is related to the type of consumers. Doctors and pharmacists are indirect customers that are like middle men between the patient and the company. This should not prevent companies from leveraging brands as we consider that doctors should be viewed as consumers. Doctors if are convinced on the quality, efficacy and reliability of the products, they do not hesitate recommending. They operate based on limited information and are influenced by the image of the company, their attitude towards the disease and their patients' feedback. Pharmaceutical branding very often trails fast moving consumer goods (FMCG) due to the variety and diverse techniques utilized by the FMCG counterparts. In the FMCG industry, organizations incorporate branding activities early in the product development process and ensure that the entire organization works towards developing a consistent brand image (Schuiling and Moss, 2003)

THE ADVANTAGES OF A PHARMACEUTICAL BRANDING STRATEGY

The pharmaceutical industry is one of the biggest markets in the world, they must focus more on their marketing strategies to successfully market their products. The time, money and effort that it takes to research and identify a market, develop a formulation for the drug, integrate operational systems, run clinical trials and focus on branding is huge, therefore it is essential to have a good pharmaceutical marketing strategy in place (Targis, 2001). Pharmaceutical companies depend majorly on their doctors to act as brand ambassadors. Their key brand strategy has been where the sales representative would promote a drug to the doctor and then follow up with reminders through various different modes (Babu et al., 2018).

The branding of Pharmaceutical products helps to create awareness among potential customers about the benefits of the drugs and medicines. It is also an important way to generate interest and increase confidence among potential customers which in the Pharmaceutical Industry include doctors. The marketing process and brand give the customers a point of differentiation amongst many other similar products in the market. In addition, the entire branding process adds value for a company as it helps the business to focus on, enhance and be consistent with its message. It also helps a company to see if the message is being received in the right way. A brand is a name that will register the product in the minds of the consumers as a set of tangible and intangible benefits(Blackett & Harrison, 2001). As a marketing tool, branding is not just a case of placing a symbol or name onto products to identify the manufacturer, a brand is a set of attributes that have a meaning, an image and produce associations with the product when a person is considering that brand. Retailers, value branding because consumers shop at stores that carry their favourite brands. For example, incase of a fever the patients immediately ask for a 'Crocin' in India. The main purpose of branding is product identification, building of trust and credibility thereby increasing profitability through the general acceptability of the product. Branding is important to both customers and marketers. From consumers standpoint, branding simplifies product choice. Without brands, consumers would have the task of having to evaluate the non-branded products in a product category whenever they went shopping and would never be at ease when using the product. Similarly in the case of OTC drugs the consumers would always prefer a known brand and in the case of prescription drugs the Doctors would recommend a brand that has gained their trust. Branding also brings in ease in product selection and a choice which is an added value to the consumer in his product search and evaluation(Costea, Bend, Chou, & King, n.d.). Organisations with strong brands have the luxury of charging premium price even in the face of mounting competition as customers would pay for the reassurance and an unspoken safety and quality. Especially when it comes to healthcare, consumers don't take a second chance Branding also serve as entry barrier.

1. Relationship With Customers

A powerful brand provides the platform on which to build an individual relationship with customers, and for the manufacturer to 'reach over the shoulder of the middle man', as H.G. Wells famously wrote, 'direct to the consumer'. The strength of the Nike brand with consumers has made the Nike range a 'must have' for any shoe retailer, and no retailers worth their salt can afford not to stock the brand. Pharmaceutical manufacturers whose brands enjoy 'must have' status with health authorities, prescribers and healthcare professionals can enjoy similar advantages, this is especially true in the case of Non prescription drugs and OTC's. The rise of DTC advertising and the ubiquity of the Internet can help brand owners create such a relationship and there is little that those government and regulatory bodies that wish to resist the encroaching tide of information can do about it.

2. Competitive Differentiation

A powerful brand provides significant competitive differentiation of a type that is extremely difficult for rivals to copy.Recognition is gradually being given to the role that branding can play in the post-patent stage of a product's life, as strong branding may confer additional time for the owner to maximise return on its original investment. For a major brand with sales of US$1bn a year, the extension of its primacy by only 100 days would be sufficient to recover the total cost of its R&D. The patent to Glaxo Wellcome's aciclovir has now expired. As a result, topical Zovirax, Glaxo Wellcome's OTC treatment for cold sores, is starting to feel the effect of generic competition. Bayer launched Soothelip (topical aciclovir) in December 1997 but Glaxo Wellcome, by managing the heritage and established recognition of Zovirax as the prescribed product, made it significantly more difficult for Bayer to compete in this sector.

3. Crossing the Borders of Countries and Markets

A powerful brand can cross the borders of countries and markets. Virgin is a classic example of a brand that has successfully translated into a number of sectors air travel, record shops, financial services, mobile telephony often on an international basis. Brands with broad-based appeal can provide a cost-effective way of leveraging value for their owners, and a guarantee of consistency of satisfaction for their customers. In the pharmaceutical market, the opportunity to carry brand value over into new market sectors through exports is becoming increasingly attractive with the growth of the OTC sector. Examples of brands that have managed the transition are Diflucan, Canesten and Zovirax. The jury is perhaps still out with Zantac and Tagamet.

4. Influencing Behavior and Attitudes

A powerful brand can influence behaviour and attitudes. As consumer attitudes towards personal computers have changed radically since the advent of Microsoft software, so attitudes towards depression have undergone a transformation since the introduction of Prozac in the late 1980s. Books have been written about the 'Prozac generation' and this immensely successful brand has acquired almost iconic status, which should help it to withstand some of the worst ravages of the post-patent era.

5. Customer Loyalty

A powerful brand that attracts customer loyalty can provide one of the greatest sources of wealth for a business, by its ability to secure, through customer commitment, more predictable cash flows. Branding has now become a management tool and, through financial evaluation techniques, it is now possible to measure the value creation performance of brands within a given portfolio, and to plan marketing investment accordingly. As has been demonstrated in so many other industries, successful brands can deliver enhanced shareholder value and add significantly to the worth of the business.

Intensive merger and acquisition activities in the pharmaceutical industry can also be interpreted from the aspect of branding. Mergers and acquisitions in other industries are often caused by the objective opportunity of using a successful (or less successful but familiar) brands for entry into a particular market. Mergers and acquisitions in pharmaceutical industry are induced by synergy in R&D, marketing or sale, which is another evidence of the industry's lack of focus on brand management. Brand equity is almost non-existent; instead, product value is expressed by its therapeutic value and patent protection. In the OTC product segment, the industry has shown that it is not unfamiliar with branding logic and practices. Important OTC brands have been present on the market for a considerable number of years, and their structure (by the length of market presence) is very similar to that of consumer goods industries. One of the conclusions is that all the roles in the decision-making process on the purchase and/or use of products are 'returned' into the hands of final consumers, which distinguishes them from ethical drugs, so that in this case branding logics is very similar to the one present in consumer goods. Successful OTC brands crossed national borders long ago, and are almost comparable with global consumer goods giants such as Coca Cola, Orbit or Pringles. Without the intention to rank or give a comprehensive list of all products, we shall mention only some, familiar to any 'average' consumer in Serbia: Aspirin (Bayer), which has celebrated the centenary of market presence; Centrum (Wyeth) or Supradyn (Roche) vitamin supplements; Strepsils (Boots) lozenges; Efferalgan (UPSA) paracetamol and many other. Advil (ibuprofen), another Wyeth's brand, one of the most popular pain killers in the USA, is gaining market share in Europe as well. This brand is well positioned in most neighboring countries, and it is only a matter of time when it will appear in our pharmacies, and pose the question of its impact on the generic product versions available on our market. Strengthening the role of final consumers and/or patients on the pharmaceutical market, dynamic changes in the position of prescribers and payers, and strengthening the role of other stakeholders on this market place the focus of interest on the question whether it is possible (and/or necessary) to develop successful ethical drug brands. To this question, Donahue (2007) adds the question whether it is possible to develop an ethical pharmaceutical brand in such a way as to promote trust in the product, the company and the industry itself, as this is one of the key concepts when considering this market. Blackett (2001) highlights the importance of dealing with ethical drug brands with the fact that their share in the total sales value of pharmaceuticals accounts for about 90%. What is the reason for inadequate engagement of pharmaceutical companies in brand development and management? The sources usually state the following reasons: High degree of regulation within the industry, with a with a strong influence of the state and politics. A constant cycle of improvement leading to the introduction of new brands at the expense of the existing ones. The tradename, i.e. brand cannot be extended to a new active pharmaceutical ingredient, as the new entity has to be registered under a unique name (Moss, Schuiling, 2001).Innovative ethical drug producers compete through R&D rather than by marketing or pricing practices (Liddell, 2001). Companies on the pharmaceutical market are primarily focused on patents guaranteeing them a period of exclusivity on a certain market. Patent protection expiry is followed by generic erosion and a large number of producers enter the market with bioequivalent products. Another reason resides in the nature of the industry itself, which is orientated to the R&D process in constant search of more efficient and safer products, which may lead to the appearance of a pharmacologically superior product even before patent expiry, which will mean the end of the inferior drug's lifecycle. Misconception that buyers/consumers are only interested in the product's technical attributes (Moss, 2001). The presence of an 'additional layer' – prescribers and pharmacists (Moss, Schuiling, 2004) and payers – between the pharmaceutical industry and the final consumer/patient. Moss (2011) views brands in pharmaceutical industry at three hierarchical levels. The first level is the corporate brand. A well-positioned corporate brand is in the function of raising a company's credibility level, strengthening the public's and/or the consumers' trust in the company, the credibility of R&D process, and a foothold facilitating access to prescribers for the company's sales force. A high failure rate of new pharmaceuticals in some cases has a discouraging impact on the idea of corporate brand development. Merck's fiasco with Vioxx explicitly shows a situation when a company would 'pay any cost' to keep the negative publicity of one drug extending to other products in its range. The therapeutic class brand represents a particular company's specific highlight on its superiority in the treatment of a particular disease.(Executive & Vol, 1999) The company's specialization in 'a single problem', a single therapeutic class, guarantees to the consumer continuous care of a particular problem, continuity of research, and thus the quality of its product or therapy. The trademark or brand name is the basic level, where the brand is developed around an individual product. The basic specific feature refers to the fact that each pharmaceutical product has at least two names – the innovator's original name and the generic name. The same product may be available on the same and/or different markets under the same generic name and different brand names. For instance, OM Pharma sells its drug Dexium (calcium dobesilate) under this brand name in Germany, and the same drug is sold in Argentina under the names Duflemina and Eflevar in Argentina, or DoxiOM in Portugal. Johnson&Johnson have licensed their Remicade to Japanese company Tnabe, so that the drug is sold on this market under the same name. Also, when licensing a drug to another company (or during joint product development), it is not uncommon for a drug to get different brand names on different markets; e.g., Valeant Pharmaceuticals licensed Virazol (ribavirin) to Schering Plough, who sold the drug on the American market under then name Rebetol, while Roche markets this drug on the European market under a separate license and the name Copegas. (Dickov & Kuzman 2011b)

6. Counterfeiting in The Pharmaceutical Sector

The commonness of fake, spurious and low quality drugs has become a major issue in the pharmaceutical industry thereby affecting the delivery of quality healthcare. This issue has turned into a menace in the recent years and is found to be more prevalent, especially in the low and middle income countries. These medicines are some of the major cause of unnecessary morbidity and mortality of the poor people in the low- and middle-income countries. This results in the loss of public confidence in the Pharmaceutical Industry(Anabila & Awunyo-vitor, 2014). Counterfeit drugs are products intentionally manufactured to resemble a brand name of a patented drug. They may not necessarily contain any active ingredients or may contain different ingredients as compared to the original drug. This issue with drugs is more in countries where the regulatory bodies do not strictly monitor and have weak quality control standards. WHO listed factors responsible for the rising wave of counterfeiting as lack of political will, lack or inadequate legislation prohibiting counterfeiting of drugs, absences or weak national drug regulatory authority, shortage or erratic supply of drugs, high cost of medicines, inefficient co-operation among stakeholders, trade involving several intermediaries, corruption and conflict of interest. The prevalence of counterfeit drugs continues to move out of control and in some parts of Africa and Asia the figure even exceeds 50-60%(Executive & Vol, 1999).Governments of these countries are gradually improving vigilance, for example, spurious drugs Imported from India by a pharmaceutical company in Ghana resulted in the shutting down of that company by the Ghana FDA, which is a step in the right direction. In order to maintain competitive edge in the industry, pharmaceutical companies have had to identify winning marketing strategies that provide competitive advantage on a sustainable basis. Pharmaceutical companies will not be able to rely exclusively on the their traditional success and will have to move towards building a strong brand. They will need to push for higher levels of monitoring to ensure protection from the spurious drugs.

BUILDING BRAND STRATEGY

The classic approach to developing brand strategy involves a series of stages in which the following are defined(Blackett & Harrison, 2001):

1. Brand positioning
2. Brand personality
3. Brand values
4. Unique values of the brand that support the values
5. How the brand appears to its audience

1. Brand Positioning

To beat competition, brands must be different. They must possess characteristics that make them stand out to customers to be unique and attractive. These characteristics may be functional based on product attributes and performance, or emotional based on perceived benefits or pleasure that flow from the brand experience. Positioning is the analytical process that helps to define the competitive space available to the brand and then states, as the foundation of all subsequent branding activity, how this will be filled. The most successful brands occupy positions in the minds of their customers that are unique and defensible; the positioning process is to do with putting the brands in place and keeping them there. This cannot be put in the same category as FMCG goods as the characteristics are different. Customers in Pharma Industry don't choose to fall sick, they are prescribed. So the positioning should focus on the highly involved patient concerned about their health decisions.

2. Personality

Brand personality builds on the emotional appeals of brands and is the medium through which these, in advertising and through visual brand identity, are expressed. Therefore, brand personality is an important differentiating factor in positioning brands. Brands can be positioned as masculine or feminine, young or old, authoritative or light-hearted, radical or conservative, according to how advertising and visual identity are used. Brands can reflect human personality traits and can align themselves closely with the aspirations of their target audience.

Advertising in medical magazines is abounding with beaming geriatrics epitomizing the merits of the latest treatment for urinary incontinence yet another example is of amorous middle-aged male whose marital bliss has been restored by a stiff dose of the latest male impotence corrective. Such crass stereotyping may be effective in capturing the attention of time-pressed doctors, but the industry must appreciate that only a subtler touch is likely to succeed with modern consumers especially in a world that is full of skepticism.

3. Brand Values

Brand values are the glue that binds the customer to the brand. They must be linked to the brand's attributes the reality of the offer they will have absolutely no credibility. Moments of truth are critical to the brand customer relationship. Several of the pharmaceutical brand advertising, focuses on product attributes, and very little focuses on patients' emotional needs. What it highlights is that while the functional needs of doctors and their patients are very similar, there is a whole layer of additional support, reassurance, and emotional support that the patient needs.

4. Unique Qualities of The Brand That Support the Values

Along with prescription, products there should be abundant scientific evidence that the claims made for the product are true, this is mandatory. A number of official and quasi-official bodies exist in countries such as the UK to ensure that no bogus products enter the market. With OTC products, the same applies and as many OTC products have been on the market for decades, longevity and the trust built up over the years can provide powerful emotional justification. Once these checks are in place the Pharma products use these certifications for branding their products and giving customers a security of assured quality.

5. How the Brand Appears to Its Audience

This is the visual manifestation of the brand's role and purpose. It comprises brand name, packaging design and advertising. Not only should these represent the brand's identity and positioning, they should help to express the brand's personality. The extent to which they can do this depends on whether the brand is available as a prescription-only product or OTC. Far fewer restrictions apply to the design and advertising of OTC brands; but the prescription sector, for the time being, remains tightly regulated.

Of all the elements in the brand "mix," the name remains the most important. It is just about the only component of the mix through which it permits the brand owner to convey brand positioning to all audiences. The choice of the brand name therefore is critical, particularly if they earmark the brand for the OTC market. Example, Prozac and Viagra are successfully branded pharma products. Regulating the name is also a part of the regulatory bodies because of the errors that misunderstood names can cause.(Morton, 2000)

Creating a culture where the importance of branding is understood is critical. No amount of careful market analysis, brand building and testing will succeed unless we accept it within the organizations top management that branding is of genuine commercial value and can help to optimize scientific success. Achieving this recognition is the greatest task that confronts brand "evangelists."

GLOBAL CHALLENGES TO BRANDING IN THE PHARMA INDUSTRY

Marketing is important but it is moving down the priority list of CEOs. The fault of this is not with the CEOs but the marketers and brand managers, as many have let their brands become commodities rather than highly differentiated brands due to poor marketing(Defibaugh, 2019). There is a study, which pointed out something notable that pharmaceutical brands including Cialis/Viagra, Allegra/Claritin, Nexium/Prevacid, Vytorin/Crestor were seen as highly commoditized compared with brands like Dunkin' Donuts/Starbucks.

When brands are highly commoditized and the perceived product differences no longer exist, then price becomes an important factor(Costea et al., n.d.). When you understand this, you can see how generics can come straight in and claim a large share of the market. In fact, in Pharmaceutical markets that have become highly commoditized, where the product itself has little intrinsic value, biosimilars were able to have a highly successful uptake. On the other hand, in other categories where the product value proposition was seen as higher for example somatropin and the products were more highly differentiated, the biosimilars were not able to achieve the same level of success(Morton, 2000).

The need for a clearer idea of the brand's role, not only in the pharma industry but in patients' lives. Branding has barely existed in the pharmaceutical industry, yet the word 'brand' is used indiscriminately and largely inaccurately. So far, branding appears to be the act of finding a trademark for a new product, launching it into the marketplace, throwing some advertising at it and then giving up all support when the patent lapses(Value & Prescribing, n.d.).

In the world of consumer goods and services, companies have for decades used branding techniques to achieve competitive advantage. Such techniques involve the development of a set of distinguishing characteristics in the product, which are capable of creating a strong and distinctive impression with the customer. If this impression is positive and other factors typically price and availability are in place, then a purchase decision that favors the brand will generally arise(Gielens & Steenkamp, 2019).

One often sees sluggish marketing where the marketers find an obvious differentiator, and base all their marketing on that simple, evident variant. This may be successful, but only if the marketers have securely knotted that differentiator to a strong driver, such as efficacy. If not, the results hoped for will not be imminent.

An example for the above is when a certain brand had great clinical data on efficacy, a minimal side effect profile and strong safety but was just failing to thrive. Two years post launch and it still had a single digit market share and was not growing. When looking at the data, it didn't look like a particularly effective drug, so the thinking was that it would have to be positioned for mild cases of the condition. However, when analyzing the data further, it was found to be a highly effective drug and the marketing team had neglected to even discuss efficacy as a message as they felt the fact it was launched and approved meant it was highly effective(Evolution, 2010). They had decided to focus on the secondary messages such as 'lack of weight gain' and completely neglected efficacy, which was the number one driver message. By changing their messaging to analytics-identified driver messages, they were able to double their market share in 6 months with the same budget, something they had not been able to achieve in the preceding years. It is so important to really get to grips with the data and base your marketing on that.

Due to the stringent regulations in the pharmaceutical sector many of the strategies used to market consumer products are considered objectionable practices. There are regulations that dissuade companies from obtaining physician loyalty by the use of expensive gifts or trips. It is unethical to use publicity techniques to convince the common people. However, the manner in which the Healthcare organisations must convince an audience that only their product are superior and meet their needs or that it deserves to be priced at a premium, is the same whether it is a FMCG or a drug being sold.

SUCCESSFUL BRANDING STORIES IN THE PHARMACEUTICAL INDUSTRY

The Marketing manager for Pfizer, in charge of Benadryl, Benylin and Sudafed, said that he focused on personalities for their brands and treated them like FMCG products, using a wide range of marketing techniques. Another brand manager of Schering Healthcare working on the OTC emergency contraception Levonelle also confirmed that there was a shift to using FMCG and consumer marketing principles (Anabila & Awunyo-vitor, 2014).

Pharma companies have hired marketing people from the FMCG industry since FMCG branding can be easily adopted into the pharmaceutical industry by taking into account the regulations. There is much to learn from FMCG where the consumer has always been king. FMCG companies know how to create brands very quickly while consumer healthcare is very slow to market.(Evolution, 2010) Furthermore, branded drugs should explore educating the consumer and to justify the extra cost rather than go for generic drugs.

Bayer's successful launch of its anticoagulant drug Xarelto highlights the power of effective messaging. Even though Xarelto was second to market and many stakeholders did not consider it the most effective compound in its class at the time of launch, it rapidly became a market leader.

FUTURE TRENDS AND CONCLUSION

Therefore, with the steady decline in the patent's influence to secure future business retributions, and the upsurge in power of the patient due to the advances in IT and the accessibility of medicines, the brand will play a progressively vital role. There are Pharmaceutical companies already working in the direction of setting up patient support programs where assistance to customers to find and select products suitable for their health needs is provided. If pharmaceutical companies prioritize the need for branding and identify the most effective ways to brand, time and resources could be allocated accordingly. Given an appropriate level of support, a brand can generate and secure profit far beyond the patent expiry.

For OTC or non-prescription drugs, pharmaceutical companies use the same branding techniques as FMCG marketers. On the other hand, branding of prescription drugs have a potential risk ahead. In branding process, marketers should ensure balance of message instead of mass promotion. The best way to achieve this balance is by taking responsibility to the public to act in an ethical manner.

The current approach adopted by most pharmaceutical companies tacitly shows the incapability of pharmaceutical companies to survive competition from generic entrants following patent expiry. However, there is strong evidence to believe that a more long-term, brand-sensitive approach may prove more profitable, given both current and expected market conditions.

This chapter gives a clear understanding of the history of how branding has evolved in the Pharmaceutical Industry over time and the rising importance of Pharma Branding inorder to have a longer success in the market beyond the patent phase. It also shows the differences between FMCG goods and what Pharma companies need to do so as to build a successful brand.

REFERENCES

Anabila, P., & Awunyo-vitor, D. (2014). Assessing the role of branding in the marketing of pharmaceutical products in Ghana : A case of three pharmaceutical companies. doi:10.5897/AJBM2013.7297

Babu, B. K., Lakshmaiah, K., Foundation, E., Lakshmaiah, K., Foundation, E., Pradesh, A., & Pradesh, A. (2018). *Pharmaceutical Branding Strategies and Communication*. Academic Press.

Blackett, T., & Harrison, T. (2001). *Brand medicine : Use and future potential of branding in pharmaceutical markets*. Academic Press.

Costea, D., Bend, S., Chou, S., & King, A. (n.d.). Is Advertising Effective or Not ? Evidence from the Pharmaceutical Market. Academic Press.

Defibaugh, S. (2019). Discourse, Context & Media "I talked to my doctor": Constructing the neoliberal patient-consumer in direct-to-consumer pharmaceutical advertising. *Discourse*, Context & Media, 28, 1–7. doi:10.1016/j.dcm.2018.12.001

Evolution, B. (2010). *The Changing Roles of Brand Management*. Academic Press.

Executive, R. P., & Vol, D. (1999). *Rx branding : A brand new culture*. Academic Press.

Gielens, K., & Steenkamp, J. E. M. (2019). Branding in the era of digital (dis) intermediation. International Journal of Research in Marketing, 1–18. doi:10.1016/j.ijresmar.2019.01.005

Morton, F. M. S. (2000). *Barriers to entry, brand advertising, and generic entry in the US pharmaceutical industry*. Academic Press.

Moss, G. D., Moss, G. D., & Bouleaux, A. (2007). What can the pharmaceutical world learn from consumer branding practice? Consumer and Pharmaceutical, 7(4), 315–320. doi:10.1057/palgrave.jmm.5050102

Panigyrakis, G. G. (1999). *Brand managers in the pharmaceutical industry : are they any different*. Academic Press.

Schuiling, I., & Moss, G. (2004). *How different are branding strategies in the pharmaceutical industry and the fast-moving consumer goods sector*. Academic Press.

Sciences, L. (2020). *Pharma 2020 : Marketing the future Which path will you take*. Academic Press.

Targis, P. W. (2001). *The role of advertising in branding pharmaceuticals*. Academic Press.

Value, I., & Prescribing, F. I. (n.d.). Its Value and Role as One of Many. Academic Press.

Chapter 4
Pharmaceutical Promotion:
A Literature Review and Research Agenda

Harindranath R. M.
Great Lakes Institute of Management, India

Bharadhwaj Sivakumaran
Great Lakes Instiitute of Management, India

ABSTRACT

The literature on promotional inputs has accumulated over time but continues to be fragmented. While there is a plethora of insights and findings, these are dispersed necessitating a one-stop-shop literature review to cover the ever-increasing research stream. This chapter addresses this gap by organizing and synthesizing the findings of the literature. This review paper covers all the important promotional instruments, such as "free drug samples," "gifts," "CME sponsor," "journal advertising," and "honorarium." The chapter develops a novel strategic contribution called "promotional inputs distribution framework," which gives tips to practitioners regarding promotional inputs; following this framework, salespeople can optimize the promotional cost and increase sales as well. Another novel contribution is the "detailing process" that characterizes the importance of information used to effectively develop the detailing story (or presentation) to physicians. This research also identifies a wider spectrum of research gaps available in the domain to advance knowledge development.

INTRODUCTION

Sales promotion helps increase the sales of products or services. In the pharmaceutical industry, sales promotion is quite different from that in consumer product industries as a majority of the promotional efforts are not directed to end-users but at physicians. Owing to the gatekeeper role of the physicians, pharmaceutical companies concentrate on physicians, promote their products and dispense promotional inputs to them

DOI: 10.4018/978-1-7998-3034-4.ch004

Studies have found that there is a strong positive link between exposure of products to a physician and their prescribing behavior (e.g. Kremer, Bijmolt, Leeflang, & Wieringa, 2008; Tsakiridou, Boutsouki, Zotos, & Mattas, 2008) and consequently, promotion becomes crucial for pharma firms. There are other reasons too for a higher level of promotions: fewer number of blockbuster drugs (brands whose sales potential in excess of $1 billion) in the firm's new product pipeline, pharma firms find it difficult to find new drugs that can sustain growth and to balance the lost revenue, and finally, new products have greater compressed product life cycles (Spiller & Wymer, 2001). Additionally, the systematic literature review performed by Stros and Lee (2015) indicated that in pharmaceutical marketing, the promotion "p" is very important, perhaps more important vis-à-vis the other Ps (such as price, product and physical distribution) of marketing. Not just review studies, empirical studies too have concluded that promotion is vital in pharma. For instance, the study performed by Hurwitz and Caves (1988) states that "the pharmaceuticals industry promotes its products heavily" (p.302) and these promotion efforts can help differentiate products, enhance brand loyalty, and check price competition (Rizzo, 1999). Thus, an important role of promotional inputs is to help to build brand equity (Osinga, Leeflang, Srinivasan, & Wieringa, 2011).

Building the brand is vital to a firm's success, due to a large number of drugs available for prescriptions. Hence, branding can play a leading role in product differentiation (Moss, 2016). Branding is critical in the pharmaceutical industry as it creates and enhances the awareness of the brand and further helps in generating a competitive advantage. The development of brand name is primarily of two types; either originating the name from the generic name (e.g. the brand name "Amoxil" from Amoxicillin) or with no association with the generic name (e.g. Zantac is the brand name of Ranitidine) (Sudovar, 1992). Branding coupled with the marketing process can provide information about products that helps create a distinction for the brand among the competitors of that product category. However, the product positioning of a drug will depend on its characteristics such as indications for which the drug is used, safety, efficacy and tolerability (Schuiling & Moss, 2004). Pharma companies need to find methods to communicate the benefits of the drug to the customers and this can be usually accomplished by a mix of promotional inputs such as detailing, advertisement in the medical journal, conference participation, continuing medical education (CME), symposium, drug sample, etc. (Nath Sanyal, Datta Saroj, & Banerjee Asok, 2013). Thus an assortment of promotional inputs dispensed to a salesperson can help build the brand. In general, in other industries, brands can be built with a combination of advertising and sales promotion. Further, in almost every industry, advertising is targeted at the consumer and sales promotion at both the consumers and the trade. However, a unique feature of the pharma industry is that advertising targeting the consumer is banned with the exception of 1-2 countries. The physician plays a very powerful role, much more than say the role of a plumber in choosing a brand of bathroom equipment. Hence, promotions too are targeted almost exclusively at the physician. Additionally, firms spend billions of dollars developing a drug. Hence, its brand needs to be built and reinforced. The only way of building the brand (apart from its performance) is by giving promotional inputs to physicians.

Broadly, pharmaceutical drug companies engage in two methods of promotion, one approach aims at physicians (direct-to-physician or DTP) and the other direct-to-consumer (DTC) or end-users. The DTC approach uses a pull strategy operating directly on end-users and a significant departure from the traditional form of promotion (i.e. DTP). For example, DTC advertising is directed to customers through media like television, newspapers, radio, the internet, and outdoor advertising and so on. Studies (e.g. Gilbody, Wilson, & Watt, 2005) have indicated that DTC advertising has led to an increased number of prescriptions for the advertised product. DTC promotions can influence the patients to ask for specific brands with their physicians and subsequently, they are forced to prescribe these brands. In the USA, there is an increased expenditure by pharmaceutical firms on DTC advertising and this can complement the effort of DTP as well (Albliwi, Antony, Abdul Halim Lim, & van der Wiele, 2014), but DTC advertising is employed on a smaller number of drugs and not all brands are advertised (Wind, Mahajan, & Bayless, 1990). However, there are benefits that the DTC advertisement offers. For instance, the study of Gilbody et al. (2005) concludes that DTC advertising positively impacts patient demand and the prescription behavior of the physicians, and provides patient education. The disadvantage of DTC advertising is that it can distort the relationship between the patient and physician, and change the prescribing practice with no positive relation to improvement in health outcomes (Gilbody et al., 2005). However, we do not dwell much in this chapter on DTC due to the fact that DTC promotion is rather limited and permitted only in two countries, i.e. the USA and New Zealand. In contrast, DTP promotion is practiced in all countries and hence this method has a global presence. The traditional method of promotion that is focussed on physicians (i.e. DTP) is important (Rosenthal Meredith, Berndt Ernst, Donohue Julie, Epstein Arnold, & Frank Richard, 2003) and the purpose of DTP promotion is to provide information on possible treatment choices, help to establish the communication between physicians and patients, and to enhance the physician-patient contact. Owing to its multiple objectives, the DTP expenditure is the major component (83%) of the promotion budget (Datta & Dave, 2017).

However, despite the importance of DTP, to our knowledge, there is no comprehensive literature review paper available on promotional inputs. This is the first literature review paper on pharmaceutical promotional inputs, such as free drug samples, gifts, continuing medical education (CME), honorarium, etc. The primary objective of the paper is to review the promotional inputs given by pharmaceutical companies and conclude with future research directions. Further, we came out with the Promotion Inputs Distribution Framework (PIDF) (Fig 1), with two axes; promotional input cost and prescription potential of physicians. These axes are further divided as "high" and "low" on both the axes, forming four quadrants, namely "no-hopers", "potentials", "low hanging fruit" and "key customers". This framework will assist pharma marketers regarding the type of promotional inputs allocated to physicians on the basis of their PIDF.

Furthermore, we developed a model for the detailing process (Fig 2), which shows that information can flow from sources such as pharmacies, salespeople and supervisors, and this information can help in the effectiveness of detailing leading to prescription loyalty. The relationship between detailing and prescription loyalty can be altered (or moderated) positively with promotional inputs. Future research can test these relationships shown in the model (Fig 2) empirically. Some of the research gaps identified are: influence of promotional inputs or support on salespeople attitudes and behavior; comparison of promotional support between the emerging and developed countries; promotional inputs distributed to salespeople can lead to unethical business practices; the impact of promotional support on the transaction-oriented role of the salespeople; and the allocation of promotional inputs on different therapeutic segments (such as cardiac issues, skincare etc.).

The chapter discusses the following; methodology, various promotional tools such as detailing, gifts and the like, the importance of promotional support given to salespeople, promotion vs. research expenditures, social and ethical implications. The chapter concludes with future research.

Figure 1. Promotion Inputs Distribution Framework

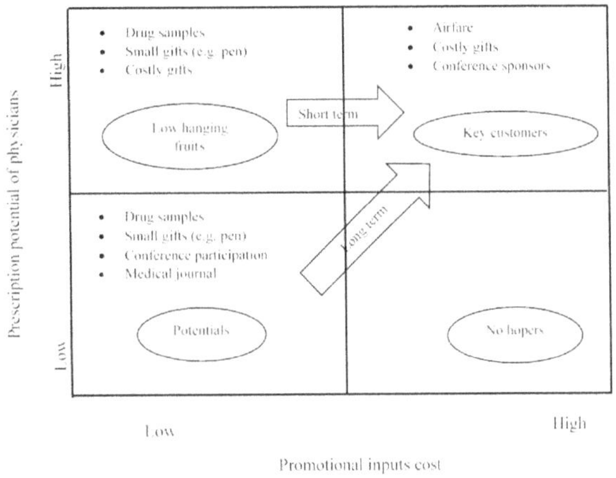

Figure 2. Detailing Process

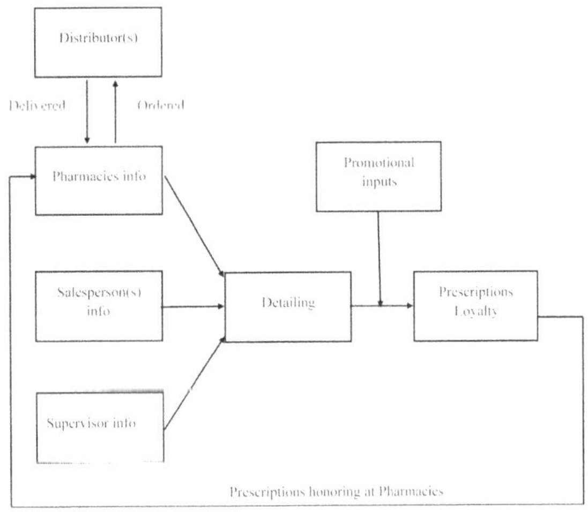

METHODOLOGY

We first performed the literature search, followed by the literature review as suggested by Boell and Cecez-Kecmanovic (2015). We searched the database of Scopus, which is comprehensive covering all the databases, and thus, our method adopted is rigorous and replicable (Boell & Cecez-Kecmanovic, 2015). The selection of research articles is based on the addition and exclusion criterion and this will help readers understand the reasons for excluding certain articles in this research (Booth, Sutton, & Papaioannou, 2016). To select the articles, we first reviewed the title and if we found it interesting, we read the abstract and this procedure helps to save our time as well as effort (Albliwi et al., 2014). If the paper found was relevant then we included it for literature review. The literature search (i.e. searching the Scopus database) yielded 1310 hits and using the exclusion criteria, we dropped 1245 research articles. Hence, the final number of articles found suitable is 65. Our search used the following keywords; "drug samples"; "gifts"; "continuing medical education sponsor or CME sponsor"; and "honorarium".

PROMOTION INPUTS DISTRIBUTION FRAMEWORK

This chapter develops a promotion inputs distribution framework and its purpose is to provide a guideline for pharmaceuticals marketers on the kind of promotional inputs that can be dispensed to physicians. Specifically, this framework assists the pharma marketers in planning the distribution of inputs to their customers (i.e. physicians) and in other words, the matrix helps in mapping customers to a particular strategy. This tool is evolved using two dimensions: physicians' potential and the promotional inputs' cost incurred by companies. The physician's potential is measured based on the average number of patients per day multiplied by the cost involved in each prescription. The promotional input cost is a direct measure. Each quadrant is named based on their characteristics, and they are "key customers" (high physicians' potential and high promotional input cost), "low hanging fruits", (high physicians' potential and low promotional input cost) "potentials" (low physicians' potential and low promotional input cost) and "no-hopers" (low physicians' potential and high promotional input cost) (see the figure above).

An important quadrant for a pharmaceutical marketing professional is "key customers" as these customers ensure maximum revenue to the firm. Based on this, pharmaceutical marketers need to concentrate to a greater extent on these "key customers" so as to get a continuous flow of prescriptions from this segment. These "key customers" can be allocated expensive promotional inputs like costly gifts, airfare, and sponsor to an international conference, among others as they provide maximum business to the firms. This could be in agreement with the Pareto principle that 20 percent of the prescribers give to an extent close to 80 percent business and the remaining (80%) contributes to business to around 20 percent.

The next important segment to concentrate on firms is the "low hanging fruits" segment. This category of physicians has prescription potential but untapped for a particular company. Since the cost of promotional inputs is low for them, they can be targeted to the same extent as "key customers".

The next segment is the "potentials" one. The promotional input cost is low for this segment and while the potential is low, it could be that some physicians here could be developed into "low hanging fruits" or even "key customers". The last quadrant, "no-hopers" can be ignored completely since they have low potential but are high cost. The obvious strategy for companies is to remove slowly the "no-hopers" from their customer list. Hence, we suggest by following the PIDF, the salespersons will become "promotional inputs wise" and save cost.

ROLE AND IMPORTANCE OF PROMOTIONAL INSTRUMENTS

The pharmaceutical industry dispenses promotional inputs to a greater extent to specialists when compared with family physicians (Campbell et al., 2007). Companies prefer to give importance to top prescribers, not just by detailing, but also through other forms of promotions (Gönül & Jr, 2012). Importantly, the promotional instruments dispensed by a firm has the role to enhance the competitive advantage in the market place. Promotional inputs can be beneficial in many ways. For example, they can act as a brand reminder (Gönül, Carter, Petrova, & Srinivasan, 2001), enhance the access to physicians, and free drugs samples can help initiate drug therapy. Above all, physicians expect promotional inputs from pharmaceutical companies. These promotional inputs are expected to play key two roles: information and persuasion. The informational role is due to the promotional intensity of new products and the persuasion is due to intense promotion (Leffler, 1981).

New product success is important for a firm for the reason that close to 25 percent of the revenue of firms was from the sales of new products (Wind et al., 1990). Companies recognize that the continuous launch and development of new products is necessary to guarantee the long-term success of the firm (Powpaka, 1996), and for new products' success, firms should provide continuous support for promotional support for salespeople. Not just new products, even for the existing products, the quantity of promotional inputs is based on the stages of the product life cycle. In other words, the promotional expenditures of a drug cannot be the same during their entire product life cycle. To conclude, the promotional expenditures are greater for a new launch, when the product is at the introductory and growth phase, and the sales volume is low (Kremer et al., 2008).

According to the social exchange theory (Blau, 1964), there exists a reciprocal exchange (Cropanzano & Mitchell, 2005); the salespeople dispenses promotional inputs to the physicians, and the physicians after receiving them, may prescribe the brand (Harindranath & Jacob, 2017). The resource bases view of a firm indicates the promotional inputs can lead to the development of brand equity and therefore an intangible market-based asset (Srivastava, Fahey, & Christensen, 2001).

PROMOTIONAL INSTRUMENTS TYPES

Detailing

Detailing is a visit by a salesperson to a physician's office and an age-old practice in the pharma industry. This promotional method is practiced by all companies and is the most expensive cum most extensively studied form of promotion (Kremer et al., 2008). The foremost component of the promotion budget is detailing (e.g. Hurwitz & Caves, 1988), for example, in the US, $15 billion is spent on detailing (Shapiro, 2018). Pharma companies' salespeople begin the process of detailing by collecting information from the pharmacy (i.e. retail audit), other companies' salespeople and their supervisor. This information helps compose the detailing story (i.e. developing message) as per the needs of each physician and then this is presented to physicians and this is akin to the concept of adaptive selling (Spiro & Weitz, 1990), but this rarely, if at all, is discussed in the pharmaceutical marketing literature. The message presented to physicians contains information on the benefits of drugs, which may lead to new prescriptions (Datta & Dave, 2017). Promotional instruments can act as a positive moderator in the relationship between detailing and prescription loyalty (refer fig.2) and it is likely that the detailing combined with the dispensing of right kind of promotional inputs can lead to a greater number of prescriptions. The appropriate combinations of the detailing story and promotional inputs for each physician can positively influence the volume of prescriptions. The prescriptions given will be honoured in the pharmacy and based on these, the pharmacy can provide new information to pharma companies' salespeople. Thus, the salespeople's prior belief is updated (refer to fig.2).

The pharmacy retailer's salesman plays a key role in providing vital information to pharma companies' salespeople about the prescription behavior of physicians, but to our knowledge, there is no research available that explains the role of a pharma retailer's salesman. There is another deficit in the literature. We find to our knowledge that no study connects the information collected from the retailers (or pharmacies) and the scripts developed by salespeople, based on this information. During an appointment, the representatives typically detail not just one, but a few drugs (Capella, Taylor, Campbell, & Longwell,

2009). Even though research has indicated that the salespeople may detail many product, to our knowledge, it is silent on the optimum number of products to be promoted in a single episode of detailing.

Once the detailing is over, salespeople assign promotional inputs based on the prescription potential of the physicians and these probably can change the prescribing behavior of physicians. Literature reveals that promotional inputs influence generating the prescriptions, but in the literature, there is little research that suggests the types of promotional inputs (say drug samples, gifts, honorarium, etc.) that are more effective compared to others. There are some basic questions unanswered in the literature like: does the physician still depend on detailing for information on drugs and therapies or is does (s) he to use say the Internet? Additionally, what is the role of detailing in developed vs. developing countries? What is the effect of culture on detailing?

The business potential of physicians varies and marketers (i.e. pharma companies) need to categorize them. One approach is from the diffusion literature. The diffusion literature reveals that physicians can be categorized as either imitators or influencers (e.g. Glass & Rosenthal, 2004) and the influencers mostly consist of specialists. The influencers are the highest volume prescribers of drugs and consequently, the salespeople give due importance in detailing and assigns greater promotional inputs to influencers (Gönül & Jr, 2012). The influencers are the key customers of pharma firms. This is in accordance with the critical mass theory (Oliver, Marwell, & Teixeira, 1985). However, in the literature, there is little discussion on the allocation and effectiveness of promotional inputs between imitators and imitators and influencers.

E-Detailing

The physician's time is demanding and salespeople calling on physicians becomes difficult. Hence, the pharma industry has come up with electronic-detailing. E-detailing is a variant of traditional detailing with digital features. Electronic detailing is a communication channel using digital technology to promote drugs to physicians. Martin E. Elling (2002) showed that only eight salespeople out of every 100 can meet the physicians. Similarly, the study of Group (1999) has given a breakup of how many salespeople meet physicians; 7 percent of the salespeople visit the physicians and take more than 2 minutes, fifty percent of salespeople take less than 2 minutes and 43 percent salespeople reach the physician's office but are unable to meet physicians. Hence, studies have concluded that there is immense competition for a physician's time (Alkhateeb & Doucette, 2008) and owing to this, electronic detailing would be a worthy option to fall back on. There are two types of electronic detailing and they are interactive or virtual e-detailing and video e-detailing. Physicians can access the (interactive) or virtual e-detailing when they want and the duration for the presentation is normally in the range of 5 to 15 minutes. Virtual e-detailing is commonly used in countries such as the USA, the UK, and France. Video e-detailing is a face-to-face approach between the salespeople and physicians. The video image of a salesperson is displayed along with audio communications and the physicians can raise questions and the salespeople can clear doubts if any (Alkhateeb & Doucette, 2008). Video e-detailing is closer to traditional e-detailing, and so a study is possibly needed to examine its effectiveness. However, researches have pointed out that electronic detailing has a stronger influence on the prescribing behavior of physicians than the traditional one and more importantly, it is cost-effective (Trucco & Amirkhanova, 2006). For certain cultures, the personal relationship between a salesperson and a physician works better. A cross-cultural study comparing the effectiveness of e-detailing across developed and emerging countries physicians would be useful in both a theoretical and practical sense.

Drug firms have many kinds of promotion strategies (Donohue & Berndt, 2004). There are many methods of promotion or interactions with the physicians: personal interactions with physicians known as detailing and providing gifts like drug samples, sponsored conferences, sponsored meals, research funds, honoraria, and continuing medical education (CME) programs. These interactions influence the prescribing behavior of physicians (Magnusson Maria, Arvola, Koivisto Hursti, Åberg, & Sjödén, 2001). These inputs can act as an inducement and will help in prescription loyalty. These assortments given are not the same for all companies and are based on the type of product the firms market. Moreover, the requirements of promotional inputs could be different for different sales territories, as each sales territory can have a unique mix of physicians. For instance, some sales territories can have a greater percentage of family physicians and others dominated by consultants or super-specialists. This section discusses the various types of promotional instruments, such as free drug samples, gifts, CME, among others and their characteristics.

Free Drug Samples

A time-tested and commonly used promotional tool is providing drug samples (Chew et al., 2000) and the dispensing of drug samples to physicians can increase the flow of new prescriptions (Lim & Kirikoshi, 2008; Mizik & Jacobson, 2004). The majority of physicians use drug samples to initiate the treatment for their patients (Okoli & Schabram, 2010). Lee and Begley (2016), in a study with a large sample (N=4720), found that drug samples are the most common form of promotion. Drug samples can influence new prescriptions (Adair & Holmgren, 2005). The samples may have a continuing effect on physicians as they may help increase tangibility to salespeople presentations (Gönül et al., 2001). Physicians who have access to free drug samples are unlikely to pick unadvertised drugs (Adair & Holmgren, 2005). The drug samples are not dispensed by every company. Some companies have banned them and others have no limit on the number of free drug samples (Chew et al., 2000). The sampling intensity varies across therapeutic segments (e.g. cardiac, skin, etc.) (Backer, Lebsack, Van Tonder, & Crabtree, 2000).

Firms need to be careful regarding the excess quantity of drug samples, which may have the tendency to cannibalize sales, even if they can increase the trial of products (Dong, Li, & Xie, 2013). Physicians who may not wish to meet salespeople want drug samples and patients also want drug samples (Fugh-Berman & Ahari, 2007). Mainly, the samples are dispensed by salespeople, but of late the samples are distributed through electronic mode also; the physicians can send the requirement for samples through an email to the company and based on the request, the drug samples are sent. The free drug samples have many advantages such as they help to initiate drug therapy, useful for indigent patients, serve as a brand reminder, can help to access the physician's office, can replace expensive prescriptions, lower the medication costs and patients can straightaway adopt the treatment. Nonetheless, drug samples don't bring benefits always, like free drug samples can raise the cost of treatment, can cannibalize the sales, among others. There is little research on the effectiveness of samples for new vs. existing products, and research can therefore, study this.

Gifts

Pharmaceutical firms present gifts regularly to physicians. The gifts range from an article of low value (e.g. a pen stand) to a higher value item like a flight ticket for a foreign trip (Madhavan, Amonkar, Elliott, Burke, & Gore, 1997). Not all gifts are given to every physician. The gifts with a low price are distributed often and contrarily, expensive gifts are offered to a few top prescribers. The benefits of dispensing gifts are that these gifts can serve as a brand reminder of a product/company, and the physicians who receive the gifts are inclined to prescribe the brand (Madhavan et al., 1997). A study with a sample of 2029 patients shows that physicians who accept gifts from pharmaceutical companies will have a lower level of trust among patients (Grande, Shea, & Armstrong, 2012). Research is silent on whether this lack of trust may lead to lower psychological satisfaction with the treatment and therefore, a slower recovery. Research can study this.

Journal Advertising

Pharmaceutical companies provide product advertisements in medical journals whose readers are physicians. Interestingly, the healthcare sector spends more on print media than other sectors (Sinha, Kesselheim, & Darrow, 2018). Journal advertisements in medical journals allow drug firms to target physicians in a precise manner. They remain attractive to pharmaceutical companies as this mode reaches over 90 percent of physicians (Sinha et al., 2018). The advertisements in journals influence sales (Kremer et al., 2008) as top-notch physicians acquire information on drugs and therapy from the journals (Haug, 1997).

Continuing Medical Education (CME) Programs

CME is an activity that maintains and enhances the knowledge, performance, and skills of physicians and the physicians, in turn, use this to render better services to the patients and the community at large (VanNieuwenborg, Goossens, De Lepeleire, & Schoenmakers, 2016). The main aim of the CME program is to maintain and to improve clinical performance. However, the trend may be changing and the focus of CME is shifting to patients' safety (Balmer, 2013). Therefore, the purpose of every CME program is to arm physicians with the latest knowledge and CME has transformed from a simple attendance or credit system to a comprehensive continuing education in the USA (Balmer, 2013). Thus the CME program has gone from strength to strength.

It has transformed from mere participation to something more: the CME has narrowed the gap between what ought to be and what is done in patient and community health (Stevenson & Moore, 2018). The CME program has increasingly helped fill the professional gaps between currently what physicians are actually doing and what they should be doing (Stevenson & Moore, 2018). The sponsorship of CME programs to physicians has a positive effect on the number of prescriptions (Goffee & Nicholson, 1994) and the sponsoring drug firms highlight their drugs (Wazana, 2000). Thus, physicians expect sponsorship for CME programs from pharmaceutical companies (Andaleeb & Tallman, 1996) and it is an important promotional instrument (Relman, 2001) to generate a greater number of prescriptions. Research has been done on the role of CME in developed countries, particularly in the USA (Balmer, 2013) and Europe (Farrow, Gillgrass, Pearlstone, Torr, & Pozniak, 2012), and there is scant research in emerging economies. An interesting research option is to understand the role of CME in new product success.

PROMOTIONAL SUPPORT TO SALESPEOPLE

The job of a pharmaceutical salesperson is to promote his products to physicians (Andaleeb & Tallman, 1996) and dispense promotional inputs. The salespeople require an assortment of promotional inputs (e.g. the free drug samples) of varying kinds as the physicians expect promotional inputs during the salespeople visit (Waheed, Jaleel, & Laeequddin, 2011). The aim of assigning promotional inputs by the firm is to give support to salespeople to achieve the sales target and alleviate the threat due to competition. All salespeople have sales quotas, which is an outcome-based control instrument (Anderson & Oliver, 1987) and on achieving the quota/target, he/she may get financial incentives. To achieve the sales quota, salespeople require promotional inputs assortments regularly from their firms. In line with previous studies (Harindranath & Jacob, 2017; Rezai, Kit Teng, Mohamed, & Shamsudin, 2014), this study has also conceptualized the promotional instruments as "job resources" of salespeople based on the job demand resource (JD-R) theory (Bakker & Demerouti, 2007). This is because the promotional inputs (as job resources) can reduce the deleterious effect of job demands and motivate the salespeople to call on more physicians. According to the Effort-recovery (ER) theory (Padilla Bravo, Cordts, Schulze, & Spiller, 2013), allocating promotional inputs to salespeople can increase their ability to achieve via dedication and ability (Rezai et al., 2014). Thus, as per the ER theory, offering promotional resources to salespeople will increase their achievement through dedication and even ability. These are job resources because they have the ability to create other resources (i.e. sales) as per the conservation of resource (COR) theory (Hobfoll, 1989). Based on these, one can argue that pharmaceutical salespeople need promotional support from their firms periodically. Promotional support is "the extent to which pharmaceutical organization offers promotional instruments (gifts, drug sample, etc.) as a resource to their sales personnel for periodic distribution to the physicians, intending to generate customer loyalty" (Harindranath & Jacob, 2017, p.98). A reflective scale was developed as a perceptual impact of promotional support (PIPS) and tested with the pharmaceutical salespeople and found to possess psychometric properties (Rezai et al., 2014). This study further tested a model and found that PIPS influence positively the salesmanship skills, sales effort, and sales performance.

ROLE OF PHARMACY RETAILERS AND DISTRIBUTORS

The pharmacy retailers have a key role in pharmaceutical marketing and salespeople provide the link between the retail pharmacy and the distributors (i.e. physicians). The salespeople need to motivate pharmacy retailers to keep adequate stocks of existing products as well as the stocks of new product(s). Their support is important to the success of firms. Many companies plan and distribute promotional inputs for pharmacy retailers and these inputs are low-value items (e.g. pens, pads, etc.). The relationship between salespeople and retailers needs to be built and promotional inputs may help to enhance the relationship further. This relationship will help salespeople to obtain information about the movements of products, information about nearing expiry goods, competitor information, prescribing habits in terms of brand name(s) and the number of tablets by an individual physician, new product introduction, among others. This information may be useful in preparing the messages for presentation for an individual physician, which could be adaptive selling (Spiro & Weitz, 1990). Knowing their importance, it will be highly useful for managers to have some metrics on the retailer coverage by the pharma sales representatives. For instance, what is the percentage of key pharmacies covered over a specific period?

Another important entity in the marketing of pharmaceuticals is the distributors or wholesalers and they provide a key link in the supply chain. The distributors supply to the retail pharmacies (refer fig.2) and thus they also have an important role in the success of firms. Distributors can provide information on customers, competitors, and new trends in the market. Once the order is received, it is processed and the distributor's salesman delivers to the retail pharmacy. Accordingly, the distributor's salesman has regular contact with the pharmacies that can be converted to a long-term relationship. Therefore, they are important to the pharmaceutical companies. Many pharma firms develop certain marketing programs suitable for a distributor's salesman. The programs could be sales contests, compliments, and events to discuss the new product(s).

PROMOTIONAL VS. RESEARCH EXPENDITURE

There is a widening gap between research expenditure and the number of new products developed (Jarvis, 2001). In pharmaceutical marketing, the expenditure exceeds the expenditure on research. For instance, spending on promotion is almost twice that of research in the USA (Gagnon & Lexchin, 2008). The ratio of mean marketing spending to research expenditure has some cut-off/threshold values i.e. less than 0.5 is good and above 1 is alarming (Datta & Dave, 2017). Does the same ratio of research to promotion expenditure hold good for other countries? Hitherto there is no literature available on these topics. Future research can compare this ratio between developed vs. emerging countries. The widely held criticism regarding pharmaceutical firms is that they are mere marketing machines (Angell, 2006). If the research from other countries finds that the ratio is reasonable in other countries, the finding (that pharma companies are marketing machines) could be specific for countries like the USA.

SOCIAL AND ETHICAL IMPLICATIONS

The mix of promotional inputs is a double-edged weapon; it can boost the welfare of physicians (e.g. CME program) and also contribute to a higher cost of treatment. Pharma promotions help educate doctors (Goffee & Nicholson, 1994), and thereby, increase sales (Wieringa & Leeflang, 2012). However, these promotions may also make doctors to prescribe irrational medicines that patients may not require (e.g. prescribing unnecessary antibiotics) (Magnusson Maria et al., 2001). Grande et al. (2012) reveal that patients have low trust in physicians that accept gifts from the drug companies. An increase of prescription rate (3 times) for two firms' drugs was witnessed when the physicians were sponsored to participate in a firm-sponsored symposium (Magnusson Maria et al., 2001); thus there can be a chance for physicians prescribe irrationally or even unethically. Most pharmaceutical salespeople functioning under outcome-based control and they have sales quotas. These salespeople are directly accountable for their sales performance, but they are free to choose the approaches of achievement (Good & Schwepker, 2012). Contrarily, some big companies (e.g. GlaxoSmithKline) have scrapped the sales budget for individual salespeople and instead they provide greater quality information to physicians that help to treat their patients (Harrison, 2013). Salespeople can follow the unethical route to meet sales quotas by luring the physicians by way of distributing expensive promotional inputs. The study of Barsky (2008) shows that when salespeople are exposed to difficult sales goals, they are inclined to behave unethically. These drug promotions may lead to higher-profit making through unethical means (Jacob, 2018). Some companies provide excessive promotional inputs to their salespeople, which can lead to unethical practices. Studies have reported that physicians may perhaps find it difficult to differentiate between scientific evidence and promotion information (Ziegler, Lew, & Singer, 1995). The conclusion from the results of empirical studies reveals that drug promotion escalates the entry drug cost, lowers price competition by enhancing the apparent product differentiation (Rosenthal Meredith et al., 2003).

Prescription drugs have an important influence on consumer welfare and public health. The spending on prescription drugs is a rapidly growing constituent of healthcare expenditure. The dispensing of gifts make the rule of reciprocity that develop a sense of indebtedness to the receiver along with the intention to reciprocate the favour (Dana & Loewenstein, 2003). Physicians after receiving the promotional inputs (such as gifts) may become indebted to the pharma firms and they prescribe the firm's drugs rather than the one best suited for the patients (Rogers, Mansfield, Braunack-Mayer, & Jureidini, 2004). The bigger gifts (e.g. sponsor for international conference) given to physicians can create a feeling of not just higher materialistic benefits but also the experience of pleasure, which may cloud the decision making of the physician. However, exploiting an individual is unethical and not compatible in developing the moral character that is required for good patient's care. Thus, gift-getting is a physician's conscious decision that will tend to compromise the interest towards patient's care.

Many developed countries have enacted laws to regulate the interactions of physicians and pharmaceuticals to curb the unethical act. For example, the bribery act of the UK, enacted in 2009, will penalize for any bribery and the Sunshine Act of the US, forces the pharmaceutical firms to disclose all the payments given to physicians. Many multinational pharmaceutical companies have developed and framed their ethical code, which suggest the ways to conduct with the physicians.

FUTURE RESEARCH

The literature review done so far suggests that the pharmaceutical promotion domain is a fertile area of research as specified by Stremersch (2008). Thus, in general, the scope for research in pharmaceutical promotion is enormous is general and more so in emerging and developing countries. While we have specified several avenues for research in the preceding paragraphs, we provide a few more below as well:

- Promotional support (Harindranath & Jacob, 2017) is the perception of salespeople on the allocation of a sufficient quantity of promotional inputs. A key avenue of future research is to integrate the promotional support as an antecedent to key variables of personal selling like adaptive selling behavior (Spiro & Weitz, 1990), sales and customer orientation (SOCO) (Saxe & Weitz, 1982), selling skills (Rentz, Shepherd, Tashchian, Dabholkar, & Ladd, 2002), among others. Do promotional inputs enhance adaptive selling and customer orientation or do they make salespeople more transaction-oriented and decrease these? Another interesting research area is to examine the interaction of promotional inputs and adaptive selling behavior and their influence on sales performance.
- The human capital theory (Becker, 1962), argues that an increase in experience for salespersons can help to develop greater job knowledge and that can further lead to enhanced job performance (Harindranath, Sivakumaran, & Jacob, 2019). An interesting avenue for research is to explore the moderating role of sales experience (e.g. Harindranath et al., 2019) on the relationship between the perceived impact of promotional support (PIPS) (Harindranath & Sivakumaran, 2020) and sales performance.
- Since the competition for a doctor's time is quite intense (Alkhateeb & Doucette, 2008), practicing adaptive selling (or detailing) inside the physician's chamber could be difficult for salespeople. The

salespeople are knowledge brokers as per the meta-study of Verbeke, Dietz, and Verwaal (2011), contrarily, in the context of pharmaceutical selling, the knowledge broker role of salespeople is diminishing as the physicians don't depend the salespeople for drug information. Recently, the physicians-salespersons relationship is increasingly become transaction-oriented and hence, the domain of personal selling may change in the pharma sector (Datta, 2016). This phenomenon indicates a paradigm shift in the job role of salespeople in the pharmaceutical sector. So the research question is "Precisely, what will be the role of pharma promotion in such a changing scenario?"

- Pharmaceutical firms organize their marketing operations based on the therapeutic segment or divisions, such as cardiac, derma or skincare, critical care, gynaecology, paediatrics, respiratory and so on. The promotional inputs for each division can be different from the other, owing to the difference in the needs of clientele. Thus a study is needed to identify the kinds of promotional inputs in such major therapeutic segments. Thus our research question is "Can different therapeutic segments require different promotional inputs?"
- Some authors (e.g. Hurwitz & Caves, 1988; Leffler, 1981) have found evidence that pharmaceutical promotion has a higher effect on persuasion level vis-à-vis information and future research can be planned on the type of promotional inputs (e.g. gifts) and its effect on persuasion compared with information levels offered. Though DTC is not prominent on a global level, research is needed to examine the economic and clinical impact of DTC advertising on the healthcare system (Gilbody et al., 2005). Future research may differentiate between the influence of DTC advertising for pharma firms that launches many new products and the firms use DTC advertising to help existing brands (Osinga et al., 2011). Another avenue for research could be checking the interaction effect of DTP and DTC on objective sales performance.
- Do promotional inputs helps in influencing the job engagement of salespersons? The promotional inputs has the potential to motivate the salesperson being a job resource and thus help in achieving the sales quota. Research perform can understand how these job resources (i.e. promotional inputs) helps in inducing the job engagement of salespeople.
- The firms can map the relationship between an individual promotional inputs (e.g. gifts) and its impact on sales. The higher the beta for a promotional input, the more influence it has on sales. This will be useful for practitioners and academia, as this approach can cut the cost due to unnecessary promotion.

RESEARCH OPPORTUNITIES IN EMERGING MARKETS

Emerging markets can advance in offering new opportunities for research, thus help to develop new perspectives in pharmaceutical marketing (Sheth, 2011). These authors argues that emerging markets are heterogeneous, lack of resources, unbranded competition level are higher, etc. We discuss below some research gaps suitable to test in emerging markets.

- The comparison on the type of promotional inputs dispensed to salespeople of emerging vs. developed countries varies, and this could be a key research direction. Example, the comparison could be the most common promotional inputs given to physicians of emerging and developed markets. This could be interesting as the resources found are scarce in emerging markets.

- Due to the stress of financial economies in emerging markets (Tota & Shehu, 2012), the promotional inputs given to salespeople can possibly trigger some unethical sales practices. For instance, firms like Insys Therapeutics have been accused of offered money to physicians for prescribing their drugs (Hannah Kuchler, 2020).
- Development of country specific policy on drug promotion have evolved over time; a research on these developments among emerging markets could be a key contribution.

SUMMARY AND CONCLUSION

Promotion is important in the pharma sector. Promotion is like a double-edged weapon; promotions can affect the sales positively, but promotion in excess can increase the treatment cost for the patients and lead to social and ethical concerns. This chapter summarises the literature in this area for the period 1980 to 2020. The various facets of promotion such as free drug samples, gifts, CME sponsors, and honorarium are discussed. Further, it develops a framework (PIDF) that will be of use to practitioners in the pharma sector. The framework suggests that the distribution of promotional inputs will be based on the potential of physicians. Thus, the framework will help in an optimal distribution of promotional inputs to physicians and thereby save the cost of promotion. It also details the social and ethical concerns in this area and outlines specific avenues for future research.

REFERENCES

Adair, R. F., & Holmgren, L. R. (2005). Do drug samples influence resident prescribing behavior? A randomized trial. *The American Journal of Medicine*, *118*(8), 881–884. doi:10.1016/j.amjmed.2005.02.031 PMID:16084181

Albliwi, S., Antony, J., & Lim, A. H. (2014). Critical failure factors of Lean Six Sigma: A systematic literature review. *International Journal of Quality & Reliability Management*, *31*(9), 1012–1030. doi:10.1108/IJQRM-09-2013-0147

Alkhateeb, F. M., & Doucette, W. R. (2008). Electronic detailing (e-detailing) of pharmaceuticals to physicians: A review. *International Journal of Pharmaceutical and Healthcare Marketing*, *2*(3), 235–245. doi:10.1108/17506120810903999

Andaleeb, S. S., & Tallman, R. F. (1996). Relationships of physicians with pharmaceutical sales representatives and pharmaceutical companies: An exploratory study. *Health Marketing Quarterly*, *13*(4), 79–89. doi:10.1300/J026v13n04_07 PMID:10159647

Anderson, E., & Oliver, R. L. (1987). Perspectives on Behavior-Based versus Outcome-Based Salesforce Control Systems. *Journal of Marketing*, *51*(4), 76–88. doi:10.1177/002224298705100407

Angell, M. (2006). The truth about the drug companies. *Trial (Boston, Mass.)*, *42*(7), 66.

Backer, E. L., Lebsack, J. A., Van Tonder, R. J., & Crabtree, B. F. (2000). The value of pharmaceutical representative visits and medication samples in community-based family practices. *The Journal of Family Practice*, *49*(9), 811–811. PMID:11032205

Bakker, A. B., & Demerouti, E. (2007). The job demands-resources model: State of the art. *Journal of Managerial Psychology*, *22*(3), 309–328. doi:10.1108/02683940710733115

Balmer, J. T. (2013). The transformation of continuing medical education (CME) in the United States. *Advances in Medical Education and Practice*, *4*, 171–182. doi:10.2147/AMEP.S35087 PMID:24101887

Barsky, A. (2008). Understanding the Ethical Cost of Organizational Goal-Setting: A Review and Theory Development. *Journal of Business Ethics*, *81*(1), 63–81. doi:10.100710551-007-9481-6

Becker, G. S. (1962). Investment in human capital: A theoretical analysis. *Journal of Political Economy*, *70*(5), 9–49. doi:10.1086/258724

Blau, P. M. (1964). *Exchange and power in social life*. Transaction Publishers.

Boell, S. K., & Cecez-Kecmanovic, D. (2015). On being 'systematic' in literature reviews. In L. P. Willcocks, C. Sauer, & M. C. Lacity (Eds.), *Formulating Research Methods for Information Systems* (Vol. 2, pp. 48–78). Palgrave Macmillan UK. doi:10.1057/9781137509888_3

Booth, A., Sutton, A., & Papaioannou, D. (2016). Systematic approaches to a successful literature review. *Sage (Atlanta, Ga.)*.

Bravo, P., Carlos, C., & Anette, S. (2013). Assessing determinants of organic food consumption using data from the German National Nutrition Survey II. *Food Quality and Preference*, *28*(1), 60–70. doi:10.1016/j.foodqual.2012.08.010

Campbell, E. G., Gruen, R. L., Mountford, J., Miller, L. G., Cleary, P. D., & Blumenthal, D. (2007). A National Survey of Physician–Industry Relationships. *The New England Journal of Medicine*, *356*(17), 1742–1750. doi:10.1056/NEJMsa064508 PMID:17460228

Capella, M. L., Taylor, C. R., Campbell, R. C., & Longwell, L. S. (2009). Do Pharmaceutical Marketing Activities Raise Prices? Evidence from Five Major Therapeutic Classes. *Journal of Public Policy & Marketing*, *28*(2), 146–161. doi:10.1509/jppm.28.2.146

Chew, L. D., O'Young, T. S., Hazlet, T. K., Bradley, K. A., Maynard, C., & Lessler, D. S. (2000). A physician survey of the effect of drug sample availability on physicians' behavior. *Journal of General Internal Medicine*, *15*(7), 478–483. doi:10.1046/j.1525-1497.2000.08014.x PMID:10940134

Cropanzano, R., & Mitchell, M. S. (2005). Social exchange theory: An interdisciplinary review. *Journal of Management*, *31*(6), 874–900. doi:10.1177/0149206305279602

Dana, J., & Loewenstein, G. (2003). A social science perspective on gifts to physicians from industry. *Journal of the American Medical Association*, *290*(2), 252–255. doi:10.1001/jama.290.2.252 PMID:12851281

Datta, A., & Dave, D. (2017). Effects of Physician-directed Pharmaceutical Promotion on Prescription Behaviors: Longitudinal Evidence. *Health Economics*, *26*(4), 450–468. doi:10.1002/hec.3323 PMID:26893065

Datta, P. T. (2016). Medical rep's suicide raises concern over sales pressure. *The Hindu Business Line*.

Dong, X., Li, M., & Xie, Y. (2013). Understanding Sample Usage and Sampling as a Promotion Tool: State of Industry Practice and Current Research. In M. Ding, J. Eliashberg, & S. Stremersch (Eds.), *Innovation and Marketing in the Pharmaceutical Industry: Emerging Practices, Research, and Policies* (Vol. 20, pp. 507–530). Springer Science & Business Media. doi:10.1007/978-1-4614-7801-0_17

Donohue, J. M., & Berndt, E. R. (2004). Effects of direct-to-consumer advertising on medication choice: The case of antidepressants. *Journal of Public Policy & Marketing*, *23*(2), 115–127. doi:10.1509/jppm.23.2.115.51395

Elling, M. E., Fogle, H. J., McKhann, C. S., & Simon, C. (2002). Making more of pharma's sales force: Pharmaceutical companies have lost their focus on doctors. The key to higher sales is regaining it. *The McKinsey Quarterly*, *3*, 86–95.

Farrow, S., Gillgrass, D., Pearlstone, A., Torr, J., & Pozniak, E. (2012). Setting CME standards in Europe: Guiding principles for medical education. *Current Medical Research and Opinion*, *28*(11), 1861–1871. doi:10.1185/03007995.2012.738191 PMID:23043468

Fugh-Berman, A., & Ahari, S. (2007). Following the Script: How Drug Reps Make Friends and Influence Doctors. *PLoS Medicine*, *4*(4), e150. doi:10.1371/journal.pmed.0040150 PMID:17455991

Gagnon, M.-A., & Lexchin, J. (2008). The cost of pushing pills: A new estimate of pharmaceutical promotion expenditures in the United States. *PLoS Medicine*, *5*(1), e1. doi:10.1371/journal.pmed.0050001 PMID:18177202

Gilbody, S., Wilson, P., & Watt, I. (2005). Benefits and harms of direct to consumer advertising: A systematic review. *Quality & Safety in Health Care*, *14*(4), 246–250. doi:10.1136/qshc.2004.012781 PMID:16076787

Glass, H. E., & Rosenthal, B. (2004). Demographics, practices, and prescribing characteristics of physicians who are early adopters of new drugs. *P&T*, *29*, 699–708.

Goffee, Rob, & Nicholson, N. (1994). Career development in male and female managers–convergence or collapse. *Women in management: Current research issues*, 80-92.

Gönül, F. F., Carter, F., Petrova, E., & Srinivasan, K. (2001). Promotion of prescription drugs and its impact on physicians' choice behavior. *Journal of Marketing*, *65*(3), 79–90. doi:10.1509/jmkg.65.3.79.18329

Gönül, F. F., & Jr, F. J. (2012). Estimation of promotional strategies for newer vs older drugs based on physician prescribing data. *International Journal of Pharmaceutical and Healthcare Marketing*, *6*(1), 39–54. doi:10.1108/17506121211216897

Good, D. J., & Schwepker, C. H. (2012). Sales Quotas: Unintended Consequences on Trust in Organization, Customer-Oriented Selling, and Sales Performance. *Journal of Marketing Theory and Practice*, *20*(4), 437–452. doi:10.2753/MTP1069-6679200406

Grande, D., Shea, J. A., & Armstrong, K. (2012). Pharmaceutical Industry Gifts to Physicians: Patient Beliefs and Trust in Physicians and the Health Care System. *Journal of General Internal Medicine*, *27*(3), 274–279. doi:10.100711606-011-1760-3 PMID:21671130

Group, Health Strategies. (1999). *Access to high prescribers: the world of doorknob details*. Author.

Harindranath, R. M., & Jacob, J. (2017). Promotional support: A formative scale development. *International Journal of Pharmaceutical and Healthcare Marketing*, *11*(1), 97–110. doi:10.1108/IJPHM-04-2016-0023

Harindranath, R. M., Sivakumaran, B., & Jacob, J. (2019). The moderating role of sales experience in adaptive selling, customer orientation and job satisfaction in a unionized setting. *Journal of Business and Industrial Marketing*, *34*(8), 1724–1735. doi:10.1108/JBIM-08-2018-0233

Harindranath, R. M., & Sivakumaran, B. (2021). Perceived Impact of Promotional Support: Issues and Scale. *Journal of Promotion Management, 27*(1), 77-102, doi:10.1080/10496491.2020.1809592.

Harrison, V. (2013). *GSK to scrap targets for sales reps*. Retrieved 31-05-2019, from https://money.cnn.com/2013/12/17/news/companies/gsk-sales-targets/index.html

Haug, J. D. (1997). Physicians' preferences for information sources: A meta-analytic study. *Bulletin of the Medical Library Association*, *85*(3), 223–232. PMID:9285121

Hobfoll, S. E. (1989). Conservation of resources: A new attempt at conceptualizing stress. *The American Psychologist*, *44*(3), 513–524. doi:10.1037/0003-066X.44.3.513 PMID:2648906

Hurwitz, M. A., & Caves, R. E. (1988). Persuasion or Information? Promotion and the Shares of Brand Name and Generic Pharmaceuticals. *The Journal of Law & Economics*, *31*(2), 299–320. doi:10.1086/467158

Jacob, N. T. (2018). Drug promotion practices: A review. *British Journal of Clinical Pharmacology*, *84*(8), 1659–1667. doi:10.1111/bcp.13513 PMID:29349812

Jarvis, L. (2001). Productivity of big pharma falls after consolidation. *Chemical Market Reporter, 259*(5).

Kremer, S., Bijmolt, T. H. A., Leeflang, P. S. H., & Wieringa, J. E. (2008). Generalizations on the effectiveness of pharmaceutical promotional expenditures. *International Journal of Research in Marketing*, *25*(4), 234–246. doi:10.1016/j.ijresmar.2008.08.001

Kuchler, H., Verbitsky, N., Jennings, T., & Connaire, S. (2020). Opioid executive admits to 'no morals' ahead of prison term. *Financial Times*. Retrieved from https://www.ft.com/insys

Lee, D., & Begley, C. E. (2016). Physician report of industry gifts and quality of care. *Health Care Management Review*, *41*(3), 275–283. doi:10.1097/HMR.0000000000000042 PMID:25427138

Leffler, K. B. (1981). Persuasion or information-the economics of prescription drug advertising. *The Journal of Law & Economics*, *24*(1), 45–74. doi:10.1086/466973

Lim, C. W., & Kirikoshi, T. (2008). Understanding the effects of pharmaceutical promotion: a neural network approach guided by genetic algorithm-partial least squares. *Health Care Management Science, 11*(4), 359-372. doi:10.100710729-008-9053-z

Madhavan, S., Amonkar, M. M., Elliott, D., Burke, K., & Gore, P. (1997). The gift relationship between pharmaceutical companies and physicians: An exploratory survey of physicians. *Journal of Clinical Pharmacy and Therapeutics*, *22*(3), 207–218. doi:10.1046/j.1365-2710.1997.94975949.x PMID:9447476

Magnusson Maria, K. (2001). Attitudes towards organic foods among Swedish consumers. *British Food Journal*, *103*(3), 209–227. doi:10.1108/00070700110386755

Mizik, N., & Jacobson, R. (2004). Arc physicians "easy marks"? Quantifying the effects of detailing and sampling on new prescriptions. *Management Science*, *50*(12), 1704–1715. doi:10.1287/mnsc.1040.0281

Moss, G. D. (2016). *Pharmaceuticals-Where's the Brand Logic? Branding Lessons and Strategy*. CRC Press. doi:10.1201/b14470

Okoli, C., & Schabram, K. (2010). *A guide to conducting a systematic literature review of information systems research*. Academic Press.

Oliver, P., Marwell, G., & Teixeira, R. (1985). A Theory of the Critical Mass. I. Interdependence, Group Heterogeneity, and the Production of Collective Action. *American Journal of Sociology*, *91*(3), 522–556. doi:10.1086/228313

Osinga, E. C., Leeflang, P. S. H., Srinivasan, S., & Wieringa, J. E. (2011). Why Do Firms Invest in Consumer Advertising with Limited Sales Response? A Shareholder Perspective. *Journal of Marketing*, *75*(1), 109–124. doi:10.1509/jm.75.1.109

Powpaka, S. (1996). Factors Affecting the Doctor's Adoption of a New Pharmaceutical Product: An Empirical Investigation. *Journal of Pharmaceutical Marketing & Management*, *11*(2), 67–97. doi:10.3109/J058v11n02_05

Relman, A. S. (2001). Separating continuing medical education from pharmaceutical marketing. *Journal of the American Medical Association*, *285*(15), 2009–2012. doi:10.1001/jama.285.15.2009 PMID:11308441

Rentz, J. O., Shepherd, C. D., Tashchian, A., Dabholkar, P. A., & Ladd, R. T. (2002). A Measure of Selling Skill: Scale Development and Validation. *Journal of Personal Selling & Sales Management*, *22*(1), 13–21. doi:10.1080/08853134.2002.10754289

Rezai, Teng, Phuah, Zainalabidin, & Shamsudin. (2014). Structural Equation Modeling of Consumer Purchase Intention Toward Synthetic Functional Foods. *Journal of Food Products Marketing*, *20*(sup1), 13-34. doi:10.1080/10454446.2014.921868

Rizzo, J. A. (1999). Advertising and competition in the ethical pharmaceutical industry: The case of antihypertensive drugs. *The Journal of Law & Economics*, *42*(1), 89–116. doi:10.1086/467419

Rogers, W. A., Mansfield, P. R., Braunack-Mayer, A. J., & Jureidini, J. N. (2004). The ethics of pharmaceutical industry relationships with medical students. *The Medical Journal of Australia*, *180*(8), 411–414. doi:10.5694/j.1326-5377.2004.tb05995.x PMID:15089733

Rosenthal Meredith, B., Berndt Ernst, R., Donohue Julie, M., Epstein Arnold, M., & Frank Richard, G. (2003). Demand Effects of Recent Changes in Prescription Drug Promotion. *Forum for Health Economics & Policy*, *6*(1). Advance online publication. doi:10.2202/1558-9544.1044

Sanyal, N., & Shamindra, D. S. (2013). Conceptualisation of branding: Strategy based on the Indian pharma sector. *International Journal of Pharmaceutical and Healthcare Marketing*, *7*(2), 175–198. doi:10.1108/IJPHM-04-2013-0013

Saxe, R., & Weitz, B. A. (1982). The SOCO scale: A measure of the customer orientation of salespeople. *JMR, Journal of Marketing Research*, *19*(3), 343–351. doi:10.1177/002224378201900307

Schuiling, I., & Moss, G. (2004). How different are branding strategies in the pharmaceutical industry and the fast-moving consumer goods sector? *Journal of Brand Management*, *11*(5), 366–380. doi:10.1057/palgrave.bm.2540182

Shapiro, B. T. (2018). Informational Shocks, Off-Label Prescribing, and the Effects of Physician Detailing. *Management Science*, *64*(12), 5925–5945. doi:10.1287/mnsc.2017.2899

Sheth, J. N. (2011). Impact of Emerging Markets on Marketing: Rethinking Existing Perspectives and Practices. *Journal of Marketing*, *75*(4), 166–182. doi:10.1509/jmkg.75.4.166

Sinha, M. S., Kesselheim, A. S., & Darrow, J. J. (2018). Pharmaceutical Advertising in Medical Journals: Revisiting a Long-Standing Relationship. *Chest*, *153*(1), 9–11. doi:10.1016/j.chest.2017.09.048 PMID:29307432

Spiller, L. D., & Wymer, W. W. Jr. (2001). Physicians' Perceptions and Uses of Commercial Drug Information Sources. *Health Marketing Quarterly*, *19*(1), 91–106. doi:10.1300/J026v19n01_07 PMID:11727295

Spiro, R. L., & Weitz, B. A. (1990). Adaptive selling: Conceptualization, measurement, and nomological validity. *JMR, Journal of Marketing Research*, *27*(1), 61–69. doi:10.1177/002224379002700106

Srivastava, R. K., Fahey, L., & Christensen, H. K. (2001). The resource-based view and marketing: The role of market-based assets in gaining competitive advantage. *Journal of Management*, *27*(6), 777–802. doi:10.1177/014920630102700610

Stevenson, R., & Moore, D. E. Jr. (2018). Ascent to the Summit of the CME PyramidDefining Outcomes for CME ActivityDefining Outcomes for CME Activity. *Journal of the American Medical Association*, *319*(6), 543–544. doi:10.1001/jama.2017.19791 PMID:29356817

Stremersch, S. (2008). Health and marketing: The emergence of a new field of research. *International Journal of Research in Marketing*, *25*(4), 229–233. doi:10.1016/j.ijresmar.2008.09.002

Stros, M., & Lee, N. (2015). Marketing dimensions in the prescription pharmaceutical industry: A systematic literature review. *Journal of Strategic Marketing*, *23*(4), 318–336. doi:10.1080/0965254X.2014.931878

Sudovar, B. (1992). Branding in the Pharmaceutical Industry. In J. M. Murphy (Ed.), *Branding: A Key Marketing Tool* (pp. 130–137). Palgrave Macmillan UK. doi:10.1007/978-1-349-12628-6_13

Tota, I., & Shehu, H. (2012). The Dilemma of Business Ethics. *Procedia Economics and Finance*, *3*, 555–559. doi:10.1016/S2212-5671(12)00195-5

Trucco, M. Y., & Amirkhanova, S. (2006). *Transforming Pharmaceutical Marketing Through e-detailing: Case Studies and Recommendations.* Paper presented at the 8th IEEE International Conference on E-Commerce Technology and the 3rd IEEE International Conference on Enterprise Computing, E-Commerce, and E-Services (CEC/EEE'06).

Tsakiridou, E., Boutsouki, C., Zotos, Y., & Mattas, K. (2008). Attitudes and behaviour towards organic products: An exploratory study. *International Journal of Retail & Distribution Management*, *36*(2), 158–175. doi:10.1108/09590550810853093

VanNieuwenborg, L., Goossens, M., De Lepeleire, J., & Schoenmakers, B. (2016). Continuing medical education for general practitioners: A practice format. *Postgraduate Medical Journal*, *92*(1086), 217–222. doi:10.1136/postgradmedj-2015-133662 PMID:26850504

Verbeke, W., Dietz, B., & Verwaal, E. (2011). Drivers of sales performance: A contemporary meta-analysis. Have salespeople become knowledge brokers? *Journal of the Academy of Marketing Science*, *39*(3), 407–428. doi:10.100711747-010-0211-8

Waheed, K. A., Jaleel, M., & Laeequddin, M. (2011). Prescription loyalty behavior of physicians: An empirical study in India. *International Journal of Pharmaceutical and Healthcare Marketing*, *5*(4), 279–298. doi:10.1108/17506121111190112

Wazana, A. (2000). Physicians and the pharmaceutical industry: Is a gift ever just a gift? *Journal of the American Medical Association*, *283*(3), 373–380. doi:10.1001/jama.283.3.373 PMID:10647801

Wieringa, J. E., & Leeflang, P. S. H. (2012). Modelling the effects of promotion expenditures on sales of pharmaceuticals. *Applied Economics*, *45*(24), 3389–3399. doi:10.1080/00036846.2012.711940

Wind, J., Mahajan, V., & Bayless, J.L. (1990). *The role of new product models in supporting and improving the new product development process: Some preliminary results.* Cambridge, MA: The Marketing Science Institute.

Ziegler, M. G., Lew, P., & Singer, B. C. (1995). The Accuracy of Drug Information From Pharmaceutical Sales Representatives. *Journal of the American Medical Association*, *273*(16), 1296–1298. doi:10.1001/jama.1995.03520400066047 PMID:7715044

Chapter 5
Going for Silver-Senior Consumers' Reviews of Medical Tourism

Helena Rodrigues
ISCTE, Instituto Universitário de Lisboa, Portugal

Ana Brochado
ISCTE, Instituto Universitário de Lisboa, Portugal

ABSTRACT

Senior medical tourism is a growing niche market. Senior citizens are increasingly traveling abroad with the stated intent of accessing medical treatment. This study sought to identify the main dimensions of overall experiences in senior medical tourism. Data based on senior citizens' comments and ratings were retrieved from the treatment abroad website, with a focus on customers over 54 years old. Content analyses identified eight major themes in medical tourism reviewers. The themes of happiness (with the results) and treatment are predominant in senior consumers. The results are relevant to managers and marketing researchers who run medical tourism businesses, providing them with a deeper understanding of the senior market on services and identifying which services' quality most significantly influence customers' recommendations.

INTRODUCTION

Referred to as being in their "third age" in some regions of the world, older individuals are turning senior medical tourism into a hot market with the potential for lucrative business development (Han & Hyun, 2015). This sector's growth is directly correlated to the aging of baby-boomer medical tourism consumers who have the time and means to travel for longer periods in other countries (Alén, Losada, & Domínguez, 2016). Although the sector has not been extremely significant in past decades, its importance is currently growing as more senior consumers are traveling abroad with the stated intent of accessing

DOI: 10.4018/978-1-7998-3034-4.ch005

medical treatment. This demographic trend is growing, and it is tied to an increase in senior medical tourism (Lunt & Carrera, 2010). Medical tourism is an expanding niche market that encourages destination countries' economic growth mainly in non-OECD countries, promotes related employment beyond the high season, and extends seniors' quality of life and health (Bristow & Yang, 2015; Laesser, 2011; Baladi, Chao, Ee & Hollas, 2019). In addition, medical tourism has a positive effect on local communities' wellbeing promoting local commerce and creating jobs in the health industry in both public and private sectors (Suess, Baloglu & Busser, 2018; Ganguli & Ebrahim, 2017). Medical tourism increases tourism's overall intensity, mostly because specific senior populations are characterized by extensive tourism experiences. In addition, these tourists and those who travel with them have time for tourism activities that include hotels, restaurants, shops, museums, transportation systems, and airlines, which all greatly benefit from this industry (Alén, Losada, & Domínguez, 2016; Connel, 2006).

Past studies have highlighted the usefulness of Web reviews in terms of understanding patients' experiences in health tourism (Rodrigues, Brochado, Troilo, & Mohsin, 2017; Gohosh & Mandal, 2019. Furthermore, a significant number of researchers found that user-generated content are a reliable source for research in tourism and have significant impact to influence tourists' decisions at any stage of their travel arrangements (Lu & Stepchenkova, 2015; Leung, Law, van Hoof, & Buhalis, 2013). Nevertheless, there is a dearth of studies that examine the effect of web reviews on a senior population. Considering this, the present research sought to add to the previous studies' findings by providing a fuller understanding of senior medical tourism based on an analysis of consumers' online posts on the Treatment Abroad website, in particular those that emphasize senior cosmetic procedures. This study aimed to answer the following research questions:

1. What are the main dimensions of senior medical tourism experiences in narratives shared online in the post-purchase phase of medical treatments?
2. What are the main themes linked with male versus female patients?
3. What are the main dimensions of senior medical tourism experiences linked with recommendations?

The research below is structured as follows. The next section discusses trends in medical tourism and the senior market. Then, the methods section presents the research context and data collection and analysis procedures. The section on results includes the context analysis results for online reviews shared by senior medical tourists in the post-purchase phase of their experiences. The paper concludes with the study's findings, limitations, and future avenues of research.

LITERATURE REVIEW

Medical Tourism Trends

The medical tourism industry is relatively new, but it is considered to be one of the fastest growing sectors globally due to massive migrations of tourists from developing nations to less developed nations that offer reasonable options for price-conscious tourists (Alleman, Luger, Reisinger, Martin, Horowitz & Cram; Seetanah, 2011). The World Tourism Organization has listed among the 2020 future market trends for medical tourism 1) an increase in tourists' age, 2) a change from active vacations to experience-based holidays, and 3) an increasingly complex market segmentation required to satisfy with tourists' different objectives. The last trend of relevance in this context is the varied purposes of traditional trips (e.g., travel to destinations, honeymoons, and cultural or cruise-related visits).

In general, medical tourism is currently experiencing an increase in overall demand among tourists over 54 years of age, with most individuals opting for cosmetic surgical procedures (Holliday et al., 2013). Health-related spending is thus expected to accelerate (Deloitte, 2015). This tendency is placing enormous pressures on governments, healthcare delivery systems, insurers, and consumers in both developed and emerging markets due to related factors such as aging populations and the expansion of cosmetic surgery services (Deloitte, 2014). Reduced mortality rates and decreased infectious diseases have resulted in a life expectancy beyond the 60s worldwide (World Health Organization, 2015).

In Europe, more people are now over 65 years old than are children. Overall, Europeans are living longer and are expected to continue to age due to unprecedented medical advances (European Commission, 2014). The number of individuals aged 65 or older is thus projected to grow from an estimated 524 million in 2010 to nearly 1.5 billion in 2050, with developing countries accounting for most of this increase (World Health Organization, 2011). In this context, an increased number elderly citizens are likely to opt for cosmetic surgical procedures to maintain a much younger appearance (Salehahmadi & Rafie, 2012).

A key observation regarding the tourism industry and individual tourists that can be made based on the above trends is the growing importance of the market segment formed by older people because of the aging population. This segment is expected to expand continually into the future (Bloom, Canning, & Fink, 2010). Multiple studies have found that the elderly's motivations to travel abroad are related to health, so the increase in senior medical tourism is necessarily directly linked to more accessible tourist facilities because disability is often directly related to age (Chen, Wu, & Cheng, 2013). Senior medical tourism is becoming particularly important due to elderly tourists' total expenditure abroad, and this market's expansion is widely considered an opportunity to create more potential tourism revenue (Alén, Domínguez & Losada, 2002)

The "Me" Generation Wellbeing

American journalist Tom Wolfe coined the term "the Me Generation" when he noted the growing narcissism of baby boomers. This generation was born approximately between 1946 and1964, taking an increasingly prominent place among the general population as this generation has aged (Metz & Underwood, 2005). It now includes people who were between 52 and 70 years old in 2016. Baby boomers have become part of the mature population, thus more attention is being paid to seniors as consumers (Norman, Daniels, & Norman, 2001). This segment's importance in the markets has grown as baby boomers are increasingly giving travel expenditure priority in their retirement plans mainly because they feel healthier, have more money to spend, are better educated, and are more independent due to fewer family obligations than those of younger generations. Baby boomers can also travel during low seasons since seniors in their 50s often choose to travel from August to November (Patterson & Pegg, 2009);(You & O'leary, 1999). The entire tourism industry's infrastructure (e.g., travel agents, airlines, hotels, and taxis) benefits considerably from this segment's new demands (Connell, 2006).

Seniors' wellbeing—whether objective or subjective—and its causal factors are broadly discussed in the literature (Böhnke & Kohler, 2010; Gerdtham & Johannesson, 2001), including how quality of life has become a crucial element in evaluations of economic and social progress overall (European

Commission, 2014). Among the determinants of wellbeing, individual characteristics such as health, education, marriage status, living conditions, and financial situation are considered the most significant (Steptoe, Deaton, & Stone, 2015). Single factors affecting the aging population's wellbeing have also been investigated (Heun, Bonsignore, Barkow, & Jessen, 2001; Heun, Burkart, Maier, & Bech, 1999; Locker, Clarke, & Payne, 2000; Oliveira, Brochado, & Correia, 2018). Health plays a prominent role, with cosmetic improvements in health depending on socioeconomic status, which is most affected by gender, behavioral factors, and education levels (Groot & Van Den Brink, 2007). As levels of education have improved and gender differences in human capital have declined, further improvements in health can be expected among the elderly in the future (Oliveira et al., 2018). Seniors are, therefore, a richer aging population in good health, characterized by a desire to travel (Oliveira et al., 2018). However, unlike work-related travel, health and wellness tourists' choices are voluntary since each individual seeks to meet desired objectives by selecting among the hospitals, clinics, or tratments that range from cosmetic surgery to diagnostics and check-ups (De la Hoz-Correa, Muñoz-Leiva & Bakucz (2018). More specifically, travel focused on health, medical, and wellness care is a function of healthcare systems, population characteristics, health behaviors, and individuals' perceived health status (Andersen, 1995). Appearance and beauty have always been important in European culture and have become even more so to the Me Generation. The generation that once vowed never to trust anyone over 30 is entering its mature years (O'Bannon, 2001). Based on attitude, health, appearance, and lifestyle, these individuals will behave and appear on average 7 to 10 years younger than their actual, chronological age. Baby boomers are not planning to "age gracefully" but instead "age beautifully." They intend to go into maturity kicking and screaming all the way, and they will do whatever they can to challenge the stereotypes—and realities—of aging (Macik-Frey, 2013). This resistance is facilitated by rising per capita spending across developed countries and increasing discretionary incomes in developing countries, which are driving global growth (BioMedTrends, 2016).

According to a recent American Academy of Cosmetic Dentistry (AACD) (2015) survey, most procedures have experienced phenomenal growth in demand, typically in excess of 200%. Whitening and/or bleaching is the most requested procedures, while veneers; tooth-colored inlays, onlays, and/or crowns; and bonding are the top five. According to the AACD, most cosmetic patients fall into the 40–49 age category (26.88%), followed by the 50+ segment (25.09%). Females represent 71% of these patients and lead in terms of demand, while baby boomers represent (32%) of cosmetic dentistry patients. The double-digit rise in cosmetic surgical procedures suggests that customers are choosing to spend on treatments with a proven track record, such as facelifts and liposuction, which remain the gold standard for facial rejuvenation and body contouring (Deloitte, 2014; International Trade Centre, 2014).

METHODS

Source and Data Collection

The data were collected from the Treatment Abroad medical tourism website. This website (see www.treatmentabroad.com) was established in 2004 in response to inquiries from individuals in the United Kingdom (UK) and from clinics and/or hospitals overseas seeking to promote themselves to UK patients. The website developed a "Code of Practice for Medical Tourism" to ensure the best practices are followed by agencies, patients, and healthcare providers. A systematic review of medical tourism websites conducted by Lunt and Carrera (2011) found that, out of 50 websites, www.treatmentabroad.com was among the top three in terms of satisfying research quality guidelines and earning the Health on the Net label (see www.hon.ch).

Medical tourism consumers are increasingly seeking information on insider experiences and positive comments from online medical tourism reviews when planning trips for medical treatment abroad. Thus, the Treatment Abroad website is potentially a valuable source of information for medical tourism consumers. The data collected consisted of medical tourism reviews of 23 clinics (i.e., 8 dental and 15 cosmetic) posted in English by seniors 54 years old and over, for a 10-year period from 2008 to 2018 during autumn and winter months. The data included patients' gender, age, country of origin, treatment type, and satisfaction rating from 0 to 5 stars, which assessed outcome of treatment, quality of care, value for money, patient communication, and hospital and/or clinic environment. A total of 468 reviews were collected (266 from females and 202 from males) with 36,488 words (25,934 for dental clinics and 10,554 for cosmetic clinics).

Data Analysis

Leximancer software was used to analyze the medical tourism consumers' reviews of their clinical experiences. Leximancer is a relatively new method for transforming lexical co-occurrence data from natural language into semantic patterns in an unsupervised manner. This program's procedures are based on Bayesian statistical theory in which fragmented pieces of evidence can be used to map what is occurring in a given system (Smith & Humphreys, 2006). Leximancer is designed to move text analysis "from words to meaning to insight" (Leximancer, 2013). In essence, the software uses a quantitative approach to conduct qualitative analysis (Indulska, Hovorka, & Recker, 2011).

Leximancer employs two stages of co-occurrence information extraction—semantic and relational—using a different algorithm for each stage (Rodrigues et al., 2019). The program identifies relationships within the text in order to generate concepts and word roots from the uploaded documents (Cretchley, Gallois, Chenery, & Smith, 2010). This procedure delivers the added benefit of recognizing themes that may be overlooked if texts are coded manually (Crofts & Bisman, 2010). As in previous studies using Leximancer (Rodrigues et al., 2017, 2019), the present research complemented the concept map generated by conducting a narrative analysis of each theme. Finally, a sentiment analysis was also performed. Sentiment is generally modelled after the researcher introduces a list of typical sentiment or emotive seed words to help "steer" the software used to determine or profile sentiment in the texts in question (Leximancer Pty Ltd, 2016).

Leximancer has thus been designed to be an effective and mostly language independent system for tagging, mapping, and mining conceptual information from large text collections. The system seeks to emulate many content analysis techniques, including a conceptual overview of the data, trend discovery, and a top-down data analysis approach, which provides greater access to the source text's information. Leximancer was selected because of the overabundance of text information in the Treatment Abroad website's reviews (see https://reviews.treatmentabroad.com/) and the lack of adequate tools to analyze what consumers have written online. The numerical data gathered were then examined using Statistical Package for the Social Sciences software to obtain descriptive statistics with frequencies and valid data on the reviewers' five-star ratings and the different medical treatment types experienced by these consumers.

RESULTS AND DISCUSSION

Treatment Types

Regarding the medical treatments, the reviews mention more than 20 different cosmetic procedures. The top medical treatments selected by female consumers are face, eye, and breast lifts. The males' most popular cosmetic treatment is eye lifts. More than 20 different dental procedures were also identified. The top treatment selected by both males and females is dental implants, crowns, and bridges.

Content Analysis

Leximancer's analyses identified eight major themes. In order of importance or strength, these are happy (with results) (223 hits), treatment (201 hits), professional (staff) (119 hits), results (58 hits), surgery (35 hits), pain (22 hits), cost (19 hits), confidence (18 hits) (see Figure 1).

Figure 1.Concept map of medical tourism experiences

At the macro level, these themes offer insights into senior consumers' views on medical tourism after they pass the age of 54". In the concept map the recommend concept is associated with "professional (staff), consistent with the sentiment analysis that rank there to concepts on the top of favorable appraisal. The "tags" indicate that female senior consumers' focus on the importance of treatments that bring happiness; women are more willing to recommend the cosmetic surgery and the good results they have achieved then man.

The "tags" that are closer to man and Dental treatment indicate that man need to have confidence in the clinic they chose, and express concern for the pain they might experience and the cost of the dental treatment.

The identified concepts reflect how the reviewers' narratives focus on the eight themes throughout their written comments (see Table 1 below).

Table 1. Reviewers' comments linked with each theme

Theme	Hit_text
Happy (with the results) (223 hits)	I had Botox (36 units) and fillers at [Clinic X] during my Bali holiday in June 2013. I was so impressed by [the] lovely staff, the beautiful environment and also with [Dr. X] who administered my treatments.
	He gave me and my daughter lots of information that made our stay in Lithuania a very enjoyable [o]ne. I am 57 years old and people tell . . . me I look like [I am in my] mid to late thirty [sic]. All in all, I am ecstatic with the results and would like to first thank my wonderful surgeon and also . . . [express] my appreciation to his team.
	I can['t say enough about the whole procedure, their courte[ous] . . . service . . . [during] every appointment, the friendliest of all the staff and my beautiful smile to prove it. A big thank you to all at . . . [Clinic X].
	Unfortunately my jaw bone is almost gone, so Mark suggested [I] needed a bone graft or just 2 implants placed at the front, which is what [I] had done[. H]e built up the gum part of the denture so now [I] show my bottom teeth a little, and my upper denture looks amazing and so natural. Thanks[,] Mark and the team[,] for returning my smile and confidence[. I] am more than happy and would say don[']t wait any longer—just go for it!
	I got the work done at [Clinic X. T]he service and standard where [sic] higher than in Norway, and the price are [sic] UNDER [sic] half of [all] Norwegian prices. I am very happy with the clinic and the staff[. I] will come back asap [sic].
Treatment (201 hits)	They are willing to work late to ensure that your treatment will be completed on schedule. The clinic is modern and the technology . . . up to date from computers to [x]-rays, not to mention the dental equipment itself.
	Do you have dental fears or other physical/psychological[issues? The] clinic offers a general anesthetic where you are awake during the treatment, and it [the anesthesia] . . . [has] no after effects or discomfort. I've even used it.
	I completed a treatment plan at the dental clinic . . . 2 months ago. Though 3 trips were needed for all the work to be finished I still made considerable savings on the quote given to me by my local UK dentist.
	With [Clinic X] I felt in control throughout and [did] not [feel] that the treatment was being inflicted on me.
	My first visit was back in 2005 for implants. . . . I have since had further treatment[s] at their new clinic.
Professional (staff) (119 hits),	He is a very professional and very good surgeon who gives . . . good advice.
	[This clinic offers v]ery professional service from start to finish.
	I chose it because it sounded the most professional and [I] wasn't disappointed with that. I will go back in a year for a check[-]up as there are guarantees with the teeth so I need to keep the appointment.
	[I had an a]mazing surgeon and anaesthetist, [in a] clean modern hospital. [It was a p]rofessional process from start to finish.
	I had dental implants and [b]ridge work done in 2005 in [Clinic X] and found the clinic very professional and the standards extremely high. So much so that I returned to the clinic this year with my husband who is also receiving dental implants.
Results (58 hits)	Prices are most affordable and [I] am now booking some overseas girlfriends in for their treatments prior to their arrival. [I a] m sure they will be more than pleased with the results.
	The final results is therefore a bit difficult to say. I will answer the first line rating according to this fact.
	The results seems [sic] very good, so I will be back later for the implants work.
	I am now 3 weeks post op and most of the swelling and bruising has gone and [I] am pleased with the results. I just have some tightness on [sic] the neck area due to the lipo[. T]his is normal and should go within a month or so.
	I[']m now 4 months post op and delighted with the results[. M]y breasts are soft and natural looking and the scars are fading away and my recurring nightmares of my implants falling out are all but a distant memory.

continues on following page

Table 1. Continued

Theme	Hit_text
Surgery (35 hits	My local surgery removed my eye stitches . . . a week later[, b]ut there was a problem with the main facial stitches (2 weeks later) in that they were so small and tight (necessary to ensure no scarring) that [my] local surgery did not have the correct cosmetic stitch removal instruments.
	I have uses [sic] [Dr. X] again and I have and will continue to recommended him. I couldn[']t have afforded to have this surgery in the UK.
	[For a f]acelift using fat as dermal filler I chose the very reasonably priced [Clinic X] for my surgery, instead of cheaper options further afield, as it enabled me to travel by Eurotunnel with my car and family supporters. I chose my surgeon on the basis of extensive research.
	[Dr. X] performed my facelift surgery back in October 2010. It is now coming up to 12 weeks since my trip to [Clinic X].
	I would not hesitate to return to [Dr. X] should I decide on anymore [sic] surgery in the future.
Pain (22 hits)	I . . . [was] given painkillers. I did not need them, however[,] because I had almost no pain.
	I had to go there 3 times in all, starting last April. I had 4 extractions first which was horrible but pain free.
	I was given antibiotics and pain killers when I left. The pain killers are still in the box [in which] they were given to me.
	The only bit of pain I suffered was the initial injection. After that, 2 sessions of 3 hours each prepping the teeth for the crowns was [sic] completely painless.
	There was virtually no pain during or after the treatments. I was given all appropriate medications which I have never experienced in [the] UK.
Cost (19 hits)	[The f]inal price match[ed] . . . [the] upfront cost.
	[The reason for going abroad] was purely the cost and the difficulty of finding an [NHS] dentist.
	In the end the only options were Poland and Hungary. Having looked at the major practices in both countries it came down to elimination not because of cost, but who I felt most comfortable with.
	Their expertise is superb.
	In total I had 5 implants and 27 crowns at a total cost of X.
Confidence (18 hits)	My husband and I visited a number of cosmetic surgeons before we met [Dr. X]. He was the first one in whom we had real confidence and he prepared me very well for the operation—in every way.
	[T]he treatment was more important than having a holiday. [The e]ase of [my] initial consultation in the UK to establish . . . face[-]to[-]face contact gave me [the] confidence to go-ahead [sic] with the treatment.
	I have had the notion of implants (so as to renew the way I used to look) for the longest while but didn't have enough confidence in the practice and technology as well as my wallet. . . . [A]s a young man I lost several of my teeth to an unscrupulous Caribbean dentist whose interest was purely financial.
	During my last visit my wife had a free consultation there and she is now planning to undergo restorative treatment with [Clinic X], so . . . [that] is a measure of our confidence! On a selfish basis it will be good to re-visit the apartment and enjoy Budapest's thermal baths once more!
	[Clinic X] is so modern and clean, that [I] never felt it [was] like a chore going to the dentist and now [I] am showing my teeth again with confidence.

Note: To guarantee anonymity, prices, personal names, and clinic names were removed or replace by phrases using "X."

Mentions of cosmetic clinics are more closely related to female consumers and are associated with the happy theme. Dental clinics are more often mentioned in connection with males and are associated with the pain, treatment, and cost themes.

Sentiment Lens

The Leximancer automatic sentiment lens feature was used to determine whether consumers react positively or negatively to medical tourism experiences. Further analysis of selected concepts was conducted with this software to assess medical tourism concepts' associations with positive or negative terms, thereby providing additional insights into the texts' contents (see Table 2).

Table 2. Sentiment lens analysis

Selected Concept: Favorable (202)		Selected Concept: Unfavorable (21)	
Related Tags	**Likelihood**	**Related Tags**	**Likelihood**
Medical specialization: dental clinic	39%	Medical specialization: dental clinic	5%
Gender: female	38%	Gender: female	5%
Gender: male	35%	Gender: male	3%
Medical specialization: cosmetic clinic	31%	Medical specialization: cosmetic clinic	2%
Related Word	**Likelihood**	**Related Word**	**Likelihood**
Staff	68%	Care	6%
Recommend	65%	Results	6%
Professional	62%	Confidence	6%
Care	56%	Staff	5%
Happy	54%	Treatment	5%
Treatment	49%	Pain	5%
Hotel	48%	Recommend	4%
Feel	46%	Feel	4%
Clinic	45%	Clinic	3%
Results	44%	Surgery	3%
Surgery	43%	Happy	2%
Confidence	33%		
Pain	23%		
Cost	21%		

The sentiment analysis revealed that medical tourism consumers' comments are significantly more favorable than unfavorable for all concepts. The main positive concepts are related to staff, recommend(ation), and professional (staff) are the most positive (68%, 65%, and 62% likelihood, respectively). The concepts of care, results, and confidence are the most negative (6% likelihood for all). These results indicate that medical tourism consumers appear to be more positive than negative about their experiences.

Leximancer generates concept maps with themes, creating lines that show the most likely path between concepts. Leximancer also provides data about themes, concepts, and words associated with concepts through an assessment of their connectivity (i.e., count and likelihood %), which is identified as paths. The concepts' likelihood is given as the percentage of the text segments containing a certain concept that will also contain another concept, while the count is given as the number of segments in which the concepts occur.

These Leximancer statistics provide information that defines both directions of conditional probability between concept paths and related themes to help the researcher investigate and assess their relevance and trustworthiness. In the present study, this part of the analysis highlighted significant paths that offer additional insights into the consumers' views and provide a deeper understanding of medical tourists' recommendations based on path analysis of experiences running from treatment to recommendation.

Based on the concepts and their related words (i.e., count and likelihood %), 20 different paths were identified for the themes that cover experiences from treatment to recommendation, using the 5 concepts with the highest count for each theme (see Table 3). These paths provide insights into medical tourism consumers' perceptions of the desired clinic treatments that lead to positive overall experiences and post-purchase recommendations. Individuals trust product and brand recommendations made by other consumers and friends and family on social media channels more than they trust traditional media or advertising channels. Therefore, social media recommendations are currently service providers' most powerful marketing asset (Jurgens, Berthon, Edelman, & Pitt, 2016).

Table 3. Concept paths from treatment to recommendation

Path Number	Concept-Word Links	Concept Number
1.	Treatment → Professional → Recommend	3
2.	Treatment → Professional → Staff → Recommend	4
3.	Treatment → Professional → Feel → Recommend	4
4.	Treatment → Professional → Feel → Happy → Recommend	5
5.	Treatment → Professional → Pain → Feel → Recommend	5
6.	Treatment → Professional → Feel → Confidence → Happy → Recommend	6
7.	Treatment → Care → Recommend	3
8.	Treatment → Care → Surgery → Recommend	4
9.	Treatment → Care → Pain → Feel → Recommend	5
10.	Treatment → Care → Surgery → Happy → Recommend	5
11.	Treatment → Care → Surgery → Results → Recommend	5
12.	Treatment → Care → Surgery → Results → Happy → Recommend	6
13.	Treatment → Cost → Surgery → Recommend	4
14.	Treatment → Cost → Hotel → Recommend	4
15.	Treatment → Cost → Hotel → Surgery → Recommend	5
16.	Treatment → Clinic → Hotel → Recommend	4
17.	Treatment → Clinic → Staff → Recommend	4
18.	Treatment → Clinic → Confidence → Happy → Recommend	5
19.	Treatment → Clinic → Staff → Results → Happy → Recommend	6
20.	Treatment → Clinic → Confidence → Results → Happy → Recommend	6

All the paths developed have a common starting point in the most important concept of treatment (148 counts) and end with the third most significant concept of recommend(ation) (93 counts). The second most important concept is happy (with the results) (116 counts). Based on the simplified model of semantic patterns extracted by Leximancer (Crofts & Bisman, 2010), an investigation was conducted of how these three concepts are linked across other concepts. The additional concepts were staff (91 counts), clinic (89 counts), professional (staff) (42 counts), results (36 counts), surgery (35 counts), care (34 counts), feel(ing) (24 counts), hotel (23 counts), pain (22 counts), cost (19 counts), and confidence (18 counts). The analysis's results include a path diagram with 20 paths from treatment to recommendation (see Figure 2).

Figure 2.Twenty paths from treatment to recommendation

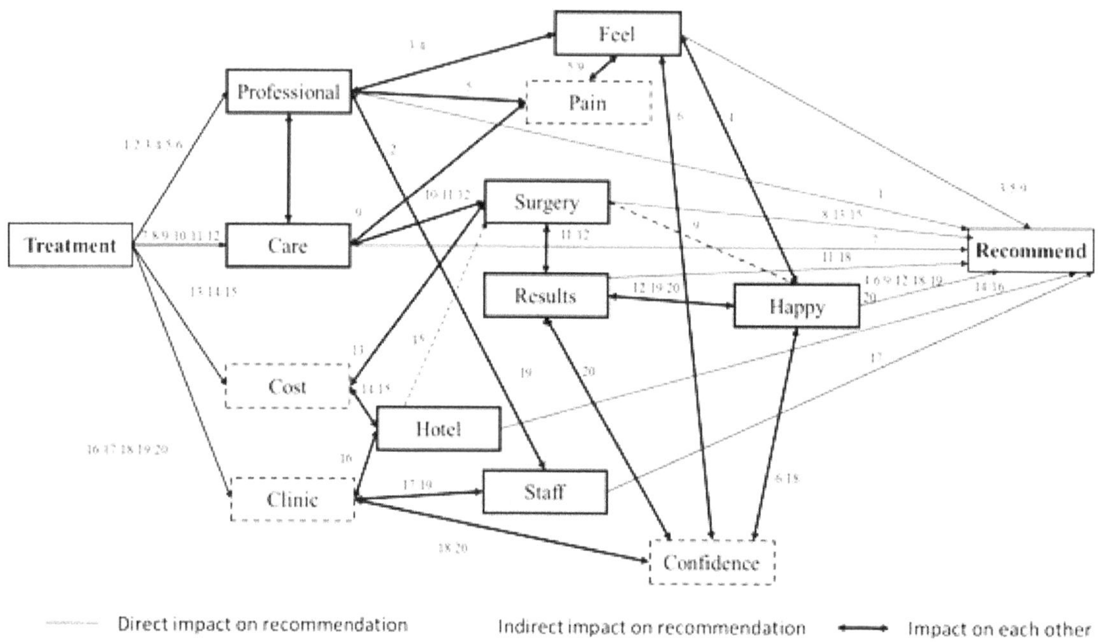

The path diagram extracted via the semantic pattern procedure highlights the two most important concepts that have a direct impact on recommendations: professional (staff) and care. The concepts of cost and clinic are also significant, but they depend on other concepts to get to the recommend(ation) concept. The concepts of pain and confidence play a moderately important role by influencing other concepts. For example, pain moderates feel(ing), professional (staff), and care. Confidence moderates clinic, results, feel(ing), and happy (with the results).

CONCLUSION

This study sought to identify the main dimensions of senior medical tourists' experiences shared online by patients in the post-purchase phase. In answer to the first research question, the content analyses revealed the following themes: happy (with the results), treatment, professional (staff), results, surgery, pain, cost and confidence

The relationship between tourism and happiness is extremely important to tourists' motivations (Liu, 2013). For most medical tourism consumers in the current research, medical treatments are the most important factor in decisions to undergo cosmetic surgery. This finding was well supported by the data as the treatment and happy (with results) themes identified are quite closely linked with confidence in treatments and procedures and professional staff and care, respectively.

In addition, the consumers also highlight the importance of hotel facilities, food, and accommodations, as well as their feelings about how they look after cosmetic procedures, which appear to be an easy way to shave years off their age. Senior consumers decide to have cosmetic surgery not to look merely normal but to look perfect. The feeling or belief that treatments (i.e., medical procedures) go well or succeed (i.e., confidence) is just as important since, if medical tourists conclude that medical treatments are ineffective, their lack of confidence limits their satisfaction with the treatments (Marple et al., 2007; Sackett, 1989; Thom, Kravitz, Bell, Krupat, & Azari, 2002).

Selecting the appropriate clinic is generally considered a significant decision when choosing a medical facility, although most medical tourism consumers choose a clinic based on a combination of interest in destinations and medical service (Carabello, 2008; Rahman, 2019). Overall, reviewers' ratings of dental clinics reflected globally higher satisfaction levels than ratings of cosmetic clinics in terms of the treatments' outcomes, hospital and/or clinic environment, and patient-staff communication. However, cosmetic clinics received higher ratings than dental clinics did regarding quality of care and value for money. One possible recommendation is that Clinics should understand tourists' needs and focus on customer orientation strategies to deliver high standards of medical tourism (Cham et al., 2020). Cosmetic plastic surgery is a specialty that aims at enhancing patients' sense of wellness and wholeness. Individuals need to feel comfortable in their body as this is a critical part of holistic health. The main theme related to gender indicate that more women than men seek plastic surgery because they are unhappy with some aspect of their physical self. A full 90% of plastic surgery patients are women according to the American Society of Plastic Surgeons (2016). Regarding the present study's second research question, many women's reviews provide insights into how they relate to their improved physical appearance, which can strengthen their chances of achieving renewed confidence in their bodies. In contrast, women and men are similar in their quest for dental procedures. Overall, cosmetic clinics are more closely related to females and, in turn, with the happy theme, while dental clinics have a closer relationship with males and the pain, treatment, and cost themes.

The results for the third research question highlight the importance of the path from treatments to happiness with results (e.g., experiences) and recommendations. The path diagram and the 20 paths detected from treatment to recommendation strongly support the conclusion that professional staff and care are the most important concepts in medical tourism, which suggests a closer investigation is needed of the happy (with the results) concept. The concepts of cost and clinic create paths ending in recommendations, but these paths rely on other concepts such as surgery, hotel, staff, confidence, and happy (with the results) to reach the recommend(ation) concept. Thus, cost is not necessarily a key driver in medical tourism, and others drivers such as service quality may be the main factors in many medical tourists' decisions (Ehrbeck, Guevara, & Mango, 2008; Veerasoontorn, Beise-Zee, & Sivayathorn, 2011). The results also indicate that the pain and confidence concepts need other linked concepts to influence consumers' feelings and happiness with results, respectively.

This study contributes to the literature in five ways. First, the research examined one of most popular international tourism sectors, medical care, in which few studies of consumer motivation and satisfaction have been undertaken. Second, the research focused on medical tourists' experiences in a extremely popular medical tourism market in Europe. Third, the study was based on medical tourists' spontaneously generated reviews rather than on data whose existence depends on external stimuli from researchers. Fourth, the study used Leximancer in a computer-assisted quantitative approach to conduct content analyses of qualitative data. Last, the results include concept paths from treatment to happiness with results (i.e., the happy concept), which then produces recommendations.

This research's findings confirm that good cosmetic treatments and consumer satisfaction (i.e., happiness) are essential to consumers' recommendations of clinics and/or medical tourism businesses to other consumers, friends and family (Mathijsen, 2019).

In addition to these implications, this study's results provide insights into the optimal way to undertake behavioral studies of medical tourists undergoing cosmetic surgery who use social media, especially online reviews, as a pre-purchase information source. Finally, the research produced a concept path diagram with 20 paths running from treatment to recommendation, in which professional staff and care as the most important concepts that directly influence customers' recommendations. The path diagram also shows how other concepts can affect each other. For example, the concepts of cost and clinic are significant, but alone they do not function as determinants or directly influence the recommendation concept.

This study had inherent limitations. First, not all senior patients write online reviews after their treatment. Second, the responses themselves are written in prose narratives in the post-purchase phase, which precludes direct observations of the medical tourism experiences in question. Future research could focus on identifying other themes and concept paths in medical tourism from consumers' reviews since medical tourism reviewers' comments provide a rich context for conducting further studies. More research is needed in the future to investigate the overall influence of the concepts of pain and confidence and their impact on other concepts such as feeling and happiness, respectively.

Medical Tourism Post Covid-19: Where Do We Go From Here?

Medical tourism once a lucrative business for countries who positioned themselves as niche markets face uncertainty due to the current Covid-19 pandemic (BMJ, 2020). Many countries maintain their borders closed, impose Covid-19 test and quarantine measures on tourists (HTI, 2020). The post Covid-19 era will bring each country to a starting point (Abbaspour, Soltani, & Tham, 2020; Bagga et.al., 2020). The ability to recover from the pandemic will depend on:

- Perceived trust: Tourists will seek safety rather than price.
- Quality: Maintaining high standards of treatment are crucial.
- Staff: Attracting and retaining highly trained health personnel.
- Communication: Provide international and local safety information in several languages.
- Partnerships: Integrated services that promote safety standards from arrival to departure (e.g., transportation from airport to clinic, local tours, shopping experiences and wellness treatments).
- Reopening plan: Until an effective cure or vaccine is found, countries that continue to implement sanitary measures to prevent the spread of the virus will be seen as safer (e.g., Social distancing, less crowded facilities, less infected population and low number of deceased).

- Medical tourism destinations: Tourist will rely on the reputation of the clinic, state of the art medical technology and overall facilities.

Yet, the future is hazy for medical tourism and lessons from the past will shape the future of the industry.

REFERENCES

Abbaspour, F., Soltani, S., & Tham, A. (2020). *Medical tourism for COVID-19 post-crisis recovery?* Anatolia. doi:10.1080/13032917.2020.1815067

Alén, E., Domínguez, T., & Losada, N. (2002). New Opportunities for the Tourism Market : Senior Tourism and Accessible Tourism. In Visions for Global Tourism Industry-Creating and Sustaining Competitive Strategies (pp. 140–166). Academic Press.

Alén, E., Losada, N., & Domínguez, T. (2016). The impact of ageing on the tourism industry: An approach to the senior tourist profile. *Social Indicators Research, 127*(1), 303–322. doi:10.100711205-015-0966-x

American Academy of Cosmetic Dentistry (AACD). (2015). *Cosmetic dentistry state of the industry survey 2015.* Retrieved from http://www.aacd.com/proxy/files/Publications%20and%20Resources/AACD%20State%20of%20the%20Cosmetic%20Dentistry%20Industry%202015.pdf

American Society of Plastic Surgeons. (2016). *Plastic surgery statistics report (2015).* Retrieved from https://www.plasticsurgery.org/Documents/news-resources/statistics/2015-statistics/2015-plastic-surgery-statistics-report.pdf

Andersen, R. (1995). Revisiting the behavioral model and access to medical care: Does it matter? *Journal of Health and Social Behavior, 36*(1), 1–10. doi:10.2307/2137284 PMID:7738325

Bagga, T., Vishnoi, S. K., Jain, S., & Sharma, R. (2020). Medical Tourism: Treatment, Therapy & Tourism. *International Journal Of Scientific & Technology Research, 9*(3), 4447–4453.

Beladi, H., Chao, C. C., Ee, M. S., & Hollas, D. (2019). Does medical tourism promote economic growth? A cross-country analysis. *Journal of Travel Research, 58*(1), 121–135. doi:10.1177/0047287517735909

BioMedTrends. (2016). *Dental business trends & latest market research.* Retrieved from http://www.biomedtrends.com/GetDetails.asp?CatName=Dental

Bloom, D. E., Canning, D., & Fink, G. (2010). Implications of population ageing for economic growth. *Oxford Review of Economic Policy, 26*(4), 583–612. doi:10.1093/oxrep/grq038

BMJ. (2020). Will medical tourism survive covid-19? *BMJ, 370.* doi:10.1136/bmj.m2677

Böhnke, P., & Kohler, U. (2010). Well-being and inequality. In S. Immerfall, & G. Therborn (Eds.), Handbook of European societies (pp. 629–666). Berlin: Springer Science + Business Media. doi:10.1007/978-0-387-88199-7_20

Bristow, R. S., & Yang, W. T. (2015). Sea, sun, sand and.... Selecting surgery: An exploration of health, medical and wellness tourist's mobility. *Human Geographies, 9*(2), 117–129. doi:10.5719/hgeo.2015.92.1

Cham, T. H., Lim, Y. M., Sia, B. C., Cheah, J. H., & Ting, H. (2020). Medical tourism destination image and its relationship with the intention to revisit: A study of Chinese medical tourists in Malaysia. *Journal of China Tourism Research*, 1–29. doi:10.1080/19388160.2020.1734514

Chen, C.-H., Wu, M.-H., & Cheng, J.-S. (2013). Service Demand of Senior for Spa on Wellness Tourism: An Explorative Study. *International Proceedings of Economics Development and Research*, *67*(6), 178–183. doi:10.7763/IPEDR

Conference, H. T. I. (2020). *Tourism post-Covid19 – What got you here, won't get you there!* Academic Press.

Connell, J. (2006). Medical tourism: Sea, sun, sand and ... surgery. *Tourism Management*, *27*(6), 1093–1100. doi:10.1016/j.tourman.2005.11.005

Cretchley, J., Gallois, C., Chenery, H., & Smith, A. (2010). Conversations between carers and people with schizophrenia: A qualitative analysis using Leximancer. *Qualitative Health Research*, *20*(12), 1611–1628. doi:10.1177/1049732310378297 PMID:20675536

Crofts, K., & Bisman, J. (2010). Interrogating accountability: An illustration of the use of Leximancer software for qualitative data analysis. *Qualitative Research in Accounting & Management*, *7*(2), 180–207. doi:10.1108/11766091011050859

De la Hoz-Correa, A., Muñoz-Leiva, F., & Bakucz, M. (2018). Past themes and future trends in medical tourism research: A co-word analysis. *Tourism Management*, *65*, 200–211. doi:10.1016/j.tourman.2017.10.001

Deloitte. (2014). *Global health care outlook: Shared challenges, shared opportunities*. Retrieved from https://www2.deloitte.com/content/dam/Deloitte/global/Documents/Life-Sciences-Health-Care/dttl-lshc-2014-global-health-care-sector-report.pdf

Deloitte. (2015). *Global health care outlook: Common goals, competing priorities*. Retrieved from https://www2.deloitte.com/content/dam/Deloitte/global/Documents/Life-Sciences-Health-Care/gx-lshc-2015-health-care-outlook-global.pdf

Ehrbeck, T., Guevara, C., & Mango, P. D. (2008). Mapping the market for medical travel. *The McKinsey Quarterly*, *11*. https://www.researchgate.net/publication/265184262_Mapping_the_market_for_medical_travel

European Commission. (2014). *Population ageing in Europe*. Retrieved from https://ec.europa.eu/research/social-sciences/pdf/policy_reviews/kina26426enc.pdf

Ganguli, S., & Ebrahim, A. H. (2017). A qualitative analysis of Singapore's medical tourism competitiveness. *Tourism Management Perspectives*, *21*, 74–84. doi:10.1016/j.tmp.2016.12.002

Gerdtham, U. G., & Johannesson, M. (2001). The relationship between happiness, health, and socio-economic factors: Results based on Swedish microdata. *Journal of Socio-Economics*, *30*(6), 553–557. doi:10.1016/S1053-5357(01)00118-4

Ghosh, T., & Mandal, S. (2019). Medical tourism experience: Conceptualization, scale development, and validation. *Journal of Travel Research*, *58*(8), 1288–1301. doi:10.1177/0047287518813469

Groot, W., & Van Den Brink, H. M. (2007). The health effects of education. *Economics of Education Review, 26*(2), 186–200. doi:10.1016/j.econedurev.2005.09.002

Han, H., & Hyun, S. S. (2015, February). Customer retention in the medical tourism industry: Impact of quality, satisfaction, trust, and price reasonableness. *Tourism Management, 46*, 20–29. doi:10.1016/j.tourman.2014.06.003

Heun, R., Bonsignore, M., Barkow, K., & Jessen, F. (2001). Validity of the five-item WHO Well-Being Index (WHO-5) in an elderly population. *European Archives of Psychiatry and Clinical Neuroscience, 251*(2), 27–31. doi:10.1007/BF03035123 PMID:11824831

Heun, R., Burkart, M., Maier, W., & Bech, P. (1999). Internal and external validity of the WHO Well-Being Scale in the elderly general population. *Acta Psychiatrica Scandinavica, 99*(3), 171–178. doi:10.1111/j.1600-0447.1999.tb00973.x PMID:10100911

Holliday, R., Bell, D., Jones, M., Hardy, K., Hunter, E., Probyn, E., & Taylor, J. S. (2013). *Beautiful face, beautiful place: relational geographies and gender in cosmetic surgery tourism websites. Gender, Place & Culture*. Taylor & Francis., doi:10.1080/0966369X.2013.832655

Indulska, M., Hovorka, D. S., & Recker, J. (2011). Quantitative approaches to content analysis: Identifying conceptual drift across publication outlets. *European Journal of Information Systems, 21*(1), 49–69. https://www.hticonference.com/medical-tourism-post-covid19-what-got-you-here-wont-get-you-there/Medical

International Trade Centre. (2014). *Medical and Wellness Tourism: Lessons From Asia*. Author.

Jurgens, M., Berthon, P., Edelman, L., & Pitt, L. (2016). Social media revolutions: The influence of secondary stakeholders. *Business Horizons, 59*(2), 129–136. doi:10.1016/j.bushor.2015.11.010

Laesser, C. (2011). Health travel motivation and activities: Insights from a mature market – Switzerland. *Tourism Review, 66*(1/2), 83–89. doi:10.1108/16605371111127251

Leung, D., Law, R., van Hoof, H., & Buhalis, D. (2013). Social Media in Tourism and Hospitality: A Literature Review. *Journal of Travel & Tourism Marketing, 30*(1–2), 3–22. doi:10.1080/10548408.2013.750919

Leximancer. (2013). *Leximancer: From words to meaning*. Retrieved from http://www.leximancer.com/cms/

Leximancer Pty Ltd. (2016). *Leximancer User Guide, Release 4.5*. Author.

Liu, K. (2013). Happiness and tourism. *International Journal of Business and Social Science, 4*(15). https://ijbssnet.com/journals/Vol_4_No_15_Special_Issue_November_2013/8.pdf

Locker, D., Clarke, M., & Payne, B. (2000). Self-perceived oral health status, psychological well-being, and life satisfaction in an older adult population. *Journal of Dental Research, 79*(4), 970–975. doi:10.1177/00220345000790041301 PMID:10831100

Lu, W., & Stepchenkova, S. (2015). User-Generated Content as a Research Mode in Tourism and Hospitality Applications: Topics, Methods, and Software. *Journal of Hospitality Marketing & Management*, *24*(2), 119–154. doi:10.1080/19368623.2014.907758

Lunt, N., & Carrera, P. (2010). Medical tourism : Assessing the evidence on treatment abroad. *Maturitas*, *66*(1), 27–32. doi:10.1016/j.maturitas.2010.01.017 PMID:20185254

Lunt, N., & Carrera, P. (2011). Systematic review of web sites for prospective medical tourists. *Tourism Review*, *66*(1/2), 57–67. doi:10.1108/16605371111127224

Ma, L. S. H. (2008). A medical tourism primer for US physicians. The Journal of medical practice management. *MPM*, *23*(5), 291. PMID:18472606

Macik-Frey, M. (2013). The age wave crests during economic crisis: New challenges for older workers. *Journal of Management and Marketing Research*, *12*, 1. http://www.aabri.com/manuscripts/121295.pdf

Marple, B. F., Fornadley, J. A., Patel, A. A., Fineman, S. M., Fromer, L., Krouse, J. H., Lanier, B. Q., & Penna, P.American Academy of Otolaryngic Allergy Working Group on Allergic Rhinitis. (2007). Keys to successful management of patients with allergic rhinitis: Focus on patient confidence, compliance, and satisfaction. *Otolaryngology - Head and Neck Surgery*, *136*(6), S107–S124. doi:10.1016/j.otohns.2007.02.031 PMID:17512862

Mathijsen, A. (2019). Home, sweet home? Understanding diasporic medical tourism behaviour. Exploratory research of Polish immigrants in Belgium. *Tourism Management*, *72*, 373–385. doi:10.1016/j.tourman.2018.12.009

Metz, D., & Underwood, M. (2005). *Older, richer, fitter: Identifying the consumer needs of Britain's ageing population*. Age Concern England.

Moghavvemi, S., Ormond, M., Musa, G., Isa, C. R. M., Thirumoorthi, T., Mustapha, M. Z. B., & Chandy, J. J. C. (2017). Connecting with prospective medical tourists online: A cross-sectional analysis of private hospital websites promoting medical tourism in India, Malaysia and Thailand. *Tourism Management*, *58*, 154–163. doi:10.1016/j.tourman.2016.10.010

Norman, W. C., Daniels, M. J., McGuire, F., & Norman, C. A. (2001). Wither the mature market: An empirical examination of the travel motivations of neo-mature and veteran-mature markets. *Journal of Hospitality & Leisure Marketing*, *8*(3/4), 113–130. doi:10.1300/J150v08n03_08

O'Bannon, G. (2001). Managing our future: The generation X factor. *Public Personnel Management*, *30*(1), 95–110. doi:10.1177/009102600103000109

Oliveira, C., Brochado, A., & Correia, A. (2018). Seniors in international residential tourism: Looking for quality of life. *Anatolia*, *29*(1), 11–23. doi:10.1080/13032917.2017.1358189

Patterson, I., & Pegg, S. (2009). Marketing the Leisure Experience to Baby Boomers and Older Tourists. *Journal of Hospitality Marketing & Management*, *18*(2–3), 254–272. doi:10.1080/19368620802594136

Rahman, M. K. (2019). Medical tourism: Tourists' perceived services and satisfaction lessons from Malaysian hospitals. *Tourism Review*, *74*(3), 739–758. doi:10.1108/TR-01-2018-0006

Rodrigues, H., Brochado, A., & Troilo, M. (2019). Listening to the murmur of water: Essential satisfaction and dissatisfaction attributes of thermal and mineral spas. *Journal of Travel & Tourism Marketing*, *24*, 16–25. doi:10.1080/10548408.2019.1633986

Rodrigues, H., Brochado, A., Troilo, M., & Mohsin, A. (2017). Mirror, mirror on the wall, who's the fairest of the mall? A critical content analysis on medical tourism. *Tourism Management Perspectives*, *24*, 16–25. doi:10.1016/j.tmp.2017.07.004

Sackett, D. L. (1989). Rules of evidence and clinical recommendations on the use of antithrombotic agents. *CHEST Journal*, *95*(2, Supplement), 2S–4S. doi:10.1378/chest.95.2_Supplement.2S PMID:2914516

Sadacharan, C. M. (2016). Vertical and horizontal facial proportions of Indian American men. *Anatomy & Cell Biology*, *49*(2), 125–131. doi:10.5115/acb.2016.49.2.125 PMID:27382514

Salehahmadi, Z., & Rafie, S. R. (2012). Factors Affecting Patients Undergoing Cosmetic Surgery in Bushehr, Southern Iran. *World Journal of Plastic Surgery*, *1*(2), 99–106. PMID:25734051

Seetanah, B. (2011). Assessing the dynamic economic impact of tourism for island economies. *Annals of Tourism Research*, *38*(1), 291–308. doi:10.1016/j.annals.2010.08.009

Smith, A. E., & Humphreys, M. S. (2006). Evaluation of unsupervised semantic mapping of natural language with Leximancer concept mapping. *Behavior Research Methods*, *38*(2), 262–279. doi:10.3758/BF03192778 PMID:16956103

Steptoe, A., Deaton, A., & Stone, A. A. (2015). Subjective wellbeing, health, and ageing. *Lancet*, *385*(9968), 640–648. doi:10.1016/S0140-6736(13)61489-0 PMID:25468152

Suess, C., Baloglu, S., & Busser, J. A. (2018). Perceived impacts of medical tourism development on community wellbeing. *Tourism Management*, *69*, 232–245. doi:10.1016/j.tourman.2018.06.006

Thom, D. H., Kravitz, R. L., Bell, R. A., Krupat, E., & Azari, R. (2002). Patient trust in the physician: Relationship to patient requests. *Family Practice*, *19*(5), 476–483. doi:10.1093/fampra/19.5.476 PMID:12356698

Veerasoontorn, R., Beise-Zee, R., & Sivayathorn, A. (2011). Service quality as a key driver of medical tourism: The case of Bumrungrad International Hospital in Thailand. *International Journal of Leisure and Tourism Marketing*, *2*(2), 140–158. doi:10.1504/IJLTM.2011.038886

World Health Organization. (2011). *Global health and aging*. Retrieved from https://www.who.int/ageing/publications/global_health.pdf

World Health Organization. (2015). *World Report on Ageing and Health*. WHO.

You, X., & O'leary, J. T. (1999). Destination behaviour of older UK travellers. *Tourism Recreation Research*, *1*(24), 23–34. doi:10.1080/02508281.1999.11014854

ADDITIONAL READING

Abbaspour, F., Soltani, S., & Tham, A. (2020). *Medical tourism for COVID-19 post-crisis recovery?* Anatolia., doi:10.1080/13032917.2020.1815067

Bagga, T., Vishnoi, S. K., Jain, S., & Sharma, R. (2020). Medical Tourism: Treatment, Therapy & Tourism. *International Journal Of Scientific & Technology Research*, *9*(3), 4447–4453.

Beladi, H., Chao, C. C., Ee, M. S., & Hollas, D. (2019). Does medical tourism promote economic growth? A cross-country analysis. *Journal of Travel Research*, *58*(1), 121–135.

BMJ (2020) Will medical tourism survive covid-19?bBMJ 2020; 370 doi: (Published 10 July 2020) doi:10.1136/bmj.m2677

Cham, T. H., Lim, Y. M., Sia, B. C., Cheah, J. H., & Ting, H. (2020). Medical tourism destination image and its relationship with the intention to revisit: A study of Chinese medical tourists in Malaysia. *Journal of China Tourism Research*, 1–29.

Conference, H. T. I. (2020) https://www.hticonference.com/medical-tourism-post-covid19-what-got-you-here-wont-get-you-there/Medical tourism post-Covid19 – What got you here, won't get you there!

De la Hoz-Correa, A., Muñoz-Leiva, F., & Bakucz, M. (2018). Past themes and future trends in medical tourism research: A co-word analysis. *Tourism Management*, *65*, 200–211.

Ganguli, S., & Ebrahim, A. H. (2017). A qualitative analysis of Singapore's medical tourism competitiveness. *Tourism Management Perspectives*, *21*, 74–84.

Ghosh, T., & Mandal, S. (2019). Medical tourism experience: Conceptualization, scale development, and validation. *Journal of Travel Research*, *58*(8), 1288–1301.

Leung, D., Law, R., van Hoof, H., & Buhalis, D. (2013). Social Media in Tourism and Hospitality: A Literature Review. *Journal of Travel & Tourism Marketing*, *30*(1–2), 3–22. https://doi.org/10.1080/10548408.2013.750919

Lu, W., & Stepchenkova, S. (2015). User-Generated Content as a Research Mode in Tourism and Hospitality Applications: Topics, Methods, and Software. *Journal of Hospitality Marketing & Management*, *24*(2), 119–154. https://doi.org/10.1080/19368623.2014.907758

Mathijsen, A. (2019). Home, sweet home? Understanding diasporic medical tourism behaviour. Exploratory research of Polish immigrants in Belgium. *Tourism Management*, *72*, 373–385.

Moghavvemi, S., Ormond, M., Musa, G., Isa, C. R. M., Thirumoorthi, T., Mustapha, M. Z. B., & Chandy, J. J. C. (2017). Connecting with prospective medical tourists online: A cross-sectional analysis of private hospital websites promoting medical tourism in India, Malaysia and Thailand. *Tourism Management*, *58*, 154–163.

Rahman, M. K. (2019). Medical tourism: Tourists' perceived services and satisfaction lessons from Malaysian hospitals. *Tourism Review*.

Suess, C., Baloglu, S., & Busser, J. A. (2018). Perceived impacts of medical tourism development on community wellbeing. *Tourism Management*, *69*, 232–245.

KEY TERMS AND DEFINITIONS

Appalachia: A geographic and cultural region of the Mideastern United States. The population in media is portrayed as suspicious, backward, and isolated.

Chapter 6
Medical Tourism:
Analysis and Expectations Worldwide

Silvia Adela Garrote Andújar
University of Vigo, Spain

Noelia Araújo Vila
https://orcid.org/0000-0002-3395-8536
University of Vigo, Spain

José Antonio Fraiz Brea
University of Vigo, Spain

Arthur Filipe de Araújo
Universidade de Aveiro, Portugal

ABSTRACT

There is no general agreement within the academic community regarding where medical tourism fits within tourism types and segments. Considering this scenario, the present work conceptualises medical tourism as a sub-segment of health tourism. Medical tourism is generally not well developed, and consequently, not enough studies have addressed it in statistical terms. In this context, the empirical component of this study consists of producing a snapshot of medical tourism in the countries that first started to capitalise on it. Results indicate that the activity is still in an initial phase of development, and provided destinations and businesses continue to provide quality infrastructures and services, it will grow significantly within the following years.

INTRODUCTION

There is not yet a universally accepted definition for health tourism, neither there is a generally agreed upon conceptualization for it (Gaines, 2019). In countries like Turkey, health tourism was understood as a synonymous with medical tourism (which refers to the therapeutic aspect). More recently, the concept has been examined under a more comprehensive perspective, according to which, it is viewed as a

DOI: 10.4018/978-1-7998-3034-4.ch006

generic term that incorporates different sub-products (Şencan et al., 2012), each catering to a specific motivation (Seow et al., 2020).

In other countries, such as Argentina, for instance, health tourism is exclusively linked to thermal activities (Turismo Argentina, 2014). In Mexico, however, the concept includes three different typologies: medical tourism, alternative and complementary medicine tourism, and wellness tourism. In this context, health tourism is defined as the activities carried out by people away from their places of residency, for more than one day and less than one year, mainly or secondarily motivated by receiving some kind of health or wellness service, or to accompany someone who will (De la Rosa, 2012). In other words, it is not limited to medical treatments, to a specific type of activity, or even to the person who carries out health-related activities, as it also includes his/her companion. And in Spain, this is understood as the process by which a person travels to receive health services in a country other than the one in which they reside. The reason for the trip is the search for these health services, in a broad sense. It is a complex and widely discussed term. It is complex because it involves two industries, health and tourism, which are traditionally not very close; as well as because of the diversity of services that the term health can integrate (Escuela de Organización Industrial, 2013). Spain ranks sixth in Europe and eighth worldwide as a medical tourism destination.

It should also be taken into account that this is a sector with certain regulations in some aspects. For example, in the European Union there is Directive 2011/24/EU of the European Parliament and of the Council of 9 March 2011. This aims to ensure patient mobility, establish rules to facilitate access to safe and high-quality health care in the European Union.

Health tourism is defined under different perspectives, including not only thermal activities, but also wellness and medical tourism. In this vein, health tourism is defined as a set of sub-products, which are divided into two basic categories: preventive health tourism, and healing health tourism (AUREN Consulters and EOI, 2013), whereas each includes more specific sub-categories, as summarised in Figure 1. Within this conceptualisation, medical tourism is a particular form of patient mobility, where patients travel across borders or to overseas destinations to receive treatments including fertility, cosmetic, dental, transplantation and elective surgery (Ghost & Mandal, 2019; Lunt et al., 2016, p.38).

It must be observed that such conceptualisation only considers cross-border displacements, limiting the concept of health tourism to the context of foreign tourists. However, as showed by Familitur's research (on Spanish tourists' travels), in 2012, domestic trips motivated by voluntary health-related activities were already growing significantly (IET, 2012). Therefore, the domestic portion of health tourism should not be overlooked.

Other authors differentiate two aspects of health tourism: medical tourism and wellness tourism. Within this perspective, the terms, "healing" and "prevention" are directly related to medical tourism, and not to general health tourism, as in the previously addressed conceptualisation. In sum, as showed in Figure 2, these authors consider wellness and medical wellness activities as a sub-category wellness tourism, which also includes thermal activities (T&L, 2013).

Considering the different perspectives addressed, it becomes clear that there is no international consensus regarding the classification of health tourism sub-products, neither there is a unanimous definition accepted in most countries. Some authors argue that, the concept of health tourism must be understood as encompassing two aspects: therapeutic and touristic (Bonfada et al., 2011). The former refers to trips made mainly to undergo medical treatment in medical facilities. Its relationship with tourism is limited to travellers' use of tourist services, such as transports, accommodation and restaurants. The latter, on the other hand, refers to trips motivated by activities that, although having a therapeutic aspect, are mainly

Figure 1. Sub-sectors encompassed by health tourism
Source: adapted from AUREN Consulters and EOI (2013)

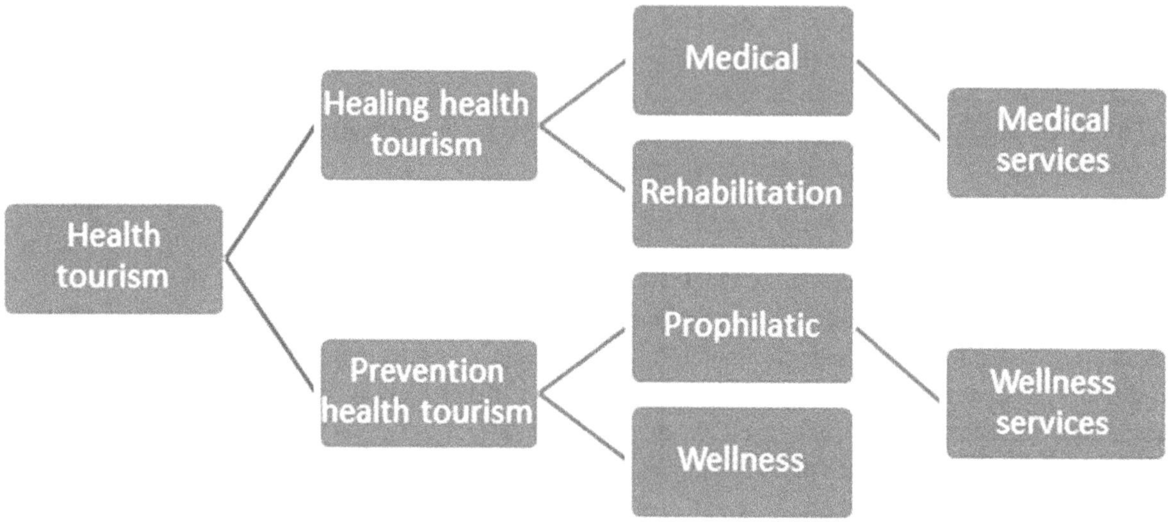

Figure 2. Health tourism definitions, including its medical and wellness components
Source: adapted from T&L (2013)

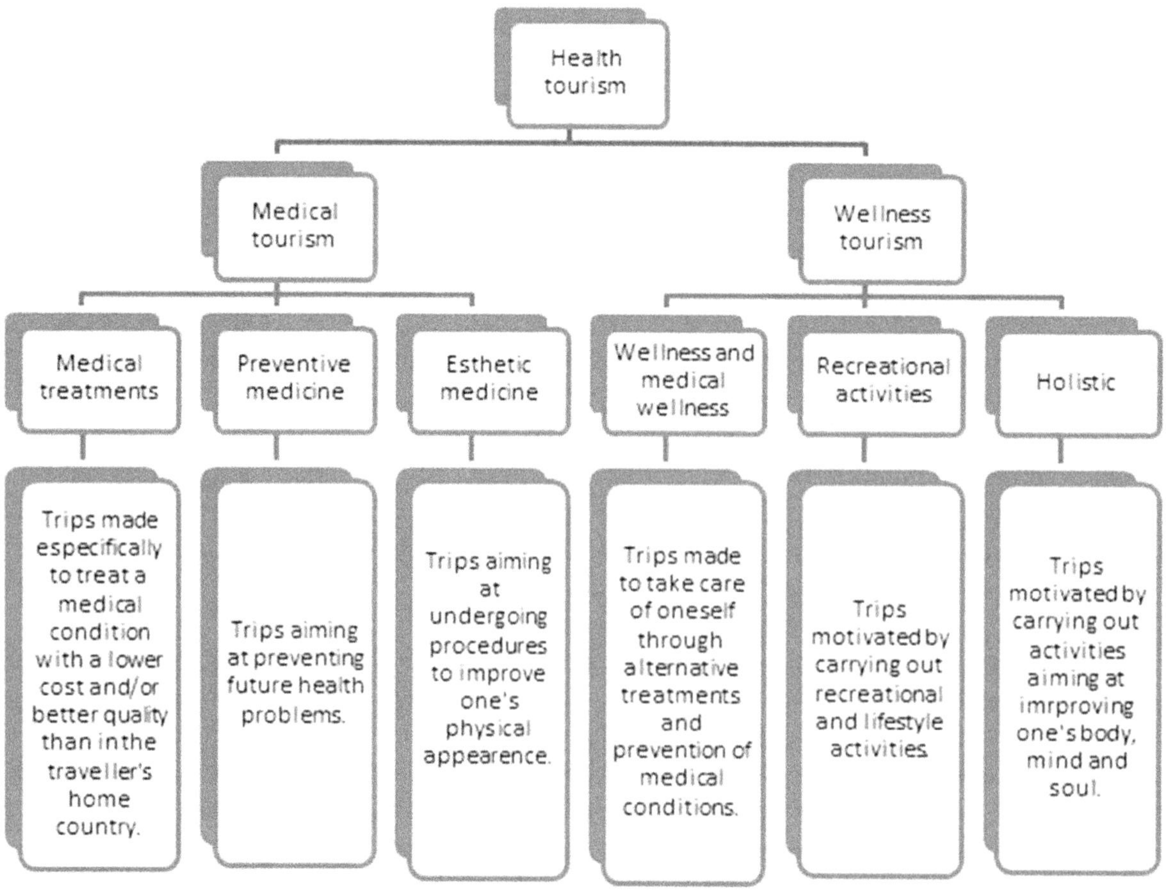

of a leisure or wellness nature. Those include going to spas, water resorts, thalassotherapy centres, and thermal facilities.

In sum, there is an infinity of classifications within health tourism. Amongst those, the present work focuses on medical or sanitary tourism, which includes trips aiming to improve one's health or recover from a medical condition by undergoing medical treatment (Carrera & Lunt, 2010). Medical tourism itself is also considered a general term that encompasses a broad array of health services, geographical contexts, health systems, and patients' personal circumstances. It implies a displacement to outside one's national health jurisdiction, for more than one day and less than one year, with the goal of receiving medical treatment. Therefore, it excludes treatments received by excursionists, expatriates, and long-term foreign residents (Lunt et al., 2013).

There are two more relevant aspects that must be considered in the context of medical tourism. The first refers to the person who pays for the treatment, which can be the government, the patient himself/herself, or a third party. The second refers to the direction of the tourist flow, that is, whether the tourist-patient travels from a poor country to a rich country or vice-versa (Lunt et al., 2013). In this context, whether a tourist-patient decides to travel to a certain destination in order to receive his/her treatment depends on each country's health system. Therefore, it is common for American, Australian, Asian, and European tourist-patients to travel to lower-income countries in order to avoid the high costs or the long waiting lists for medical treatments in their home countries (Lunt et al., 2013). However, the motivations of patients from the US and Europe, for instance, are arguably distinct, as the public health systems in both places are significantly different (Lunt et al., 2013).

In some countries, people face several difficulties when trying to receive specialised medical attention, such as prohibitively expensive private medical services or long waiting lines on the public health system. For these reasons, many chose to travel to certain countries in order to obtain a specific treatment (Ngamvichaikit & Beise-Zee, 2014). Aesthetic treatments, for instance, are commonly sought by medical tourists, as they are typically not covered by public health assistance or medical insurance, and costs on private clinics vary significantly among different countries. In this context, certain places' capacity to attract travellers who consume medical services becomes a competitive advantage for their tourism industry (Gray & Poland, 2008). For this reason, destination managers have increasingly acknowledged medical tourism's potential to diversify the local tourism offer, and thus generate economic gains, create jobs and increase tax revenue, as well as improve local medical systems (Suess et al., 2018). In sum, medical tourism is a consolidated global phenomenon, which has grown exponentially in these first decades of the XXI century (Chew & Darmasaputra, 2015), and consequently, aroused the interest of specialists.

Medical tourism, as well as health tourism in general, have not received enough academic attention. In this context, the present investigation aims to contribute to the knowledge of this segment. To this end, an analysis of the medical tourism scenario in countries that have actively worked towards its success is carried out. Medical tourism development was analysed by examining the cases of 14 countries in Europe, America, and Asia, where the segment presents higher growth numbers.

METHODOLOGY

The present investigation aims to contribute to the knowledge of this segment in the country.

The authors faced some challenges regarding the definition of a theoretical foundation for the present work, mainly due to the confusion in the terminology employed. The absence of studies in the literature posed an additional difficulty. In this context, further investigating the practical reality of medical tourism has been deemed an interesting and relevant research path. Considering this, the paper focus literature reviews, which critique and summarise a body of literature about the topic, concerning different countries. Medical tourism development was analysed by examining the cases of 14 countries in Europe, America, and Asia, where the segment presents higher growth numbers (Table 1). Some of the characteristics that were considered in the revision are: health system, kind of medical services offered, type of users or type of facilities.

It should also be noted that in the analysis carried out, any trip motivated by preventive, recreational or curative health treatment is used as a concept of medical tourism.

Table 1. Analysed countries

<table>
<tr><th>America</th><th>Asia</th><th>Europe</th></tr>
<tr><td>United States</td><td>India</td><td>Turkey</td></tr>
<tr><td>Venezuela</td><td>Thailand</td><td>Hungary</td></tr>
<tr><td>Brazil</td><td rowspan="3">Singapore</td><td>Germany</td></tr>
<tr><td>México</td><td>United Kingdom</td></tr>
<tr><td>Other countries in South America</td><td>Spain</td></tr>
</table>

RESULTS

United States

Due to the country's relatively expensive private health services, the cost to tourists might be considerably higher than in other countries, especially when expenses with transports and accommodation are considered. Nevertheless, the United states are a very popular destination due to the quality of the doctors and their equipment. However, the mentioned high cost has led 250,000 Americans to travel abroad in order to receive health care. Therefore, it is also considered an important medical tourist generating country (PRWeb, 2013). The country's fame as a medical tourism destination has been associated with the advances in medical technology, as well as the excellence of medical schools. Those factors have attracted patients from all over the world, who attend major hospitals, such as Hopkins University Hospital. The country's high prices have always had a pulling effect towards the higher income segments. However, due to the proliferation of medical attention, some hospitals and clinics have lowered their prices to attract other market segments, both domestic and foreign (Medicaltourism, 2013). According to McKinsey & Co., in 2008, 85,000 medical tourists visited the United States. From those, 40% sought advanced medical technologies, 32% needed to receive a treatment that was not available in their own country, and 9% aimed to receive a certain treatment at a lower cost (Treatmentabroad, 2014).

Venezuela

This type of tourism is increasingly common in Venezuela, as local medical professionals are internationally renowned for their outstanding performance and experience[1]. Due to the country's internal situation, Venezuela can be a less inclusive alternative, as tourists' freedom is somewhat limited. Admittedly, the country does not currently offer an ideal scenario for the reception of international tourists. Nevertheless, Venezuela aims to position itself globally and maintain a respectable share of the medical tourism market, which will hopefully help it overcome the major shortcomings in its the tourism industry.

Years before the problems currently face by the country escalated, medical initiatives aiming to develop this type of tourism had already been carried out. For instance, in 2011, the website www.medicalvenezuela.com was created. The portal was initially focused on medical tourism related to cosmetic surgery procedures, in which the country is a major reference. However, in face of the frequent queries about more complex procedures (cardiology, neurosurgery, surgery treatment for obesity, etc.) other specialties were included. The website had partnerships with specialised travel and tourism services, in order to provide travel organisation services and assistance to foreign patients. The idea is simple: the patient is brought to the country, his/her check-up is done all in one day, the surgery is appointed, and the patient is hospitalized. Upon leaving the hospital, the patient stays for a certain period in a hotel until he/she is discharged and sent back to his/her country. Some patients prefer to arrive some days prior to their appointment and visit some tourist attractions. The most demanded destinations are Salto Angel, Margarita and Los Roques[2].

Even with the current political and economic crisis, Venezuela is still a very attractive destination for foreigners in search of medical services at a lower cost. According to M. Enrique Meneses, president of the Clinics' and Hospitals' Association, "*Venezuela is still attractive due to the quality of its professionals. The country is renowned for the quality medicine practiced in its institutions, which are on the highest level, despite the difficulties in repairing and innovation on medical equipment. We wish to correct such problem with the project of the Tourism to Health Association*" [3]

Brazil

Brazil is one of the world's top 5 medical tourism destinations. Although the country also attracts patients seeking treatments for diseases and conditions, most of the medical tourists who visit Brazil seek elective surgery operations (aesthetical or cosmetic) (Edmonds, 201). Hence, this type of tourism in Brazil is frequently referred to as "*turismo de bisturi*" (scalpel tourism).

In this context, Brazil's success is not due to low-cost medical services, but to the country's tradition and expertise in plastic surgery. In fact, Brazil is a destination of choice for plastic surgeons from all over the world aiming to practice their abilities. In this context, some authors point out that the country faces ethical issues (some even qualify them as human rights' violations), as low-cost aesthetical operations are often undertaken by insufficiently experienced professionals, who basically charge just enough to cover the costs of materials and anaesthesia. In this context, low-mid class patients serve as medical practice tools for these recently graduated surgeons, so that they can gain the necessary experience to perform surgery for the rich in the future (Edmonds, 2011).

Notwithstanding, Brazilian media acclaims the country as the "champion" of the plastic surgery world (Edmonds, 2011, p.298) and as a scalpel empire. They often brag that the number of cosmetic procedures per capita is much higher in Brazil than in North America or Europe, which is made possible by the odd, but increasing, presence of foreigners in the plastic surgery clinics (Edmonds, 2011).

México

Mexico receives a great number of residents considered medical tourists from bordering American states (California, Texas and Arizona). However, over 70% of those visitors are Hispanic, mostly Mexican, who have emigrated to the United States, but do not have medical insurance there (Flores, 2013; Labonté et al., 2013). Therefore, they resort to their own country of origin to obtain medical treatment at a lower cost (Woodman, 2010). Procedures undergone by medical tourists in Mexico range from surgeries to dental and orthopaedic treatments (Flores, 2013).

Although some authors state that Mexico is a world leader in medical tourism, the country did not have a plan for the sector up until very recently. This changed in 2013, when the Mexican Secretariat of Tourism (SECTUR) released a strategy for medical tourism's development and promotion. The strategy is based on the more comprehensive concept of health tourism, rather than exclusively focused on visitors seeking medical services (SECTUR, 2013). The document defined several guidelines for the establishment of a medical and health tourism offer. It also includes the creation of an information system that provides reliable statistics on medical and health tourists' numbers and economic impact.

In addition to the more than 21 million uninsured Hispanics residing in bordering US states (Flores, 2013), medical tourism in Mexico also appeals to foreigners seeking aesthetic surgeries.

Other South American Countries

Other South American countries have started to focus on specific offers to potential medical tourists. Chile, for instance, often receives patients from neighbouring countries, such as Bolivia, Ecuador or Peru (Labonté et al., 2013), and the latter has also begun to develop an offer of their own. Accordingly, Panama has been attracting patient-tourists mostly for cosmetic surgery, although visitors are increasingly seeking knee, hip, dental and cardiovascular surgery as well (Labonté et al., 2013).

Latin American countries are creating a platform for networking and business, education and culture collaboration between health care providers, in order to jointly develop their health services.

Likewise, Colombia is undertaking a solid strategy to attract medical tourists from all over the world (de Pacheco, 2017). Their goal is to "*provide health services comparable to those of a first world country, in a third world country*". In this context, they plan to be recognized as a leading destination in medical tourism by 2032, which should result in "*over six billion dollars in profits per year*" (Labonté et al., 2013, p.196). Some cities in Colombia have build (or are building) "*health cities*", that is, areas in which both public and private hospitals concentrate on serving medical tourists (Labonté et al., 2013, p. 196). Medellín, for instance, is implementing a strategy that includes bringing tourists from Bogotá airport in private planes (Labonté *et al.*, 2013, p.196). However, Colombia has many social problems, such as a high level a social inequality, which is reflected in their health system. Moreover, the real estate speculation caused precisely by the construction of health centres has resulted in private investors constantly pressuring municipalities to demolish low-income neighbourhoods' housing complexes in order to build high-end apartments close to these facilities (Labonté *et al.*, 2013). The high altitude in some parts of the country (over 2600m above sea level, in certain points) is an additional inconvenience for patients who need anaesthesia, as they have to be in the country two to three days prior to the intervention in order to acclimatise (Sáenz, 2010).

At last, Cuba should also be mentioned. The country has one doctor for each 148 inhabitants, and receives a significant volume of international medical tourists, including important politicians from other South American and even African countries. Currently, analogous to other countries, Cuba does not have official data on medical tourism. Therefore, they can only address it from the supply side, that is, the treatments they offer. In this regard, the main programs focus on ophthalmology or rehabilitation treatments for chemical dependents (Cubanacan, 2014). A very interesting aspect of Cuban health services is the possibility of requesting a budget and booking medical appointments through a simple Web form, in which the patient can also attach results previous exams, so the doctor has access to them beforehand. The website is provided by the Tourism and Health Organization (former Cubanacan), which offers combined medical and accommodations/tourism services throughout the country (Servimedcuba, 2012).

India

Medical tourism in India has been through a big change in recent years. Private companies have contributed to the creation of a favourable environment for patients by providing improved facilities, which has attracted many medical tourists. According to India's Ministry of Tourism, the country received around six hundred thousand patients-tourists in 2010, with a total expenditure of approximately 4,500 million Rupees (just over 53 million Euros). These patients come mainly from around 30 countries, including United States, Canada, United Kingdom, Russia and some of Central Asian countries (IMTD, 2012). India is referred to as the world leader in Medical Tourism in Some Web sites. The country is a pioneer in this sector and sustains a growth of 30%. Contributing to this success, Indian hospitals are comparable to those in the US, even though they offer the same treatments at a much lower price (approximately 10% of the American price and 40% of the British) (Medical Tourism Resource Guide, 2011).

Most tourists who travel to India for medical treatment come from South Asia (9.3% - mainly from the Maldives (59.3%), followed by Afghanistan (16.5%)), Africa (8.5%, mainly from Nigeria (29%) and Tanzania (13.7%)), and West Asia (8.4%, mainly from Iraq (33.3%), Oman (11.4%), and Yemen (10.5%)). Western European countries represent around 0.3% - 0.4% each. Eastern European countries, on the other hand, represent 1.9% each in average. Amongst those, Russia stands out with 3,3% of medical tourists to India (India Tourism Statistics, 2012, p.38-41).

Thailand

Medical tourism in Thailand, not unlike tourism in general in the country, has been continuously growing since 2010. In fact, the number of medical tourist arrivals in 2012 is almost twice as big as in 2012 (almost 3 million, compared to just over 1.5 million) (Mymedholiday.com, 2013).

Medical tourists represent one of the main market segments of Thailand's tourism industry. According to official sources, health tourism is rapidly growing. In 2010, Thailand received over 1,5 million international medical tourists, some of which needed to undergo specific treatments, while others sought preventive measures, meditation or natural therapies. The country's hospitals are well prepared and accredited by the Joint Commission International (JCI), an international quality certification for hospitals).

According to the website *Medical Tourism in Thailand*, in 2012, the country received around 2.5 million international medical tourists who underwent treatments in accredited hospitals and clinics (NaRanong & NaRanong, 2011). This represents 10% of the total annual tourist arrivals to Thailand, making it the world's main international medical tourism destination (Thailand Med Tourism, 2013).

Japan is the main medical tourism market to Thailand, followed by the countries encompassed by the Southeast Asian Nations Association (Burma, Brunei, Cambodia, Philippines, Indonesia, Laos, Malasia, Singapore and Vietnam – besides Thailand itself) (ASEAN, 2014). Other important markets are middle eastern countries, United States and United Kingdom. Residents from all of these counties go to Thailand in search of quality treatments at a lower price (Thailand Med Tourism, 2013). However, in 2012, there was a slight change in the list of countries whose residents travelled to Thailand for medical reasons. In this context, Japan kept it's leading position, followed, however, by United States, United Kingdom, some Arab countries and Australia (Mymedholiday.com, 2013).

Singapur

Although more expensive than in India or Thailand, medical services in Singapore are still considerably cheaper (around 50%) than in the United States. The country has 15 hospitals and medical centres accredited by the JCI, which offer treatments in many different areas, such as orthopaedics, urology, dermatology, cardiology, sports medicine, endocrinology, ophthalmology, odontology, cosmetics, and alternative medicine (traditional Chinese medicine), encompassing acupuncture and herbal natural remedies (Medicaltourism, 2013e). In 2012, Singapore received around 850 thousand foreign patients, which generated 3.5 billion dollars in revenue (Kelley, 2013, p.23).

Turkey

Turkey is one of the countries with the greatest number of hospitals, clinics and medical centres accredited by the JCI in Europe (Woodman, 2010). Besides, Turkish medical centres also have other accreditations, such as those from Joint Commission on Accreditation of Healthcare Organizations (JCAOH)[4] and the International Organization for Standardization (ISO) (Turkeyhealthguide, 2011). Prices of medical treatments in Turkey are comparable to those in Asian countries, while hospitals' personnel are typically from western countries (Woodman, 2010). In addition, turkish medical facilities, technology and professionals meet high quality standards due to governmental regulations (Woodman, 2010; Erdogan & Yilmaz, 2012, p.1054).

Turkey promotes medical tourism as part of its health tourism offer, which also includes thermal spas and hotels with wellness facilities (Turkeyhealthguide, 2011). In this vein, the strategies adopted by the government for medical tourism are organised under several areas: international coordination, health tourism, thermal and wellness tourism, and senior and accessible tourism (Gültüvin & Cengiz, 2013). Accordingly, regulations, mobility and international coordination issues (visas, taxes and air fares) have been prioritised to facilitate the arrival of medical tourists (Gültüvin & Cengiz, 2013).

Turkish Ministry of Health highlights five key competitivity elements for health tourism (they do not refer specifically to medical tourism, but to the broader typology of health tourism): high quality standards, personalised services, competitive prices, short waiting times and a rich cultural heritage (Gültüvin & Cengiz, 2013, p.429).

Currently, Turkey is a preferred destination for many European patients, namely those from the United Kingdom, Netherlands, Romania, Kosovo, Bulgaria, Azerbaijan and Russia. However, patients from countries outside Europe, such as Bahrain, are also common.

Hungary

Hungary is famous for having many dental clinics. Therefore, the country attracts numerous residents from the European Union in search of treatments such as restorations and implants. Additionally, many tourists also seek cosmetic mouth surgery in Hungary (Woodman, 2010), where they typically cost between 40% and 70% of what they do in the United States (Barnato, 2014; Szabó, ND). Hungary has been trying to promote other areas of medicine for medical tourists (IMTJ, 2013), such as fertility, facial cosmetic surgery, ophthalmology, abdominal surgery, breast implants and orthopaedic prostheses. The country is also a reference in thermal tourism, due to its many spas and mineral water sources, which are also associated with beauty and nutrition therapies (Szabó, ND).

Just like Turkey, Hungary has facilities accredited by official entities. Most accreditations are given by national organisms, although some centres are also accredited by the United Kingdom Care Quality Commission and by ISO (Hungarian Tourism, 2014).

Regarding medical tourism statistics, like in many other countries, relevant data regarding the demand for medical tourism and medical tourists' motivations are limited or inexistent, as service providers do not collect them. Therefore, the little information available mostly concerns health tourism in general and thermal tourism (Michalkó, Rátz y Hinek, 2012, p.35-36).

Germany

Germany is known as a destination for patients seeking advanced medical technologies, safety and high quality, while avoiding waiting lists. The country manages to offer all this due to its high density of hospitals. Moreover, medical treatments usually cost half of what they would in the United States (Medicaltourism, 2013).

The 27 hospitals featured in the medical tourism section of Germany's official tourism website offer treatments in areas such as oncology, neurology, transplants and cardiology. The website features a map with the hospitals' locations and the respective treatments they offer (Germany.travel, 2013b).

Regarding statistics, once again, there is a shortage of relevant data. Although some information on health tourism is available, reliable sources of specific medical tourism data are limited. Some webpages show statistical data from the German Government, according to which the country received about 77,000 foreign patients 2010, which generated more than 950 million euros in revenue (Infosalus, 2013). However, the source of this information has not been correctly defined, which suggests a certain lack of credibility. In fact, the German official tourism website does not feature any information regarding the number of medical tourists or the revenue they generated in its annual statistical report. The only information regarding medical tourism refers to the number of preventive medicine and rehabilitation clinics (Germany.travel, 2014).

Therefore, although medical tourism is of some relevance to Germany, as in most other destinations, it still lacks reliable relevant data.

United Kingdom

The UK is seen much more as a medical tourist generating country than as a destination. In 2010, the number of British tourists who travelled abroad to undergo medical treatment was 20% higher than that of foreign tourists who entered the UK for the same purpose (Jack & Neville, 2013).

As in most countries, the UK lacks information on the number, characteristics, motivations and experiences of medical tourists. Therefore, local authorities carried out an extensive research to support decision-making regarding policies and management in this area. The study revealed that, from 2000 to 2010, the number of British who travelled abroad to receive medical treatment increased six-fold. Meanwhile the number of international medical tourists entering the United Kingdom in the same period was much more stable (Hanefeld, Horsfall, Lunt, & Smith, 2013).

The study also included data regarding the revenue from all medical tourists who had travelled to the United Kingdom. It was calculated by separating the treatment expenses from the rest of the expenses. To this end, some factors were considered, such as the fact that the patients probably arrived a few days before the treatment and stayed a few days later to fully recover, during which they likely visited some tourist attractions. Therefore, it has been estimated that medical tourists' expenses contribute with 219 million pounds per year (about 270 million euros) to the British economy. This is not so much a result of the sheer number of tourists traveling to the United Kingdom to receive medical treatment (which is significantly lower than that of British patients traveling abroad), but of the expenses that each of these tourists have in the United Kingdom, which are typically high (Hanefeld, Horsfall, Lunt, & Smith, 2013). Nevertheless, the mentioned study has some limitations. For instance, it does not differentiate between tourists who use the private or the public health systems.

Spain

Spain is hardly seen as a big player in the field of medical tourism, although they country has recently taken some steps to establish itself in this market. Some webpages specialised in medical trips highlight that Spain has a good health system. Accordingly, Spain ranks seventh on the World Health Organization's list of countries with the best health care services (Medicaltourism, 2013d), and has 20 hospitals and clinics accredited by the JCI[5], which offer modern facilities and qualified doctors. Some health centres offer interpreters to facilitate the communication with foreign patients, although most doctors speak English fluently. The most demanded medical procedures by international patients in Spain include odontology, eye surgery, orthopaedic surgery, and surgery treatments for obesity disorders (Medicaltourism, 2013d). In this context, the number of medical tourists coming to Spain has increased in recent years. Nevertheless, until very recently, Spanish authorities have shown an extremely negative attitude towards the concept of medical tourism. This situation, was caused by some problems related to the European health card, especially in provinces bordering other European countries, where the card's purpose was supposedly corrupted (Diariocrítico, 2012).

Regarding statistics, reliable data are still scarce. Some communication media feature data up from 2012, which, according to which Spain received 22,000 foreign tourist-patients that year. Regarding medical tourists' origin, Germany, United Kingdom and France are the main markets. A significant number of tourist-patients also comes from Russia, Belgium, Norway, Algeria, Tunisia, Morocco, the Middle East and Latin America (Pasamontes, 2013).

Although medical tourism numbers in Spain are relatively low, some authors argue that the country has a significant potential in this area. This is not only because Spain is an internationally recognized destination, but also due to the good reputation of its sanitary services, although this mostly refers to the private health system (Pasamontes, 2013). In general, Spain is described as an excellent destination to combine wellbeing and medical treatments, with competitive prices and modern facilities (Treatmentabroad, ND).

There is, however, a long way to go to position Spain as a benchmark medical tourism destination. To this end, it is essential to correctly define what medical tourism is, and then adopt clear goals for this market, as well as a consistent plan of action to achieve them. This is, without a doubt, essential to promote Spain as a medical tourism destination under the umbrella of medical health tourism.

SWOT Analysis

As a final point of this analysis, the results obtained in a SWOT analysis are grouped together. The reader can thus observe in a global way the analysis carried out and see the situation of medical tourism. In general terms, it is a growing sector, with a target audience interested in health, aesthetics and body care; a growing trend in today's society. These are all opportunities that are joined by a greater number of people interested in investing in this sector and the technological advances in medicine. The latter brings greater quality and safety to treatments, with faster recoveries.

As negative points, there is the high price of some countries for this type of treatment. This makes it unaffordable for the entire public. The greatest current threat is the problem of mobility between countries due to the current health pandemic. The current crisis derived from the COVID19 has affected the tourism sector and especially medical tourism. Consumers are not taking the risk of consuming medicine outside their country, thus paralysing such travel.

Finally, as strengths of the sector once this health crisis is over, they are that it is a sector with good facilities and with some specialization of treatments by countries or destinations. In addition, cooperation between companies began to emerge, strengthening this sector. Each of the countries analyzed tends to be a reference in some type of medicine (some aesthetic treatment, dentistry, digestive treatments, etc.).

Table 2. SWOT

Weaknesses	Threats
• No common definition. • High price in some countries.	• Low mobility between countries due to COVID-19.
Strengths	**Opportunities**
• Specialization by country. • Promotion. • Collaboration between companies. • Quality of facilities and service.	• Advances in medical technology. • Growing demand. • Growing interest in health and personal care. • Investors interested in the sector.

CONCLUSION

There is no unanimous and unique definition of medical tourism, neither in terms of the places where the phenomenon takes place, nor in terms of the authors that address it. Precisely defining medical tourism is not a simple task, as it depends on how each country sees it, as well as on their own legislation, health system and social benefits. It is unsurprising that, typically, tourists from richer countries travel to less developed ones to receive medical treatment at a lower cost. This is the case of Thailand and India, for instance, to where a significant number of foreign tourists travel in order to have access to more affordable medical services.

As each country adopts the definition that best fits its reality, it is difficult to establish a consistent definition of medical tourism. In this context, the demand normally determines what the term includes within justifiable limits. For instance, some authors consider medical tourism as trips primarily motivated by using the destination country's public health system. This definition, however, is not exempt from debate. In the case of Spain, for example, the use of the public health system by non-residents, is seen as a negative phenomenon, especially when it is the main purpose of their trip. However, the evolution of this market, which is currently still incipient, will lead to a better definition of the concept. There is no doubt, however, that tourism is an economic activity, and therefore, needs to generate income for the companies that make up the tourism industry, and in this case, also for those in the health sector.

The literature on medical tourists' motivations are still scarce or non-existent. The few studies available state that having access to less expensive medical services is by far the most common motivation. Other often relevant reasons are the quality of the medical centre, and the medical specialities and specific treatments they offer – which are often not found in the tourists' place of residence. In this context, international quality accreditations gained a particular importance in the context of medical tourism.

Although many countries are promoting medical tourism, some factors hinder the reliability of the available data on the phenomenon. In terms of statistics, it cannot be categorically stated that medical tourism motivates a significant number of tourists. Therefore, the segment is often interesting more due to the amount of income it generates than because of the sheer number of tourists it generates. Some classic medical destinations (those that have long been marketing medical services for tourists, such as the United States and the United Kingdom) seem to be strongly labelled by high prices of treatments. Although this may be viewed as a differentiation factor by the tourists who can afford it, these countries have been increasingly seen as medical tourist senders, rather than important destinations. Others have focused their strategy on pursuing lower income market segments, which in turn, has also led to an image of lower quality standards.

In the case of Spain, although private medical centres have been marketing their services to foreigners for some time, the country is not yet a reference in medical tourism. Not only more facilities, services and high-quality medical care are needed, but other factors are also missing. In such competitive market, Spain should differentiate itself not only through the good international reputation of its tourism and health sectors, but also by providing potential medical tourists a favourable and safe environment.

But the analysis carried out not only serves as a reference for Spain, but for many other countries where medical tourism is developed or developing. Medical tourism is a growing sector, due to the new possibilities offered by health tourism, such as qualitative and quantitative changes in patient mobility, new trends, and even the birth of various types of health tourism. There are countries and clinics interested in attracting a foreign target audience, but they need to know more about the impact of medical tourism on a national and international level in order to commit to this new activity in the sector. In countries such as Germany, Austria and Switzerland, the health tourism market is almost saturated. Already in 2017, Germany had more than 500 wellness hotels catering for a significant volume of patients. In other countries such as Malta and Cyprus, health tourism is still taking its first steps. This particular and continuously developing scenario requires a digital transformation for all those clinics that want to reach international customers and not be left behind by their competitors. The preparation of services for health tourism requires not only having the necessary equipment and professionals to cover this new demand, but also an efficient marketing strategy to enter the foreign market correctly.

Finally, certain medical tourism trends that have been shaping this market since 2010 will apparently continue. This is the case of the demand for high quality standards, medical centres specialised in certain pathologies and the growth of domestic markets.

REFERENCES

Asean. (2014). *Asean Member States*. Available in: https://www.asean.org/asean/asean-member-states

Auren Consultores & EOI. (2013). *Turismo de salud en España*. Secretaría de Estado de Turismo, Ministerio de Industria, Energía y Turismo.

Barnato, K. (2014). *Top destinations for health tourism*. CNBC. Available in: https://www.cnbc.com/id/101487998/page/10

Bonfada, P. L. B., Bonfada, M. R. H., González, M. E. A., & Gândara, J. M. G. (2011). El turismo de salud y el uso terapéutico del agua. *Estudios y Perspectivas en Turismo*, *20*(2), 462–477.

Carrera, P., & Lunt, N. (2010). A European perspective on medical tourism: The need for a knowledge base. *International Journal of Health Services*, *40*(3), 469–484. doi:10.2190/HS.40.3.e PMID:20799671

Chew, Y. T., & Darmasaputra, A. (2015). 12 Identifying research gaps in medical tourism. *Destination Marketing: An international perspective*, 119.

Cubanacan. (2014). *Cubanacan Turismo y Salud*. Available in: http://www.cubanacan.cu/index.php/es/component/content/article/118-cubanacan-turismo-y-salud

de la Puente Pacheco, M. A. (2017). Turismo médico comparado en Colombia y Singapur: Estudio sectorial y perspectivas de desarrollo. *Revista de derecho. División de Ciencias Jurídicas de la Universidad del Norte*, (47), 290–309.

De la Rosa, R. (2012). *Turismo de Salud*. México: Asociación Mexicana de Turismo de Salud. Disponible en: https://turespacio.com/blogs/turismo-de-salud/

Diariocritico. (2012). Cifras del ‘turismo sanitario’: España facturó en un sólo año 441 millones a los países europeos, frente a los 46 que pagó por los gastos de españoles en el extranjero. *Diario Crítico*. Available in: https://www.diariocritico.com/economia/sanidad/tribunal-de-cuentas/extranjeros/410713

Edmonds, A. (2011, Winter). Almost Invisible Scars. *Medical Tourism to Brazil*, *36*(2), 297–302. PMID:21114074

Erdogan, S., & Yilmaz, E. (2012). Medical Tourism: an assessment on Turkey. In *International Joint Conference of 10th, International Conference on Knowledge, Economy and Management; 11th International Conference of the ASIA Chapter of the AHRD & 2nd International Conference of the MENA Chapter of the AHRD. Proceedings*. Istanbul Medeniyet Üniversitesi.

Escuela de Organización Industrial. (2013). *El turismo de Salud en España*. Gobierno de España.

Flores, L. (2013). *Un mercado muy sano*. CNEExpansion. Available in: http://www.cnnexpansion.com/economia/2013/06/26/un-mercado-muy-sano

Gaines, J., & Lee, C. V. (2019). Medical tourism. In *Travel Medicine* (pp. 371–375). Elsevier. doi:10.1016/B978-0-323-54696-6.00039-2

Germany.travel. (2013). *Hospitals in Germany*. Available in: https://www.germany.travel/es/viajes-tematicos/turismo-medicinal/hospitals/clinicas.html (09.05.2017).

Germany.travel. (2014). *German National Tourist Board. Incoming-Tourism. Germany Facts and Figures 2013, Germany, the travel destination.* Alemania. Available in: https://www.germany.travel/media/pdf/dzt_marktforschung/GNTB-Incoming-Tourism-Germany-2014.pdf

Ghosh, T., & Mandal, S. (2019). Medical tourism experience: Conceptualization, scale development, and validation. *Journal of Travel Research*, *58*(8), 1288–1301. doi:10.1177/0047287518813469

Gray, H. H., & Poland, S. C. (2008). Medical tourism: Crossing borders to access health care. *Kennedy Institute of Ethics Journal*, *18*(2), 193–201. doi:10.1353/ken.0.0006 PMID:18610785

Gültüvin, E., & Cengiz, E. (2013). Health Tourism in Turkey: Opportunities and Threats. *Mediterranean Journal of Social Sciences*, *4*(10).

Hanefeld, J., Horsfall, D., Lunt, N., & Smith, R. (2013). Medical Tourism: A Cost or Benefit to the NHS? *PLoS One*, *8*(10).

Hungarian Tourism. (2014). *Medical Tourism in Hungary, Spa Hungary*. Hungría. Available in: http://spa.gotohungary.com/en_GB/about-medical-tourism1

IMTD. (2012). *Industry Overview*. India Medical Tourism and Wellness Destination (IMTD). India. Available in: http://www.imtd.in/industry-overview/

IMTJ. (2013). Hungary: Hungarian Tourism promotes medical tourism. *International Medical Travel Journal*. Available in: https://www.imtj.com/news/?entryid82=416494

INFOSALUS. (2013). *Alemania.- El turismo médico crece un 20 por ciento cada año a pesar de ser un todavía "un mercado sin explotar"*. Available in: https://www.infosalus.com/actualidad/noticia-alemania-turismo-medico-crece-20-ciento-cada-ano-pesar-ser-todavia-mercado-explotar-20130307143011.html

Instituto de Estudios Turísticos. (2012). Informe anual 2012. Movimientos turísticos de los españoles (FAMILITUR). Madrid: Instituto de Turismo de España, Ministerio de Industria, Energía y Turismo.

Jack, A., & Neville, S. (2013). More medical tourists leave UK than come to country, says study. *The Financial Times*. Available in: http://www.ft.com/cms/s/0/6e27935e-3cc0-11e3-86ef-00144feab7de.html#axzz36NzrUhlx

Kelley, E., & Lunt, N. (2013). *Medical tourism.* WTO Patient Safety Programme.

Labonté, R., Runnels, V., Packer, C., & Deonandan, R. (Eds.). (2013). *Travelling Well: Essays in Medical Tourism. Transdisciplinary Studies in Population Health Series* (p. 20). Institute of Population Health, University of Ottawa.

Lunt, N., Horsfall, D., & Hanefeld, J. (2016). Medical tourism: A snapshot of evidence on treatment abroad. *Maturitas, 88*, 37–44. doi:10.1016/j.maturitas.2016.03.001 PMID:27105695

Lunt, N., Horsfall, D., Smith, R., Exworthy, M., Hanefeld, J., & Mannion, R. (2014). Market size, market share and market strategy: Three myths of medical tourism. *Policy and Politics, 42*(4), 597–614. doi:10.1332/030557312X655918

Lunt, N. T., Mannion, R., & Exworthy, M. (2013). A framework for exploring the policy implications of UK medical tourism and international patient flows. *Social Policy and Administration, 47*(1), 1–25. doi:10.1111/j.1467-9515.2011.00833.x

Medical Tourism Resource Guide. (2011). *India Medical Tourism. India.* Available in: https://www.medicaltourismresourceguide.com/india-medical-tourism

Medicaltourism. (2013a). *United States Medical Tourism. United States Medical Tourism offers the latest and best technology, as well as the best medical schools, teaching hospitals and research centers.* Medical Tourism Association. Available in: https://www.medicaltourism.com/en/destination/united-states.html

Medicaltourism. (2013b). *Singapore Medical Tourism.* Available in: https://www.medicaltourism.com/en/destination/singapore.html

Michalkó, G., Rátz, T., & Hinel, M. (2012). Spatial differences in Hungarian medical tourism supply based on service providers' online presence. *Hungarian Geographical Bulleton, 61*(1), 31–47.

Mymedholiday.com. (2013). *Thailand's medical tourism statistics: a look at the international patient numbers.* Tailandia. Available in: http://www.mymedholiday.com/blog/2013/10/793/thailands-medical-tourism-statistics-a-look-at-the-international-patient-numbers/

NaRanong, A., & NaRanong, V. (2011). The effects of medical tourism: Thailand's experience. Bulletin of the World Health Organization, *89*, 336-344.

Ngamvichaikit, A., & Beise-Zee, R. (2014). Communication needs of medical tourists: An exploratory study in Thailand. *International Journal of Pharmaceutical and Healthcare Marketing, 8*(1), 98–117. doi:10.1108/IJPHM-10-2012-0010

Pasamontes, J. C. (2013). *España multiplicará por 40 el negocio del turismo de salud.* 02b.com. Available in: http://www.02b.com/es/notices/2013/09/espana_multiplicara_por_40_el_negocio_del_turismo_de_salud_7345.php

PRWEB. (2013). *HealthcareAbroad.com Launches Medical Tourism Directory.* Author.

Sáenz, G. (2010). *Colombia como destino de turismo médico.* Conexión Colombia. Available in: https://www.conexioncolombia.com/colombia-como-destino-de-turismo-medico

SECTUR. (2013). *Impulso al turismo médico*. Presidencia de la República. Available in: http://www.presidencia.gob.mx/impulso-al-turismo-medico/

Şencan, I., Aydin, D., Constantinides, C., Mike, C., Yilmaz, C., Genç, A. & Lanyi, A. (2012). Definitions and Descriptions regarding Heatlh Tourism. Turquía: General Directorate of Health Services, Department of Health Tourism, Ministry of Health.

Seow, A. N., Choong, Y. O., Moorthy, K., & Choong, C. K. (2020). Predicting medical tourism behavioural intention using social cognition models. *Tourism Review*. Advance online publication. doi:10.1108/TR-06-2019-0267

Servimedcuba. (2012). *Quienes somos*. http://www.servimedcuba.com/index.php?option=com_content&view=article&id=72&Itemid=30 (20.05.2018).

Suess, C., Baloglu, S., & Busser, J. A. (2018). Perceived impacts of medical tourism development on community wellbeing. *Tourism Management*, *69*, 232–245. doi:10.1016/j.tourman.2018.06.006

Szabó, A. (n.d.). Hungary the leading elite in Medical tourism. Medical tourism and spas in Hungary. *Hungarian Tourism Plc.*

Tat news. (2013). *World Travel Market (WTM) 2012*. Tailandia: Tourism Authority of Thailand Newsroom. Available in: https://www.tatnews.org/world-travel-market-wtm-2012/

Thailand Med Tourism. (2013). *Thailand's Medical Tourism Statistics: A Look at the International Patient Numbers*. Available in: http://www.thailandmedtourism.com/NewsArticleDetail/108/8856/Thailands-Medical-Tourism-Statistics-A-Look-at-the-International-Patient-Numbers

T&L. (2013). *Plan de negocios para el subsector de Turismo de Bienestar en Colombia*. T&L Tourism Leisure and Sports, Europraxis, Grupo Aviatur.

Treatmentabroad. (2014). *The healthcare system and hospital facilities in the USA*. Treatmentabroad. Available in: http://www.treatmentabroad.com/destinations/usa/travel-and-accommodation-0

Treatmentabroad. (n.d.). Why consider Spain for medical tourism? Spain: TreatmenAbroad.com Available in: http://www.treatmentabroad.com/destinations/spain/why-choose-spain (10.05.2018).

Turismo Argentina. (2014). *Turismo Salud, Productos Turísticos*. http://www.turismo.gov.ar/

Turkeyhealthguide. (2011). *You're invited to Turkey for medical tourism*. turkeyhealthguide.com. Available in: http://www.turkeyhealthguide.com/you_are_invited_to_turkey_for_medical_tourism.asp (09.05.18).

Woodman, J. (2010). *The Top 10 Medical Travel Destinations*. Internationalliving. Available in: https://internationalliving.com/2010/06/the-top-10-medical-travel-destinations/

ADDITIONAL READING

Connell, J. (2011). *Medical tourism*. Cabi. doi:10.1079/9781845936600.0000

Connell, J. (2013). Contemporary medical tourism: Conceptualisation, culture and commodification. *Tourism Management*, *34*, 1–13. doi:10.1016/j.tourman.2012.05.009

Crooks, V. A., Kingsbury, P., Snyder, J., & Johnston, R. (2010). What is known about the patient's experience of medical tourism? A scoping review. *BMC Health Services Research*, *10*(1), 266. doi:10.1186/1472-6963-10-266 PMID:20825667

Crooks, V. A., Turner, L., Snyder, J., Johnston, R., & Kingsbury, P. (2011). Promoting medical tourism to India: Messages, images, and the marketing of international patient travel. *Social Science & Medicine*, *72*(5), 726–732. doi:10.1016/j.socscimed.2010.12.022 PMID:21310519

Hall, C. M. (2011). Health and medical tourism: A kill or cure for global public health? *Tourism Review*, *66*(1/2), 4–15. doi:10.1108/16605371111127198

Han, H., & Hyun, S. S. (2015). Customer retention in the medical tourism industry: Impact of quality, satisfaction, trust, and price reasonableness. *Tourism Management*, *46*, 20–29. doi:10.1016/j.tourman.2014.06.003

Heung, V. C., Kucukusta, D., & Song, H. (2010). A conceptual model of medical tourism: Implications for future research. *Journal of Travel & Tourism Marketing*, *27*(3), 236–251. doi:10.1080/10548401003744677

Hopkins, L., Labonté, R., Runnels, V., & Packer, C. (2010). Medical tourism today: What is the state of existing knowledge? *Journal of Public Health Policy*, *31*(2), 185–198. doi:10.1057/jphp.2010.10 PMID:20535101

Lunt, N., & Carrera, P. (2010). Medical tourism: Assessing the evidence on treatment abroad. *Maturitas*, *66*(1), 27–32. doi:10.1016/j.maturitas.2010.01.017 PMID:20185254

Yu, J. Y., & Ko, T. G. (2012). A cross-cultural study of perceptions of medical tourism among Chinese, Japanese and Korean tourists in Korea. *Tourism Management*, *33*(1), 80–88. doi:10.1016/j.tourman.2011.02.002

KEY TERMS AND DEFINITIONS

Aesthetic Medicine: Comprises all medical procedures that aim to improve the patient's physical appearance using non-invasive, or minimally invasive, cosmetic procedures.

Medical Tourism: The practice of travelling abroad in order to receive medical treatment.

Medical Treatments: Actions and procedures necessary to combat a disease or disorder.

Prevention Health: Action taken in advance to make decrease one's chances of developing a disease. Often based on popular knowledge.

Prophylactic: A medicine or course of action used to prevent disease.

Rehabilitation: The act of restoring one's health or normal life through training and therapy after imprisonment, addiction, or illness.

Wellness: General state of good health and wellbeing, especially as an actively pursued goal.

ENDNOTES

1. https://www.hosteltur.com/comunidad/005015_turismo-de-salud-es-posible-en-venezuela.html
2. https://informe21.com/
3. http://www.caraotadigital.net
4. Analogous to the JCI, the JCAOH is a non-profit, independent organisation for accreditation and certification of the quality and continuous improvement of medical organisations; More information on https://www.jointcommission.org/about_us/about_the_joint_commission_main.aspx
5. The division of the JCI responsible for the accreditation and quality improvement of medical centres worldwide.

Chapter 7
The Importance of Happiness and Well-Being Experience in Health:
The Case of Vidago Palace Thermal Spa

Carlos Alberto Martins
Lusíada University of Porto, Portugal

Paula Rodrigues
https://orcid.org/0000-0003-2967-2583
Lusíada University of Porto, Portugal

ABSTRACT

This research explains the importance of happiness and well-being in unique health experience and the effect on satisfaction and loyalty in consumer's health thermal spa through a qualitative methodology. The brand chosen is the Vidago Palace Thermal Spa located in the north of Portugal. The combination of different options creates some unique health experiences, which follow the major trends of happiness and well-being, and contributes to a better health and lifestyle. Those attributes built great experiences and support consumer satisfaction and loyalty in health thermal spas.

INTRODUCTION

Brand experience has emerged in recent years as a very important topic in marketing and consumer behaviour research. Indeed, brand experience is increasingly recognised as important in managerial practice (Andreini, Pedeliento, Zarantonelo & Solerio, 2019). Brakus, Schmitt and Zarantonello (2009) operationalised and defined brand experience based on an experiential marketing approach (Schmitt, 1999). However, as Brakus et al's (2009) work suggested, consumption changes in the market, that is, the proliferation of, for example, themed vacations, conferences, dinners, etc. held in different contexts, among them thermal spas, suggests the need for more research into brand experience and a more critical look at the marketing management of the construct (Schmitt, Brakus & Zarantonello, 2014).

DOI: 10.4018/978-1-7998-3034-4.ch007

Hall (2011:6) defined health tourism as "a commercial phenomenon of industrial society which involves a person travelling overnight away from a normal home environment for the express benefit of maintaining or improving health, and the supply and promotion facilities of destinations which seek to provide such benefits". This type of tourism aims at achieving better physical and mental well-being. Cunha (2006) distinguished between groups; those seeking therapeutic treatments, groups looking to achieve well-being, and a third group seeking health resorts to rest in, to escape the harshness of everyday life, and to relax in natural environments. The wellness and spa sector is a multi-million euro global industry that is expected to continue to grow (GWI, 2018). The spa industry can be viewing as a homogenous entity; research has demonstrated that consumers use spas for several reasons, namely: health, sport, tourism and recreation (Baloglu, Busser & Cain, 2019; Dryglasa & Salamaga, 2017).

In recent years the health and wellness tourism sector has become more challenging and interesting for business managers. "Tourism is currently developing based on the search for new spaces and environments" (Guerra, 2016:114). Tourist destinations need to develop new and distinct offers, with an emphasis on rest, leisure and, above all, emotional stimuli, and to propose novel experiences. Health tourism is associated with other areas, such as beauty and slimming treatments, cosmetic surgery, and with thermal resorts; in the Portuguese case thermal resorts were, in the latter part of the 20th century, abandoned or declined over time. Many have since progressively been recovered and adapted to new requirements and trends. Recent health and physical concerns have (Stephen, 2016) triggered a debate between medicine and tourism (Smith & Puckzo, 2009), as this area of tourism integrates mental and physical health. Thus, some authors find difficulty in establishing a clear difference between health/medical tourism and wellness tourism (Berg, 2008; Smith & Puckzo, 2009). The Tourism of Portugal report (2006) even distinguishes between three types of health and well-being: health tourism, general well-being and specific well-being. These designations were extended into the Report of the Portuguese Association of Tourism and Welfare (2013), thus explicitly integrating medical tourism, thermal spas, thalassotherapy, aesthetic tourism, health and wellness resorts.

A health spa experience has been defined as a series of interconnected events facilitated by a company in order to engage a consumer in a memorable and unique way (Pine & Gilmore, 1998). This memorable and unique heathy experience leads to more satisfied and loyal consumers.

This work is made up of three parts. The first is a general introduction to the themes of happiness, well-being and brand experience, highlighting their importance for health. The second develops the basic concepts of happiness, well-being and brand experience, and their influence on health. The third part presents data on the welfare sector in global terms and in relation to Portugal. Finally, the chapter ends with a case study – the Vidago Palace Thermal SPA, and outlines some challenges, and presents some recommendations, related to the theme.

CONCEPTUAL BACKGROUND

Happiness

Happiness has been examined from different angles, from an undifferentiated approach (Layard, 2005), from a subjective perspective that reflects different states for different people (Gilbert, 2006), and even from the viewpoint that happiness varies with age and culture (Mogilner, Kamvar, & Aaker, 2011; Tsai 2006). Mogilner (2012:430) argued that happiness can be understood as "excitement, elation and enthusiasm" or the "calm, peacefulness, and serenity" that transmits positive emotions. Temporal issues tend to influence the experience of happiness. When the individual is focussed on the future, the excitement (s)he feels tends to be considered as a state of happiness. When (s)he focusses on the present, feelings of calmness are seen to represent as a state of happiness. These temporal perspectives tend to influence purchasing decisions (Mogilner, Kamvar & Aaker, 2012). On the other hand, individuals with humour, and/or positive attitudes, are more optimistic, more creative and focus on the long term (Schwartz & Close, 1983; Adaval, 2003; Labroo & Patrick, 2009). Purchasing decisions can, thus, be influenced by emotions (happiness). When the individual is more excited, (s)he tends to choose more challenging or adventurous activities; when (s)he is calm, (s)he tends to prefer relaxing and wellness activities (Kim, Park & Schwarz, 2010). While a focus on the future can trigger the acquisition of more exciting products/services, concerns about the present tend to focus on calmer products/activities (Fingerman & Permultter, 1995; Mogilner et al., 2012).

From another perspective, Aknin et al. (2018) established a relationship between income and happiness. They concluded that consumers make a portion of their income available for purchases that offer experiences – free time, self-expression and generosity. A positive relationship does exist between income and happiness, however this association is often overrated (Akin, Norton & Donn, 2009). The poor are not always miserable, and the rich are not always happy (Aknin, Wiwad, & Hanniball, 2018). This reveals that the interconnection between income and happiness is less evident than was once thought (Cone & Gilovich, 2010). The relationship between time and money raises an intriguing question, because an analysis of the relationship between time and happiness shows that time influences happiness (Whillans, Dunn, Smeets, Bekkers & Norton, 2012).

The importance of age for the happiness dimension varies throughout life (Mogilner, et al., 2011). For younger people happiness means excitement and enthusiasm, for older people happiness is synonymous with calm and peace. Young people relate happiness to new social interactions, new information and exciting choices. For the elderly, perceived time left, family social relationships, emotions, and peaceful consumption choices are important. As this group has less time left in life, more ordinary experiences become extraordinary (Aknin et al., 2018), but it is unclear what provides continuing happiness; some findings suggest that shared experiences are more fun than individual experiences (Caprariello & Reis, 2013). Bhattacharjee and Mogilner (2014:2) contrasted ordinary and extraordinary experiences; "ordinary experiences as those that are common, frequent, and within the reality of everyday life. Extraordinary experiences, on the other hand, are uncommon, infrequent, and beyond the realm of everyday life".

Zauberman et al. (2009:715) argued that happiness often comes from extraordinary experiences "whereas memories of mundane experiences help individuals navigate through daily life, memories of extraordinary and meaningful life events have important consequences for self-definition, well-being and life satisfaction". In contrast, another line of research proposes that mundane, ordinary experiences are also a source of happiness (De Voe & House, 2012). It is recognised that happiness varies throughout life, depending on age, and if an experience is ordinary or extraordinary (Bhattacharjee & Mogilner, 2014). Thus we propose that brand experience provides happiness and leads consumers to experience positive emotions and well-being (Bhattacharjee & Mogilner, 2014; Gilovich, Kumar & Jampol, 2015; Kim & Ko, 2011; Schmitt, Brakus & Zarantonello, 2014). Acquisitions can be material or experiential. While the former involves the acquisition of tangible goods, experiential purchases involve an intention to access a life experience (Van Boden & Gilovich, 2003). This distinction leads us to propose that experiential purchases give greater satisfaction than material purchases. These shopping experiences are commonly enjoyed in social environments (i.e. with friends or family). Other aspects of experiential acquisitions are more directly related to personal identity (Carter & Gilovich, 2012). Thus, we posit that:

P1. The consumer's happiness has a positive effect on the unique health thermal spa experience.

Well-Being

Stephen (2016) argued that the notion of well-being covers a concern for the body, mind, spirit (wellness) and physical fitness (fitness). Other authors have argued that well-being represents a balance between the physical, psychological, social and intellectual dimensions, the individual's life sense and occupational dimensions (Hettler, 1980). Another research stream has shown that an individual's lifestyle can be related to healthy activities, such as spa experiences, which shows the importance that health has for the consumer (Chen & Hsieh, 2010; Goldman, Bunnell & Posner, 2014).

Well-being is influenced by three psychological needs: autonomy, competence and social connections (Ryan & Deci, 2000). These have a positive impact on performance, job satisfaction, sports' results and physical well-being. Baloglu Busser and Cain (2019) identified five motivational factors and two experiential dimensions. People use spas for health, tourist, recreational and cultural reasons (Baloglu, Busser & Cain, 2019). Recent trends suggest that consumers choose to visit spas for emotional well-being (EWB). Drylasa and Salamaga (2017) identified three target segments: individuals concerned with nature and culture, with social relationships and with well-being. Self-determination theory (SDT) proposes that motivation and its variants influence the quality of experiences and emotions (Deci & Ryan, 2008). SDT identifies three types of motivation: autonomous, controlled and amotivation. Autonomous/intrinsic motivation conditions behaviours through the satisfaction that the individual derives from an activity. Controlled motivation "exerts pressure on people to act in a certain way based on external rewards or punishment, internalized as shame or fear" (Baloglu, Busser & Cain, 2019:429). On the other hand, SDT proposes that amotivation is the lowest level of motivation, that is, lack of motivation, or the lack of intent to engage in an experience. For Baloglu, Busser and Cain (2019:429) "SPA service is a wellness activity and typically a positive and self-enhancing experience, intrinsic motivation is the most likely type of motivation that would drive SPA visitation". Positive emotional experiences can also provoke intrinsic motivational factors, leading to a desire to try new experiences and triggering loyalty (Reicheld & Sassen, 1990). Thus, we posit that:

P2. Well-being is the objective of a undergoing a unique health consumer experience.

Unique Health Experiences and Loyalty

The rise of experiential marketing approaches has been defined as one of the key developments in post-modern consumer culture (Pine & Gilmore, 2011). This research line has been very strongly associated with consumer culture theory (CCT), and includes an exploration of the multi-sensory, experiential and emotive dimensions of consumption behaviour (Holbrook & Hirschman, 1982). Several CCT studies have explored extraordinary and unique experiences.

Unique and extraordinary experiences have a set of characteristics, such as positive and collaborative interpersonal interactions among people who share similar goals, attenuated boundaries, and a sacred nature which escapes the logic of the marketplace (Tumbat & Belk, 2011). These experiences have been defined as special types of hedonic consumption that are emotionally intense, unique, memorable and transformative (Husemann et al., 2016; Tumbat & Belk, 2011).

A wellness experience consists of a combination of multiple dimensions that induce emotions. These dimensions allow unique moments (Mossberg, 2007) of social interaction and generate expectations (Oh, Fiore, & Jeoung, 2007), an escape from the routine and monotony of daily life (Quan & Wang, 2004), and involvement in thermal spa/wellness experiences may surprise the consumer. These experiences can also consolidate memories of stimuli (joy and pleasure) and rewarding moments (Larsen, 2003). These experiences represent the confluence between experiences lived (emotional, spiritual, physical) moment-to-moment, and experiences felt.

Getz (2012) argued that these experiences can be influenced by a cognitive dimension (memories, perceptions, learning) and an affective dimension (feelings, emotions, values). The difficulty in evaluating experiences is due to consumers' underlying motivations which, because they are subjective, hinder the identification of what may condition a pleasure stimulus (Stephen, 2016). Brakus, Schmitt and Zarantonello (2009) defined brand experience as subjective consumer responses evoked by brand-related stimuli when consumers interact with the brand. These interactions involve multi-sensory and emotive aspects of brand use beyond mere utilitarian function (Holbrook & Hirchman, 1982; Gentile, Spiller & Noci, 2007). The economic development of modern society, in terms of service offerings, has led to the initial service being undifferentiated, and to the provision of services (Pine & Gilmore, 1998).

The field of customer experience has been addressed by several authors in recent years (Reicheld, 1996). Nevertheless, memorable and unique experiences require an ingredient absent in most studies into emotions (Thomke, 2019). More than price and other functional attributes, memorable and unique experiences require emotional magic. "The essential difference between emotion and reason, is that emotion leads to action while reason leads to conclusions" (Thomke, 2019:2). Most companies focus on eliminating unpleasant experiences, and on reducing variations in experiences to remove outliers. Outliers represent positive emotional experiences, which leave affective memories. It is these experiences that reinforce loyalty and determine choice (Reicheld, 1996). For this reason, Thomke (2019:5) suggested that "you might think that every company would be trying to create dynamic, delightful customer journeys infused with emotion".

Several studies have related motivational effects to customer experience. "Customer experience" has been defined in various ways; as an educational experience (Oh, Fiore & Jeoung, 2007), an *escapist* experience and a sensory experience (memory). Together these form the experience (Pine & Gilmore, 1998). These memories can also determine loyalty (Kim, 2010; Kim & Ritchie, 2014).

Healthcare is one of the most important and personalised consumer experiences service (Kemp, Jillapali & Becerra, 2014). According to these authors "healthcare branding requires a solid, organized commitment to delivering unique standards of consistency through the institution's products and services" (Kemp et al., 2014, 126).

Thermal spas offer various types of therapies that provide health benefits. These therapies can address rheumatic disorders and diseases of the nervous, respiratory and digestive systems, among others. Thermal resorts are sun/beach-based alternatives, far from today's urban confusion (Guerra, 2016).

Brand experiences occur when consumers interact with a product or service. In services, experiences take place when there is contact with a physical store, its staff and/or its operations (Kerin, Jan & Howard, 2002). The various stimuli presented by the brand, such as its colours, shape, design, slogans, mascots, packaging, communications, its points of sale (where consumers can view it), are the elements that determine the consumers' experience of the brand. Meanwhile, Brand experience, thus, can vary between intense, durable and positive forms, or more superficial, spontaneous or even negative forms. This gradation influences brand loyalty (Reicheld, 1996). Brand experiences also include "specific sensations, feeling, cognitions and behavioral responses triggered by specific brand related stimuli" (Brakus et al., 2009:53). Another difference between brand experience and constructs such as brand image and brand identification is the involvement consumers establish with the brand, which is based on their needs, values and interests. It is understood that high involvement with the brand does not necessarily lead to intense experiences: "Brand experience is not an emotional relationship concept. According to Keller (1993), brand experience is distinct from brand associations and brand image. Brand experience may be conditioned by sensory, affective, intellectual and behavioural factors.

Some studies have examined the correlation between behavioural variables such as purchase intention, word-of-mouth and willingness to pay a price premium, and psychological variables such as satisfaction and loyalty intentions (Oliver, 2010). Loyalty has been defined as the consumer's internalised commitment to consistently support an establishment in the future irrespective of situational or external influences (Oliver, 2010; Kandampully, Zhang, & Bilgihan, 2015). Loyalty is characterised by a deep commitment to repurchasing a product or a service. Zhong, Busser and Baloglu's (2017) study suggested that there may be a link between emotionally exciting positive unique experiences and consumer loyalty. Spa companies are very dependent on loyal and satisfied consumers to drive revenue (Baloglu, Busser & Cain, 2019). Thus, we posit that:

P3. A unique health experience leads to a more satisfied and loyal consumer.

RESEARCH DESIGN

The research objective is to evaluate how moments of happiness and well-being create unique experiences and loyal customers.

The data collection method was based on a qualitative descriptive study, through a group discussion, comprising representatives of 10 families of different ages and compositions; and through semi-structured interviews. The discussion took place in a hotel conference room with: (a) two couples (under 30 years old) without children (b) three couples (30 to 50 years old) with children; and (c) 5 couples (seniors - over 50 years old) also without children. Thereafter, three semi-structured interviews were conducted with a representative from each of the three groups of families; the object here was to go further into the experiences they highlighted and their probability of returning to the hotel.

CASE STUDY

Global Well-Being Industry

"The Global Wellness Institute (GWI) defines wellness as the active pursuit of activities, choices, and lifestyles that lead to a state of holistic health. Wellness is multi-dimensional and preventive; it relies on individual responsibility to integrate a holistic health paradigm into everyday life – how we live, eat, work, play, travel, maintain vitality, deal with stress, and respond to the first signs of illness" (GWI, 2018:4). According to the GWI, the welfare economy "has grown from $3.7 trillion in 2015 to $4.2

trillion in 2017, representing 5.3% of global economic output (Table 1). By comparison, global health expenditures were estimated at $7.3 trillion in 2015 (the most recent year for which data are available)" (GWI, 2108:4).

Through 2015-2017 the wellness economy grew by 6.4% annually, a growth rate nearly twice as high as global economic growth (3.6% annually) (Table 2). The wellness sectors that have experienced the fastest growth rates are spas, wellness tourism, and wellness real estate (GWI, 2018:4).

Table 1. Market size

Market Size	2015	2017	Average Annual Growth Rate
Personal Care, Beauty, Anti-Aging	$999.0	$1,082.9	4.1%
Healthy Eating, Nutrition, Weight Loss	$647.8	$702.1	4.1%
Wellness Tourism	$563.2	$639.4	6.5%
Fitness & Mind-Body	$542.0	$595.4	4.8%
Preventive & Personalised Medicine and Public Health	$534.3	$574.8	3.7%
Traditional & Complementary Medicine**	**$199.0	**$359.7	**
Wellness Real Estate/Properties***	$118.6	$134.3	6.4%
Spa Economy *(Spa Facilities)*	$98.6 *($77.6)*	$118.8 *($93.6)*	****9.8% ****(9.9%)
Thermal/Mineral Springs	$51.0	$56.2	4.9%
Workplace Wellness	$43.3	$47.5	4.8%
Wellness economy	*$3,724.4	*$4,220.2	6.4%

Source: Global Wellness Institute estimates, based on economic and industry sector projections from the IMF, ILO, Euromonitor and the GWI's data and projection model.

Table 2. Wellness growth projections 2017-2022

Projected Market Size (US$ billions) 2017 – 2022	2017	2022	Projected Average Annual Growth Rate
Wellness Real Estate/Properties	$134.3	$197.4	8.0%
Workplace Wellness	$47.5	$65.6	6.7%
Wellness Tourism	$639.4	$919.4	7.5%
Spa Facilities	$93.6	$127.6	6.4%
Thermal/Mineral Springs	$56.2	$77.1	6.5%

Source: Global Wellness Institute estimates, based on economic and industry sector projections from the IMF, ILO, Euromonitor, and the GWI's data and projection model.

Wellness Trends

In the experience economy "personal achievement, the search to become the people we dream of being in terms of well-being and health (physical, mental and emotional) are fundamental parts of this process" (Lima, 2016:1). Taking this approach into account we highlight here some trends.

One of the recent trends is to live slowly (slow living) and more simply. This way of life is associated with status and environmental activism (BCSD, 2019). This lifestyle began in the 1980s. With the growing information available to consumers and their consequent greater awareness, a trend has been unleashed where individuals seek a life more connected with others "in order to have richer and more satisfying experiences, and to feel that life and the way we live it has a purpose" (BCSD, 2019:2). An evolution has been seen from slow food and slow fashion which has infected other areas – for example, slow fitness and slow tourism. Slow living is characterised by a resumption of artisanship and a growing concern for well-being and achieving a work/life balance (BSCD, 2019). However, even as these priorities have developed, new consumers do not despise speed and instantaneity. This finding takes into account the awareness that speed requires more resources and, thus, higher prices. Technologies have also appeared that are associated with "slower" lifestyles, such as robotics, IoT, artificial intelligence and augmented reality (Lima, 2016; BCSD, 2019).

Modern societies have increased life expectancy due to improved living conditions. In developed countries people are living longer but are having less children. Another change is the transition from the concept of health being focused on the disease, to a much greater focus on prevention and the adoption of healthier lifestyles which meet the current economic context where the state fosters preventive, rather than curative, care approaches (Mendes, 2013:61).

Anxiety, on the other hand, is a mega tendency caused by individuals' perceptions that the future looks unstable and their struggle to achieve happiness. This megatrend has the following characteristics: increased obesity, the pursuit of healthy longevity, increased chronic diseases, home health control systems, and technological developments, a more comprehensive view of health, a focus on healthy lifestyles and wellness treatments, stress management, and declining fertility (which is linked to population aging) (Mendes, 2013:62).

Finally, the importance of technology has grown, and will continue to grow, in the health sector. The consolidation of individual and personalised health management (Lima, 2016), and further developments in electronic medicine, will impact on the control of chronic diseases, the maintenance, or even the adoption, of healthier lifestyles, and increase interaction between patients and physicians. "The development of telepresence, with monitoring systems for older people living alone, contributes among other reasons for a lower development of isolation-related diseases" (Mendes, 2013:63). In this context, despite the growing importance of technology, human contact will remain at the top of the health and well-being pyramid. Other related trends are: wellness spaces, balanced health, virtual self-realisation, health-related impact indicators, and distributed diagnosis (Lima, 2016).

Portuguese Spa Market and Competition

All segments of the Portuguese tourist market grew in the years from 2010. This was particularly evident in the leisure and family segment. The latest results indicate that the main tourist age segments visiting Portugal were people between 25 and 64 years (54%), and above 65 (16%). The main reasons given for

Table 3. Total trips to Portugal

Unit: thousands	Total trips, with duration of at least one night						
	Total	Leisure and holidays	Visiting family and friends	Business	Health	Religion	Others
2009	18 048	9 245	6 802	1 554	54	126	267
2010	15 373	7 476	6 026	1 156	24	186	506
2011	15 191	6 927	6 489	991	49	186	549
2012	17 098	7 201	7 870	1 236	55	198	538
2013	17 861	7 405	8 370	1 306	47	206	527
2014	17891	7262	8238	1549	60	236	547
2015	19 147	8 084	8 594	1 663	68	191	548
2016	20 182	8 837	8 901	1 650	39	227	528
2017	21 188	9 577	9 326	1 502	60	235	489
2018	22 079	10 263	9 137	1 832	40	215	592

Source: INE - Tourism Statistics, Portugal (2019).

their visits were leisure and holidays (45%), and to visit family and friends (40%). These segments have grown since 2010 (Tables 3 and 4).

There is a strong spa/thermal sector in Portugal, with most of the offer being concentrated in the north (Ferreira & Vieira, 2016). The Vidago Palace Thermal SPA is located in the north. Thus, the main competitors were chosen based on geographic criteria, that is, they are located in the north of Portugal.

Table 4. Total trips by age

Age 2018	Total trips, with duration of at least one night						
	Total	Leisure and holidays	Visiting family and friends	Business	Health	Religion	Others
Total	22 079.0	10 262.7	9 136.9	1 832.3	39.6	215,1	592.4
0 - 14 years	3 797.3	1 979.7	1 634.4	71.8	x	43,1	67.5
15 - 24 years	2 042.0	1 023.8	777.4	167.0	x	36,9	35.6
25 - 44 years	6 384.8	2 900.6	2 618.3	716.1	4.5	27,9	117.4
45 - 64 years	6 094.1	2 598.3	2 659.9	633.4	8.3	60,0	134.1
65 or + years	3 760.9	1 760.3	1 446.9	244.0	24.7	47,2	237.8

Source: INE - Tourism Statistics, Portugal (2019).

The experiential map below (Figure 1) features the Vidago Palace (V), the Chaves (C), the Pedras Salgadas (PS), the Boticas (B), the Termas Taipas Termal (TC), and the Termas de S. Vicente (TSV) thermal spas.

To assess the different positioning of the various competitors we took into account two dimensions, the diversity of services offered and experiential diversity. The first dimension was based on the following criteria: therapeutic recommendations, medical programmes, wellness programmes, and the techniques involved in the provision of services. The second dimension covers accommodation, historical heritage, the availability of tennis courts and golf courses, private gardens, the surrounding nature and landscape and the diversity of the leisure programmes on offer. Using these criteria, it is possible to distinguish three groupings.

The first group offers a limited variety of services and experiences. A second group, comprising three units (TC, TSV, PS), offers a greater variety of services and experiences. Finally, Vidago is distinguished by offering a greater variety of services and experiences to its visitors.

Figure 1. Experiential Map

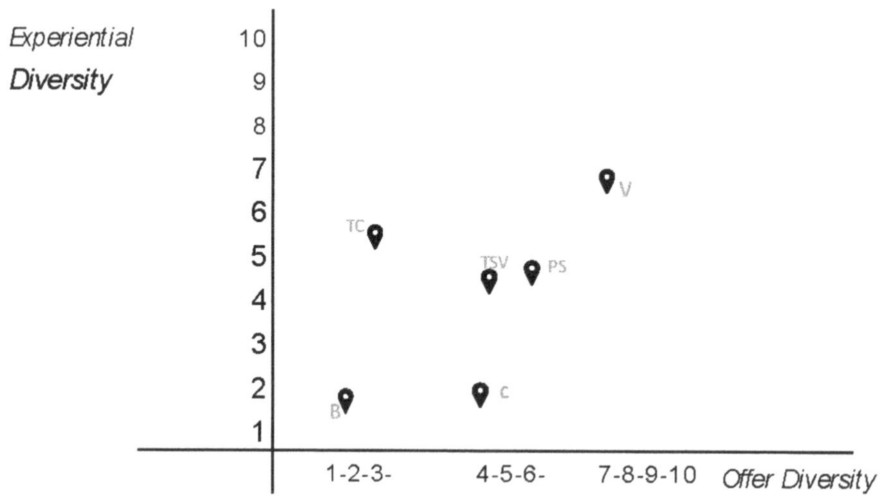

Vidago Palace: Thermal SPA

The history of the Vidago Palace takes us back to the beginning of the last century to the reign of King Carlos I, when the hotel project began. The King wanted a luxurious space where he could accommodate his family and visitors and tourists coming in search of the therapeutic effects of the mineral waters in the region. In the event, the Vidago Palace opened its doors on October 6, 1910, after the assassination of the king and the beginning of the revolution of 1910. The hotel eventually became one of the most prestigious European resorts, especially during the period from the start of World War II until the end of the 1960s. During the following decades the appearance of more diversified offers, and higher luxury standards, caused the palace to close in 2006 (Vidago Palace, s.d.).

One hundred years after it first opened, and preserving the architectural heritage and identity of the resort, the hotel reopened in 2010. The remodelling of the Vidago Palace Hotel was undertaken by interior architects José Pedro Lopes Vieira & Diogo Rosa Lã, and architect Álvaro Siza Vieira, who created the new Spa and Club House (Roof Magazine, 2016).

Located in the magnificent "Centenary Park", with its extensive botanical richness, where magnolias, plane trees, camellias, holly, pines and lavender mix in a lush combination with a lake, water mirrors and thermal water sources, the Vidago Palace Hotel is a reminder of past times. The hotel retains its charming period details, with fine materials lining its corridors, sumptuous furniture, lush fabrics, Venetian-style chandeliers, and silk wallpaper with expressive motifs in the style of a grand manor house resplendent with soul and history. When one enters the Vidago Palace Hotel, one finds comfort, beauty and nobility.

For these reasons, and more, the hotel has over the years received several national and international awards, the most recent being awarded by Condé Nast Traveler, in 2016. The Spanish edition of Condé Nast Traveler highlights "a gravel path between the trees" that leads "to a pink facade with Romeo and Juliet balconies", the palatial environment and the magnificent swimming pool (Condé Nast Traveler, 2016).

The Vidago Palace Hotel was also in 2013 recognised by the reservation website booking.com in its 7 Star Global Luxury Awards scheme, which rates the most luxurious and exclusive hotels in the world, in the Hotels & Resorts category. The hotel was granted its +8 award, based on the opinions of visitors who booked through the service (Idealista, 2013). In 2017 the UNICER group, which owns the hotel, changed its name to the Super Bock Group: the group sales manager noted.. (the group).. "also owns the Pedras Salgadas Spa & Nature Park resort, and wants to consolidate its leisure segment – its main revenue earner - and to reinforce the MICE segment (meetings, incentives, conferences, exhibitions), using the hotel's conference centre, with capacity for some 500 people, its eight meeting rooms and its auditorium". The creation of the Kids Club, and improvements made to the restaurant and bar service, represent a further enhancement in service quality.

The Super Bock Group is the largest Portuguese drinks company, with a multi-brand and multimarket strategy, whose core activity is the beer and bottled water business. The group is also present in the soft drinks and wine segments, in the production and marketing of malt, and in the tourism business; it owns two flagship assets in the Trás-os-Montes region, the Vidago and Pedras Salgadas thermal resorts. The company is majority Portuguese owned, the VIACER Group holding 56%, Carlsberg owning the other 44% (Super Bock Group, s.d.)

In 2005 the group launched a major tourist sector investment. The majestic Vidago Palace Hotel was restored (reopened 2010), with an updated thermal spa, golf course and conference centre; and the Pedras Salgadas Spa & Nature Park was developed (opened 2012).

The Vidago Palace Hotel is located in northern Portugal, by road about an hour away from Porto and 15 minutes from Chaves. Considered one of the most famous historic luxury hotels in Portugal, the Vidago Palace is imposing, yet inviting, combining the grandeur of a palace with the cosy atmosphere of a country house (Super Bock Group, s.d.).

The Vidago Palace Hotel complex has 77 rooms and suites, some with private patios, a thermal spa, and 20 rooms used for relaxation, well-being and beauty treatments; the Vidago mineral water provided is a differentiating element. It offers also an indoor pool and an outdoor pool, a sauna, gym, and an 18-hole golf course (6,308 metres, designed by Mackenzie Ross) (Idealista, 2013).

The Vidago Palace Thermal SPA provides an excellent offer and service; Vidago mineral water is used in various treatments. The spa is noted for its innovation and strong commitment to ultramodern technology, and offers exclusive treatments in Portugal, such as Iyashi Dôme (of Japanese origin), that combines three important concepts: purification, weight loss and cell regeneration. It has an integrated offer featuring the most varied therapies, and is a true holistic spa (Ambitur, 2016).

The spa offers a unique technique, used only by major international brands such as Evian, Vichy and Intercontinental Moscow. It has an installation which emits long infrared rays (IRL), of organic plant origin, similar to the heat radiated by the sun; this system is also used in maternity ward incubators.

The main function of the system is to purify the body by the elimination of toxins. The Iyashi Dôme technology purifies and sculpts the body, as it supports the elimination of fat reserves, transforming them into energy. A thirty-minute session is equivalent to a twenty-kilometre run; approximately six hundred calories of energy are used. The first fifteen minutes are similar to a "sunbath", and the second fifteen minutes are compared to an "intense sports activity". Effective results are obtained after about five sessions; the device acts on three different curative levels: weight, anti-aging and detox. The client easily detects an improvement in the density, homogeneity, luminosity and elasticity of his/her skin, and a reduction in skin roughness.

"The investment in Iyashi Dôme allows the hotel to be at the forefront of beauty and wellness techniques used worldwide. Its exclusive technology - unique in Portugal - facilitates treatments until now non-existent in the country, but in high demand abroad. The selection of this device is related to a holistic philosophy of well-being practiced in the Vidago Palace SPA and which seeks to offer integrated health solutions. This is undoubtedly a solution that naturally and deeply rebalances the body, so that it can find harmony and general well-being again. We are, therefore, confident in the demand of the national market, as well as in the results presented by the device, always having as our main objective the total satisfaction of our client" (See Portugal, 2015).

In partnership with the Clarins brand, the European leader in face and body products, which operates a beauty-treatment institute that offers excellent training, the Vidago Thermal SPA provides its guests with various wellness treatments, using the best products. Clients can enjoy temperature contrast experiences, such as the sauna and the ice fountain and can revitalise their bodies in the outdoor vitality pool. At the Vidago Palace Thermal SPA, in an environment of pure tranquillity, one can enjoy unique and unforgettable moments that balance the body and the mind. The hotel offers techniques, culture and international influences that provide wellness treatments designed to fit its clients' needs. The Vidago mineral water programmes have therapeutic and curative properties. The water is abstracted directly from deep layers of granitic rock. Among the water's benefits are its positive effects on the metabolic, cardiovascular, digestive and musculoskeletal systems, and the skin.

The spa offers revivification, in balanced, natural, health services. These are described below.

SPA included. Enjoy a luxurious stay with a free Spa credit. Minimum stay of two nights with breakfast included; One spa treatment per room, per stay. One can choose a treatment from the Spa menu which includes: a natural juice after treatments; access to the Vidago Spa circuit (vitality pool, indoor pool, sauna, hammam, ice fountain and fully equipped gym); and activities, hiking, cycling, golf and tennis.

Vidago revives. In its harmonious combination with nature the palace aims to convey a sense of vitality. Therapies are widely employed. Two nights of accommodation with breakfast included. A morning walk on the "Hot Springs Route"; a taste of natural mineral water from the hot springs; an exfoliating natural mineral water shower and massage. Body and face moisturizing and a balancing massage. Guests have access to the Vidago Spa circuit (vitality pool, indoor pool, sauna, hammam, two experience showers, ice fountain and fully equipped gym), and Vidago Palace activities;(hiking, cycling, golf and tennis.

Vidago in balance. This reflects simplicity and tranquillity, everything you need to rebalance yourself. A three-night accommodation package with breakfast included. A taste of natural mineral water in the hot springs; a yoga session and a meditation session; a whirlpool with natural Vidago mineral water; a honey, ginger and coconut milk ritual; a mystic massage (body massage with the sound of Tibetan gongs; access to the Vidago Spa circuit (vitality pool, indoor pool, sauna, hammam, ice fountain and gym; and Vidago Palace activities, hiking, cycling, golf and tennis.

Vidago nature. A focus on the light that surrounds the palace, and the enjoyment of peaceful moments. Includes: four nights' accommodation with breakfast; a twelve kilometre nature trail accompanied by a personal trainer (Vidago Palace-Pedras Salgadas Spa & Nature Park); a picnic at the Pedras Salgadas Spa & Nature Park; a tree climbing session at the Pedras Salgadas Spa & Nature Park; transfer from Pedras Salgadas to Vidago Palace Hotel; a jet shower with Vidago natural mineral water; a massage shower with natural Vidago mineral water; a balanced massage with essential oils; a deep tissue massage; access to the Vidago Spa circuit (vitality pool, indoor pool, sauna, hammam, ice fountain and gym, and Vidago Palace activities, hiking, cycling, golf and tennis.

Vidago healthy silhouette. The perfect place to re-educate the body through the use of spring mineral water direct from its source, personalised physical exercise and nutrition. This programme includes: five nights' accommodation with breakfast; spa cuisine menu (full board based on a diet plan prescribed by the nutritionist; includes non-alcoholic drinks); a taste of natural mineral water from the hot springs; a 40-km bicycle tour along the "Linha do Corgo" (Vidago-Chaves-Vidago); a session of HIT Pilates (high intensity physical training with Pilates recovery session); an intensive GAP session (physical training of the glutes, abs and legs); an essential detox treatment; a jet shower with natural Vidago mineral water; two Iyashi Dôme + Jet Blitz; a tri-active body treatment - intense firmness; a tri-active body treatment - slimming efficacy; access to the Vidago Spa circuit (vitality pool, indoor pool, sauna, hammam, ice fountain and gym); and Vidago Palace activities, hiking, cycling, golf and tennis.

The spa's thermal offer features two different techniques, including: Hydroponia; jet shower, simple immersion bath, hydromassage bath, hydromassage bath with underwater jet, general/partial massage shower; and complementary techniques including transdermal mesotherapy and electronic lymphatic drainage treatments, aromatherapy treatments, facial and body beauty treatments, traditional massages - shiatsu, reflexology, manual lymphatic drainage, Indian head massage; other therapies - traditional acupuncture, and "Day Spa" and nutrition packages. The Wellness Programme aims to provide a complete wellness experience. A variety of programmes effective for rejuvenating the body and mind are available. Among them the Vidago Mineral Water Programme, with its therapeutic and healing properties, stands out. The water is abstracted directly from deep layers of granitic rock. Among the water's benefits are its positive effects on the metabolic, cardiovascular, digestive and musculoskeletal systems, and the skin.

Medical programmes seek to provide a complete wellness experience. They offer a variety of programmes effective in rejuvenating the body and mind. The water has benefits for the metabolic, cardiovascular, digestive and musculoskeletal systems, and the skin. Personalised programmes are available, based on a medical consultation, a nutritional consultation, biometric evaluation, and physical and cardiorespiratory evaluations; these are developed individually to find the "perfect treatment" for the body and mind. Services are available for both adults and children; the little ones are pampered in unforgettable spa experiences. Services are available for specific treatments from the age of 2. The children may be accompanied by adults.

Finally, body and facial beauty treatments are also available. These are based on many small procedures: movement, relaxation, beauty treatments, healthy/balanced food and skin purification. The experience aims to help one find perfect harmony, the ideal balance of all the elements that make up beauty! Skin purification and detoxification form the basis of the treatments one can choose during the stay, and thus one can immediately appreciate the results of the incredible nutrition and sensations.

Depending on the packages selected, the prices of the main treatment categories are shown below (Table 5).

Table 5. Price list

Treatment type	*Duration (minutes)*	*Price Range (euros)*
Thermal Treatment	10-40 m	20-50€
T. Shower and Massages	25-80 m	50-125€
T. of the world	25-110 m	70-160€
Clarins		
Face	75 m	90€
Body	50 m	80€
Massages & body	50-55 m	80€
Body & face	80 m	115€
Packages	110-200 m	170-300€
Beauty	-	35-50€
Well-being		
Treat. & well-being	50-80 m	80-115€
Couple experience	110-180 m	250-450€
Exfoliation	30 m	40€
Fitness & leisure	50m-6hours	45-200€
Thermal programmes	-	407-637€

The Vidago Palace possesses a set of unique and exclusive attributes that give it a distinct position, based on the opinion of its customers (Figure 1). These attributes are evident in terms of the variety of services offered in the wellness programmes and techniques used, and the diversity of experiences dimension is evident in the architectural beauty of the facilities, their location, the landscape, the tranquillity provided by nature, the golf course and the gastronomic offer (Table 6).

Table 6. Satisfaction index

Source	**Number of Evaluations**	**Rating**
TripAdvisor	870	Excellence (732)
Hotels.com	50	9.8
Central de Reservas	n.a.	9.3
Logitravel	n.a.	10

The resort features a fundamental strategic resource, both in therapeutic and curative terms - Vidago Natural Mineral Water.

The Vidago Palace has responded to some of the trends observed in the sector by introducing varied therapeutic programmes which give its visitors different and memorable experiences in terms of both health and well-being (Table 7).

Table 7. Vidago Palace uniqueness

Drivers	The unique experiences	How The Vidago Palace Thermal SPA builds unique experiences
Major Trends	• Slow living – the importance of how to live life; the exploration of different and enriching experiences; work-life balance. • Aging - improving conditions and lifestyles to guarantee longevity. • Reduced anxiety - the search for happiness and relaxation. • Future of betterman - health and well-being at the top of the pyramid; technology-based personalisation (digitisation).	▪ SPA inclusive - programme per room ▪ Yoga sessions ▪ Hydromassages ▪ Vidago SPA Circuit ▪ Personalised medical programmes
Happiness and well-being	• The pursuit of excitement and enthusiasm • The search for calm and serenity • Purchases that allow access to extraordinary experiences.	▪ Bicycle tours ▪ HIT Pilates ▪ Body treatments ▪ SPA cuisine menu ▪ Intensive GAP sessions
Brand experience	• Contact and service provision • Environment identity and design • The location and its context • Brand communication	▪ Architectural space ▪ Botanical richness ▪ New design (after 2010)
Customer experience	• Memorable moments • Positive emotional experiences	▪ Mineral water programmes that rejuvenate the body and mind ▪ Hiking, water tasting, cycling, golf, tennis, sauna, massages etc.
Health importance	• Health of body and mind • Therapeutics	▪ Medical consultations ▪ Benefits for the digestive, cardiovascular systems and skin, among others.

CURRENT CHALLENGES AND RECOMMENDATIONS

The challenge for The Vidago Palace and other thermal spas, in terms of developing a loyal customer base, is to successfully create consumption experiences that are emotionally intense, memorable, unique and transformative.

Customer loyalty is driven more by emotional factors than by logical and rational factors. Service users expect to enjoy emotional, cognitive and motivational experiences. These factors can result in stories/narratives, memories and feelings. Through these experiential paths terrible or exceptional experiences can arise. Only memorable experiences give rise to positive emotions and are remembered as unique. Users develop loyalty based on unique and memorable experiences.

In the Vidago case some of its distinguishing factors are clear and difficult to copy/imitate. Among these are Vidago mineral water, the beautiful architecture of the hotel and its setting in the landscape. To these tangible aspects can be added the variety of spa treatments on offer, the golf course, the calmness and serenity of the setting, the bicycle tours and walks, and the various customised leisure and medical programmes. This differentiated offer is based on high prices, which require customers with greater purchasing power and, consequently, involves less visitors. On the other hand, this small group of customers requires increased innovation and high quality of service provision. These requirements impact on the company's cost structure, which represents a major challenge.

This research has some limitations. The spa's geographical location limits its ability to attract customers, which results in a less than desirable occupancy rate. The hotel might develop a set of actions to address this limitation; based on the brand's positioning it might develop varied programmes to attract new national and international customers. Finding new international partners, and the development of digital channels, are strategic priorities. A brand reinforcement and promotion programme should be designed for the domestic market and for new foreign markets, both to consolidate the brand and to attract new customers.

FUTURE RESEARCH DIRECTIONS

It will be necessary to development a quantitative analysis to confirm the main assumptions of this study. Measures should be taken to clarify whether the constructs of happiness (ordinary, extraordinary and memorable experiences) and wellness (memories and feelings) have a relationship with unique experiences and loyalty in the thermal and health spa sector.

CONCLUSION

Happiness depends on various factors; genetic, activities undertaken, life stability, age and the type of experiences one undergoes. Most of the families interviewed believed that some medical services, facilities, meals and accommodation belong to ordinary experiences, while thermal programmes, bicycle tours, tennis, saunas and massages were excellent experiences. Reported as memorable experiences were golf, the mineral water and the spa programmes, and the walking tours. It was not clear to the families that happiness was based on specific joyful moments (Caprariello & Reis, 2013), because they had great experiences without any social contacts outside the family. The families also stated that great experiences could result from ordinary aspects/situations. Unique experiences result from the sum of all experiences (Bhattacharjee & Mogilner, 2014; De Voe & House, 2012). The importance of happiness to families based on age wasn't confirmed, because all the families (the young and the seniors) enjoyed the uniqueness of the hotel, which was perceived to be a calm and peaceful place (Mogilner, Kamvar & Aaker, 2011; Akin, Wiwad & Hanniball, 2018).

Wellness is related to memories, feelings and emotions. All the families indicated that the local landscape, and the hotel architecture, were distinct and unique factors. These features are strongly related to brand identity. The surrounding nature gave the clients serenity and the resulting feelings reduced the anxieties of daily life and provided positive emotions (Getz, 2012). These experiences, based on cognitive and affective factors, were the basis of unique experiences for all these families and supported medium- and long-term loyalty.

ACKNOWLEDGMENT

This work is supported by national funding's of FCT - Fundação para a Ciência e a Tecnologia, I.P., in the project «UIDB/04005/2020.

REFERENCES

Adaval, R. (2003). How good bets better and bad gets worse: Understanding the impact of affect on evaluations of known brands. *The Journal of Consumer Research*, *30*(December), 352–367. doi:10.1086/378614

Aknin, L. B., Norton, M., & Dunn, E. W. (2009). From wealth to well-being? Money matters, but less than people think. *The Journal of Positive Psychology*, *4*(6), 523–527. doi:10.1080/17439760903271421

Aknin, L. B., Wiwad, D., & Hanniball, K. (2018). *Buying well-being: spending behavior and happiness*. Academic Press.

Ambitur. (2016). Obtido de Ambitur: http://www.ambitur.pt

Andreine, D., Pedeliento, G., Zarantonello, L., & Solero, C. (2019). Reprint of "A renaissance of brand experience: Advancing the concept through a multi-perspective analysis". *Journal of Business Research*, *96*, 355–365. doi:10.1016/j.jbusres.2018.05.047

Baloglu, S., Busser, J., & Cain, L. (2019). Impact of experience on emotional well-being and loyalty. *Journal of Hospitality Marketing & Management*, *28*(4), 427–445. doi:10.1080/19368623.2019.1527269

BCSD. (2019). Tendencias uma questão de velocidade. BCSD Conselho Empresarial para o Desenvolvimento Sustentável, 1-4.

Berg. (2008). *Health tourism and Wellness tourism*. Munchen: Oldenbourg Publisher.

Bhattacharjee, A., & Mogilner, C. (2014). Happiness from ordinary and extraordinary experiences. *The Journal of Consumer Research*, *41*(1), 1–17. doi:10.1086/674724

Brakus, J. J., Schmitt, B. H., & Zarantonello, L. (2009). Brand experience: What is it? How is it Measured? Does it affect Loyalty. *Journal of Marketing*, *73*(3), 52–68. doi:10.1509/jmkg.73.3.052

Caprariello, P., & Reis, H. T. (2013). To do, to have or to share? Valuing experiences over material possessions depends on the involvement of others. *Journal of Personality and Social Psychology*, *104*(2), 199–215. doi:10.1037/a0030953 PMID:23276272

Carter, T. J., & Gilovich, T. (2012). I am what I do, not what I have: The differential centrality of experiential and material and purchases to the self. *Journal of Personality and Social Psychology*, *98*(1), 1304–1317. doi:10.1037/a0027407 PMID:22369046

Chen, Y.-K., & Hsieh, T. (2010). A study of the relationship among experiential marketing, experiential value and customer satisfaction. *Journal of Statistics and Management Systems*, *13*(6), 1283–1303. do i:10.1080/09720510.2010.10701534

Cone, J., & Gilovich, T. (2010). Understand money limits: People's beliefs about the income-happiness correlation. *The Journal of Positive Psychology*, *5*(4), 294–301. doi:10.1080/17439760.2010.498620

Cunha, L. (2006). *Turismo de Saude - Conceito e mercados*. Revista Lusófona de Humanidades e Tecnologias.

Deci, E., & Ryan, R. (2008). Self-determination theory: Macrotheory of human motivation development and health. *Canadian Psychology*, *49*(3), 182–185. doi:10.1037/a0012801

DeVoe, S., & House, J. (2012). Time, money and happiness: How does putting a price on time affect our ability to smell the roses? *Journal of Experimental Psychology*, *48*(2), 466–467.

Dryglasa, D., & Salamaga, M. (2017). Applying destination attribute segmentation to health tourists: A case study of Polish spa resorts. *Journal of Travel & Tourism Marketing*, *34*(4), 503–514. doi:10.1080/10548408.2016.1193102

Estar, A. d. (2013). *Associação de Turismo e Bem Estar.* Academic Press.

Estevão, H. F. (2016). *O Turismo de Experiencia no âmbito da Saúde e Bem-Estar; Orientação à Turismoterapia.* Dissertação - Instituto Politecnico de Tomar.

Ferreira, S., & Vieira, T. (2016). *Termas Norte de Portugal.* Academic Press.

Fingerman, K. L., & Perlmutter, M. (1995). Future time perspective and life events across adulthood. *The Journal of General Psychology*, *122*(1), 95–111. doi:10.1080/00221309.1995.9921225 PMID:7714506

Gentile, C., Spiller, N., & Noci, G. (2007). How to Sustain the Customer Experience: An Overview of Experience Components that Co-create Value with the Customer. *European Management Journal*, *25*(5), 395–410. doi:10.1016/j.emj.2007.08.005

Getz, D. (2012). *Event Studies. Theory, Research and Policy for Planned Events.* Routledge.

Gilbert, D. T. (2006). *Stumbling on Happiness.* Knof.

Gilovich, T., Kumar, A., & Jampol, L. (2015). A Wonderful Life: Experiential Consumption and the Pursuit of Happiness. *Journal of Consumer Psychology*, *25*(1), 152–165. doi:10.1016/j.jcps.2014.08.004

Goodman, R. A., Bunnell, R., & Posner, S. F. (2014). What is "community health"? Examining the meaning of an evolving field in public health. *Preventive Medicine*, *67*, 28–61. doi:10.1016/j.ypmed.2014.07.028 PMID:25069043

Guerra, R. J. (2016). *Turismo de Saude e Bem-Estar - estratégia de desenvolvimento local para as Caldas da Cavaca.* Tese de Doutoramento da Universidade de Coimbra.

Hall, C. M. (2011). Health and medical tourism: Kill or cure for global public health? *Tourism Review*, *66*(1/2), 4–15. doi:10.1108/16605371111127198

Hettler, B. (1980). Wellness promotion on a university campus. *Family & Community Health*, *3*(1), 77–95. doi:10.1097/00003727-198005000-00008 PMID:10246133

Holbrook, M. B., & Hirschman, E. C. (1982). The experiential aspects of consumption: Consumer fantasies, feelings, and fun. *The Journal of Consumer Research*, *9*(September), 132–140. doi:10.1086/208906

Husemann, K., Eckhardt, G., Grohs, R., & Saceanu, R. (2016). The dynamic interplay between structure, anastructure and antistructure in extraordinary experiences. *Journal of Business Research*, *69*(9), 3361–3370. doi:10.1016/j.jbusres.2016.02.008

Idealista. (2013). Obtido de Idealista: http://www.idealista.pt

Institute, G. W. (2018). *Empowering Wellness Worldwide.* Author.

Isen, A. M. (2003). *Positive Affect as a Source of Human Strength. In A Psychology of Human Strengths.* American Psychological Associations.

Kandampully, J., Zhang, T., & Bilgihan, A. (2015). Customer loyalty: A review and future directions with a special focus on the hospitality industry. *International Journal of Contemporary Hospitality Management*, *27*(3), 379–414. doi:10.1108/IJCHM-03-2014-0151

Keller, K. L. (1993). Conceptualizing, measuring and managing customer-based brand equity. *Journal of Marketing*, *57*(1), 1–22. doi:10.1177/002224299305700101

Kemp, E., Jillappalli, R., & Becerra, E. (2014). Healthcare branding: Developing emotionally based consumer brand relationship. *Journal of Services Marketing*, *28*(2), 126–137. doi:10.1108/JSM-08-2012-0157

Kerin, R. A., Jain, A., & Howard, D. (2002). Store shopping experience and consumer price-quality-value perceptions. *Journal of Retailing*, *68*(4), 376–397.

Kim, A., & Ko, E. (2011). Do social media marketing activities enhance customer equity? An empirical study of luxury fashion brand. *Journal of Business Research*, *65*(10), 1480–1486. doi:10.1016/j.jbusres.2011.10.014

Kim, H., Park, K., & Schwarz, N. (2010). Will this trip really be exciting? The role of incidental emotions in product evaluation. *The Journal of Consumer Research*, *36*(6), 983–991. doi:10.1086/644763

Kim, J.-H. (2010). Determining the factors affecting the memorable nature of travel experiences. *Journal of Travel & Tourism Marketing*, *36*(April), 780–796. doi:10.1080/10548408.2010.526897

Kim, J.-H., & Ritchie, B. (2014). Cross Cultural validation of a memorable tourism experience scale. *Journal of Travel Research*, *53*(3), 323–335. doi:10.1177/0047287513496468

Labroo, A. A., & Patrick, V. M. (2009). Providing a moment of respite: Why a positive mood helps seeing the big picture. *The Journal of Consumer Research*, *35*(5), 800–809. doi:10.1086/593683

Larsen, J. (2003). Tourism Mobilities and the Travel Glance:Experiences of Being on the Move. *Scandinavian Journal of Hospitality and Tourism*, *1*(2), 81–98.

Layard, R. (2005). *Hppiness: Lessons from a new science*. Penguin.

Lima, M. (2016). *Saude e Bem Estar como Tendencia - o futuro do aperfeiçoamento (The Future of Betterman)*. Academic Press.

Luxury Magazine. (2016). Obtido de Fluxury Magazine: http://www.fluxurymagazine.com

Lyubomirsky, S., Seldon, K., & Schkade, D. (2005). Pursuing happiness: The architecture of sustainable change. *Review of General Psychology*, *9*(2), 111–131. doi:10.1037/1089-2680.9.2.111

Marketeer. (2016). Obtido de Marketeer: http://marketeer.pt

Mendes. (2013). *O cluster da Saude e Bem-Estar: uma aposta de futuro.* Lisboa: CCP-Confederação de Comercio e Serviços de Portugal.

Mogilner, C., Kamvar, D., & Aaker, J. (2011). The shifting meaning of happiness. *Social Psychological & Personality Science*, *2*(4), 395–402. doi:10.1177/1948550610393987

Mogilner, C., Kamvar, S., & Aaker, J. (2012). How happiness affects choice. *The Journal of Consumer Research*, *39*(2), 429–443. doi:10.1086/663774

Mossberg, L. (2007). A marketing approach to the tourist experience. *Scandinavian Journal of Hospitality and Tourism*, *7*(1), 59–74. doi:10.1080/15022250701231915

Oh, H., Fiore, A., & Jeoung, M. (2007). Measuring experience economy concepts: Tourism applications. *Journal of Travel Research*, *46*(2), 119–132. doi:10.1177/0047287507304039

Oliver, R. L. (2010). *Satisfaction: A behavioral perspective on the consumer* (2nd ed.). M.E. Sharpe.

Piece of Moments. (2016). Obtido de Piece of Moments: http://piece-of-moments.webnode.pt

Pine, B., & Gilmore, J. (2011). The experience economy. Boston: Harvard Business Review Press.

Pine, B., & Gilmore, J. H. (1998). Welcome to the experience economy. *Harvard Business Review*, 97–105. PMID:10181589

Portugal, T. d. (2006). *Saúde e Bem-Estar*. Trismo de Portugal.

Publituris. (2016). Obtido de Publituris: http://www.publituris.pt

Quan, S., & Wang, N. (2004). Towards a structural model of the tourist experience: An illustration from food experiences in tourism. *Tourism Management*, *25*(3), 297–305. doi:10.1016/S0261-5177(03)00130-4

Reicheld, F. (1996). *The loyalty effect: The hidden force behind growth, profits and lasting value*. Harvard Business Review School Press.

Reicheld, F., & Sasser, W. E. (1990). Zero defections: Quality comes to services. *Harvard Business Review*, 105-111.

Roof Magazine. (2016). Obtido de Roof Magazine: http://roof-magazine.com

Ryan, R., & Deci, E. (2000). Self-determination theory and facilitation of intrinsic motivation, social development and well-being. *The American Psychologist*, *55*(1), 68–78. doi:10.1037/0003-066X.55.1.68 PMID:11392867

Schmitt, B. (1999). Experiential marketing. *Journal of Marketing Management*, *15*(1–3), 53–67. doi:10.1362/026725799784870496

Schmitt, B. H., Brakus, J., & Zarantonello, L. (2014). The current state and future of brand experience. *Journal of Brand Management*, *21*(9), 727–733. doi:10.1057/bm.2014.34

Schwarz, N., & Clore, G. L. (1983). Mood, misattribution and judgments of well-being: Informative and directive functions of affective states. *Journal of Personality and Social Psychology*, *45*(3), 512–523. doi:10.1037/0022-3514.45.3.513

Smith, M. K., & Puckzo, L. (2009). *Health and Wellness tourism*. Butterworth-Heinemann.

Superbock Group. (n.d.). Obtido de https://www.superbockgroup.com/detalhe/about-the-group/

Thomke, S. (2019). *The magic that makes customer experiences stick*. MIT- Management Review.

Time Out. (2016). Obtido de Time Out: http://timeout.pt

Tumbat, G., & Belk, R. (2011). Marketplace tensions in extraordinary experiences. *The Journal of Consumer Research*, *38*(1), 42–61. doi:10.1086/658220

Van Boven, L., & Gilovich, T. (2003). To do or to have? That is the question. *Journal of Personality and Social Psychology*, *85*(6), 1193–1202. doi:10.1037/0022-3514.85.6.1193 PMID:14674824

Ver Portugal. (2015). Obtido de Ver Portugal: http://www.verportugal.net

Vidago Palace. (n.d.). Obtido de https://www.vidagopalace.com/pt/

Whillans, A., Dunn, E., Smeets, P., Bekkers, R., & Norton, M. (2012). Bying the time promotes happiness. *Proceedings of the National Academy of Sciences*.

Zauberman, G., Rebecca, K. R., & Kim, K. B. (2009). Memories as assets: Strategic memory protection in choice over time. *The Journal of Consumer Research*, *35*(5), 715–728. doi:10.1086/592943

Zhong, Y. Y., Busser, J., & Baloglu, S. (2017). A model of memorable tourism experience: The effects on satisfaction, affective commitment, and storytelling. *Tourism Analysis*, *22*(2), 201–217. doi:10.3727/108354217X14888192562366

KEY TERMS AND DEFINITIONS

Happiness: The state of being happy.

Health: Good physical and emotional condition.

Loyalty: The consumer's internalised commitment to consistently support an establishment in the future irrespective of situational or external influences.

Unique Experience: Characteristic of one person or thing, and so serving to distinguish it from others.

Well-Being: The state of being comfortable, healthy.

Chapter 8
Understanding the Brand Management and Rebranding Processes in Specific Contexts of Medical Tourism

Gisela Maria Alves
Centro de Estudos de Comunicação e Sociedade, Universidade do Minho, Portugal & UNIDCOM, IADE, Portugal

Bruno Barbosa Sousa
https://orcid.org/0000-0002-8588-2422
Polytechinc Institude of Cávado and Ave (IPCA), Portugal

Maria Belino
Instituto Português de Administração de Marketing (IPAM), Portugal

ABSTRACT

With this chapter, the authors intend to understand the importance of brand management (specifically rebranding) in specific contexts of medical tourism and health and wellness. The case study will include an example of the medical tourism segment in Portugal. This research is particularly relevant for Portugal because it is necessary to ensure the sustainability of the health system, as health expenditures are mostly publicly funded. Models and best rebranding practices will be studied in the health and wellness sector in Portugal (e.g., medical tourism). The chapter starts with a conceptual framework based on branding and rebranding models. From this theoretical base, the concepts and models are derived. This study aims at discussing brand management in healthcare management and medical tourism contexts. From an interdisciplinary perspective, this research brings together inputs from relationship marketing, medical tourism, and healthcare management (service excellence).

DOI: 10.4018/978-1-7998-3034-4.ch008

1. INTRODUCTION

Nowadays, companies take their presence in the online world as imperative, be it to reach new customers, promote the brand, better know their customers, stay competitive or to maintain their relevance. In this context, a (digital) brand is not limited to creating value for the consumer, but also for the company, becoming an active, having a social value and a financial value. Overall, much of the financial value of a company is based on its intangible assets. The brand is a special intangible asset. In many companies is the most important asset (Kapferer, 2012). Building a brand driven culture is a lifelong commitment to a mindset and a way of life that takes time, planning and perseverance. it produces intangible outputs, which include greater customer satisfaction and loyalty (repetition), reduced price sensitivity, fewer customer defections, a greater share of customers' wallets and more referrals (Sousa & Silva, 2015). The main drivers of rebranding occur because of the need for repositioning and / or the need for a change in brand image (Muzellec & Lambkin, 2006). According to Muzellec & Lambkin (2006), these authors explain that the change of the brand name is a risk, insofar as: it may lead to losing the brand's reputation and all the time it has led to market positioning. Being the knowledge of the essential component name of the brand, this action could undermine brand equity. Changing the name can undermine the brand as well as destroy it. Thus, a rebranding involving a name change may clear the consumer's mental image of the brand (Aaker, 1991). The first key concept is brand building, so we have the strategic analysis of the brand, the definition of brand identity and finally the implementation of brand identity. Next we have two key concepts that we must take into account, the brand image and the value of the brand. And as the main and ultimate key concept we will address the rebranding, its definition, its causes, the elements that make up the rebranding-mix, and the existing rebranding models and processes.

According to Pinho, Borges and Zahariev (2017), health systems sustainability is one of the major challenges public policymakers in developed countries face. Since the second half of the 20th century, health expenditure has been increasing at a faster pace than national income levels all over the world. For instance, in specific tourism contexts, the practice of healthcare management and medical tourism depends on successfully informing potential patients about procedure options, service excellence, treatment facilities, tourism opportunities, travel benefits and destination choice and corporate social responsibility (CSR) (Rodrigues, Real, Vitorino and Cantista, 2011; Rodrigues and Borges, 2015). As a niche tourism example, medical tourism is becoming an increasingly popular option for patients looking to access procedures that are seemingly unavailable to them in their home countries due to lack of affordability, lack of availability or lengthy waiting lists (Sousa & Alves, 2019). Medical tourism and its related businesses and organizations have been regarded as one of the most lucrative hospitality sectors for many destination countries and cities, in specific developing ones (Han, 2013; Heung et al., 2011; Van Niekerk, 2014; Demicco, 2016). Reviewing the research on medical tourism, not to mention domestic medical tourism, is challenging due to the novelty of the concept, lack of specific data, and somewhat amorphous nature of the concept (Hudson & Shephard, 1998; Chambers & McIntosh, 2008; Hudson & Li, 2012; Cham et al., 2020). The demand for global healthcare services is experiencing tremendous growth. The ease of seeking medical treatment and services overseas contributes to the globalization of the healthcare market. According to Smith and Forgione (2007), the growing trend of medical tourism is not merely seen on an individual patient basis - many corporations are also investigating the potential benefits.

With this chapter, we intend to understand the importance of brand management (specifically rebranding) in specific contexts of medical tourism and health and wellness. The case study will include an example of the medical tourism segment. This research is particularly relevant because it is necessary to ensure the sustainability of the health system, as health expenditures are mostly publicly funded (Pinho and Borges, 2015). Models and best rebranding practices will be studied in the health and wellness sector (e.g. medical tourism). This chapter focuses on medical tourism and healthcare management. The authors also consider some implications for management, as well as give suggestions for future lines of research. The paper starts from a conceptual framework based on branding and rebranding models. From this theoretical base the concepts and models are derived. This study aims at discussing the brand management in healthcare management and medical tourism contexts. For instance, the study addresses the predisposition for the destination and the influence of relationship marketing on behavioural intentions. Under an interdisciplinary perspective, this research brings together inputs from relationship marketing, medical tourism and healthcare management (service excellence).

2. BACKGROUND: BRAND MANAGEMENT AND REBRANDING PROCESS

2.1 Brand Management

According to Jankovic (2012), organizations in competitive markets need to pay attention to marketing strategies and brand identity, as the process of building brand identity in these markets is more difficult and requires the help of communication tools, development of shares marketing strategies and a brand orientation for a specific audience. In accordance with Farhana (2014), defining brand identity is crucial for products with a targeted audience allowing consumers to identify with the brand and thus build a relationship. Aaker (1996) establishes three moments for brand building, the first, strategic brand analysis, then the definition of brand identity, and finally the implementation of brand identity. Branding has taken a relevant role in organizations' marketing strategies and is no longer just an element of identifying goods and services (Day, 1994). The brand starts to gain weight in the purchase decision process and becomes a differentiation strategy against the competition (De Chernatony, Drury, & Segal-Horn, 2004). For Kotler and Armstrom (2007, p. 206), a brand is a name, term, sign, symbol or design or a combination of all, intended to identify a supplier's goods or services to differentiate them from other competitors. Martind (1997) adds that the organization needs to take care of its brand, as an endless and integrated part of the management in order to obtain an improvement, recognition and loyalty from its consumers that will consequently experience, like and repeat the act of buying, recommending it positively. According to Farhana (2014), brand identity influences the buying decision process of customers as sales of the organization and can help in building brand equity. Through brand identity, this can be an element for differentiating yourself from competing products, expressing the organization's purpose and value, adding product value, and guiding the development of the organization's marketing strategies. For Lencastre (1999) brand is defined as "a triadic concept that is defined by the signs it has (name, logo, slogan), by what counts (brand object and mission) and does (marketing mix) and by the reflection of the construction of this brand. consumer identity (image and public mix) ".

Lencastre's model of the triangle of the brand (1999), the brand is seen in the first pillar as a sign (name and identity mix) consisting of elements such as brand name, of which the logo, lettering, coloring and trade mark that corresponds to an organization's badge and its products. Marketing mix is the second pillar and refers to the product mix (because the goal of the brand is the product) and all communication, distribution and price strategies in order to analyze their coherence. These signals are issued to the third pillar, the brand public mix where the brand targets are receiving these emissions, through different brand images, the image mix. Thus, when well worked, brand signs facilitate the formation of associations and promote brand awareness, crucial for establishing its value. In short, regarding the identity mix of the brand we must characterize the name, the logo, the slogan and the characters. When it comes to marketing mix, mission, product, price, communication and distribution are important. And finally the receiving pillar of the public and image mix we must characterize the associations and brand awareness among their audiences. In this way we begin to analyze the elements to be taken into account when defining brand identity.

Upshaw (1995) defines strong brand identity as digital printing that makes a distinctive, unique and different brand that aids in developing the creation of loyalty in the minds of consumers and the creation of lasting bonds. According to Aaker (2010) brand identity is a set of unique associations that the organization proposes in relation to the brand and represents a promise to customers of what it intends to accomplish. The essence, identity, positioning and personality are the elements that constitute the brand identity in an interesting approach by Kapfere (1992). The mission, values, reputation and competencies that are part of the brand that are consumed by consumers and belong to the essence of the brand according to Macrae (1996). So the core identity of the essence is all those associations based on promise and future prospects that are meaningful and successful for the brand. What makes the brand unique and unique, and sets it apart from others is identity. Identity is the aspiration, and it reflects the perceptions that must be developed and reinforced for it to last. Brand positioning corresponds to the "part of identity and value proposition that is actively communicated to the target audience and represents advantages over competing brands" (D. A. Aaker, 1996, p. 176).

Authors Chernatony, Drury, Segal-Horn (2004) and Geuens, Weijters and De Wulf (2009) clarify the differences between brand identity and brand positioning, and these two concepts complement each other in brand management as part of a organization's strategy. Brand identity is the intended projection of the organization in the consumer's mind and brand positioning is the effective projection of the brand in relation to the competition in the consumer's mind.

Brand personality adds the "set of human characteristics associated with the brand" (Aaker, 1997, p. 347), with which the consumer identifies, seeking in the brand the expression of his own personality. Kapferer (1997) developed a methodology through a prism that allows explaining the brand identity. . This diagram consists of two dimensions: constructed sender versus constructed recipient - because the brand must be seen as a person (constructed emitter: physical and personality) and also as a characterized user (constructed recipient: reflection and self-image); and externalization versus internalization - a brand is composed of social aspects that define its external expression. According to Kepferer (1997) to the set of external logo-shaped elements in the consumer's mind that are spontaneously evoked when the brand is mentioned, he called the brand physical, the character of the brand from the moment it communicates through a Specific style of color scheme, writing and design or even by association with symbolic characters calls brand personality. Kapfere argues that it is necessary to create a system of values and basic principles on which the brand bases its behavior, we are in the presence of the brand culture. It also argues that the role of the brand as a means of relationship between the products and the target audience is crucial in defining the relationship with the brand. It mentions the reflection of the brand that should reference the target audience of the brand or reflect the image of the consumer - source of identification with the brand. Finally, it refers to the self-image of the brand, which translates to the consumer an association so close to the brand leading him to associate with his own image. In short, the brand identity prism allows you to assess brand strengths and weaknesses and help you find ways to build brand loyalty and value. Kapferer (2012) simplified the prism by introducing within a three-part pyramid, the Brand Kernel, which is the essence or core of brand identity, brand style that causes brand personality and its interaction with the brand. stakeholders and lastly the brand theme, that is, the way the brand expresses itself. Implementing the brand identity that will integrate communication must be realistic for external and internal customers, have durability, that is, stability over time and consistency creating interaction between customers and the brand (Jankovic, 2012; Lang & Hyde, 2013). Jankovic (2012) also adds that communication efforts are relevant, especially due to the advancement of technologies, such as the internet and new media in marketing strategies.

According to Aaker's brand building proposal (2010) is the implementation that integrates communication, media selection and actions that enhance relationship experiences and evaluation with a view to continuous improvement in the brand / company / customer relationship, that when necessary it should change or innovate. Thus, according to Lencastre (1999), in a first moment of brand building, the sources of value management that allow raising the consumer differential response to the brand are the two emission pillars, the brand identity mix and the product and marketing mix. It is now up to analyze the brand image and public mix that correspond to the third pillar. Visual identity is the visual and verbal representation of the formal elements of a brand. Usually this set of elements is the logo or visual symbol that is recognized by consumers (Biricik, 2006). The brand is also surrounded by emotional attributes at its core, personality traits of the brand. According to Gobé (2002, p. 19) the best way to emotionally connect products to consumers is by communicating at the senses and emotions level, focusing on the strongest aspect of the human character.

2.2 Rebranding: Process and Motivations

The need for branding in companies arises for several reasons (Wheeler, 2009). These include the need for rebranding that we will address next. We start with the definition of the term and the reasons why we invest in rebranding, the rebranding mix and finally the phases of rebranding models. Rebranding is recommended when something needs to be improved on brand performance in order for the existing brand to reach its full potential. It involves changing not only the visual identity of the organization but also the level of real changes within the organization (Muzellec, Doogan, & Lambkin, 2003). According to Goi and Goi (2011, p. 445) Muzellec, Doonga and Lambkin (2003) defined rebranding as "the practice of building a new name representing a differentiated position in the mindset of stakeholders and a distinct identity of the competitor". In the same sense Daly and Moloney (2004) explain that rebranding consists of changing some or all tangible (physical expression of the brand) and intangible (value, image and feelings) elements of a brand. This is changing the existing brand name if necessary and modifying and enhancing your logo. Muzellec and Lambkin (2006) defined rebranding as a change in an organization's self-identity and / or an attempt to change image perceptions among stakeholders.

Rebranding can only be limited to a slight change, or a deeper change that makes the brand virtually unrecognizable (Miller et al., 2014). On the other hand, rebranding can be a process of redefining a name, a logo, or an identity, or even renewing all three elements of a brand at the same time, whether it is a product, service or organization to add value to the brand or strengthen the existing image (Stuart & Muzellec, 2004). The authors argue that when all elements are addressed simultaneously, we are facing a revolutionary rebranding strategy with major graphic changes. When only one of the elements, logo and / or slogan is changed, we are dealing with an evolutionary rebranding strategy that relies on small modifications that may not be noticeable to consumers, but which eventually update or revitalize the brand itself. Tevi and Otubanjo (2013, p. 89) confirm that each has a different goal. The evolutionary one is "building on the equity of the same corporate organization" and the revolutionary's goal is "to transfer the previous heritage and build a completely new one". Although revolutionary rebranding is the most studied, evolutionary rebranding is the most common (Miller et al., 2014).

In the event that we have a strong brand in the market that does not face scandal-like situations, you should only update your image to improve and strengthen your position in the market. On the other hand, brands that have not been able to assert themselves in the market have a greater need to make profound changes in order to try to create notoriety and improve their value (Goi & Goi, 2011). The main drivers of rebranding are due to the need for repositioning and or the need for a change in brand image (Muzellec & Lambkin, 2006). These situations may arise due to acquisitions, mergers or business separations that lead to the creation of a new identity that fits the new business structure. Others, due to pressure from new competitors, brand or product portfolio changes, or the attempt to rejuvenate or globalize visual identity and spread a new vision on the part of the company (Muzellec et al., 2003 Stuart & Muzellec, 2004). According to Baker and Balmer (1997), for a company's visual identity to be renewed, structural, strategic or management change, regulatory transformations, external and internal disagreements and / or competitiveness among others are required.

However Stuart and Muzellec (2004) state that there are two reasons why the company changes its logo. First because the company has changed its name, then it needs to change the logo, and second because it needs to update the logo for image change and new strategies. Williams (2006) explains some situations that cause rebranding as the case of scandals where the intention is to erase the previous brand identity and replace it with a new image and message. The case where the brand is simply out of date, or needs to be updated, due to an increase in new products or services requires adjustment because it is not intended to eliminate the value of the existing brand, but only to make a small change or adjustment. to make it a broad brand.

For rebranding, Muzellec and Lambkin (2006) defined four categories of main rebranding motives.

Company structure change:
- Acquisition, union or separation between companies;
- Creation of new sectors (new innovative products and services or sub-brands);
- Change between public and private services.

Company strategy change:
- Change (diversification or reduction) of portfolio of brands, products or services;
- Internationalization;
- Location.

Change in market position:
- Loss of market position;
- Reputation issues;
- Old and outdated image.

Change by external factors:
- legal reasons;
- Economic crises and disasters.

The authors Goi and Goi (2011) also added the following motivations: concern with the company's image in relation to its activities (transparency and environmental and social concern); union of several brands within a global one; cultural reasons; upgrade the brand to new means and existing possibilities. However Banerjee (2016, p. 63) still propose a simple model on the causes referred to above as internal and external imperatives that give rise to the new logo. Where external imperatives are legal decisions; consumer change; exposure fatigue; competitive disorganization; technological changes; cultural misfit. To succeed in the new implementation Muzellec, Doogan and Lambkin (2003) created a classification of the different phases of rebranding that generated the four elements of rebranding-mix that must be analyzed by companies.

Figure 1. Rebranding- Mix
Source: Based on Muzellec et al., (2003)

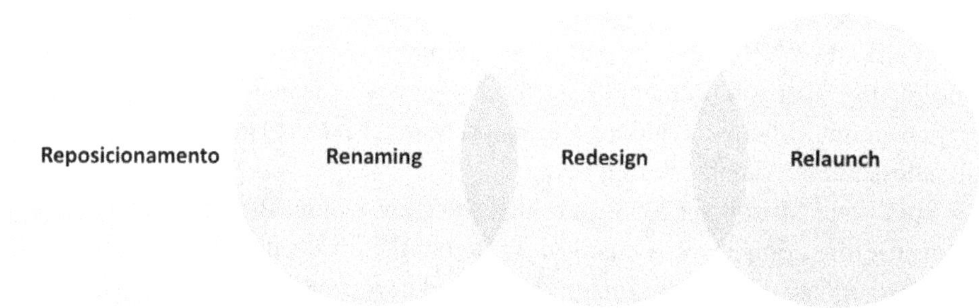

Repositioning refers to the definition of objectives for the company's new repositioning strategy in the minds of consumers, competitors and stakeholders. This step is dynamic or can only be radically adjusted or changed over time so that the company can keep up with the competitive evolution of the market as well as external situations (Muzellec et al., 2003). Renaming refers to changing the brand name which can damage years of efforts or even destroying brand heritage (Muzellec & Lambkin, 2006). This process automatically falls into a revolutionary rebranding case (Daly & Moloney, 2004; Muzellec & Lambkin, 2006) and can be a risky strategy if you lose brand awareness, but on the other hand you can also create a strong and memorable brand. (Muzellec et al., 2003). Redesign encompasses all aesthetic change of the brand image. Which brings us to an evolutionary rebranding where there is the change that can consist only of changing corporate colors, the font used, communication, characters, or other features or elements. These changes eventually involve high costs due to changes in all uniform materials, stores and products and other investments due to the same upgrade as intended (Muzellec et al., 2003; Stuart & Muzellec, 2004). Re-launching is a new brand launch, the communication that must be made to convey changes, both to the stakeholders involved, employees, investors, shareholders and other important transmitters of information to the company, as they are the ones that also give the face and voice for the company (Muzellec et al., 2003; Stuart & Muzellec, 2004). These members should be knowledgeable about the transformation before and after its release as they are active members and can assist in the rebranding process (Daly & Moloney, 2004). This internal communication should be made through meetings, workshops, newspapers or pamphlets. On the other hand relaunch can be broadcast by press conference through various media, and / or through various advertising and merchandising companies (Muzellec et al., 2003). In the corporate rebranding management study by Daly and Moloney (2004) is a different model and argues that the rebranding process is divided into three phases: analysis, planning and finally evaluation. The analysis should involve a detailed analysis of the current situation of the company and the market where it operates, based on market studies, data sources and focused on various stakeholders (Daly & Moloney, 2004). Within this framework, the determination of the problems and the reasons why there is a need to modify the brand, the objectives and the possible strategies to achieve them, a research on the opinions, needs and desires of the users must be identified. stakeholders, and other studies that may support the intended strategy (Daly & Moloney, 2004). The next process takes a long time and the budget for the whole methodology needs to be defined and shared, the graphical and operational development of the new identity, the continuity of market studies and analysis, in order to create alternatives if things are not. go as planned (Daly & Moloney, 2004). Following the launch, it is necessary to analyze the results and market reactions, as well as to conduct stakeholder studies in order to get feedback on whether there is a need to adopt evolutionary rebranding strategies. At this stage of the evaluation, the investment is not only for the launch of the new brand, but it is necessary to eliminate the existence of the old one (Daly & Moloney, 2004). However, the model limits external audiences to "customers" and neglects other external stakeholders who have a link to the brand. In contrast to Daly and Moloney (2004), Muzellez and Lambkin (2006) present a model where communication covers all stakeholders, not just customers. This model contributed to a better understanding of the concept and it identifies three phases: (1) rebranding factors (2) rebranding goals and (3) rebranding process. The model highlights the involvement of internal employees in cultural image creation and external stakeholders in image creation. Lomax (2002) presents a model that has some similarities to the model of Muzellec and Lambkin (2006). It first identifies and solves the reasons for rebranding, then evaluates the original brand and then identifies the purpose of rebranding (developing a new image or for greater employee involvement) and finally what differs from the model of Muzellec and Lambkin (2006).) is the involvement of the project management team in monitoring, control and follow-up.

According to Tevi and Otubanjo (2013, p. 89) the ultimate goal of the rebranding phenomenon is to survive and thrive. In this way brands adapt to their environment by corporate rebranding. Given that the environment of an organism is internal and external, the causes of rebranding must be inside and outside an organization according to Goi and Goi (2011). Based on the studies by Muzellec, Doogan and Lambkin (2003) and Daly and Moloney (2004), a new, even more detailed step model was proposed by three other authors (Juntunen et al., 2009). From this model we can conclude that: motivation- consists of the reasons that lead to realize a rebranding strategy; analysis - consists of all studies performed to understand the current market, competition and company situation; planning- programming of the entire strategy, including the repositioning, renaming, redesigning and restructuring (if internal restructuring is necessary) steps; preparation - consists of preparing the plan and pre-theses for the launch; launch - internal and external disclosure of the new image; evaluation - development of studies to analyze the results obtained; long-term continuity- realization of promises made by the company during launch as rebranding typically adds other strategies (such as improving service quality and environmental sustainability practices). Years later Miller, Merriless, and Yakimova (2014) present a study that aimed to indicate at which stages greater attention should be paid to the main beneficial factors or obstacles to the strategy which makes the model different from those previously presented (Daly & Moloney, 2004; Juntunen et al., 2009; Muzellec & Lambkin, 2006).

To begin the process, you need to consider the reasons, objectives, and other crucial contexts in order to open the brand review. During this stage, a broad review of the strategy should be privileged, thus avoiding adequate studies that allow a good understanding of the brand. At this stage it is essential to have a good leader with the ability to anticipate possible barriers. In the next phase, in the implementation of the strategy one must start by applying the marketing plan and maintaining the gestation of all key stakeholders to the process. During the third phase it is important that there is good internal communication and that it is based on the influence of all stakeholders and the active participation of all company members to ensure continuity with the old brand elements that will be part of rebranding. Then the process is completed by monitoring the results obtained (Miller et al., 2014). For Miller, Merrilees and Yakimova (2014), according to their study, some factors benefit the rebranding strategy. Having a person with strategic experience in the area in which the brand is inserted will more easily lead to the development of a clear and in-depth understanding of all positive and negative factors of the brand. It must therefore, from the past history of the brand, so that the process is evolutionary and not a total cut with its essence. This requires the help of all employees and managers, involving them in the design of the project so that they continue to feel connected to the brand. According to the same study it appears that the biggest errors arose due to decisions made exclusively by leaders excluding other key stakeholders in the process, tensions between stakeholders lacking consensus among opinions, limited views on the strategy, the use of inadequate studies and incorrect or inappropriate consumer considerations (Miller et al., 2014).

3 MEDICAL TOURISM CONTEXT

Medical tourism and its related businesses and organizations have been regarded as one of the most lucrative hospitality sectors for many destination countries and cities, in specific developing ones (Han, 2013; Heung et al., 2011; Van Niekerk, 2014; Demicco, 2016; Sousa & Alves, 2019; Dang et al., 2020). Reviewing the research on medical tourism, not to mention domestic medical tourism, is challenging due to the novelty of the concept, lack of specific data, and somewhat amorphous nature of the concept (Hudson & Shephard, 1998; Chambers & McIntosh, 2008; Hudson & Li, 2012). Over the years there has been an increase in competition among tourism destinations (Ferreira & Sousa, 2020), leading to the need for a deeper understanding about the tourism realm, impact and management. Medical tourism is partly the result of the globalization of both healthcare and tourism, which already constitute major arenas of transnational economic activity. The process is usually facilitated by the private medical care sector, but involves both the private and public sectors of the tourism industry. Medical tourists can take advantage of having medical surgery or treatment while enjoying a stay in one of the world's popular tourist destinations (Connell, 2006; Heung, Kucukusta & Song, 2011; Demicco, 2017, 2017a). For instance, and according to Sousa and Alves (2019), employers are considering medical outsourcing as an option for their employees, in order to experience significant cost-savings. In medical tourism, citizens of highly developed nations bypass services offered in their own communities and travel to less developed areas of the world for medical care (Ormond & Sulianti, 2017). Healthcare and medical tourism is fundamentally different from the traditional model of international medical travel where patients generally journey from less developed nations to major medical centers in highly developed countries for medical treatment that is unavailable in their own communities (Horowitz et al., 2007). Figure 2 shows how the sector may be classified and segmented. Health tourism offers a more traditional tourism experience,

Figure 2. The shape of health and medical tourism (Henderson, 2004; Tresidder, 2011)

whereby the customer is pampered with the major motivation of relaxation and rejuvenation and fits within more established notions of tourism. Cosmetic tourism, although involving a medical element and often an operation, commonly mixes the procedure with usual tourist behaviour (Tresidder, 2011).

According to Sousa and Alves (2019), the practice of healthcare management and medical tourism depends on successfully informing potential patients about procedure options, service excellence, treatment facilities, tourism opportunities, travel benefits and destination choice. As a niche tourism example, medical tourism is becoming an increasingly popular option for patients looking to access procedures that are seemingly unavailable to them in their home countries due to lack of affordability, lack of availability or lengthy waiting lists. According to Lee, Han and Lockyer (2012), medical tourism has existed since at least the 19th century when people started to travel to other areas for healing and relaxation such as at spas and springs (Hunter, 2007). Modern medical tourism is grounded in what is commonly referred to as push and pull factors (Awadzi & Panda, 2005). Push factors include inflated health care costs (Hunter, 2007; Ye et al., 2008), a shortage of care personnel in the public health care system (DeMicco & Cetron, 2005; Hunter, 2007), long wait times (Wocher, 2009; Weil, 2009), and low quality care for the cost of treatment (Adams, 2005; Borman, 2004; DeMicco & Cetron, 2005; Kang & Oh, 2008; Yu, 2009; Pinto & Pinto Borges, 2019); while pull factors are favorable currency exchange rates, improvement of medical standards, and the development of air transportation (Lee et al., 2012).

4. CONTRIBUTION AND NEXT STEPS

Brand preference is important for diffusion of innovation in any context as it provides a lot of benefits such as having strong competitive power and unique position in the market (Delgado-Ballester and Munuera-Aleman, 2005). Societies all over the world have noticed recently that environmental issues are increasing steadily due to the huge amounts of environmental pollution that are produced by the industrial manufacturing (Chen, 2008; Mourad et al., 2012). Therefore, green marketing is one of the inevitable trends for companies, and its concept has been widely accepted and applied in recent years. Consequently, green marketing often allows the companies to access to new markets, to increase their profitability, and to enjoy more competitive advantages (Peneda de Oliveira & Sousa, 2019). Therefore, consumer loyalty has become one of the principal lines of research in marketing. Emerging perspectives explored include targeting profitable customers, using the strongest possible strategies for customer bonding, marketing to employees and other stakeholders, and building trust as a marketing tool in healthcare management and medical tourism contexts. Despite the phenomenal growth in medical tourism, little is known about the role of satisfaction, trust, cooperation and commitment in explaining international patient-travelers' post-purchase behavior. The main purpose of this chapter, therefore, was to present a theoretical contribute that clearly explicates overseas medical travelers' intention formation by considering the impact of perceived medical and brand management and rebranding process and motivations. This study is a preliminary contribution towards a greater understanding regarding the relationship between the relationship marketing and rebranding process in specific contexts of healthcare and medical tourism.

With this chapter, we intended to understand the importance of brand management (specifically rebranding) in specific contexts of medical tourism and health and wellness. The case study included an example of the medical tourism segment (i.e. theoretical background). This research was particularly relevant, also, because it is necessary to ensure the sustainability of the health system, as health expenditures are mostly publicly funded (Pinho and Borges, 2015). Models and best rebranding practices were presented in this specific research topic (e.g. health and wellness sector and medical tourism). This chapter focused on medical tourism and healthcare management. The authors also considered some implications for management, as well as give suggestions for future lines of research. The chapter started from a conceptual framework based on branding and rebranding models. From this theoretical base the concepts and models were derived. This study aimed at discussing the brand management in healthcare management and medical tourism contexts. For instance, the study addressed the predisposition for the destination and the influence of relationship marketing on behavioural intentions. Under an interdisciplinary perspective, this research brings together inputs from relationship marketing, medical tourism and healthcare management (service excellence).

For future research, the ethnographic experience of the researchers allowed them to understand the phenomena of brand attachment with the medical tourisms and the consequent effect on satisfaction and loyalty (Sousa & Magalhães, 2019; Sousa & Rocha, 2019). These conclusions are based on the researchers' perception derived from the ethnographic research. Future research might also profitably concentrate on the further development of the several constructs, particularly the emotional dimension of medical tourism organizations.. Therefore, future studies can set forth toward the longitudinal study to find out the differences of medical tourism brand image, satisfaction, trust, and brand equity in the different stages of the environmental regulations in the world. With the insights from this study it is expected that future studies can contribute to the development of empirical studies to address the developed propositions. In particular it is expected that future research explores the relationship between brand attachment, satisfaction and loyalty of medical tourism products and services. It is important to reveal the individual attributes that cause satisfaction and/or dissatisfaction, and shed light on the most determinant and critical attributes in explaining the tourist experience, in the specific the case of niche tourism perspective (e.g. medical tourism). Studies could further develop a questionnaire to be applied to participants to capture a cross-sectional view of the relationships among the constructs gauging their impact.

ACKNOWLEDGMENT

This chapter is a tribute to Gisela Maria Alves, the researcher, colleague and friend who started this project (in 2019).

REFERENCES

Aaker, D. (2010). *Building Strong Brands*. P. Book.

Aaker, D. A. (1996). Measuring brand equity across products and markets. *California Management Review*, *38*(3), 102–120. doi:10.2307/41165845

Aaker, D. A., & Equity, M. B. (1991). Capitalizing on the Value of a Brand Name. New York, 28, 35-37.

Aaker, J. (1997). Dimensions of Brand Personality. *JMR, Journal of Marketing Research*, *34*(3), 347–356. doi:10.1177/002224379703400304

Bagozzi, R. P., Batra, R., & Ahuvia, A. (2017). Brand love: Development and validation of a practical scale. *Marketing Letters*, *28*(1), 1 14. doi:10.100711002-016-9406-1

Baker, M. J., & Balmer, J. M. T. (1997). Visual identity: Trappings or substance? *European Journal of Marketing*, *31*(5/6), 366–382. doi:10.1108/eb060637

Ballester, E. D. (2004). Applicability of a brand trust scale across product categories. *European Journal of Marketing*, *38*(5/6), 573–592. doi:10.1108/03090560410529222

Ballester, E. D., & Alemán, J. L. M. (2001). Brand trust in the context of consumer loyalty. *European Journal of Marketing*, *35*(11/12), 1238–1258. doi:10.1108/EUM0000000006475

Banerjee, S. (2016). Logo Change : Little Image Touch up or Serious Overhaul! Imperatives and Scanning Parameters. *Journal of Marketing Communications*, *4*(1), 59–70.

Bastos, D. H., Moura, L. R. C., & Christino, J. M. M. (2015). Measurement, testing and confidence validation in brand. *Revista Capital Científico-Eletrônica, 13*.

Bastos, D. H., Rodrigo, L., Moura, C., Maria, J., & Christino, M. (2015). Measurement, testing and confidence validation in brand. *Revista Capital Científico-Eletrônica, 13*.

Batra, R., Ahuvia, A., & Bagozzi, R. P. (2012). Brand Love. *Journal of Marketing*, *76*(2), 1–16. doi:10.1509/jm.09.0339

Biricik, A. (2006). *The role of logo design in creating brand emotion: a semiotic comparison of the Apple and IBM logos*. School of Engineering and Sciences of İzmir Institute of Technology.

Boyett, J. H., & Boyett, J. T. (2003). The Guru Guide to Marketing: A Concise Guide to the Best Ideas from Today's Top Marketers (1a Edição). John Wiley & Sons, Inc.

Carroll, B. A., & Ahuvia, A. C. (2006). Some antecedents and outcomes of brand love. *Marketing Letters, 17*(2), 79–89. doi:10.100711002-006-4219-2

Cham, T. H., Lim, Y. M., Sia, B. C., Cheah, J. H., & Ting, H. (2020). Medical tourism destination image and its relationship with the intention to revisit: A study of Chinese medical tourists in Malaysia. *Journal of China Tourism Research*, 1–29. doi:10.1080/19388160.2020.1734514

Chambers, D., & McIntosh, B. (2008). Using authenticity to achieve competitive advantage in medical tourism in the English-speaking Caribbean. *Third World Quarterly, 29*(5), 919–937. doi:10.1080/01436590802106056

Cheng, A. C. L., Gursoy, D., & Lu, C. Y. (2015). Authenticity perceptions, brand equity and brand choice intention: The case of ethnic restaurants. *International Journal of Hospitality Management, 50*, 36–45. doi:10.1016/j.ijhm.2015.07.008

Daly, A., & Moloney, D. (2004). Managing Corporate Rebranding. *Irish Marketing Review, 17*, 30–36.

Dang, H. S., Nguyen, T. M. T., Wang, C. N., Day, J. D., & Dang, T. M. H. (2020). Grey System Theory in the Study of Medical Tourism Industry and Its Economic Impact. *International Journal of Environmental Research and Public Health, 17*(3), 961. doi:10.3390/ijerph17030961 PMID:32033177

Day, G. S. (1994). The of Market-Drive Capabilities Organizations. *Journal of Marketing, 58*(4), 37–52. doi:10.1177/002224299405800404

De Chernatony, L., Drury, S., & Segal-Horn, S. (2004). Identifying and sustaining services brands' values. *Journal of Marketing Communications, 10*(2), 73–93. doi:10.1080/13527260410001693785

de Lencastre, P. (1999). A marca: O sinal, a missão e a imagem. *Revista Portuguesa de Marketing*, (June), 23–71.

de Toni, D., & Mazzon, J. A. (2014). Teste de um modelo teórico sobre o valor percebido do preço de um produto. *Revista ADM, 49*(3), 549–565. doi:10.5700/rausp1167

DeMicco, F. J. (2016). A Disney strategic approach to patient/guest services in Hospitality Bridging Healthcare (H2H) and medical tourism and wellness. The Routledge Handbook of Health Tourism, 261.

DeMicco, F. J. (Ed.). (2017). *Medical Tourism and Wellness: Hospitality Bridging Healthcare (H2H)*. CRC Press. doi:10.1201/9781315365671

DeMicco, F. J. (2017a). A Disney Approach to Medical Tourism and Wellness. In *Medical Tourism and Wellness* (pp. 135–142). Apple Academic Press. doi:10.1201/9781315365671-5

DeMicco, F. J., & Reid, R. D. (1988). Older workers: A hiring resource for the hospitality industry. *The Cornell Hotel and Restaurant Administration Quarterly, 29*(1), 56–61. doi:10.1177/001088048802900116

Farhana, M. (2014). Implication of Brand Identity Facets on Marketing Communication of Lifestyle Magazine: Case Study of A Swedish Brand. *Journal of Applied Economics & Business Research*, *4*(1), 23–41. http://search.ebscohost.com/login.aspx?direct=true&db=buh&AN=94709306&site=ehost-live

Ferreira, J., & Sousa, B. (2020). Experiential Marketing as Leverage for Growth of Creative Tourism: A Co-creative Process. In Advances in Tourism, Technology and Smart Systems. Smart Innovation, Systems and Technologies, (vol. 171, pp. 567-577). Springer. doi:10.1007/978-981-15-2024-2_49

Geuens, M., Weijters, B., & De Wulf, K. (2009). A new measure of brand personality. *International Journal of Research in Marketing*, *26*(2), 97–107. doi:10.1016/j.ijresmar.2008.12.002

Ghaseminezhad, M. (2016). Investigating the impact of rebranded experience on purchase intention and rebranded evaluation. *International Journal of Humanities and Cultural Studies.*

Gobé, M. (2002). *A emoção das marcas: conectando marcas às pessoas*. Campus.

Goi, C., & Goi, M. (2011). Review on Models and Reasons of Rebranding. *International Conference on Social Science and Humanity*, *5*, 445–449.

Han, H. (2013). The healthcare hotel: Distinctive attributes for international medical travelers. *Tourism Management*, *36*, 257–268. doi:10.1016/j.tourman.2012.11.016

Heung, V. C., Kucukusta, D., & Song, H. (2011). Medical tourism development in Hong Kong: An assessment of the barriers. *Tourism Management*, *32*(5), 995–1005. doi:10.1016/j.tourman.2010.08.012

Hudson, S., & Li, X. (2012). Domestic medical tourism: A neglected dimension of medical tourism research. *Journal of Hospitality Marketing & Management*, *21*(3), 227–246. doi:10.1080/19368623.2011.615018

Hudson, S., & Shephard, G. W. (1998). Measuring service quality at tourist destinations: An application of importance-performance analysis to an alpine ski resort. *Journal of Travel & Tourism Marketing*, *7*(3), 61–77. doi:10.1300/J073v07n03_04

Hunter, W. C. (2007). Medical tourism: A new global niche. *International Journal of Tourism Science*, *7*(1), 129–140. doi:10.1080/15980634.2007.11434599

Jafari, J., & Aaser, D. (1988). Tourism as the subject of doctoral dissertations. *Annals of Tourism Research*, *15*(3), 407–429. doi:10.1016/0160-7383(88)90030-8

Jankovic, M. (2012). Integrated marketing communications and brand identity development. *Management*, *17*(63), 91–100. doi:10.7595/management.fon.2012.0015

Jones, M. A., Reynolds, K. E., Mothersbaugh, D. L., & Beatty, S. E. (2007). The positive and negative effects of switching costs on relational outcomes. *Journal of Service Research*, *9*(4), 335–355. doi:10.1177/1094670507299382

Juntunen, M., Saraniemi, S., & Jussila, R. (2009). Corporate re-branding as a process. *Proceedings of the 5th Thought Leaders International Conference on Brand Management*, (April), 6–7.

Kapferer, J.-N. (1992). *Stractegic brand management, new approaches to creating and evaluating brand equity*. Free Press.

Kapferer, J. N. (1997). *Strategic Brand Management: Creating and Sustaining Brand Equity Long Term*. P. Konga.

Kapferer, J.-N. (2008). *The New Strategic Brand Management: Creating and sustaining brand equity long term*. K. Page.

Kapferer, J.-N. (2012). *The New Strategic Brand Management Advanced Insights and Strategic Thinking*. K. Page.

Kapferer, J. N. (2012). *The new strategic brand management: Advanced insights and strategic thinking*. Kogan Page Publishers.

Keller, K. L. (1993). Conceptualizing, Measuring, and Managing Customer-Based Brand Equity. *Source Journal of Marketing, 57*(1), 1–22. doi:10.1177/002224299305700101

Keller, K. L. (1998). *Strategic brand management*. Prentice-Hall.

Keller, K. L., & Machado, M. (2006). *Gestão estratégica de Marcas*. Pearson.

Kotler, P., & Armstrong, G. (2007). *Princípios de Marketing*. Pearson Prentice Hall.

Kotler, P., & Keller, K. (2006). Administração de Marketing. São Paulo: Pearson.

Kotler, P., & Keller, K. (2013). Administração de Marketing (10aEdição). São Paulo: Academic Press.

Kotler, P., & Pfoertsch, W. (2006). *B2B Brand Managemet*. Springer-Verlag Berlin Heidelberg.

Kucukusta, D., & Guillet, B. D. (2014). Measuring spa-goers' preferences: A conjoint analysis approach. *International Journal of Hospitality Management, 41*, 115–124. doi:10.1016/j.ijhm.2014.05.008

Kucukusta, D., Mak, A., & Chan, X. (2013). Corporate social responsibility practices in four and five-star hotels: Perspectives from Hong Kong visitors. *International Journal of Hospitality Management, 34*, 19–30. doi:10.1016/j.ijhm.2013.01.010

Kucukusta, D., Pang, L., & Chui, S. (2013). Inbound travelers' selection criteria for hotel spas in Hong Kong. *Journal of Travel & Tourism Marketing, 30*(6), 557–576. doi:10.1080/10548408.2013.810995

Lakatos, E. M., & Marconi, M. A. (2007). *Técnicas de pesquisa: Planejamento e execução de pesquisas, amostragens e técnicas de pesquisa, elaboração, análise e interpretação de dados* (6th ed.). Atlas.

Lang, B., & Hyde, K. F. (2013). Word of Mouth: What We Know and What We Have Yet To Learn. *Journal of Consumer Satisfaction, Dissatisfaction & Complaining Behavior, 26*, 1–18.

Lien, C. H., Wen, M. J., Huang, L. C., & Wu, K. L. (2015). Online hotel booking: The effects of brand image, price, trust and value on purchase intentions. Elsevier.

Lomax, W., Mador, M., & Fitzhenry, A. (2002). *Corporate Rebranding : Learning from Experience*. Kingston University.

Macrae, C. (1996). *The brand chartering handbook : how brand organizations learn "living scripts."* Addison-Wesley.

Michaelidou, N., Micevshi, M., & Cadogan, J. W. (2015). An evaluation of nonprofit brand image: Towards a better conceptualization and measurement. *Journal of Business Research*, *68*(8), 43. doi:10.1016/j.jbusres.2015.03.024

Milan, G. S., De Toni, D., de Lima, V. Z., Eberle, L., Milan, G. S., De Toni, D., ... Eberle, L. (2017). Papel Moderador da Marca e Mediação do Valor Percebido na Intenção de Recompra. *Revista de Administração Contemporânea*, *21*(3), 347–372. doi:10.1590/1982-7849rac2017160062

Miller, D., Merrilees, B., & Yakimova, R. (2014). Corporate Rebranding. *An Integrative Review of Major Enablers and Barriers to the Rebranding Process*, *16*(3), 265–289. doi:10.1111/ijmr.12020

Mittal, V., Ross, W. T. Jr, & Baldasare, P. M. (1998). The Asymmetric Impact of Negative and Positive Attribute-Level Performance on Overall Satisfaction and Repurchase Intentions. *Journal of Marketing*, *62*(1), 33–47. doi:10.1177/002224299806200104

Mollerup, P. (1999). *Marks of Excelence- The history and taxonomy of trademarks*. Phaidon.

Muzellec, L., Doogan, M., & Lambkin, M. (2003). Corporate rebranding-an exploratory review. *Irish Marketing Review*, *16*, 31.

Muzellec, L., & Lambkin, M. (2006). Corporate rebranding: Destroying, transferring or creating brand equity? *European Journal of Marketing*, *40*(7/8), 803–824. doi:10.1108/03090560610670007

Muzellec, L., & Lambkin, M. (2006). *Corporate rebranding : destroying, transferring or creating brand equity?* doi:10.1108/03090560610670007

Namkung, Y., & Jang, S. (2013). Effects of restaurant green practices on brand equity formation: Do green practices really matter? *International Journal of Hospitality Management*, *33*, 11. doi:10.1016/j.ijhm.2012.06.006

Oliver, R. L. (1997). *Satisfaction: A Behavioral Perspective on the Consumer*. McGraw-Hill.

Peneda de Oliveira, C., & Sousa, B. M. (2019). Green Consumer Behavior and Its Implications on Brand Marketing Strategy. In V. Naidoo & R. Verma (Eds.), *Green Marketing as a Positive Driver Toward Business Sustainability* (pp. 69–95). IGI Global. doi:10.4018/978-1-5225-9558-8.ch004

Pinho, M., & Borges, A. (2015). Bedside healthcare rationing dilemmas: A survey from Portugal. *International Journal of Human Rights in Healthcare*, *8*(4), 233–246. doi:10.1108/IJHRH-03-2015-0008

Pinho, M., Borges, A. P., & Zahariev, B. (2017). Bedsides healthcare rationing dilemmas: A survey from Bulgaria and comparison with Portugal. *Social Theory & Health*, *15*(3), 285–301. doi:10.105741285-017-0029-2

Pinho, M., & Pinto Borges, A. (2019). The views of health care professionals and laypersons concerning the relevance of health-related behaviors in prioritizing patients. *Health Education & Behavior*, *46*(5), 728–736. doi:10.1177/1090198119853604 PMID:31204850

Rodrigues, P., & Borges, A. P. (2015). Corporate social responsibility and its impact in consumer decision-making. *Social Responsibility Journal*, *11*(4), 690–701. doi:10.1108/SRJ-02-2014-0026

Rodrigues, P., Real, E., Vitorino, F., & Cantista, I. (2011, January). The importance of corporate social responsibility in the brand image. In *10th International Marketing Trends Congress, Paris, France* (pp. 21-23). Academic Press.

Sirdeshmukh, D., Singh, J., & Sabol, B. (2002). Consumer Trust, Value, and Loyalty in Relational Exchanges. *Journal of Marketing*, *66*(1), 15–37. doi:10.1509/jmkg.66.1.15.18449

Smith, P. C., & Forgione, D. A. (2007). Global outsourcing of healthcare: A medical tourism decision model. *Journal of Information Technology Case and Application Research*, *9*(3), 19–30. doi:10.1080/15228053.2007.10856117

Sousa, B., & Alves, G. (2019). The role of relationship marketing in behavioural intentions of medical tourism services and guest experiences. *Journal of Hospitality and Tourism Insights*, *2*(3), 224–240. doi:10.1108/JHTI-05-2018-0032

Sousa, B., & Rocha, A. T. (2019). The role of attachment in public management and place marketing contexts: A case study applied to Vila de Montalegre (Portugal). *International Journal of Public Sector Performance Management*, *5*(2), 189–205. doi:10.1504/IJPSPM.2019.099094

Sousa, B., & Silva, J. (2015). The Brand Management: A perspective applied in the context of sports media. *International Journal of Marketing. Communication and New Media*, *4*(3), 118–133.

Sousa, B. B., & Magalhães, F. C. (2019). An Approach on Attachment in Public Marketing and Higher Education Management Contexts. In C. Machado & J. Davim (Eds.), *Higher Education and the Evolution of Management, Applied Sciences, and Engineering Curricula* (pp. 151–171). IGI Global. doi:10.4018/978-1-5225-7259-6.ch006

Stuart, H., & Muzellec, L. (2004). Corporate makeovers : Can a hyena be rebranded? *Journal of Brand Management*, *11*(July), 472–482. Advance online publication. doi:10.1057/palgrave.bm.2540193

Tevi, A. C., & Otubanjo, O. (2013). Understanding Corporate Rebranding. *An Evolution Theory Perspective*, *5*(3), 87–93. doi:10.5539/ijms.v5n3p87

Tresidder, R. (2011). 19 Health and Medical Tourism. *Research Themes f or Tourism*, 266.

Upshaw, L. B. (1995). *Building Brand Identity: A Strategy for Success in a Hostile Marketplace*. Wiley.

Van Niekerk, M. (2014). The role of the public sector in tourism destination management from a network relationship approach. *Tourism Analysis*, *19*(6), 701–718. doi:10.3727/108354214X14146846679402

Wheeler, A. (2009). Designing Brand Identity- an essential guide for the entire branding team (3aEdição). John Wiley & Sons, Inc.

Williams, J. (2006). *The Art of Rebranding*. Retrieved January 4, 2018, from https://www.entrepreneur.com/article/159470

Wocher, J. (2009). *Japan lags behind*. Retrieved from http://www.imtj.com/articles/2008/japan-lags-behind

Wong, A., & Sohal, A. (2002). An examination of the relationship between trust, commitment and relationship quality. *International Journal of Retail & Distribution Management*, *30*(1), 34–50. doi:10.1108/09590550210415248

Yoo, B., & Donthu, N. (2001). Developing and validating a multi-dimensional consumer based brand equity scale. *Journal of Business Research*, *10*(1), 61–67. doi:10.1016/S0148-2963(99)00098-3

Yoo, B., Donthu, N., & Lee, S. (2000). An Examination of Seiected Marketing Mix ELements and Brand Equity. *Journal of the Academy of Marketing Science*, *28*(2), 195–211. doi:10.1177/0092070300282002

Zeithaml, V. A. (1988). Consumer Perceptions of Price, Quality and Value: A Means-End Model Synthesis of Evidence. *Journal of Marketing*, *52*(July), 2–22. doi:10.1177/002224298805200302

Zeithaml, V. A., Berry, L. L., & Parasuraman, A. (1996). The Behavioral Consequences of Stroke. *The Behavioral Consequences of Serviece Quality*, *60*(April), 31–46. doi:10.1007/978-1-4614-7672-6

Zielke, S. (2010). How price image dimensions influence shopping intentions for different store formats. *European Journal of Marketing*, *44*(6), 748–770. doi:10.1108/03090561011032702

Zielke, S. (2011). Integrating Emotions in the Analysis of Retail Price Images. *Psychology & Marketing*, *28*(4), 330–359. doi:10.1002/mar

KEY TERMS AND DEFINITIONS

Brand: Is an overall experience of a customer that distinguishes an organization or product from its rivals in the perspective of the customer.

Marketing Concept: Marketing is accomplishing the objectives of a firm relies upon knowing needs of target markets.

Marketing Tools: The techniques and materials used by those who are involved in the promotion of goods and services.

Medical Tourism: Refers to people traveling abroad to obtain medical treatment. Health tourism is a wider term for travel that focuses on medical treatments and the use of healthcare services. It covers a wide field of health-oriented, tourism ranging from preventive and health-conductive treatment to rehabilitational and curative forms of travel.

Rebranding: Is the process of changing the corporate image of an organisation. It is a market strategy of giving a new name, symbol, or change in design for an already-established brand. The idea behind rebranding is to create a different identity for a brand, from its competitors, in the market.

Strategy: Describes how the ends (goals) will be achieved by the means (resources).

Chapter 9
The Brand NHS:
Undue Use and Its Consequences

Ana Maria Reis
https://orcid.org/0000-0003-0674-7327
ISAG - European Business School and Research Center in Business Sciences and Tourism (CICET – FCVC)

Bárbara Soares
Portuguese Healthcare Regulation Authority, Portugal

ABSTRACT

The brand NHS (SNS Serviço Nacional de Saúde) is a registered brand. In 2015, a new legal regime on health advertising practices was introduced. This regime set a more rigid penalty framework, including pecuniary and ancillary sanctions, applied to the undue use of the brand NHS by private providers and disloyal advertising, protecting the brand's reputation and increasing patients' trust. The objective of this chapter was to discuss the undue use of the brand NHS, in Portugal, by private providers, and its impact on brand reputation. The main conclusions are the cases of health advertising and undue use of the brand NHS have been reduced under the new regime; the sanctions applied after 2015 varied from 500 euros to 1,500 euros, which reveals a small financial impact for providers; this reduction could be justified by the negative impact on the image of the healthcare provider under an administrative offense process.

INTRODUCTION

In healthcare sector the brands are closely linked to perceived service quality, patients' emotional connection and corporate reputation (Chahal & Bala, 2012; Erbay & Esatoglu, 2017; Kemp et al., 2014; Trong Tuan, 2014). A strong brand increases patients' trust and acts as a mean of differentiation, which in turn increases brand equity (Chahal & Bala, 2012). In the healthcare sector the brand loyalty is reinforced by searching costs when patients want to find another provider (Seiler, 2013), and switching costs (Grytten & Sorensen, 2000; Strombom et al., 2002). Therefore, effective brand management is a key factor in the health sector, specifically when providers want to attract new patients.

DOI: 10.4018/978-1-7998-3034-4.ch009

The Portuguese Health System is mainly financed by public funds and coexists with public and private insurance schemes for certain professions, private voluntary health insurance and out-of-pocket payments (Barros et al., 2011; Simões et al., 2017). In 2017, 67% of the total health expenditure was funded by public sources, and the out-of-pocket reached 27% of the financial flows (PORDATA, 2018).

Within this context, the Portuguese National Health Service (NHS), based on universal, general and tending-towards-free access to health services, is fundamental in the provision of healthcare (Simões, 2010).

The brand NHS (*SNS Serviço Nacional de Saúde*) is a registered brand since May 2016. However, the management of the NHS brand has a long tradition going back to the '80s, with continuous efforts on quality improvements building NHS reputation and image. Portuguese NHS management has been focused on the identity approach, entailing corporate strategic-level brand management.

The market NHS includes, at the supply side, the private and social providers contracting with the NHS (Almeida, 2017; OECD, 1998), in complementarity with the public healthcare providers (Nunes & Ferreira, 2019). Under a contract with the NHS, the private providers are associated with the brand NHS and should meet NHS standards, in what concerns quality, reputation and image. The private providers with contract must also follow the same rules as the public providers in what concerns the access to health care and prices.

The registered brand NHS is a recognized and trusted brand that includes all the publicly funded services. Contracting with the NHS includes minimum quality standards, in most of which the payment is conditional on fulfilling these standards, reinforcing brand identity. When patients go to a public healthcare provider, or a private provider contracting with the NHS, are expecting service with specific characteristics, which they relate with the brand NHS. Therefore, NHS brand management entails an organizational identity and corporate identity that implies NHS funded services (public and private) should be clearly branded NHS and easily identified by patients. In this context, legislation can act as a brand management tool, preventing damages on NHS brand reputation, conducted by external providers.

Different types of contract between the Portuguese NHS and private providers exist, namely the Public-Private Partnerships (PPP) and the conventions. The creation of PPP granted more autonomy to organizations by conceding the management of service units of care to private entities, or by the joint investment between them and the State (Barros, 2010; Barros et al., 2011; Barros, 2016; Portuguese Health Regulation Authority, 2016a; WHO, 2018). Nowadays, three NHS hospitals are managed by private entities under a PPP – Vila Franca de Xira, Cascais, and Loures. These contracts between the NHS and private were established between 2008 and 2010. After 2010 no new PPP contract was established.

The concept 'conventions' refers to the NHS contracting with private sector, to provide specific healthcare services to NHS' patients. In most of the medical specialities, these contracts have been in place since the late 1980s. The Portuguese legal framework had imposed rigidity of the conventions' market, give that, with just a few exceptions no new private providers were allowed to contract with the NHS (Portuguese Health Regulation Authority, 2008). This legal context was responsible for a lack of competition within this subsector and the substantial cost to the NHS for such services (Portuguese Health Regulation Authority, 2006), accounting for almost 10% of the NHS total costs (Simões et al., 2017).

The difficulty in entering the conventions' market lead to competition distortions, such as the publicity of conventions by private providers that do not have any contract with the NHS, publicity and use of one convention in the improper establishment and the improper use of NHS name or logo. These undue uses of the brand NHS are justified by an economic interest in attracting NHS patients, taking advantage of the brad NHS, and related reputation.

The Portuguese legal system penalizes the undue use of the brand NHS, given that the brand identity approach implies that the providers should meet the same standards and reinforce corporate image and reputation. In this context, the Portuguese Health Regulation Authority (ERS) is the independent public body responsible for regulating the activity of healthcare providers, in Portugal. In 2015, the Portuguese Government established a new legal regime on health advertising practices, through the Decree-Law no. 238/2015, of October 14th. The law applies to public and private stakeholders that benefit from or participate in the conception or diffusion of health advertising to patients or potential healthcare users.

The legal regime includes general principles that these practices shall comply with, namely transparency, reliability and legality, objectivity and scientific rigour. Specifically, Article 4(4) of the Decree-Law no. 238/2015, of October 14th, establishes that the advertising practices carried out by healthcare providers should be beyond all doubt about the acts and healthcare services offered and about the convention or any contracts in force.

This legal regime comprises a paradigm change, from administrative interventions applied to these practices to a new penalty framework, which provides for additional sanctions, including financial penalties, as well as the suspension of rights in case of serious breaches of this regime on health advertising practices. Therefore, this regime is intended to protect patients' rights, protecting the NHS brand image and reputation.

No studies are analysing the NHS brand, in Portugal. Therefore, in this chapter, we present the value of the NHS brand, the management of the NHS brand and the impacts that it has been suffering. Considering this background, the objective of this chapter is to explore the undue use of the brand NHS by private providers, in Portugal. Practical examples of undue use of the NHS brand are used to show how private providers act and how their behaviour can compromise the NHS brand reputation. Moreover, this chapter includes an analysis of the impact of the laws on healthcare advertising, namely the Decree-Law no. 238/2015, of October 14th, on the undue use of the brand.

This is the first time that the NHS brand is analysed and presented in this perspective. The comparison of the period before and after the application of the Decree-Law no. 238/2015, of October 14th, has not been addressed in other studies. We argue that this decree-law is an important tool of brand management, contributing to the maintenance of the NHS brand reputation. Moreover, a critical analysis of the impact of this legal framework on practical cases is also a novelty of this chapter.

In what follows, this chapter is organized in 5 sections. The next section includes a methodology description. Sections 3 and 4 describe the market and the brand NHS and the legal regime on health advertising practices, respectively. In section 5, the practical cases are summarized, including a discussion and estimation of the potential consequences under the new legal regime on health advertising practices. The final two sections include the description of implications and limitations of the study and potential future research directions, as well as the fundamental conclusions.

METHODOLOGY

The methodology used includes a theoretical analysis of the Portuguese healthcare context, focusing on the role of the private healthcare providers contracting with the NHS. First, the value of the brand NHS and the brand management approach is theoretically presented and discussed.

A description of the new legal regime on health advertising practices is developed, focusing the consequences before and after the Decree-Law no. 238/2015, of October 14th. In this chapter a critical discussion is developed, considering the use of the brand NHS and its implications, using practical cases within the Portuguese context. Some descriptive statistics were used to analyse the market NHS and the undue use of the brand NHS. An estimation of the potential financial impact of the undue use of the brand NHS is also conducted.

In what concerns the data sources, we used information available online, extracted from public reports of the Portuguese Ministry of Health and the Portuguese Health Regulation Authority website.

THE MARKET AND THE BRAND NHS

The brand NHS (*SNS Serviço Nacional de Saúde*) is a registered brand since May 2016, with name and logo registered (figure 1). However, it should be noted that the NHS and its brand reputation go back at least to 1979 (Law no. 56/79, of September 15th) (Domingues, 2019; Simões, 2010).

Figure 1. Portuguese NHS' logo

Considering the seven brand approaches listed by Heding et al. (2009), which represent different perceptions of the brand (Heding et al., 2009), the identity approach is the one that bests suits the brand NHS. The identity approach relies on the concepts of organizational and corporate identity, which implies strategic-level brand management, at a corporate level, and not a product-focused perspective (Heding et al., 2009). Moreover, in the identity approach, image and reputation are key determinants of consumers' choice. This theoretical approach is consistent with the NHS, given that healthcare providers cover a wide range of products and services to improve or maintain patients' health (European Commission, 2015) and corporate reputation has a significant impact on consumers choice, satisfaction and loyalty in the healthcare market (Erbay & Esatoglu, 2017).

NHS' institutions are perceived as institutions with high-level professionals and quality standards, and brand management strategies have been based on these standards to build NHS brand reputation. The value of the NHS brand has been greatly influenced by the perceived quality and brand reputation, and a strong emotionally based consumer-brand relationships (Chahal & Bala, 2012; Erbay & Esatoglu, 2017; Kemp et al., 2014; Trong Tuan, 2014). Corporate reputation and a stronger image have an impact on patients' decisions when choosing their healthcare providers, and on their loyalty to a specific provider (Chahal & Bala, 2012; Erbay & Esatoglu, 2017).

In turn, brand reputation includes expectations on the behaviour of the organization and its member (Erbay & Esatoglu, 2017). Therefore, patients expect NHS' services to meet specific standards (quality, security, lower price). The supply side of the Portuguese NHS market includes not only the public healthcare providers but also the private providers contracting with the NHS. Patients and the public see the NHS as a single organization, and NHS services should be branded NHS. If the NHS service is being delivered by a third-party private provider, it should be identified in the providers' website or advertising. On the other hand, services that are not under contract should not use the name and NHS logo. If private providers act as NHS units unproperly (which is without having a contract), they will influence brand reputation and image. In this sense, legislation can act as a brand management tool, preventing acts of undesirable interferences on the NHS brand reputation.

In Portugal, the NHS brand management considers the protection of the registered brand NHS under the Portuguese Industrial Property Code. It also includes specific legislation, namely the establishment of specific rules the providers with a contract with the NHS should comply, and the legal regime on health advertising practices.

The conventions are the most common type of contract with the NHS, covering approximately 1300 private providers, excluding dialysis and the so-called SIGIC (Waiting List for Surgery's Integrated Management System) (figure 2) (Portuguese Ministry of Health, 2017). The contracts operate as follows: the NHS declares the terms of service and prices that the NHS is willing to pay, as well as the quality standards that private providers need to meet (Dixon, 1999). A list of all those providers who have registered is published by the competent Regional Health Administration. In principle, patients can choose from any of the providers who appear on the contracts, under the freedom of choice right in the NHS.

Under these contracts, the NHS patients pay the equivalent to the payments in the public services (called moderating fee – *taxa moderadora*) (Central Administration of the Health System, 2016; Portuguese Health Regulation Authority, 2013e), and the private are reimbursed directly by the NHS, based on the costs established by law.

However, no new private providers were allowed to contract with the NHS for some time (Simões et al., 2017). This tendency can be seen in figure 2, presenting the little movement of providers between 2010 and 2017, using data from the Central Administration of the Health System (ACSS) (Portuguese Ministry of Health, 2017). These conventions pose a considerable financial burden on NHS budget, totalling 402.048.923 euros (excluding dialysis and SIGIC), corresponding to a rise of around 2.1% from the previous year (Portuguese Ministry of Health, 2017).

Figure 2. Healthcare providers with a contract with the NHS, between 2010 and 2017

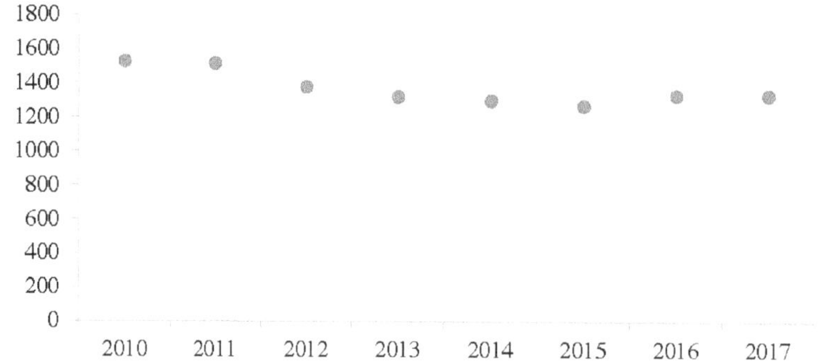

The majority of these contracts date to the 1980s (Portuguese Health Regulation Authority, 2008). The legal framework provided by the Decret-law no. 97/98, of April 18th, which established the possibility of new providers contracting with the NHS, apparently opening the conventions market, has not been implemented except for surgery, dialysis and SIGIC (Waiting List for Surgery's Integrated Management System) (OECD, 2013; Portuguese Health Regulation Authority (ERS), 2014). More recently, the Decret-law no. 139/2013, of October 9th, established the "new legal regime of conventions", designed to ensure respect for the principles of the equity, complementarity, patients' freedom of choice, transparency, equality and competition. Under the Decret-law no. 139/2013, of October 9th, the main clauses for each area of healthcare (*clausulado-tipo*) should be defined via specific legislation. However, the great majority of these legislations is missing, which prevents the entry of new providers. Exceptions were observed with the publication of the respective legislation (*clausulado-tipo*), and the opening of the conventions market, in 2017, concerning the areas of clinical analysis (Dispatch no. 3668-E/2017, of April 28th), pathological anatomy (Dispatch no. 3668-J/2017, of April 28th) and nuclear medicine (Dispatch no. 3668-F/2017, of April 28th) (Portuguese Ministry of Health, 2017).

This market rigidity led to market distortions, including the advertising of conventions by healthcare providers without a contract with the NHS. The NHS brand is used improperly by healthcare providers due to an economic interest in attracting NHS' patients. On average, each healthcare provider with a contract received 302 292.42 euros, in 2017. We estimated the average value received by each healthcare provider with convention, in 2017, based on the total amount paid and the number of providers, using data from the Central Administration of the Health System (Portuguese Ministry of Health, 2017).

Under the concept of universal NHS, all residents in Portugal are covered by the Portuguese NHS, irrespective of their socioeconomic, employment or legal status (Simões et al., 2017). When providers use the brand NHS without legitimacy, they are expecting to attract more patients, even though they may lose money, initially. As we will see later in this chapter, some private healthcare providers use not only the NHS brand improperly in advertising but also act like NHS providers without having a convention, for instance applying the moderating fee (for example 7 euros for speciality appointments), which is substantially below the private price. This behaviour reveals the reputation of the NHS brand. The private providers are available to apply a lower price because they think in it as an investment to attract NHS patients. Once this objective is achieved, it is easier to fix the patients, due to the search cost and switching costs that exist in the healthcare sector.

The healthcare services are characterized by a reduced level of health literacy (Espanha & Ávila, 2016; Pedro et al., 2016), including a lack of patients' knowledge on quality standards and their rights (Health Regulation Authority, 2017) and a strong patient-provider relationship (Phillips-Salimi et al., 2012), influencing patient's health outcomes in health. This relationship leads to search costs, when patients want to find another provider (Seiler, 2013), and switching costs (Grytten & Sorensen, 2000; Strombom et al., 2002). Switching costs include monetary costs and time lost due to necessary paperwork when switching to a new provider, uncertainty about the quality of untested brands and psychological costs, such as "brand loyalty" (Lamiraud, 2014). These costs strengthen the connection between patients and the usual private healthcare provider and reduce market competition.

If the private providers use the brand NHS without legitimacy, they compromise the legality and transparency in the economic relations between providers, funders and users. First, competition problems arise due to the use of a brand with a reputation in the market, competing unfairly by attracting patients against other providers. The users' rights are also compromised by this behaviour, namely the principle of transparency and their right to be correctly informed. Given that patients are not aware of the real quality and price of healthcare when the private providers use the brand NHS, patients will expect to be under certain quality level (Portuguese Health Regulation Authority, 2013a), specific access rules and price conditions, which they associate to the NHS brand and public services standards. Moreover, when private providers act on behalf of the NHS the users expected to be fully protected under the concept of universality and tending-towards-free access to health services, including follow-up as well as a series of procedures for sorting out possible complications. Private providers could not be financially able (or interested) in guaranteeing the safeguard of these questions, defrauding legitimate expectations and compromising patients' health. If so, the NHS brand reputation is compromised, because it relies on patients' expectations (Erbay & Esatoglu, 2017).

Moreover, the reputation of the private sector providers contracting with the NHS also influences the NHS brand reputation, given that the public see the NHS as a single organization, and their positive reputation reinforces the value of the NHS brand (Erbay & Esatoglu, 2017). The reputation of the private providers contracting with the NHS is ensured by the legal regime establishing specific rules that these providers must comply with, and its monitoring by the Portuguese Health Regulation Authority.

THE LEGAL REGIME ON HEALTH ADVERTISING PRACTICES

Adverting is a central element of consumers' rights, as provided in the Constitution of the Portuguese Republic. Following the Constitution (Article 60) advertising should be regulated by law and it prohibits all the forms of surreptitious, indirect or fraudulent. In 1990, Decree-Law 330/90, of October 23rd, approved the Portuguese Advertising Code, which currently regulates advertising activity in Portugal (Bramão & Costa, 2003; Chaves, 2005). In this context by advertising, it means the forms of communication in the field of economic activities, with the key aim of promoting goods and services, to stimulate their commercialization.

Additionally, some legislation has been approved on specific activity sectors, including the health sector. In 2014, the Portuguese Health Regulation Authority issued a Recommendation on health advertising practices, addressed to healthcare providers ((Portuguese Health Regulation Authority, 2014e). This Recommendation was motivated by several cases reported on this topic, decided individually (summarized in table 2), that justified intervention, in a more comprehensive way, for preventive proposes. This recommendation wanted to defend users' rights in what concerns the free and informed access to healthcare services but can be considered soft law.

In this sequence, the Portuguese Government constituted a working group with experts of public entities, including professional associations. This working group has the mission of summarizing the existing legislation and proposes a regulation and/or alteration of the existing legal frameworks, in what concerns the advertising practices carried out by any healthcare provider (joint Dispatch of the Ministry of Economy and the Ministry of Health no. 11344/2014). This work culminated with the approval of the Decree-Law no. 238/2015, of October 14th.

The Decree-Law no. 238/2015, of October 14th, established a new legal regime on health advertising practices. In this context, health advertising is any commercial communication, telemarketing, tele promotion, practice, or product placement. According to Article 12, this legal regime entered into force on 1 November 2015.

This regime applies to all healthcare providers as well as any agents or information services that offer information on healthcare services, namely in what concerns the protection and maintenance of health and the prevention and treatment of disease. In this context, Article 10 attributes the regulatory competence to the Portuguese Health Regulation Authority. Therefore, Regulation no. 1058/2016, published in the II Series of the Portuguese official gazette, *Diário da República,* no. 226, of November 24th, established the operational and concrete rules on the needed elements concerning the identification of the agents involved in health advertising and the content of publicized messages (fulfilling Articles 4 and 5 of the Decree-Law no. 238/2015, of October 14th).

The legal regime includes general principles that these practices shall comply with, namely transparency, reliability and legality, objectivity and scientific rigour (Article 3). It also established a set of prohibited health advertising practices (Article 7).

Among the prohibited health advertising practices listed, Article 4(2) of the Decree-Law no. 238/2015, of October 14th, specify that the health advertising practices cannot give rise to doubt about the treatments and healthcare services, nor about conventions or other existing contracts. Additionally, the message or information advertised should be clearly and accurately drafted and should contain all the adequate and needed elements, to allow the complete understanding of the issue by users of health services (Article 5(1) of the Decree-Law no. 238/2015, of October 14th). Specifically, the said adequate and required elements for users understanding comprise any possible constraints or exceptions on the duration of the conventions, arrangements or protocols for the provision of healthcare (Article 3(2) - c) of the Regulation no. 1058/2016, of 24 November 2016).

On the other hand, Article 7 includes the prohibited practices that have to be a cause for concern in terms of misleading consumers. This article includes the health advertising practices that wrongly influenced an average person in terms of knowledge/information. Specifically, practices that help to trigger a decision on the health services contracted, due to a confusing message on healthcare services, brands, trade names and other distinguishing signs or distinctive competencies of the healthcare providers, are forbidden. Additionally, Article 7 also prohibits the advertising practices that erroneously persuade the user on the alleged healthcare services quality, due to an undue use of a specific brand or their distinguishing marks (Article 7 (1) – e).

In this chapter, the references and the discussion of misleading advertising practices using NHS brand (name, logo or distinctive terms or elements) refer to the specific legal framework presented in the two previous paragraphs.

The new legal regime on health advertising practices sets up a more rigid penalty framework than the previous one, providing additional safeguards for the NHS brand and its reputation. It comprises a paradigm change, from administrative interventions applied to improper advertising practices – considered as soft law – to a new penalty framework – considered as hard law. The legal impositions are mandatory and the non-compliance with the new legal regime constitutes an administrative offence.

It includes a set of pecuniary sanctions (Article 8(1)), from 250 euros up to 3,740.98 euros (natural people); from 1000 euros up to 44,891.81 euros (legal entity). The Decree-Law no. 238/2015, of October 14th, also establishes a set of ancillary sanctions, namely: a) confiscation of equipment, objects or goods used for forbidden practices; b) temporary disqualification (up to a maximum of two years) from the professional practice or from advertising; c) deprivation of rights or benefits given by regulation authorities or public entities (up to a maximum of two years).

In table 1 a synthesis is presented, comparing the legal consequences before and after the application of the Decree-Law no. 238/2015, of October 14th. Before 2015, the Portuguese Health Regulation Authority applied the legal framework foreseen by the Decree-law no. 126/2014, of August 22nd. This framework includes the application of administrative law procedures, which ended with orders and instructions directed to the healthcare providers, in the most serious cases, or recommendations and warnings, in minor cases or where insufficient evidence has been presented.

Table 1. Comparative Synthesis of the legal consequences before and after the new legal regime on health advertising practices

Before the Decree-Law no. 238/2015, of October 14th	**Decree-Law no. 238/2015, of October 14th (Legal regime on health advertising practices)**	
Advertising Code (Decree-Law 330/90, of October 23rd, last amended by Decree-Law 66/2015, of April 29th), disperse legislation, and *soft law*.	Opening of offense processes.	
Application of administrative law procedures (Article 19th of the Decree-Law no. 126/2014, of August 22nd), which ended with: - Orders and instructions directed to the healthcare providers, in the most serious cases; - Recommendations and warnings, in minor cases or where insufficient evidence has been presented.	**Imposition of pecuniary sanctions (Article 8(1))** - from 250 euros up to 3,740.98 euros (natural people); - from 1000 euros up to 44,891.81 euros (legal entity);	**Ancillary sanctions (Article 8(3))** a) confiscation of equipment, objects or goods used for forbidden practices; b) temporary disqualification [...] (up to a maximum of two years) from the professional practice or from advertising; c) deprivation of rights or benefits given by regulation authorities or public entities (up to a maximum of two years).

Source: Elaborated by the authors.

The Portuguese Industrial Property Code also punish the misuse of a registered brand (name, logo or insignia), in its Article 335, namely imposing a fine from 3,000 euros to 30,000 euros if the offender is a legal entity, and for 750 euros to 3,740 euros, if the infraction is carried out by a natural person. In this chapter we focused the undue use of the NHS brand under the new publicity regime.

UNDUE USE OF THE BRAND NHS: PRACTICAL CASES

There are different ways of misusing the brand NHS: use of the name/logo NHS without convention; use of the convention in a different unit (not included in the contract); the convention does not covers all the medical specialities/doctors or has regional scope (does not cover all national NHS users), but the provider meets all users without distinction.

In this section, practical cases were presented and used to compare the consequences before and after the new legal regime. In the context presented before, the Portuguese Health Regulation Authority aims at delivering independent assurance about the legality and transparency in the economic relations between providers, funders and users, and it is also the competent entity to apply the new legal regime on health advertising practices.

Using public data available at the Portuguese Health Regulation Authority website this chapter summarize the scope of the infractions related to the undue use of the brand NHS. The themes of the cases were dived on: 1) Advertising; 2) Undue use of the brand NHS; 3) Advertising and undue use of the brand NHS. The cases focusing 'advertising' refers to the dissemination of incorrect messages or diffusion of information that is misleading to the consumer, by private providers using the name NHS or associated terms (such as *taxa moderadora).* The category 'undue use of the brand NHS' includes the cases of providers acting irregularly as if having a 'convention', and cases of undue use of an existing 'convention' contract (in a different location, covering medical specialities that are not included in the contract). In these cases no irregularities were found in advertising practices.

Table 2 includes the list of cases received and analysed before the application of the new legal regime. It is also resumes the consequences applicable on the date of the events in question, as well as the potential consequences as if the Decree-Law no. 238/2015, of October 14th, was already in force. In sum, 22 cases were reported and decided by the Portuguese entity empowered to punish advertising practices and the undue use of conventions. After 2015, the Portuguese Health Regulation Authority centralize the addressed complains to both public and private providers (Portuguese Health Regulation Authority, 2016c). Moreover, the Portuguese Health Regulation Authority Recommendation no. 1/2014, focusing health advertising practices, alerted the health sector's stakeholders about the practices, such as misleading advertising, which may affect both consumer and competitors' interests. This recommendation should have increased the awareness of these questions, boosting the number of related complains. In this context, the observed increase in the number of cases analysed in 2015 can be justified by these factors. Therefore, the number of cases after the application of the new regime should be compared with the ones received in 2015, due to the similar context.

Figure 3 includes the percentage of cases in each category. The majority of cases (41% of the total cases analysed) include both undue use of the brand NHS and advertising problems.

The consequences, under the soft law regime applicable before the Decree-Law no. 238/2015, of October 14th, included the application of recommendations, orders or instructions addressed to the private providers. After 2016, under the new regime on health advertising practices and the Portuguese Health Regulation Authority's Regulation no. 1058/2016, of November 24th, the number of cases has been reduced. This new legal regime on health advertising practices sets up a more rigid penalty framework. Comparing the years 2016, 2017 e 2018 with the number of cases received in 2015 about this topic, per 10,000 registered complains, a tendency of decrease was observed (figure 4). In absolute terms, between 2016 and 2018 the Portuguese Health Regulation Authority set up 5 procedures, compared with 7 cases in the single year 2015.

The five cases analysed between 2016 and 2018 leaded to application of sanctions, considering the legal framework presented before (sanctions from 1,000 euros up to 44,891.81 euros, concerning legal entities). The specific pecuniary sanction applied in each specific case is decided based on the criterions established in Article 63 of the Decree-law no. 126/2014, of August 22nd (which approved the Statutes of the Health Regulation Authority). These criterions include the duration, the impact and gravity of the infraction, the background of the offender, the offender's collaboration, the correction of the inappropriate conduct, to name a few. The financial impact was 4,750 euros (on average, 950 euros, per provider, including sanctions from 500 euros up to 1,500 euros), between 2016 and 2018. It should be noted that two of the five cases also included instructions issue, because the new regime does not exclude the application of soft law instruments. The payments below 1,000 euros result from voluntary payments, under the Regulatory Regime of Administrative Offences (Decree-Law no. 433/82, of October 27th, as amended by Decree-law no 244/95, of September 14th, and by the Law no n.º 109/2001, of December 24th).

An estimation of the potential financial impact of the new legal regime on health advertising practices is conducted, to explore to explore the consequences before and after this new legal framework. Given that all the offenders were legal entities, the estimation considered the fines applicable in those situations (fine from 1,000 euros up to 44,891.81 euros). Our estimation considered the minimum value (1,000 euros), given that we have not full information on the previous cases. In concrete terms, we are not able to verify *ex-post* the criterion established in Article 63 of the Decree-law no. 126/2014, that determine the specific sanctions applicable. If the previous cases (until 2015, listed in the table 2) were analysed within the new legal framework, it should represent a total amount collected of 13,000 euros, considering the 13 legal entities that made an improper use of the brand NHS and/or disseminate incorrect messages using the brand NHS.

Table 2. List of cases, by scope, between 2009 and 2015

Case	Scope	Consequences (date of the events)	Consequences under the new legal regime
ERS/005/2009 (Portuguese Health Regulation Authority, 2009a)	Undue use of the brand NHS	Instruction issuance	Not applicable
ERS/092/2009 (Portuguese Health Regulation Authority, 2009b)	Advertising + Undue use of the brand NHS	Order issue and instruction	Imposition of a fine from 1000 euros up to 44891.81 euros and potential application of an ancillary penalty
ERS/101/2009 (Portuguese Health Regulation Authority, 2009c)	Advertising + Undue use of the brand NHS	Instruction issuance	Imposition of a fine from 1000 euros up to 44891.81 euros and potential application of an ancillary penalty
ERS/049/2010	Advertising + Undue use of the brand NHS	Instruction issuance	Imposition of a fine from 1000 euros up to 44891.81 euros and potential application of an ancillary penalty
ERS/052/2010 (Portuguese Health Regulation Authority, 2010)	Advertising + Undue use of the brand NHS	Order issue and instruction	Imposition of a fine from 1000 euros up to 44891.81 euros and potential application of an ancillary penalty
ERS/123/2011 (Portuguese Health Regulation Authority, 2011)	Undue use of the brand NHS	Instruction issuance	Not applicable
ERS/034/2012 (Portuguese Health Regulation Authority, 2012)	Advertising	Instruction issuance	Imposition of a fine from 1000 euros up to 44891.81 euros and potential application of an ancillary penalty
ERS/040/2012 (Portuguese Health Regulation Authority, 2012b, p. 2)	Undue use of the brand NHS	Instruction issuance	Not applicable
ERS/036/2013 (Portuguese Health Regulation Authority, 2013b)	Undue use of the brand NHS	Instruction issuance directed to the private provider and recommendation directed to the Regional Health Administration	Not applicable
ERS/083/2013 (Portuguese Health Regulation Authority, 2013c)	Advertising	Order issue and instruction	Imposition of a fine from 1000 euros up to 44891.81 euros and potential application of an ancillary penalty
ERS/091/2013 (Portuguese Health Regulation Authority, 2013d)	Advertising	Order issue and instruction	Imposition of a fine from 1000 euros up to 44891.81 euros and potential application of an ancillary penalty
ERS/009/2014 (Portuguese Health Regulation Authority, 2014a)	Advertising + Undue use of the brand NHS	Instruction issuance	Imposition of a fine from 1000 euros up to 44891.81 euros and potential application of an ancillary penalty

continues on following page

Table 2. Continued

Case	Scope	Consequences (date of the events)	Consequences under the new legal regime
ERS/021/2014 (Portuguese Health Regulation Authority, 2014b)	Undue use of the brand NHS	Instruction issuance	Not applicable
ERS/051/2014 (Portuguese Health Regulation Authority, 2014c)	Advertising	Instruction issuance	Imposition of a fine from 1000 euros up to 44891.81 euros and potential application of an ancillary penalty
ERS/052/2014 (Portuguese Health Regulation Authority, 2014d)	Advertising + Undue use of the brand NHS	Instruction issuance	Imposition of a fine from 1000 euros up to 44891.81 euros and potential application of an ancillary penalty
ERS/001/2015 (Portuguese Health Regulation Authority, 2015a)	Undue use of the brand NHS	Order issue and instruction	Not applicable
ERS/014/2015 (Portuguese Health Regulation Authority, 2015b)	Undue use of the brand NHS	Order issue and instruction	Not applicable
ERS/021/2015 (Portuguese Health Regulation Authority, 2015c)	Undue use of the brand NHS	Instruction issuance	Not applicable
ERS/039/2015 (Portuguese Health Regulation Authority, 2015d)	Advertising	Instruction issuance	Imposition of a fine from 1000 euros up to 44891.81 euros and potential application of an ancillary penalty
ERS/042/2015 (Portuguese Health Regulation Authority, 2015e)	Undue use of the brand NHS	Order issue and instruction	Not applicable
ERS/043/2015 (Portuguese Health Regulation Authority, 2015f)	Advertising + Undue use of the brand NHS	Order issue and instruction	Imposition of a fine from 1000 euros up to 44891.81 euros and potential application of an ancillary penalty
ERS/067/2015 (Portuguese Health Regulation Authority, 2015g)	Advertising + Undue use of the brand NHS	Order issue and instruction	Imposition of a fine from 1000 euros up to 44891.81 euros and potential application of an ancillary penalty

Source: Elaborated by the authors using data from the Portuguese Health Regulation Authority.

Figure 3. Percentage of cases by scope
Source: Elaborated by the authors.

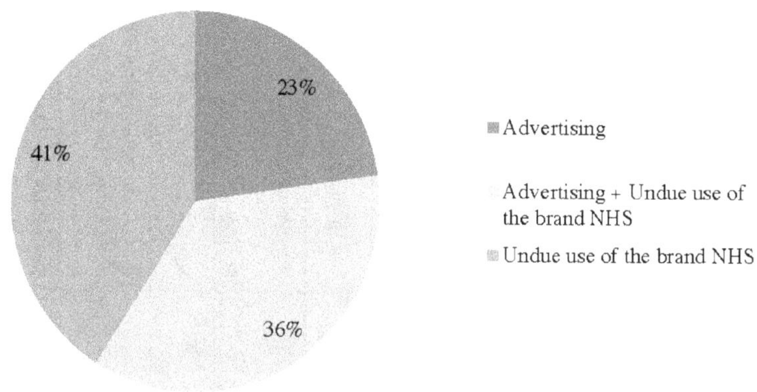

Figure 4. No. of cases per 10,000 registered complains, between 2015 and 2018
Source: Elaborated by the authors using data from the Portuguese Health Regulation Authority.

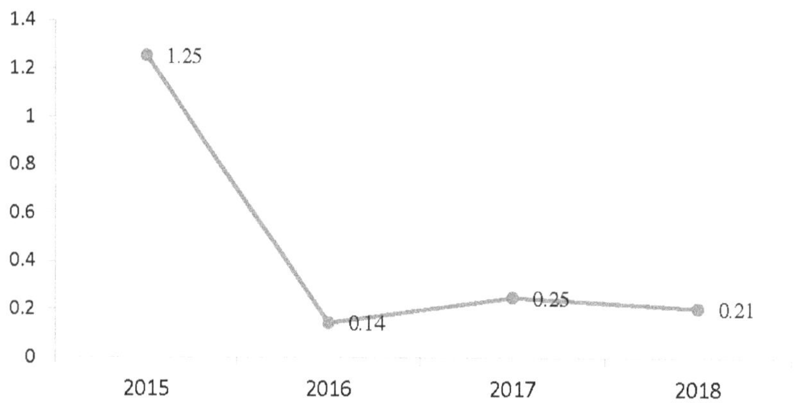

Table 3. List of cases, after 2016, and related consequences

Cases	Scope	Consequences
PCO/114/2016 (Portuguese Health Regulation Authority, 2016b)	Advertising	1500 euros sanction
PCO/160/2017 (Portuguese Health Regulation Authority, 2017)	Advertising	1000 euros santion
PCO/86/2017	Advertising + Undue use of the brand NHS	500 euros sanction
PCO/204/2018 (Portuguese Health Regulation Authority, 2018a)	Advertising	Intruction and 500 euros sanction
PCO/428/2018	Advertising	Instruction and 1250 euros sanction

Source: Elaborated by the authors using data from the Portuguese Health Regulation Authority.

FUTURE RESEARCH DIRECTIONS

Some limitations should be noted. There is a need to further analyse and quantify the financial impact for specific private providers using the brand NHS, to understand if the undue use of the brand NHS is financially rewarding.

This chapter includes an exploratory exercise on the potential impacts of the new legal regime in previous cases (before the Decree-Law no. 238/2015, of October 14th). However, we do not have full information on the context of those cases. For instance, we cannot conclude if the provider acted intentionally or with serious negligence, or unintentionally and without negligence. Then, we cannot estimate accurately and in monetary terms the real impact of the new legal regime. Moreover, the real consequences after the new regime are based on a reduced time horizon (we covered approximately only three years from its adoption). Further analyses will benefit from more years of evidence, after the effectiveness of the Decree-Law no. 238/2015, of October 14th.

In what concerns the cases presented, given that we used data available at the Portuguese Health Regulation Authority, this chapter does not account for: cases dismissed due to a lack of evidence (without instructions, orders or recommendations); or administrative infraction proceeding which had ended in acquittals due to a lack of evidence proving the infraction.

This chapter focused the consequences of the undue use of the brand NHS under the new legal regime on health advertising practices. However, some consequences may also arise from the application of the Portuguese Industrial Property Code, and these questions should be further discussed.

CONCLUSION

The brand NHS (*SNS Serviço Nacional de Saúde*) is a registered brand since May 2016, with name and logo registered. However, the NHS and its reputation go back at least to 1979 (Law no. 56/79, of September 15th). This brand has reputation and quality standards associated as well as specific rules concerning the access to healthcare services, under the concepts of universality and tending-towards-free access. When private providers act on behalf of the NHS (through a specific contract, namely 'conventions') the users recognize the brand NHS and expect to meet the standard that they associate with the brand. If the private providers use the brand NHS without legitimacy compromise the patients' rights, the brand reputation and the market competition.

The first main conclusion of this chapter is that the rigidity of the conventions' market could induce the undue use of the brand NHS. In concrete terms, in what refers to the slowness of the implementation of the new conventions' regime. The disloyal practices include the publicity of conventions by private providers that do not have any contract with the NHS, the incorrect use of a given convention, and the improper use of NHS name or logo, including misleading advertising.

This chapter included a presentation and discussion of the new legal regime on health advertising practices, introduced by the Decree-Law no. 238/2015, of October 14th. In sum, the new legal regime provides a hard law instrument that sets up a more rigid penalty framework than the previous law. Compared with the previous legal framework, mainly focused on soft law (recommendations, orders issue and instructions), the new legal regime on health advertising practices included the imposition of pecuniary sanctions that poses a financial burden on providers that use the brand NHS without legitimacy.

The Portuguese entity empowered to punish advertising practices and the undue use of conventions (the Portuguese Health Regulation Authority), registered and decided 22 cases of undue use of the brand NHS and advertising irregularities, between 2009 e 2015. Of those 22 cases reported 41% related to both misleading advertising practices and undue use of the brand NHS.

After 2016, considering the changes introduced by the Decree-Law no. 238/2015, of October 14th and the Portuguese Health Regulation Authority's Regulation no. 1058/2016, of November 24th, it was observed a decrease in the number of cases (5 between 2016 and 2018, against 7 in 2015). The application of a hard law framework is also evidenced by the increased number of administrative infractions versus instructions/orders, which suggests this could be a more effective management tool to protect brand reputation.

The financial burden after the new regime was 4,750 euros (including sanctions that vary from 500 euros up to 1,500 euros). If the new legal regime on health advertising practices was applied to the previous cases it should represent a total amount collected of 13,000 euros, between 2008 and 2015. This very small impact should not justify the tendency of reduction in the number of cases. The new regime discourages disloyal practices using the brand NHS possible due to the negative impact on the image of the healthcare provider under an administrative offence process, rather than the financial risk involved. Moreover, the ancillary sanctions set out in the Decree-Law no. 238/2015, of October 14th, could also justify the observed reduction of cases.

With think, some lessons can be learned from the Portuguese context. Managers in the health sector should not neglect the importance of the existing legal regime on brand identity and reputation. However, Portugal can also increase its NHS brand equity learning from other countries with similar NHS, such as the English NHS. The English NHS Identity includes specific guidelines and a strong image. All the NHS services should be clearly branded NHS, should adhere to the NHS Identity guidelines and be branded with their NHS organisational logo, regardless of who the provider is (NHS England, 2020). In sum, NHS brand management should combine distinct methods to reinforce brand reputation and patients' trust in NHS' services.

REFERENCES

Almeida, Á. S. (2017). The role of private non-profit healthcare organizations in NHS systems: Implications for the Portuguese hospital devolution program. *Health Policy (Amsterdam)*, *121*(6), 699–707. doi:10.1016/j.healthpol.2017.03.016 PMID:28433325

Barros, P. P. (2010). As parcerias público-privadas na saúde em Portugal [Health PublicPrivate Partnerships in Portugal]. In J. Simões (Ed.), 30 Anos do Serviço Nacional de Saúde – Um percurso comentado [30 Years of National Health Service – A commented pathway] (pp. 519–560). Almedina.

Barros, P. P. (2016). Public-private partnerships. In R. M. Scheffler (Ed.), *World Scientific handbook of global health economics and public policy*. World Scientific. doi:10.1142/9789813140530_0009

Barros, P. P., Machado, S., & Simões, J. (2011). Portugal: Health system review. *Health Systems in Transition*, *13*(4), 1–156. PMID:22222781

Bramão, M. P., & Costa, A. (2003). *Código da publicidade: Anotado e comentado*. Vida Económica.

Central Administration of the Health System. (2016). *Circular Normativa n.º 8/2016. Alteração do regulamento de aplicação de Taxas Moderadoras* [Normative Circular No. 8/2016. Changes in application rules for user charges]. Central Administration of the Health System. http://www.acss. min-saude. pt/circulares/Circular_Normativa/2016/Circular_Normativa_8_2016.pdf

Chahal, H., & Bala, M. (2012). Significant components of service brand equity in healthcare sector. *International Journal of Health Care Quality Assurance*, *25*(4), 343–362. doi:10.1108/09526861211221518 PMID:22755484

Chaves, R. M. (2005). *Regime jurídico da publicidade*. Almedina.

Dixon, A. (1999). *Health Care Systems in Transition—Portugal*. European Observatory on Health Care Systems.

Domingues, M. E. (2019). *40 Anos do SNS*. Ministerio da Saúde.

Erbay, E., & Esatoglu, A. (2017). Reputation Management in Healthcare. In Developments in Health Sciences (pp. 591–610). St. Kliment Ohridski University Press.

Espanha, R., & Ávila, P. (2016). Health Literacy Survey Portugal: A Contribution for the Knowledge on Health and Communications. *Procedia Computer Science*, *100*, 1033–1041. doi:10.1016/j.procs.2016.09.277

European Commission. (2015). *Competition among health care providers: Investigating policy options in the European Union*. Publications Office. https://data.europa.eu/doi/10.2875/867590

Grytten, J., & Sorensen, R. (2000). Competition and dental services. *Health Economics*, *9*(5), 447–461. doi:10.1002/1099-1050(200007)9:5<447::AID-HEC529>3.0.CO;2-A PMID:10903544

Health Regulation Authority. (2017). *Literacia em direitos dos utentes de cuidados de saúde* [Literacy on patients' rights in health care]. Health Regulation Authority. https://www.ers.pt/pages/171?news_id=1688

Heding, T., Knudtzen, C. F., & Bjerre, M. (2009). *Brand management: Research, theory and practice*. Routledge.

Kemp, E., Jillapalli, R., & Becerra, E. (2014). Healthcare branding: Developing emotionally based consumer brand relationships. *Journal of Services Marketing*, *28*(2), 126–137. doi:10.1108/JSM-08-2012-0157

Lamiraud, K. (2014). Switching Costs in Competitive Health Insurance Markets. In *Encyclopedia of Health Economics* (pp. 375–381). Elsevier. doi:10.1016/B978-0-12-375678-7.01312-2

NHS England. (2020). *NHS Identity Guidelines*. https://www.england.nhs.uk/nhsidentity/

Nunes, A. M., & Ferreira, D. C. (2019). Reforms in the Portuguese health care sector: Challenges and proposals. *The International Journal of Health Planning and Management*, *34*(1), e21–e33. doi:10.1002/hpm.2695 PMID:30370564

OECD. (1998). *OECD Economic Surveys: Portugal 1998*. OECD. https://www.oecd-ilibrary.org/economics/oecd-economic-surveys-portugal-1998_eco_surveys-prt-1998-en

OECD. (2013). *Waiting Time Policies in the Health Sector: What Works?* (L. Siciliani, M. Borowitz, & V. Moran, Eds.). OECD. https://www.oecd-ilibrary.org/social-issues-migration-health/waiting-times-for-elective-surgery-what-works_9789264179080-en

Pedro, A. R., Amaral, O., & Escoval, A. (2016). Literacia em saúde, dos dados à ação: Tradução, validação e aplicação do European Health Literacy Survey em Portugal. *Revista Portuguesa de Saude Publica*, *34*(3), 259–275. doi:10.1016/j.rpsp.2016.07.002

Phillips-Salimi, C. R., Haase, J. E., & Kooken, W. C. (2012). Connectedness in the context of patient-provider relationships: A concept analysis: Connectedness. *Journal of Advanced Nursing*, *68*(1), 230–245. doi:10.1111/j.1365-2648.2011.05763.x PMID:21771040

PORDATA. (2018). *Fundação Francisco Manuel dos Santos*. http://www.pordata.pt/en/Portugal

Portuguese Health Regulation Authority. (2006). *Avaliação do Modelo de Celebração de Convenções pelo SNS* [Assessment of the NHS contracting model]. Portuguese Health Regulation Authority.

Portuguese Health Regulation Authority. (2008). *Estudo sobre as Convenções em 2008* [Study on NHS coventions in 2008]. Portuguese Health Regulation Authority.

Portuguese Health Regulation Authority. (2009a). *ERS/005/2009*. https://www.ers.pt/uploads/writer_file/document/273/Deliberacao_ERS-005-09_-Hosp_Misericordia_de_Paredes.pdf

Portuguese Health Regulation Authority. (2009b). *ERS/092/2009*. https://www.ers.pt/uploads/writer_file/document/244/ERS_092_09.pdf

Portuguese Health Regulation Authority. (2009c). *ERS/101/2009*. https://www.ers.pt/uploads/writer_file/document/235/ERS_101_09.pdf

Portuguese Health Regulation Authority. (2010). *ERS/052/2010*. https://www.ers.pt/uploads/writer_file/document/234/ERS_052_10.pdf

Portuguese Health Regulation Authority. (2011). *ERS/123/2011*. https://www.ers.pt/pages/484?news_id=674

Portuguese Health Regulation Authority. (2012). *ERS/034/2012*. https://www.ers.pt/uploads/writer_file/document/821/ERS_034_12.pdf

Portuguese Health Regulation Authority. (2013a). *Acesso, Concorrência e Qualidade no Sector Convencionado com o SNS: Análises Clínicas, Diálise, Medicina Física e Reabilitação e Radiologia* [Access, competition and quality issues in the provision of services by private providers to the National Health Service: Clinical Pathology, Dialysis, Physical Medicine and Rehabilitation and Radiology]. Portuguese Health Regulation Authority.

Portuguese Health Regulation Authority. (2013b). *ERS/036/2013*. https://www.ers.pt/uploads/writer_file/document/1044/ERS_36_13.pdf

Portuguese Health Regulation Authority. (2013c). *ERS/083/2013*. https://www.ers.pt/uploads/writer_file/document/1040/ERS_083_13.pdf

Portuguese Health Regulation Authority. (2013d). *ERS/091/2013*. https://www.ers.pt/uploads/writer_file/document/989/ERS_091_13__TM__.pdf

Portuguese Health Regulation Authority. (2013e). *O novo regime jurídico das Taxas Moderadoras* [The New Legal Framework of Moderating Fees]. Author.

Portuguese Health Regulation Authority. (2014a). *ERS/009/2014*. https://www.ers.pt/uploads/writer_file/document/1583/Publica__o_-_vers_o_n_o_confidencial_-_ERS_009_14.pdf

Portuguese Health Regulation Authority. (2014b). *ERS/021/2014*. https://www.ers.pt/uploads/writer_file/document/1454/Publica__o_-_vers_o_n_o_confidencial_-_ERS_021_14.pdf

Portuguese Health Regulation Authority. (2014c). *ERS/051/2014*. https://www.ers.pt/uploads/writer_file/document/1575/Publica__o_-_vers_o_n_o_confidencial_-_ERS_051_14.pdf

Portuguese Health Regulation Authority. (2014d). *ERS/052/2014*. https://www.ers.pt/uploads/document/file/8794/Publica__o_-_vers_o_n_o_confidencial_-_ERS_052_14.pdf

Portuguese Health Regulation Authority. (2014e, September 16). *Recomendação n.º 1/2014—Recomendação da ERS relativa a práticas publicitárias dos prestadores de cuidados de saúde*. https://www.ers.pt/pt/regula%C3%A7%C3%A3o/recomenda%C3%A7%C3%B5es/hist%C3%B3rico/hist%C3%B3rico/recomendacao-n%C2%BA-12014-recomendacao-da-ers-relativa-a-praticas-publicitarias-dos-prestadores-de-cuidados-de-saude/

Portuguese Health Regulation Authority. (2015a). *ERS/001/2015*. https://www.ers.pt/uploads/writer_file/document/1459/Publica__o_-_vers_o_n_o_confidencial_-_ERS_001_15.pdf

Portuguese Health Regulation Authority. (2015b). *ERS/014/2015*. https://www.ers.pt/uploads/writer_file/document/1585/Publica__o_-_vers_o_n_o_confidencial_-_ERS_014_15.pdf

Portuguese Health Regulation Authority. (2015c). *ERS/021/2015*. https://www.ers.pt/uploads/document/file/8797/Publica__o_-_vers_o_n_o_confidencial_-_ERS_021_15.pdf

Portuguese Health Regulation Authority. (2015d). *ERS/039/2015*. https://www.ers.pt/uploads/document/file/8798/Publica__o_-_vers_o_n_o_confidencial_-_ERS_039_15.pdf

Portuguese Health Regulation Authority. (2015e). *ERS/042/2015*. https://www.ers.pt/uploads/document/file/8793/Publica__o_-_vers_o_n_o_confidencial_-_ERS_042_15.pdf

Portuguese Health Regulation Authority. (2015f). *ERS/043/2015*. https://www.ers.pt/uploads/document/file/9243/Vers_oPublica__o_ERS-43-2015.pdf

Portuguese Health Regulation Authority. (2015g). *ERS/067/2015*. https://www.ers.pt/uploads/document/file/9245/Vers_oPublica__o_ERS-67-2015.pdf

Portuguese Health Regulation Authority. (2016a). *Estudo de avaliação das parcerias público-privadas na saúde* [Assessment of public-private partnerships in the health sector]. Portuguese Health Regulation Authority.

Portuguese Health Regulation Authority. (2016b). *PCO/114/2016*. https://www.ers.pt/pages/123?news_id=1647

Portuguese Health Regulation Authority. (2016c). *Relatório do Sistema de Gestão de Reclamações—Síntese descritiva de 2015*. Health Regulation Authority. https://www.ers.pt/uploads/writer_file/document/1794/Relat_rio_RECS_2015.pdf

Portuguese Health Regulation Authority. (2017). *PCO/160/2017*. https://www.ers.pt/pages/123?news_id=2307

Portuguese Health Regulation Authority. (2018a). *PCO/204/2018*. https://www.ers.pt/pages/123?news_id=2307

Portuguese Health Regulation Authority. (2018b). *PCO/428/2018*. https://www.ers.pt/pages/123?news_id=2329

Portuguese Health Regulation Authority (ERS). (2014). *Gestão da Lista de Inscritos para Cirurgia no SNS* [Management system of the waiting list for surgery in the NHS]. Portuguese Health Regulation Authority.

Portuguese Ministry of Health. (2017). *Acesso a cuidados de saúde nos estabelecimentos do SNS e entidades convencionadas*. Author.

Seiler, S. (2013). The impact of search costs on consumer behavior: A dynamic approach. *Quantitative Marketing and Economics*, *11*(2), 155–203. doi:10.100711129-012-9126-7

Simões, J. (2010). *30 anos do Serviço Nacional de Saúde: Um percurso comentado*. Almedina.

Simões, J., Augusto, G., Fronteira, I., & Hernández-Quevedo, C. (2017). Portugal: Health system review. *Health Systems in Transition*, *19*(2), 1–184. PMID:28485714

Strombom, B. A., Buchmueller, T. C., & Feldstein, P. J. (2002). Switching costs, price sensitivity and health plan choice. *Journal of Health Economics*, *21*(1), 89–116. doi:10.1016/S0167-6296(01)00124-2 PMID:11845927

Trong Tuan, L. (2014). Clinical governance, corporate social responsibility, health service quality, and brand equity. *Clinical Governance: An International Journal*, *19*(3), 215–234. doi:10.1108/CGIJ-02-2014-0007

WHO. (2018). *Health System Review—Portugal. Phase 1 Final Report*. WHO.

Chapter 10
A New Customer Brand Engagement Framework in Social Media:
The Case of Beauti Portugal SEM Healthcare

Amélia Maria Pinto da Cunha Brandão
https://orcid.org/0000-0003-2751-7272
Faculdade de Economia, Universidade do Porto, Portugal

André Filipe Rei Lopes
Faculdade de Economia, Universidade do Porto, Portugal

Paula Rodrigues
Lusíada University of Porto, Portugal

ABSTRACT

Brand researchers and practitioners acknowledge that brands have the power to create emotional relationships between customers and enterprises. Moreover, it is known that brands can sometimes reflect the strategic vision of a firm. The aim of this chapter is to capture the creation of an identity for a new brand and to create a framework to better manage customer brand engagement in social media. To the best of this author's knowledge, this research creates a new framework that allows managers better handling their social media strategy regarding engagement. This study contributes to the lack of studies regarding brand management in SMEs, found by Krake, Wong and Merrilees, and Merrilees, and more particularly, it addresses Ojasalo et al.'s gap regarding the few literature research about brand management in SMEs. Moreover, it provides some understanding of customer brand engagement evidenced through social media, which, according to Wallace et al., continues to present challenges.

DOI: 10.4018/978-1-7998-3034-4.ch010

INTRODUCTION

The strategic management of the brand is highly aligned with the long term strategy of a firm (Kapferer, 2008; Aaker & McLoughin, 2010). "Today branding is such as strong force that hardly anything goes unbranded" (Kotler & Keller, 2011, p.261). Brands provide value to the customer and are often considered in the customer's buying process with substantial relevance (Kapferer, 2008). Furthermore, they are also value generators to all stakeholders and produce benefits internally in the firm (i.e the role of the staff) (Chernatony, 2010). Managing brands implies also building it strongly, since it produces a number of marketing advantages, enabling companies to be distinguished from competitors (Hoeffler & Keller, 2002). The principal focus of branding is to build successful brands that can be distinguished from the competitor, be admired, establish a relationship with target customers and, if possible, engage them through loyalty (Aaker, 1996; Keller, 2003).

The literature review is scarce about branding in SMEs, especially in the software business (Koporcic, 2020; Ojasalo et al., 2008; Odoom, Narteh & Boateng, 2017; M'zungu, Merreles & Miller, 2019). Branding in SME's is relatively new and is always obfuscated by daily tasks, as Krake (2005) highlights. And despite attracting academic attention in recent years, evidence suggest that studies on branding in the context of SMEs continue to be a gap in marketing literature (Odoom, Narteh & Boateng, 2017; M'zungu, Merreles & Miller, 2019). In this case study, we will analyze the influence of consumer brand engagement and social media in an online platform for beaty & wellness that operates with Business-to-Business (B2B) and Business-to-Consumer (B2C) type of activity.

The consideration of brand-consumer relationships is fast infiltrating the branding vernacular (Patterson & O'Malley, 2006). Customer brand engagement acknowledges the cognitive, emotional and behavioral dimensions of those relationships (Brodie et al., 2011; Hollebeek, 2011; Gambetti et al., 2012; Bilro & Loureiro, 2020). Social media affect brand management because consumers have become pivotal authors of brand stories (Gensler et al., 2013). Thus, social media with its ability to facilitate relationships may help realize the promise of the marketing concept, market orientation, and relationship marketing by providing the tools to better satisfy customers and build customer engagement (Sashi, 2012). Additionally, tactics and engagement are top areas marketers want to master (Stelzner, 2014). Not less important, as a brand's social network now consists of many voluntary connections from consumers, the authenticity of a brand's social identity is affected. At the same time it adds complexity to the management of brand identity (Naylor et al., 2012).

The aim of this chapter is to capture the creation of a framework for better manage customer brand engagement in social media. This investigation bridges the academia gap in the development of a framework which allows managers better handling their social media strategy regarding engagement. This chapter offers suggestions for managers seeking to enhance brand engagement through social media, embracing all channels and suggesting practices for effective social media management. The object of chapter is Beauti, a Small-Medium Enterprise (SME) technologic software product provider that is currently in the first steps of building its own brand.

This chapter contributes to the lack of studies regarding brand management in SMEs, found by Krake (2005), Wong and Merrilees (2005) and Merrilees (2007), and more particularly, it addresses Ojasalo's et al. (2008) gap regarding the few existing literature about brand management in software SMEs. Moreover, it provides some understanding of customer brand engagement evidenced through social media, which, according to Wallace et al. (2014) continues to present challenges, and take a lot of importance in SMEs.

Therefore, the challenge of this investigation lies in investigate these two research questions:

Q1: How is Beauti Portugal brand being managed?
Q2: How can Beauti.pt best manage and increase customer brand engagement?

BRAND MANAGEMENT: A LITERATURE REVIEW

Brand Management in SMEs

Despite the fact that there is not a universally standard definition of SMEs, the mainstream and more quoted one is provided by the European Commission, which considers as most determining factors the number of employees and either turnover or balance sheet total. Brand Management alongside with branding in SMEs, is at a low level of consciousness for most new entrepreneurs and even existing SMEs businesses (Merrilees, 2007). It seems to be a generalized idea that researchers overlooked the chapter of brand management, brand building and branding in SMEs even though that a considerable number of academic and empirical studies have been directed toward entrepreneurship, SMEs and marketing communication in new ventures. (Abimbola, 2001; Krake, 2005; Wong & Merrilees, 2005; Merrilees, 2007; Berthon et al., 2008; Spence & Essoussi, 2010; Bresciani & Eppler, 2010; Baumgarth, 2010; Roy & Banerjee, 2012; Asamoah, 2014). It is surprising since in most developed and developing economies, performance of small and medium sized companies is critical for economic and social development as these firms' types are effective in providing productive employment and earning opportunities. (Katz et al., 2000).

The first suggestions for building a strong brand in SMEs were addressed by Keller (2003), advocated that SMEs should concentrate on building one or two strong brands and they should be driven by creatively developed marketing programs on one or two brand associations, to serve as the source of brand equity. Moreover, some guidelines for the creation of a strong SME brand were advanced (Krake, 2005). Most of the SMEs are as well, product centered. The "funnel" model for the role of brand management in *SMEs* highlighted the factors affecting the role of brand management in SMEs (Krake, 2005).

Wong and Merrilees (2005), driven by the Urde's (1999) definition of brand orientation, explored this concept applied to the Small Mid-Size Enterprises. They found that SMEs have a narrow interpretation of what branding is, being limited to the brand name and/or logo. More researchers compelled the same line of thought of Krake's (2005) report: SMEs devote most of their time to daily routine and business pitching (Wong & Merrilees, 2005). They suggested that both SMEs and Large Organizations (LOs) apostles the idea of branding but the ways in which are carried out are different. Moreover, a branding-archetype ladder model was proposed, including three ladders:

Minimalist Brand Orientation – short-term focused based on day-to-day tasks or production approach, as opposed to marketing and brand orientation;

Embryonic Brand Orientation – Awareness of competitive advantage and positioning but the brand seems to be more an implicit, optional part of what they do business, and not necessarily critical for business success;

Integrated Brand Orientation - The brand is a more important and active part of the marketing strategy (Wong & Merrilees, 2005). Both Krake (2005) and Wong and Merrilees (2005) acknowledge that the main SMEs' problems are a lack of financial resources, managerial skills, information and knowledge, technology, processes and structures.

Berthon et al. (2008) contends that even with constrained budgets, SME marketers can creatively manage and leverage the full potential of their brands, corroborating with Krake (2005) and Wong and Merrilees (2005). Moreover, young companies should not be forced to compare their branding strategies to multinational firms (Bresciani & Eppler, 2010), in line with Wong and Mirrelees (2005) and Berthon et al. (2008). The literature review suggests a framework and key guidelines for start-up branding (Bresciani & Eppler, 2010) and recognize and emphasize the importance of online branding in their approach. Firms have widely different approaches to online branding although digital branding can be a potentially very powerful tool for businesses with low budget (Bresciani & Eppler, 2010). The internet offers a vast number of innovative branding opportunities especially suitable for start-ups, due to their relatively low cost and wide reach (Bresciani & Eppler, 2010). Internet advertising can offer a great return because it is a highly targeted form of advertising, but they can be expensive if they are not continuously monitored by competent staff (Bresciani & Eppler, 2010). Their observations regarding the absence of co-branding and partnerships are consistent previous findings in SMEs (Krake, 2005; Ojasalo et al., 2008). Some companies have created more than one brand and it is a conscious choice, similarly to what Krake (2005) has found, and partially in contrast with Keller's (2003) theoretical guidelines. New ventures should, contrary to large organizations, develop more creative, innovate and unconventional branding activities (Keller, 2003; Ojasalo et al., 2008; Bresciani & Eppler, 2010). Moreover, it can also address the problem found by Asamoah (2014) that the dominant marketing approach that has been used by SMEs over the years strongly focuses on product and price. Hence, brands in SMEs context are the continuation of the entrepreneur's vision, beliefs and values.

Brand Building in Software SMEs

The research literature on branding of software products is very scarce (Osajalo et al., 2008). Ulkuniemi and Helander (2005) examined marketing challenges in the special context of the software component business.

Moreover, some authors identified two major components of brand equity, for banking business application software: perceived value and trust (Srivastava & Mookerjee's, 2004). Others, examined the assets and capabilities of software companies from the perspectives of business models and value-creating networks (Rajala & Westerlund, 2004) concluding that brand is a key asset.

The special characteristics of brand building in software SMEs deserved research (Ojasalo et al., 2008). Four larger themes emerged:

(i) Goals and perceived benefits of brand building,
(ii) *Resources in brand*
(iii) *Internal and external cooperation in brand* and
(iv) *Means and communication in brand.*

Many of the SMEs feel that for a small company it is not possible to build both a company brand and a product brand separately. Instead, the best choice is to use the company name as the product line's "family name" and name the individual products by combining the "family name" (i.e. the company name) with a product-specific extension.

The need to maintain a certain level of "brand flexibility" was also recognized (Osajalo et al., 2008). Value-based brand building was seen to be a one helpful tool in this challenge.

Customer Brand Engagement: A Literature Review

Recently, researchers looked to explain brand engagement offering conceptual frameworks and a variety of theories (Brodie et al., 2011; Hollebeek, 2011; Gambetti et al., 2012; Brodie et al., 2013; ; Zhang, Guo, Hu, & Liu, 2017; Harrigan, Evers, Miles, & Daly, 2017; Dessart, Veloutsou & Morgan-Thomas, 2015).

The majority of these frameworks offer perspectives on how the components comprising the engagement concept relate to each other. These authors emphasize that the most useful engagement definitions acknowledge the cognitive, emotional and behavioral dimensions of the concept. For example, Hollebeek (2011) defines customer brand engagement (CBE) as "the level of a customer's cognitive, emotional, and behavioral investment in specific brand interactions" whereas Gambetti, Graffigna and Biraghi (2012) regards brand engagement as a composite of experimental and social dimensions. Gambetti et al. (2012, p. 681) define consumer brand engagement as the "interaction, participation, dialogue, co-creation, and sharing of brand-related values and content".

Customer Brand Engagement in Social Media

The typical marketing approach of mass production, developing creative mass advertising, selling products and ensuring customers are satisfied is not enough to create engaged customers (Roberts & Alpert, 2010). The interactive nature of social media has excited practitioners with its potential to better serve customers and satisfy their needs (Sashi, 2012). Engaged customers are likely to recommend products to others, e.g. by word-of-mouth, blogs, social networking, comments on web sites, etc., and even add value by providing user-generated content (Sashi, 2012). Customer engagement expands the traditional role played by customers and includes them in the value-adding process (Sashi, 2012; Dessart, Veloutsou & Morgan-Thomas, 2016).

Social media platforms should be seen as a social customer relationship management tool that enables enterprises to engage and build relationships with their consumers (Baumöl, Hollebeek & Jung, 2016; Malthouse et al., 2013; Simon & Tossan, 2018; Vickers, 2015).

Social media affect brand management because consumers have become pivotal authors of brand stories (Gensler et al., 2013; Malthouse et al., 2013). Both firm-generated and consumer-generated brand stories are told through a plethora of communication channels in a dynamic and evolving process (Gensler et al., 2013; Vickers, 2015). A network-oriented approach to branding implies that a consumer's relationship with a brand now extends into the consumer's social connections, whether it is the consumer influencing or being influenced by such social connections about the brand (Gensler et al., 2013).

There is no definitive typology of different types of social media (Kaplan & Haenlein, 2010), but it is common to differentiate among social networking (e.g. Facebook), professional networking (e.g. LinkedIn), video-sharing (e.g. YouTube), picture sharing (e.g. Flickr), social bookmarking (e.g. Delicious, Digg), social sharing of knowledge (e.g. Wikipedia), microblogging (e.g. Twitter), blogs (e.g. Blogger), and user forums (Tsimonis & Dimitriadis, 2014). The common characteristic is that these social media allow individuals and entrepreneurs to engage in social interactions, in a way and on a scale that were not possible before (Fischer & Reuber, 2011).

Consumer's online brand-related activities (COBRAs) are imperative for companies to effectively anticipate and direct consumers in a way that is in sync with business goals. (Muntinga et al., 2011). This COBRA concept can be seen as a behavioral construct that provides a unifying framework to think about consumer activity pertaining to brand-related content on social media platforms (Muntinga et al.,

2011). A set of levels of online brand-related activeness- *consuming*, *contributing* and *creating* COBRA type was typified. Entertainment as a major influencer of engagement was supported by Gummerus et al. (2012) who states that being entertained in the community is more important for the brand relationship outcome than the social activities.

Literature review suggest the use of the following formulas (Cvijikj & Michahelles, 2013) to measure the engagement on Facebook:

$$\text{FeedbackRate} = \frac{\#Likes + \#Comments}{\#Impressions}$$

$$\text{LikesRate} = \frac{\#Likes}{\#Fans\ on\ the\ day\ of\ posting}.$$

$$\text{mmentsRate} = \frac{\#Comments}{\#Fans\ on\ the\ day\ of\ posting}$$

$$\text{ShareRate} = \frac{\#Shares}{\#Fans\ on\ the\ day\ of\ posting}$$

Interaction Duration = Time of last Interaction – Time of post creation

On Facebook, the number of "likes", shares, or comments a brand's page receives is a manifest variable for brand engagement (Chauhan & Pillai, 2013; Hoffman & Fodor, 2010; Malhotra et al., 2013; Dessart, Aldás-Manzano, & Veloutsou, 2019). Consumers who select "like" for a brand may do to allow that brand to express their ideal or actual selves (Ahuvia, 2005) whereas some consumers choose brands to express a self that is not supported in their material world, since social networks allow consumers to present an "ideal self" (Schau & Gilly, 2003).

The brand engagement was explored in the literature review by eliciting the views on Facebook fans, and examining the extent to which those brands "liked" are socially self-expressive, or inner self-expressive, and the outcomes of this relationship for brand love and word-of-mouth (WOM) (Wallace et al., 2014).

The brand social network relationship quality will influence the overall brand relationship quality, which, consequently, will increase WOM (positive or negative) and the willingness to pay a premium price (Park & Kim, 2014). Previous researchers, developed and validated the customer brand engagement in specific social media settings and concluded that while consumer brand 'involvement' acts as a CBE antecedent, consumer 'self-brand connection' and 'brand usage intent' represent key CBE consequences (Hollebeek et al., 2014).

Content Marketing

Content marketing is a technique of creating and distributing relevant and valuable content to attract, acquire, and engage a clearly defined and understood target audience-with the objective of driving profitable customer action (Kho, 2014). Content marketing is a broad term that applies to everything from company newsletters and white papers, to blogs and podcasts, to virtual events, mobile apps and even consumer generated videos (Kirsten, 2012). The aim of this marketing tactic is to create and disseminate content that will engage customers and potential customers by offering them something of value (Kirsten, 2012). Ideally, the content should be valuable and engaging enough for customers that they're motivated to share it with their peers, ultimately helping to spread the marketing message and build brand awareness (Kirsten, 2012). Content marketing is important for optimal engagement and better business results (Petouhoff, 2013). Additionally, delivering relevant content will be the basis for good Searching Engine Optimization (SEO) (Kho, 2014).

Content marketing objectives must form part of a defined content strategy (Holliman & Rowley, 2014). The key objectives for content marketing are: brand awareness or reinforcement; lead conversion and nurturing; customer conversion; customer service; customer upsell and passionate subscribers (Rose & Pullizzi, 2011). To enhance trust, a content marketing strategy must shared values, interdependence, quality communication and non-opportunistic behavior (Peppers & Rogers, 2011).

Nevertheless, content marketing brand's approach to engage its customers provides a method to enrich interactions with customers at every single stage of their buying journey (Robert, 2014). Moreover, Holliman and Rowley (2014, p. 20) define digital content marketing (DCM) as "the activity associated with creating, communicating, distributing, and exchanging digital content that has value for customers, clients, partners, and the firm and its brands."

Companies with a strategy for social marketing are clearly focused on engaging customers and realize this will require increasing their efforts to reach more customers with timely and relevant content (Ascend2, 2013). Therefore, the creation and sharing of content must be prioritized.

Both Kirsten (2012) and the Content Marketing Institute (2013) provide tips and advice to achieve success and produce better marketing. It is highlighted that without a content strategy, social media will fail, the content should be short and entertaining and marketers should not forget to be helpful. However, it is important to acknowledge that the value of digital content is contextual and such that its value in use by different users on specific occasions is difficult to predict in advance (Rowley, 2008).

METHODOLOGY

The methodology inherent to this investigation is a case chapter. A case chapter allows an investigation to retain the holistic and meaningful characteristics of real-live events, such organizational and managerial processes (Yin, 2009). Single case studies, like the presented one, have been used frequently (Dyer & Wilkins, 1991). According to Grinder et al. (2010), a single industry chapter is beneficial if the industry provides a rich field of exploration into entrepreneurial practices

Phases and Stages of the Project

The aim of this investigation is to create a framework for better manage and increase, customer brand engagement in social media (see Fig. 1).

Figure 1. Stages of the Project and Methodology adopted

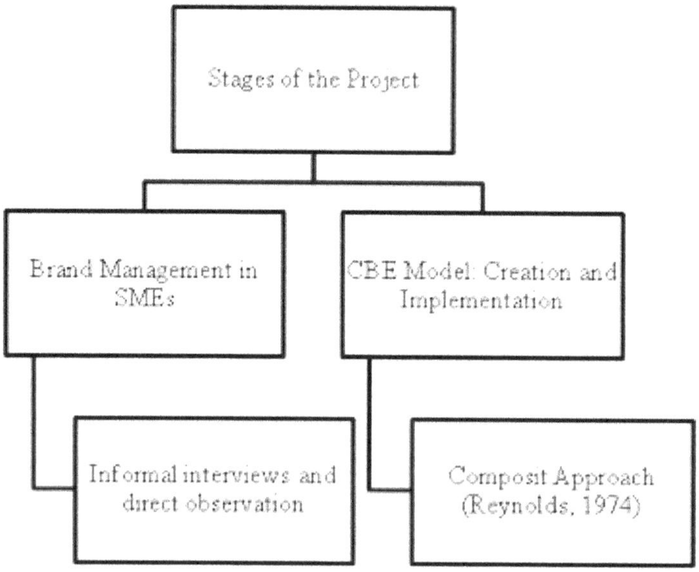

Data Collected

Secondary data was collected from Beauti's internal documents (reports, agendas and meetings) and, archival documents (online databases).

Concerning primary data, informal interviews (by e-mail) with different levels of staff and direct participation and observation. They weren't aware of which ones answer by the time they were interviewed. The multiple sources of evidence, their objectives and the interveners are synthesized in the following table 1.

Table 1. Data Collected synthesized

Source	Interveners/Place	Objective/Evidence
Documentation	Existing reports, agendas, meetings, company diagnosis	Importance of brand management in strategic decisions, Beauti's social media presence and objectives
Direct Observation	Beauti's offices - UPTEC	Importance of brand management in daily tasks
Participant Observation	Beauti's offices - UPTEC	Creation and Implementation of CBE Model
Archival Documents	Online Databases	Characterization of the Portuguese market, client profiles, targets, potential clients, social media management
Informal Interviews	All staff members (managing partner and two collaborators)/Beauti's offices - UPTEC	Perception of the importance of brand management, Beauti's perceived values, beliefs, vision, objectives, value propositions, positioning, brand essence, alignment between staff members' answers.

Source: Adapted from Mota (2014)

The Case Beauti Portugal

Beauti Portugal is an online destination for beauty & wellness professionals and clients based in Porto, Portugal (www.beauti.pt). Founded in 2013 by four entrepreneurs, this online platform operates with Business-to-Business and Business –to-Consumer type of activity. The core business attends to booking beauty salons via internet 24/7, according to the establishment and professional preferred or even service provider most adequate to consumer needs. In order for this work-flow to happen, Beauti offers, at the same time, tools to beauty & wellness professionals to grow and manage their business. Management and marketing software tools are offered, as well as, a network community between clients and consumers concerning the newest fashion trends (photos, videos and news). The business model relies on a subscription fee paid by the professionals or beauty salons meanwhile the process of booking for the consumers is free from charges.

Despite being launched only in October 2014, having a good amount of prospects and potential clients will fuel growth. Beauti is forecasted to reach the adequate amount of revenues in order to be financially stable in Portugal and promote an internationalization process in approximately one year.

Regarding the competitors, all Beauti's similar software product providers are based overseas, especially in USA or UK markets, since it was on those markets that online booking for beauty and wellness appeared. The strongest ones are Styleseat.com, Vagaro.com and Wahanda.com. In Portugal, there is only one serious competitor that is also in the first steps of building its business, named Bucmi.com. This Spanish based SME endorse the view "change is good" in a blog for users with discounts, trends and tips regarding the fashion and wellness industry. They charge a subscription fee alongside a commission per booking from 3% to 9% of the service's price. "La revolución de belleza y bienestar", as they advocate, is already possible in Portugal and in more than 1000 saloons across various Spanish cities.

Beauti's strategy is to target the "First Movers or Innovators" regarding the transactions via internet, and the "Trendy" ones concerning the beauty and wellness industry. This particular target can be analyzed with more detail: In the B2C segment, Beauti targets trendy first movers, more particularly young adults who are now initiating their professional careers and do not neglect their looks and their physical (and consequently physiologic) well-being. On the other hand, in the B2B segment, Beauti looks for salons and professionals who aren't afraid of taking risks and actually are willing to give up their traditional management system, for a new one, more developed and complex, which includes marketing tools and forward thinking.

RESULTS AND DISCUSSION

This point will answer the first research question "*How is Beauti Portugal brand being managed?*" Informal interviews and direct observation of the company's activities were the support to the results here discussed. Most of the results are due to the operational activities that the company developed so far, and their connection to the importance of brand management in small-medium enterprises.

The first thing to note is that both Krake's (2005) and Wong and Merrilees' (2005) findings are present in Beauti's brand management. Most of the time is spent improving product features and in developing commercial activities. In the case of Beauti, it is recognized that the brand is highly important but it is only seen as complement of a good product. The brand communicates an identity and helps the business to thrive but the product is still the center of the business idea, corroborating Krake's (2005) and Ojasalo's et al. (2008) research.

The main challenge found is the lack of promotional resources to increase brand awareness. It is the standardized idea among Beauti's workers that creating effective messages to directly communicate and inform the target presents the most difficult marketing communication strategy to implement. This finding complies with Krake's (2005) and Wong and Merilees' (2005) studies. The most directly and effective way to show Beauti's value propositions is by virtue of personal selling or face-to-face, but on the other hand, is also the most expensive one.

Additionally, Beauti's vision regarding branding is simple. Their strategy is to be a reference in online business in Portugal. Therefore, Beauti's efforts are channeled towards online branding activities. Internet advertising (Google AdWords, Facebook ads, SEO marketing affiliate programs and email marketing) is the highest target form of advertising for Beauti. As concluded by Bresciani and Eppler (2010) digital branding can be a potentially very powerful tool for business with low budget. Nevertheless, there are a few offline campaigns that Beauti organized such us the "launch event" and the annually "Beauti Awards". This is also supported by the literature, namely Keller (2003), Ojasalo et al. (2008) and Bresciani and Eppler (2010) who defend that new ventures should, in contrast with large organizations, develop more creative, innovative and unconventional branding activities, for instance to organize events and to develop online branding activities.

In terms of brand building within software SMEs, it is impressive to acknowledge that the five large themes emerged from Ojasalo's et al. (2008) empirical chapter also apply to Beauti Portugal. Brand building has a minor role in the overall product development activity, competitive strength in the marketplace is mostly based on a superior knowledge of IT and the customer, brand building is less important than technologic development, they have cooperative relationships with customers and partners and lastly, due to the dynamics of the operational environment and the flexibility related to the changing technology and customer needs, the content of the brand should not be too detailed and the brand must be flexible. This implies that Beauti is managing its brand very similarly to many other software SMEs.

In this sense, it was possible to identify three facts diverging from the literature: (i) emphasizing external communication disregarding the organization's internal communication, (ii) the importance of the entrepreneur and (iii) the absence of co-branding.

The internal communication at Beauti is undervalued and subdued to the external communication (i). The brand's values, beliefs and identity are not fully engrained in the all members of the staff. Despite the desire of wanting Beauti to succeed, and the general agreement concerning Beauti's marketing activities, the answers about Beauti's brand values and identity were slightly different from collaborator to collaborator and each member have its own awareness and perception of the brand.

The entrepreneur, according to Krake (2005), Wong and Merrilees (2005) and Bresciani and Eppler (2010), is sometimes the brand because it influences the passion, logic and the personification of the brand. However, this does not exactly apply to Beauti (ii). The company's brand emerged essentially from the product, and it construct is a system of trial and error in which every staff member contributes with ideas and formulates its own associations. This process makes it hard to understand what the brand clearly stands for.

Co-branding and partnerships, not only are present in Beauti, but also are of extreme importance to the company's business model (iii). The partnerships with some recognized magazines from the sector and with Expocósmetica (which hosted the "Beauti Awards" event) contradict Keller (2005) and Ojasalo et al., (2008).

Customer Brand Engagement Framework

The literature review suggests that this is possible the first framework embracing several theories and studies from multiple researchers and allowing its operationalization for management purposes. It identifies several opportunities for SMEs company managers, suggesting practices for effective social media handling and for those interested in enhancing brand engagement through social media.

This framework was built with the intent of providing tools for better managing customer brand engagement in social media, being particularly focused on Beauti Portugal. Consequently, it supplies the answer to the third research question: "*how can Beauti.pt best manage and increase customer brand engagement?*", and can also be generalized to other SMEs new ventures. Moreover, it provides some understanding of customer brand engagement evidenced through social media, which, according to Wallace *et al.,* (2014) continues to present challenges.

It is constructed based on literature extensions and adaptations, namely Muntinga et al. (2011), Wallace et al. (2014), Cvijikj and Michahelles (2013) and Park and Kim (2014). Thus, they are integrated in the framework especially because of the definitions and concepts created.

It can be segmented in five different but sequential parts in order to make the explanation more clear and understandable:

(i) The **target** category,
(ii) the **action plan** guidelines,
(iii) the **outcomes** of the action plan,
(iv) the **consequences** of the framework and,
(v) the **metrics** of evaluation.

The first three are directly related and influenced by one another. The target constitutes the basis for the action plans which in turn influences the outcomes. The consequences of the framework concern the use of the framework as a whole and the metrics of evaluation are some guidelines to assess the performance of this model.

The specificities and the functionality of this model are hereinafter explained.

The Target Categories

The target categories are an adaptation of Muntinga's et al. (2011) behavioral construct that provides a unifying framework to think about consumer activity related to branded content on social media platforms. The purpose of these target categories is to acquire consuming targets and then manage them, ultimately leading them to be contributors and to provide insights to the action plan's guidelines.

COBRAs were categorized by Muntinga et al. (2011) into three dimensions that correspond to a path of gradual involvement with brand-related content on social media, namely consuming, contributing and creating. This framework acknowledges the same terms (consuming, contributing and creating) as well as the different motivations influencing the participation of the consumers on social media platforms (information, remuneration, entertainment, personal identity, social interaction and empowerment).

Therefore, like in Muntinga's et al. (2011) COBRA type, the *consuming* category represents a minimum level of online brand-related activeness. It denotes participating without actively contributing to or creating content. It is limited by those who consume, watch the brand-related videos, "like" a picture, a comment, a post or a brand page in social media, view the product ratings and reviews that others post and the dialogues between members of brand pages in different social media platforms. The act of engaging in this consuming type is motivated by, according to Muntinga's et al. (2011), information, remuneration and entertainment.

The *contributing* category of this framework, similar to Muntinga's et al. (2011), is the middle level of online brand-related activeness. It denotes both user-to-content and user-to-user interactions about brands. People who contribute to brand-related content conversation on a social networking site, making comments on posts, videos, pictures and tagging acquaintances on brand-related content others have created. Those costumers that engage by actively contributing to brand-related content are motivated by entertainment, personal identification with the brand and social interaction with other fellow engaged customers.

The *creating* category also follows Muntinga's et al. (2011) COBRA type. It represents the ultimate level of online brand-related activeness. It denotes actively producing and publishing the brand-related content that others consume and contribute to. Consumers that create/write brand-related posts, product reviews, produce and upload branded videos, music and pictures, or write articles on brands. They directly ask for comments, "likes" or tag different people to enter the conversation acting like some sort of influencers or brand ambassadors, even though that they are only customers with no direct relation with the company. These customers are usually motivated to engage by integration and social interaction, personal identification with the brand, entertainment and also empowerment.

The Action Plan Guidelines

The action plans are the guidelines that companies, like the object brand of this investigation, may use to better manage the engagement between the customer and the brand. The customers lying on different stages of the online brand-related activeness need to be approached differently, since their motivations and their actions are different from the others. At least six distinct action plans can be designed and implemented according to the target engaged customer and the desired outcomes. The specificities of the social media platforms indicate that three main aspects are essential to perform a better action plan: The social media *channel*, the type of *content* and the *posting time/date.*

The channel to be used in any action plan must follow a careful attention since different social media are used with different purposes and objectives. For instance, Facebook and LinkedIn differ in their substance, so the way to achieve engaged customers, even if we are talking about the same brand, has to be distinct. Sometimes, they should not even be related in order to not jeopardize the target or negative influence their desired outcomes. Additionally, Instagram is great for products, pictures of staff and developments within the business (Bendror, 2013) whereas LinkedIn is much more focused business participation than many social networks and is a great place to network and do research on specific organizations and opportunities (Jantsch, 2009), meaning that the action plan for these two social media channels must be different.

With respect to the type of *content*, as mentioned before, should be valuable and engaging enough for customers that they're motivated to share it with their peers, ultimately helping to spread the marketing message and build brand awareness (Kirsten, 2012). The content is a fundamental tool to engage customers and provides a method to enrich interactions with customers at every single stage of their buying journey (Roberts, 2014), connecting with the different targets of this framework (consuming, creating, contributing).

Since it is recognized by researchers and practitioners as one of the most important drivers for customer brand engagement, the type of content that companies ultimately deliver on their action plan must be accurate with the channel to be used and, of course, with the objectives and social media strategy to be followed. Entertainment was found to be the most influential type of content (Muntinga et al., 2011; Gummerus et al., 2012; Cvijikj & Michahelles, 2013; Stelnzer, 2014) and although not applicable in every single case, it's a powerful insight in order to create more engagement within the particular targets.

Cvijikj and Michahelles's, (2013) chapter on Facebook found that posts created on workdays increase the level of comments, while posting in peak activity hours will reduce the level of engagement through liking and sharing. Their findings will lead us to the last aspect to be analyzed in these Action Plans: the *posting time/date*. Therefore, this aspect of the action plan is directly related with the social media *channel* and the type *content* since different channels have different peaks in audience. The type of content is more likely to be read in some hours/days than in others so the timing acquires great importance.

The Outcomes of the Action Plan

The outcomes are the expected results of every action plan in the different target category stages. They can be divided in two groups of outcomes: the inner-self outcomes and the ideal-self outcomes.

Wallace et al., (2014), as mentioned before, advocates that a "real" brand relationship, is when the consumer has a genuine attachment to the brand because it reflects themselves. Consequently, inner-self outcomes are the result of action plans that appeal to the consumers' actual selves (Ahuvia, 2005).

In the case of action plans expressing the inner self, consumers will experience brand love and offer positive WOM as found in Wallace's et al. (2014) research. Ultimately, these inner self outcomes will lead to more sales, higher loyalty and facility in acquiring new customers, as Tsimonis and Dimitriadis (2014) suggest.

On the contrary, the case of the ideal-self outcomes are the ones expressing a self that is not supported in consumers' material world, an "ideal self" (Schau & Gilly, 2003).

Ideal-self outcomes will induce consumers to experience brand love and accept wrongdoing, arguably because the brand is not internalized and does not really resonate with the self (Wallace et al., 2014).

These ideal-self outcomes will subsequently provide lock-in strategies and higher switching-cost towards other brand, as proposed by Tsimonis and Dimitriadis (2014).

The Consequences of the Framework

The consequences of the framework are the broadly benefits extracted from using this framework. It differs from the outcomes because those are a reflection of every action plan implemented individually and these consequences are driven by the usage of the framework as a whole.

If the social networks are an important channel for customer brand engagement (and can actually be a source of more costumer engagement) it is intuitive to expect that it will have an influence on the consumer's relationship with the brand's social network. Besides, the brand social network relationship will influence the overall brand relationship quality, which, consequently, will increase WOM (positive or negative), the willingness to pay a premium price and, of course, brand usage, similar to Park and Kim (2014) and Hollebeek et al. (2014).

The Metrics of Evaluation

The metrics are the last component of this CBE framework. They are fundamental since they help measuring the performance of this model and also the levels of customer brand engagement in social media. The metrics designed here, are an adaptation of Cvijikj and Michahelles's (2013) to measure online engagement on Facebook.

Two of them will be exactly the same, the other three (LikesRate, CommentsRate and ShareRate) will be adapted to measure the number of likes, comments and shares, compared to the totality of likes in the brand page. The UserGeneratedContentRate and the ReferralRate are two distinct metrics, newly created to accurately measure the performance of this framework. The metrics of evaluation of this CBE framework's performance are exposed below:

$$\text{FeedbackRate}=\frac{\#Likes+\#Comments}{\#Impressions}$$

$$\text{LikesRate}=\frac{\#Post\ Likes}{\#Likes\ Brand\ Page}$$

$$\text{CommentsRate}=\frac{\#Post\ Comments}{\#Likes\ Brand\ Page}$$

$$\text{ShareRate}=\frac{\#Post\ Shares}{\#Likes\ Brand\ Page}$$

$$\text{UserGeneratedContentRate}=\frac{\#Videos,\ Photos\ and\ Articles\ Posted\ by\ Consumers}{\#Total\ Brand\ Posts}$$

$$\text{ReferralRate}=\frac{\#Brand\ Referrals\ by\ Customers}{\#Likes\ Brand\ Page}$$

Interaction Duration = Time of last Interaction – Time of post creation

This way is possible to evaluate every action plan for the distinct targets, the outcomes and the consequences, as well as customer engagement in general. Additionally, there is another basic metric that will make the bridge between customer brand engagement and overall brand management, named brand usage. Brand usage is an adaptation of the definition of brand usage intent by Park and Kim (2014), which reflects the use of that specific brand opposed to a competitive one although not using the "intent" but instead actual numbers of brand users.

The indicators presented were discussed with the heads of the company, in order to be implemented later. Thus, it is not yet possible to indicate values for that metrics.

Figure 2. CBE Framework

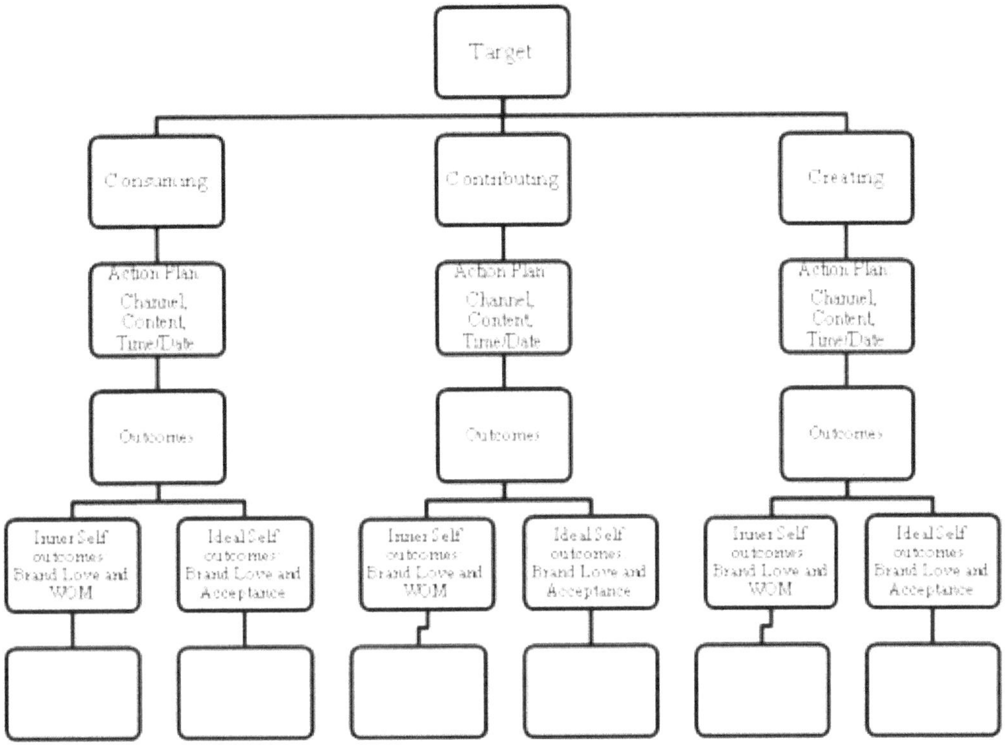

CONCLUSION

The aim of this investigation was to capture the creation of a framework for better manage customer brand engagement in social media. It fill the academia gap by the conception of a framework which allows managers better handling their social media strategy regarding engagement. This chapter offers suggestions for managers seeking to enhance brand engagement through social media, embracing all channels and suggesting practices for effective social media management. The object of chapter is Beauti Portugal. Beauti is a Small-Medium Enterprise (SME) technologic software product provider that is currently in the first steps of building its own brand.

Besides, it also presents some theoretical implications. This chapter contributes to the lack of studies regarding brand management in SMEs, found by Krake (2005), Wong and Merrilees (2005) and Merrilees (2007), and more particularly, it addresses Ojasalo's et al. (2008) gap regarding the few existing literature about brand management in software SMEs. Moreover, it provides some understanding of customer brand engagement evidenced through social media, which, according to Wallace et al. (2014) continues to present challenges.

This project was divided in two distinct but complementary parts which constitutes the basis for answering the research questions proposed. Both questions were answered using different methods but inserted in the category of a case study.

In this chapter, data were collected from Beauti's internal documents, archival documents and informal interview with different levels of staff and direct participation and observation. The key information and sources are the founder and managing partner and two co-founders, one software developer and one marketing manager. They weren't aware of which ones answer by the time they were interviewed.

The results regarding the brand management in Beauti were consonant with most of the literature discoveries with few exceptions. The company is highly focused on selling, the brand adapts to product development and technology is seen more important that brand development. There is, as well, a concern on keeping the brand flexible enough for future changes. However, three interesting facts diverge from the literature findings: Emphasizing external communication disregarding the organization's internal communication, the importance of the entrepreneur and the absence of co-branding. It can be concluded that Beauti brand management corresponds to the *Embryonic Brand Orientation* from Wong and Merilees (2005). Exists awareness of competitive advantage and positioning but the brand seems to be more an implicit, optional part of what they do business, and not necessarily critical for business success.

Additionally, a customer brand engagement framework was built with the intent of providing tools for better managing customer brand engagement in social media. The literature reviewed suggests that this is possible the first framework embracing several theories and studies from multiple researchers. It was constructed based on literature extensions and adaptations, namely Muntinga et al. (2011), Wallace et al. (2014), Cvijikj and Michahelles (2013) and Park and Kim (2014). Thus, they are integrated in the framework especially because of the definitions and concepts created. It can be segmented in five different but sequential parts: The target category (i), the action plan guidelines (ii), the outcomes of the action plans (iii), the consequences of the framework (iv) and the metrics of evaluation (v).

The first three are directly related and influenced by one another. The target constitutes the basis for the action plans which in turn influences the outcomes. The consequences of the framework concern the use of the framework as a whole and the metrics of evaluation are some guidelines to assess the performance of this model.

LIMITATIONS OF THE PROJECT AND FURTHER INVESTIGATION

This investigation possesses some limitations like any other case study. Even though that can be applicable to other SMEs in the first steps of building its own brand, the conclusions are a bit exclusive for Beauti Portugal.

The constant changing environment and the upgrades on the company business model may jeopardize the validity of this project in the near future, since the conclusions today presented may be already outdated. The fact that the investigator is participant in some of the decisions taken by the company (regarding it brand) may induce some biased findings and conclusions.

The customer brand engagement framework embraces some limitations. Being new and untested, it requires validity and possibly some alterations. It is recognized that only its utilization and evaluation will indicate the pertinence and the applicability of the framework to real business cases.

REFERENCES

Aaker, D. A. (1996). *Building Strong Brands*. The Free Press / Simon and Schuster.

Aaker, D. A., & Joachimsthaler, E. (2007). *Como construir marcas líderes;* tradução: Daniel Grassi, Porto Alegre. *The Bookman.*

Aaker, D. A., & Mcloughin, D. (2010). *Strategic Market Management: Global Perspectives.* John Wiley & Sons Ltd.

Abimbola, T. (2001). Branding as a Competitive Strategy for Demand Management in SMEs. *Journal of Research in Marketing and Entrepreneurship, 3*(2), 97–106. doi:10.1108/14715200180001480

Adjei, M., Noble, S., & Noble, C. (2010). The influence of C2C communications in online brand communities on customer purchase behavior. *Journal of the Academy of Marketing Science, 38*(5), 634–653. doi:10.100711747-009-0178-5

Ahuvia, A. C. (2005). Beyond the extended self: Loved objects and consumers' identity narratives. *The Journal of Consumer Research, 32*(1), 171–184. doi:10.1086/429607

Asamoah, E. S. (2014). Customer based brand equity (CBBE) and the competitive performance of SMEs in Ghana. *Journal of Small Business and Enterprise Development, 21*(1), 117–131. doi:10.1108/JSBED-10-2013-0154

Ascend2. (2013). *Marketing Strategy Report Social Media.* Available at: http://ascend2.com/home/wp-content/uploads/Social-Marketing-Strategy-Report-Ascend2-Edition.pdf

Awareness Inc. (2011). *11 ways to create engagement.* Available at: https://www.academia.edu/7151949/1_Strategies_to_Increase_Engagement_11_Strategies_to_Increase_Engagement_from_Awareness_Inc_Creators_of_the_Social_Marketing_Hub

Bagozzi, R. P., & Dholakia, U. M. (2006). Antecedents and purchase consequences of customer participation in small group brand communities. *International Journal of Research in Marketing, 23*(1), 45–61. doi:10.1016/j.ijresmar.2006.01.005

Baumgarth, C. (2010). "Living the brand": Brand orientation in the business-to-business sector. *European Journal of Marketing, 44*(5), 653–671. doi:10.1108/03090561011032315

Baumöl, U., Hollebeek, L., & Jung, R. (2016). Dynamics of customer interaction on social media platforms. *Electronic Markets, 26*(3), 199–202. doi:10.100712525-016-0227-0

Bendror, Y. (2013). *Which Social Media Channels Should I Use For My Business?* Available at: https://smallbusiness.yahoo.com/advisor/social-media-channels-business-223554094.html

Berthon, P., Ewing, M. T., & Napoli, J. (2008). Brand Management in small to medium-sized enterprises. *Journal of Small Business Management, 46*(1), 27–45. doi:10.1111/j.1540-627X.2007.00229.x

Bilro, R. G., & Loureiro, S. M. C. (2020). *A consumer engagement systematic review: Synthesis and research agenda.* Spanish Journal of Marketing – ESIC. doi:10.1108/SJME-01-2020-0021

Bresciani, S., & Eppler, M. J. (2010). Brand new ventures? Insights on start-ups'" branding practices. *Journal of Product and Brand Management, 19*(5), 356–366. doi:10.1108/10610421011068595

Brodie, R. J., Hollebeek, L. D., Juric´, B., & Ilic´, A. (2011). Customer engagement conceptual domain, fundamental propositions, and implications for research. *Journal of Service Research*, *14*(3), 252–271. doi:10.1177/1094670511411703

Brodie, R. J., Ilic, A., Juric, B., & Hollebeek, L. (2013). Consumer engagement in a virtual brand community: An exploratory analysis. *Journal of Business Research*, *66*(1), 105–114. doi:10.1016/j.jbusres.2011.07.029

Casaló, L. V., Flavián, C., & Guinalíu, M. (2010). Relationship quality, community promotion and brand loyalty in virtual communities: Evidence from free software communities. *International Journal of Information Management*, *30*(4), 357–367. doi:10.1016/j.ijinfomgt.2010.01.004

Chauhan, K., & Pillai, A. (2013). Role of content strategy in social media brand communities: A case of higher education institutes in India. *Journal of Product and Brand Management*, *22*(1), 40–51. doi:10.1108/10610421311298687

Cleff, T., & Rennings, K. (2012). Are there any first-mover advantages for pioneering firms? *European Journal of Innovation Management*, *15*(4), 491–513. doi:10.1108/14601061211272394

Content Marketing Institute. (2013). *The CMI Content Marketing Framework: 7 building blocks to success.* Available at: https://contentmarketinginstitute.com/wp-content/uploads/2013/03/CMI_Framework.pdf

Content Marketing Institute and MarketingProfs. (2015a). *B2B Small Business Content Marketing: 2015 Benchmarks, Budgets and Trends North-America.* Available at: https://www.slideshare.net/CMI/b2b-small-business-content-marketing-2015-benchmarks-budgets-and-trends-north-america?qid=de17404c-06e7-49ba-a457-078fdb7ac8e9&v=qf1&b=&from_search=11

Content Marketing Institute and MarketingProfs. (2015b). *B2C Content Marketing Benchmarks, Budgets, and Trends North-America.* Available at: https://www.slideshare.net/mprofs/b2c-content-marketing-2014-benchmarks-budgets-and-trendsnorth-america?qid=d4bc6ef8-b24b-4a23-8566-57e0f4bf0328&v=default&b=&from_search=1

Cvijikj, I. P., & Michahelles, F. (2013). Online Engagement Factors on Facebook Brand Pages. *Social Network Analysis and Mining*, *3*(4), 843–861. doi:10.100713278-013-0098-8

de Chernatony, L. (1999). Brand Management Through Narrowing the Gap Between Brand Identity and Brand Reputation. *Journal of Marketing Management*, *15*(1-3), 157–179. doi:10.1362/026725799784870432

de Chernatony, L. (2010). *From Brand Vision to Evaluation* (3rd ed.). Butterworth-Heinemann.

Dessart, L., Aldás-Manzano, J., & Veloutsou, C. (2019). Unveiling heterogeneous engagement-based loyalty in brand communities. *European Journal of Marketing*, *53*(9), 1854–1881. doi:10.1108/EJM-11-2017-0818

Dessart, L., Veloutsou, C., & Morgan-Thomas, A. (2015). Consumer engagement in online brand communities: A social media perspective. *Journal of Product and Brand Management*, *24*(1), 28–42. doi:10.1108/JPBM-06-2014-0635

Dessart, L., Veloutsou, C., & Morgan-Thomas, A. (2016). Capturing consumer engagement: Duality, dimensionality and measurement. *Journal of Marketing Management*, *32*(5–6), 399–426. doi:10.1080/0267257X.2015.1130738

Dilip, R., & Banerjee, S. (2012). Strategic branding roadmap for SMEs operating in business-to-business sector. *Journal of Research in Marketing and Entrepreneurship*, *14*(2), 142–163. doi:10.1108/14715201211271384

Dyer, G. Jr, & Wilkins, A. (1991). Better stories, not better constructs to generate better theory: A rejoinder to Eisenhardt. *Academy of Management Review*, *16*(3), 613–619. doi:10.5465/amr.1991.4279492

Earley, P. (2009). Work, learning and professional practice: The role of leadership apprenticeships. *School Leadership & Management: Formerly School Organisation*, *29*(3), 307–320. doi:10.1080/13632430902793718

Euromonitor – Country Report Portugal. (2014). *Internet Retailing in Portugal.* Available at: www.euromonitor.com/internet-retailing-in-portugal/report

Fischer, E., & Reuber, A. R. (2011). Social interaction via new social media: (How) can interactions on Twitter affect effectual thinking and behavior? *Journal of Business Venturing*, *26*(1), 1–18. doi:10.1016/j.jbusvent.2010.09.002

Fuller, J., Jawecki, G., & Muhlbacher, H. (2007). Innovation creation by online basket- ball communities. *Journal of Business Research*, *60*(1), 60–71. doi:10.1016/j.jbusres.2006.09.019

Gambetti, R. C., Graffigna, G., & Biraghi, S. (2012). The grounded theory approach to consumer-brand engagement: The practitioner's standpoint. *International Journal of Market Research*, *54*(5), 659–687. doi:10.2501/IJMR-54-5-659-687

Ganley, D., & Lampe, C. (2009). The ties that bind: Social network principles in online communities. *Decision Support Systems*, *47*(3), 266–274. doi:10.1016/j.dss.2009.02.013

Gensler, S., Völckner, F., Liu-Thompkins, Y., & Wiertz, C. (2013). Managing Brands in the Social Media Environment. *Journal of Interactive Marketing*, *27*(4), 242–256. doi:10.1016/j.intmar.2013.09.004

Grinder, B., Pascal, J. V., & Schwartz, G. R. (2010). Entrepreneurship and the early American clock industry. *Journal of Research in Marketing and Entrepreneurship*, *12*(1), 54–70. doi:10.1108/14715201011060885

Gummerus, J., Liljander, V., Weman, E., & Pihlström, M. (2012). Customer engagement in a Facebook brand community. *Management Research Review*, *35*(9), 857–877. doi:10.1108/01409171211256578

Harrigan, P., Evers, U., Miles, M., & Daly, T. (2017). Customer engagement with tourism social media brands. *Tourism Management*, *59*, 597–609. doi:10.1016/j.tourman.2016.09.015

Hoeffler, S., & Keller, K. L. (2002). Building brand equity through corporate societal marketing. *Journal of Public Policy & Marketing*, *21*(1), 78–89. doi:10.1509/jppm.21.1.78.17600

Hoffman, D., & Fodor, M. (2010). Can you measure the ROI of your social media marketing? *MIT Sloan Management Review*, *52*(1), 40–49.

Hollebeek, L. (2011). Exploring customer brand engagement: Definition and themes. *Journal of Strategic Marketing*, *19*(7), 555–573. doi:10.1080/0965254X.2011.599493

Hollebeek, L. D., Glynn, M. S., & Brodie, R. J. (2014). Consumer Brand Engagement in Social Media: Conceptualization, Scale Development and Validation. *Journal of Interactive Marketing*, *28*(2), 149–165. doi:10.1016/j.intmar.2013.12.002

Holliman, G., & Rowley, J. (2014). Business to business digital content marketing: Marketers' perceptions of best practice. *Journal of Research in Interactive Marketing*, *8*(4), 269–293. doi:10.1108/JRIM-02-2014-0013

Hoy, M. (2011). Building pathways to working with collections: Can internships and student work experience help? *Australian Academic and Research Libraries*, *42*(1), 29–42. doi:10.1080/00048623.2011.10722202

Jang, H., Olfman, L., Ko, I., Koh, J., & Kim, K. (2008). The influence of on-line brand community characteristics on community commitment and brand loyalty. *International Journal of Electronic Commerce*, *12*(3), 57–80. doi:10.2753/JEC1086-4415120304

Jantsch, J. (2009). *Let's Talk: Social Media for Small Business – Version 2*. Available at: https://www.ducttapemarketing.com/socialmediaforbusiness.pdf

Kaltcheva, D. V., Patino, A., Michael, V., Dennis, L., Pitta, A., & Imparato, N. (2014). Customers' relational models as determinants of customer engagement value. *Journal of Product and Brand Management*, *23*(1), 55–61. doi:10.1108/JPBM-07-2013-0353

Kapferer, J. N. (2008). *Strategic Brand Management* (4th ed.). Kogan Page.

Kaplan, A. M., & Haenlein, M. (2010). Users of the world, unite! The challenges and opportunities of social media. *Business Horizons*, *53*(1), 59–68. doi:10.1016/j.bushor.2009.09.003

Keller, K. L. (2003). *Strategic Brand Management: Building, Measuring and Managing Brand Equity*. Prentice Hall.

Keller, K. L., & Lehmann, D. R. (2006). Brands and Branding: Research Finding and Future Priorities. *Journal of Marine Science*, *25*(6), 551–765.

Kho, N. D. (2014). The State of Content Marketing. *EContent (Wilton, Conn.)*, *37*(1), 14–15.

Kirsten, K. (2012). Content creation (Core Concepts/Content Marketing). *Marketing News, 46*(2).

Koporcic, N. (2020). Interactive Network Branding: Demonstrating the importance of firm representatives for small and medium-sized enterprises in emerging markets. *Journal of Business and Industrial Marketing*, *35*(7), 1179–1189. doi:10.1108/JBIM-10-2018-0301

Kotler, P., & Keller, K. L. (2011). *Marketing Management* (13th ed.). Prentice Hall.

Krake, B. G. J. M. F. (2005). Successful brand management in SMEs: A new theory and practical hints. *Journal of Product and Brand Management*, *14*(4), 228–239. doi:10.1108/10610420510609230

Lewis, S. (2013). *Consumer Engagement Relationships in Social Media Campaigns*. Available at: https://www.american.edu/soc/communication/upload/Shani-Lewis-capstone.pdf

M'zungu, S., Merrilees, B., & Miller, D. (2019). Strategic and Operational Perspectives of SME Brand Management: A Typology. *Journal of Small Business Management*, *57*(3), 943–965. doi:10.1111/jsbm.12387

Malhotra, A., Malhotra, C. K., & See, A. (2013). How to create brand engagement on Facebook. *MIT Sloan Management Review*, *54*(2), 18–20.

Malthouse, E. C., Haenlein, M., Skiera, B., Wege, E., & Zhang, M. (2013). Managing customer relationships in the social media era: Introducing the social CRM house. *Journal of Interactive Marketing*, *27*(4), 270–280. doi:10.1016/j.intmar.2013.09.008

McAlexander, J. H., Schouten, J. W., & Koening, H. F. (2002). Building Brand Community. *Journal of Marketing*, *66*(1), 38–54. doi:10.1509/jmkg.66.1.38.18451

Mellahi, K., & Johnson, M. (2000). Does it pay to be a first mover in e.commerce? The case of Amazon.com. *Management Decision*, *38*(7), 445–452. doi:10.1108/00251740010373458

Merrilees, B. (2007). A theory of brand-led SME new venture development. *Qualitative Market Research*, *10*(4), 403–415. doi:10.1108/13522750710819739

Mota, F. (2014). *Como otimizar o modelo de compra na gestão de stocks com base num método de avaliação da quantidade económica de compra: O caso da Sonae MC*. Relatório de Estágio do Mestrado em Economia da Faculdade de Economia do Porto.

Muniz, A. Jr, & O'Guinn, T. (2001). Brand Community. *The Journal of Consumer Research*, *27*(4), 412–436. doi:10.1086/319618

Muniz, A. M. Jr, & Schau, H. J. (2005). Religiosity in the abandoned Apple Newton brand community. *The Journal of Consumer Research*, *31*(4), 737–747. doi:10.1086/426607

Muntinga, D., Moorman, M., & Smit, E. G. (2011). Introducing COBRA: Exploring Motivations for Brand-Related Social Media Use. *International Journal of Advertising*, *30*(1), 13–46. doi:10.2501/IJA-30-1-013-046

Odoom, R., Narteh, B., & Boateng, R. (2017). Branding in small- and medium-sized enterprises (SMEs): Current issues and research avenues. *Qualitative Market Research*, *20*(1), 68–89. doi:10.1108/QMR-12-2015-0091

Ojasalo, J., Nätti, S., & Olkkonen, R. (2008). Brand building in software SMEs: An empirical chapter. *Journal of Product and Brand Management*, *17*(2), 92–107. doi:10.1108/10610420810864702

Ouwersloot, H., & Odekerken-Schröder, G. (2008). Who's who in brand communities—And why? *European Journal of Marketing*, *42*(5/6), 571–585. doi:10.1108/03090560810862516

Park, H., & Kim, Y. K. (2014). The role of social network websites in the consumer–brand relationship. *Journal of Retailing and Consumer Services*, *21*(4), 460–467. doi:10.1016/j.jretconser.2014.03.011

Patterson, M., & O'Malley, L. (2006). Brands, Consumers and Relationships: A Review. *Irish Marketing Review, 18*(1/2), 10–20.

Peppers, D., & Rogers, M. (2011). *Managing Customer Relationships: A Strategic Framework* (2nd ed.). Wiley.

Petouhoff, N. (2013). *The Social Engagement Report: Competitive Brand Performance*. Available at: http://www.infinigraph.com/webinar/The_Social_Engagement_Report_2013.pdf

Porter, C., Donthu, N., MacElroy, W. H., & Wydra, D. (2011). How to foster and sustain engagement in virtual communities. *California Management Review, 53*(4), 80–110. doi:10.1525/cmr.2011.53.4.80

Rajala, R., & Westerlund, M. (2004). *Business models and networks: assets and capabilities in software business*. Paper presented at the 20th Industrial Marketing and Purchasing Conference, Copenhagen.

Reynolds, P. D. (1971). *A Primer in Theory Construction*. MacMillan Publishing Co.

Robert, R. (2014). Content Marketing Forecast. *EContent (Wilton, Conn.), 37*(9), 28–28.

Roberts, C., & Alpert, F. (2010). Total customer engagement: Designing and aligning key strategic elements to achieve growth. *Journal of Product and Brand Management, 19*(3), 198–209. doi:10.1108/10610421011046175

Rowley, J. (2008). Understanding digital content marketing. *Journal of Marketing Management, 24*(5/6), 517–540. doi:10.1362/026725708X325977

Sashi, C. M. (2012). Customer engagement, buyer-seller relationships, and social media. *Management Decision, 50*(2), 253–272. doi:10.1108/00251741211203551

Schau, H. J., & Gilly, M. C. (2003). We are what we post? Self-presentation in personal web space. *The Journal of Consumer Research, 30*(3), 385–404. doi:10.1086/378616

Simon, F., & Tossan, V. (2018). Does brand-consumer social sharing matter? A relational framework of customer engagement to brand-hosted social media. *Journal of Business Research, 85*, 175–184. doi:10.1016/j.jbusres.2017.12.050

Spence, M., & Essoussi, L. H. (2010). SME brand building and management: An exploratory chapter. *European Journal of Marketing, 44*(7/8), 1037–1054. doi:10.1108/03090561011047517

Srivastava, N. V., & Mookerjee, A. (2004). Determinants of brand equity for banking business application software products. *International Journal of Technology Management, 28*(1), 128–138. doi:10.1504/IJTM.2004.005057

Stelzner, M. A. (2014). *2014 Social Media Report*. Social Media Examiner. Available at: https://www.socialmediaexaminer.com/SocialMediaMarketingIndustryReport2014.pdf

Tsimonis, G., & Dimitriadis, S. (2014). Brand strategies in social media. *Marketing Intelligence & Planning, 32*(3), 328–344. doi:10.1108/MIP-04-2013-0056

Ulkuniemi, P. K., & Helander, N. M. (2005). *Marketing challenges in the software component business*. Paper presented at the 21st Industrial Marketing and Purchasing Conference, Rotterdam.

Vickers, M. (2015). Is your CRM system social media friendly? *CRM Magazine*, *19*(6), 7.

Vukasovic, T. (2013). *Brand Developing Relationships Through Social Media*. Available on: http://www.toknowpress.net/ISBN/978-961-6914-02-4/papers/ML13-228.pdf

Wallace, E., Buil, I., & de Chernatony, L. (2014). Consumer engagement with self-expressive brands: Brand love and WOM outcomes. *Journal of Product and Brand Management*, *23*(1), 33–42. doi:10.1108/JPBM-06-2013-0326

Walmsley, A., Thomas, R., & Jameson, S. (2012). Internships in SMEs and career intentions. *Journal of Education and Work*, *25*(2), 185–204. doi:10.1080/13639080.2011.573774

Wirtz, J., den Ambtman, A., Bloemer, J., Horváth, C., Ramaseshan, B., van de Klundert, J., Canli, Z. G., & Kandampully, J. (2013). Managing brands and customer engagement in online brand communities. *Journal of Service Management*, *24*(3), 223–244. doi:10.1108/09564231311326978

Wong, H. Y., & Merrilees, B. (2005). A brand orientation typology for SMEs: A case research approach. *Journal of Product and Brand Management*, *14*(3), 155–162. doi:10.1108/10610420510601021

Wu, S., & Fang, W. (2010). The effect of consumer-to-consumer interactions on idea generation in virtual brand community relationships. *Technovation*, *30*(4), 238–248. doi:10.1016/j.technovation.2010.07.005

Yin, R. K. (2009). *Case Chapter Research: Design and Methods* (4th ed.). Sage Publications.

Zaglia, M. E. (2013). Brand communities embedded in social networks. *Journal of Business Research*, *66*(2), 216–223. doi:10.1016/j.jbusres.2012.07.015 PMID:23564989

Zhang, M., Guo, L., Hu, M., & Liu, W. (2017). Influence of customer engagement with company social networks on stickiness: Mediating effect of customer value creation. *International Journal of Information Management*, *37*(3), 229–240. doi:10.1016/j.ijinfomgt.2016.04.010

KEY TERMS AND DEFINITIONS

Brand Usage: Reflects the use of that specific brand opposed to a competitive one although not using the "intent" but instead actual numbers of brand users.:

Consumer Brand Engagement: The level of a customer's cognitive, emotional: and behavioral investment in specific brand interactions.

Consumer Online Brand-Related Activities (COBRAs): A behavioral construct that provides a unifying framework to think about consumer activity pertaining to brand-related content on social media platforms:

Content Marketing: Is a technique of creating and distributing relevant and valuable content to attract: acquire, and engage a clearly defined and understood target audience-with the objective of driving profitable customer action.

Social Media: Is a platforms that enables enterprises to engage and build relationships with their consumers.:

Chapter 11
Consumer Decision Making From a Beloved Brand:
The Aspirin Case

Ana Pinto Borges
https://orcid.org/0000-0002-4942-079X
European Business School and Research Group, ISAG (NIDISAG), Portugal

Paula Rodrigues
https://orcid.org/0000-0003-2967-2583
Lusíada University of Porto, Portugal

ABSTRACT

The purpose of this study is to understand the main determinants that influence consumer decision-making processes applied to the purchase of the brand Aspirin. For this, a set of explanatory variables was considered that not only translated the general health habits of the population but also two variables that measure the establishment of a strong emotional relationship with the brand: self-brand engagement and brand love. The authors used a survey to collect the data, and in their treatment, they applied a factorial analysis and a logistic regression to explain consumer behavior. Emotional factors (self-brand engagement and brand love) are the most important factors in the consumer decision-making process of the Aspirin brand. The multifaceted black box of the consumer is also observed in the scope of over-the-counter (OTC) drugs, which is the case of Aspirin. Marketers, health professionals, and public policymakers face a new challenge alongside the patient's health.

1. INTRODUCTION

The paradigm of consumer brand relationship has generated a wide academic interest, namely regarding the understanding of the various relational behaviours of consumers with the brands (Fornier, 1998; Fetscherin & Heirich, 2014; Novak & Hoffam, 2019; Veloutsou, 2007; Veloutsou & Moutinho, 2009).

DOI: 10.4018/978-1-7998-3034-4.ch011

The seminal work of Fournier (1998) considers that the diversity of consumer relationships with brands can be conceptualized in a number of ways, including according to the functional and/or symbolic benefits of product/brands. The value of the functionality-based relationship considers the brand's functional role, associated with the objective benefits and inherent characteristics of brand attributes (Hwang & Kandampully, 2012; Fernandes & Moreira, 2019; Keller, 2012).

The concept of consumer brand relationship is still subject to much discussion (Dessart, Veloutsou & Morgan-Thomas, 2016; Dwivedi, 2015; Gambetti & Graffigna, 2010; Schultz, 2013; Vivek et al., 2012). In addition, consumer brand relationship nomological linkages are still underdeveloped and studies remain largely conceptual, which can create empirical opportunities to examine key relationships that have management implications (Brodie et al., 2011).

Consumer brand engagement always denotes an interaction between consumers and brands. Also, following the work of Fournier (1998) it is widely recognized that brands and consumers interact in partnership in a variety of ways. And this existing consumer brand engagement interaction is recognized by many academic authors, such as, Hollebeek et al. (2014) and Vivek et al. (2012). Thus, it can be considered that functional brands also cause interaction between consumers, leading to a strong relationship between consumers and brands, especially if there is a long time brand usage duration.

In current literature on brand love, the concept of brand love is often used as a holistic term and used for different studies (Bauer, Heinrich & Martin, 2004; Patwardhan & Balasubramanian, 2011). All of these studies make an important contribution to the understanding of the brand love conceptualization and dimensionality, but unfortunately do not warrant discussion of the appropriate relationship theory behind the construct (Fetscherin, 2014).

This is important given that the relationship is part of the consumer-brand relationship equation (Fournier, 2009) and explains the emotional connection consumers have with brands. Thus, the equation consists of three parts: the consumers, the brand, and the relationship between them.

Brand love has become a major research topic because functional differentiation across close brands and building and reinforcing emotional links between consumers and brands are becoming increasingly crucial for business management (Grissafe & Nguyen, 2011; Rodrigues & Rodrigues, 2019).

With this research, we intend to analyse what are the explanatory factors of the consumption of a functional health brand. We evaluate the Aspirin case as a brand and it was not distinguished from the existence of generic medication. The medication, as known as acetylsalicylic acid, was called for the first time Aspirin by the pharmaceutical multinational company, Bayer, in the end of the 19th century, and sold it around the word (Mann & Plummer, 1991). The Aspirin was Bayer's brand name, but the company has been selling or losing rights in several countries. In this moment, the acetylsalicylic acid is included in the list of essential medicine of the World Health Organization (WHO) as the safest and most effective medicines needed in a health system (WHO, 2019). In this paper, we evaluate the explanatory factors of the Aspirin as a brand independently of the company that market it. For this, a set of explanatory variables was considered, that not only translated the general health habits of the population but also two variables that measure the establishment of a strong emotional relationship with the brand: self-brand engagement and brand love, thus fulfilling a gap in the academic literature that little attention has attracted regarding this aspect of the consumer brand relationship.

This research contributes to the scientific advance in the brand area. There is still little empirical research on beloved brands in the pharmaceutical sector. The pharmaceutical industry is known for spending billions of dollars in marketing and advertising prescription medicines and over-the-counter (OTC) drugs. The main factor that differentiates the OTC drugs is that they do not need a doctor's prescription and consequently they are available in many places like pharmacies,, stores or gas stations. We observe a lack of literature investigating consumers' purchasing patterns of OTC drugs (Kohli & Buller, 2013) and this investigation aims to contribute to fill this gap. Furthermore, at the level of business management, this research not only considers the sociodemographic characteristics of the respondents and the consumption habits, but it also includes emotional factors related with the brand: self-brand engagement and brand love. This study provides helpful suggestions for marketers, medical professionals, and public policy makers concerning the determinants that influence the consumers and non-consumers of the Aspirin brand.

2. THEORETICAL BACKGROUND AND HYPOTHESES DEVELOPMENT

2.1. Purchase Consumption of Functional Brands

There are several types of brands and they have the capacity to satisfy different consumers' needs. Some brands satisfy hedonic or symbolic needs, as luxury brands, whereas others brands satisfy more functional needs. According to Know, Seo and Ko (2016) functional brands help to satisfy a consumer practical needs, attending an utilitarian benefit and solving their current problems. For Bairrada et al. (2018) functional benefits of the brands intends to fulfil external consumption needs. For Dhar and Wertenbroch (2000), utilitarian products/brands are brands whose purchase intention is more cognitive, instrumental and functional.

This research used the categorisation theory that posit that individuals structure their world view through categorisation, in order to simplify the environmental complexity in which they are embedded (Alba & Hutchinson, 1987; Rosch, 1978). This theory has been widely used to explain consumer behaviour (Ulkümen et al., 2010).

The information processing model assumes that consumers shape their purchase intention based on the search of information and the assessment of utility and functional attributes of a product and/or brand, which in turn are associated with tangible benefits and objective characteristics (Holbrook & Hirchaman, 1982). Therefore, consumers use the information of the functional characteristics of the products to classify and categorize brands, facilitating their decision making process and their purchase intention (Malär et al., 2012).

2.2. Consumer Brand Engagement with Functional Brands

Consumer brand engagement has emerged as an important variable in recent years, for both academic and management, largely due to the potential outcome of consumer behavior (Brandão, Pinho & Rodrigues, 2019; Dessart, Veloutsou & Morgan-Thomas, 2016; Dwivedi, 2015; Gambetti & Graffigna, 2010; Fernandes & Moreira, 2019). However, despite developments, scholars agree that the construct is not yet fully developed (Dessart, Veloutsou & Morgan-Thomas, 2016; Dwivedi, 2015; Gambetti & Graffigna, 2010; Vivek et al., 2012).

The nature of consumer brand engagement remains controversial, that is, it is still debated whether the construct is predominantly behavioural (Van Doorn et al., 2010) or contains additional emotional and cognitive aspects (Hollebeeck, 2011). Nevertheless, the tendency is to regard, independently of the underlying conceptual perspective, consumer brand engagement as a multidimensional construct

(Bowden, 2009; Bowden et al., 2017; Brodie et al., 2011; Dessart et al., 2016; Dwivedi, 2015; Hollebeek et al., 2014; Leckie et al., 2016; Vivek et al., 2012).

There are several definitions of consumer brand engagement, namely, "a customer's behavioural manifestations that have a brand or firm focus, beyond purchase, resulting from motivational drivers" (van Doorn et al., 2010, p. 254), "the level of an individual customer's motivational, brand-related and context-dependent state of mind characterized by specific levels of cognitive, emotional and behavioural activity indirect brand interactions" (Hollebeek, 2011, p. 790) or "as consumers' positive, fulfilling, brand-use-related state of mind that is characterized by vigor, dedication and absorption (Dwivedi, 2015, p. 100). There are several common aspects evident in these definitions, namely, "motivational drivers", "brand interaction", and "state of mind" (which contains cognitive, emotional and behavioural elements) as well as context specificities that seem to be central to the construct of consumer brand engagement.

Brand Engagement in Self-Concept (BESC) is defined as "an individual difference measure representing consumers' propensity to include important brands as a part of how they view themselves" (Sprott, Czellar & Spangenberg, 2009, p. 92). Sprott et al. (2009) tested the concept in five studies and found that BESC in high consumer ratings relate to consumers who have more accessible memories of favourite brands, feel strong associations between them and the brands, are more likely to remember brands they own, feel the meaning of the brand, becoming increasingly loyal to the brand than others with lower ratings. All of this can be found in functional brands and in this research we used this concept of brand engagement.

Consumer brand usage duration may influence consumer brand engagement (Dwivedi, 2015). The brand usage duration refers to the total amount of time that a consumer has and interacts with the brand (Dodds et al., 2005). It is also likely that past consumer-brand experiences stored in memory over years may have effects on relational responses, such as consumer brand engagement (Lau & Lee, 1999). In the case of functional brands, it was expected that the brand usage duration and the past consumer-brand experience affect consumer brand engagement.

2.3. Brand Love for Functional Brands

The first authors who introduced the feeling of love in marketing were Shimp and Madden (1988). They adopted, in the marketing context, Sternberg's Interpersonal Theory of Love (1986), entitled the Triangular Love Theory.

The Interpersonal Theory or Triangular Love Theory (Sternberg, 1986) adapted to the consumer context, is closely related to the construct of the emotional attachment. This theory assumes that brand love is achieved through dimensions such as passion, intimacy and commitment (Kamat & Parulikar, 2007; Keh, Pang & Peng, 2007).

Brand love is a variable that has originated a large number of academic researches (Albert, Merunka & Valette-Florence, 2008; Albert, Merunka & Valette-Florence, 2009; Batra, Ahuvia & Bagozzi, 2012; Bergkvist & Bech-Larsen, 2010; Carroll & Ahuvia, 2006; Fournier, 1998; Fetscherin & Conway, 2012; Heinrich, Albrecht & Bauer, 2012; Fetscherin, 2014; Bairrada, Coelho & Coelho, 2018; Bagozzi, Batra & Ahuvia, 2017; Delgado-Ballester, Palazón & Pelaez-Muñoz, 2017; Junaid, Hu, Hussain & Kirmani, 2019; Rodrigues & Rodrigues, 2019) and great attention in management, with the notion of love brands (Roberts, 2005).

Initially, research on brand love focused on the emotions that individuals feel for a brand. However, the research base on the brand love construct results from Belk's (1988) works that suggest that the possession of an object is an extension of the self and Fournier's (1998) work demonstrates the interpersonal relationship that may exist between brands and the individual.

However, despite the already extensive academic literature on the subject, there is still no consensus on what brand love is (Albert, Merunka & Valette-Florence, 2008). The several definitions of brand love suggest that this concept can range from one (Carroll & Ahuvia, 2006) to eleven dimensions (Albert, Merunka & Valette-Florence, 2008) with most studies presenting different conceptualizations. The equivalence of brand love and interpersonal love has led to some limitations in the research, as some authors insist that it is necessary to understand very well how consumers experience this feeling and, as such, brand love should be defined, on this basis. There is a fundamental difference between interpersonal love and love for a brand, because while the first implies a bi-directional connection, the second deals only with a one-dimensional relationship (Albert, Merunka & Valette-Florence, 2008; Albert, Merunka & Valette-Florence, 2009; Batra, Ahuvia & Bagozzi, 2012).

According to Carroll and Ahuvia (2006), the concept of brand love can be defined as the degree of emotional and passionate connection that a satisfied consumer has about a brand. So if a consumer is satisfied with a functional brand, he can create deep connections to the point of establishing a love bond. Utilitarian attributes of functional brands were considered as explanatory antecedents of consumer brand love (Rauschnabel & Ahuvia, 2014).

The concept of brand love is not independent of consumer brand experience (Garg et al., 2015; Junaid et al., 2019) whereas a positive emotional relationship can be developed over time based on factors that result from consumer brand experience (Huang, 2017; Venkatesan et al., 2018). Consumers with high brand experience may very likely develop brand love and brand engagement (Junaid et al., 2019). Therefore, long-standing functional brands are more likely to have led to consumers having a great deal of experience with them.

3. METHODOLOGY, SAMPLE DESCRIPTION AND DATA ANALYSIS

Questionnaire

We collected the data through an online survey, after a distribution using electronic addresses and available on social networks like Facebook and LinkedIn. We got 321 valid answers. The questionnaire comprises: i) the sociodemographic characteristics of the respondents – gender, age, marital status, education and net monthly income; ii) health related habits: acute illness, smoking status, alcohol consumption habits and self-reported health status; iii) consumer behaviour towards medication consumption and Aspirin purchase; and iv) to measure the brand love and the word-of-mouth were considered the Carroll and Ahuvia (2006) scales and for the self-brand engagement was used the Sprott et al. (2009) scale.

Data Analysis

For data description, descriptive statistics appropriate to the characteristics of the variables were applied. To evaluate the 14 statements of the scales we used the principal component analysis, with varimax rotation. We also considered the Kaiser-Meyer-Olkin (KMO) test of sampling adequacy and Bartlett's test of sphericity, to validate the factorability and the adequacy of the analysis. To describe the determinants that influence aspirin purchase, we used a logit regression. The analyses were performed with SPSS (version 21).

Sample Description, Health Related Habits and Consumer Behaviour

The sample contains 56,4% females and 43,6% males. The most representative age group, with 43.0%, is between 20 and 40 years old. Regarding marital status, 44,2% are married, 31,5% single, 19,3% divorced and 5,0% widowed. More than half of the sample (58%) has at least a bachelor degree. In relation to the net monthly income, 67% reported having a monthly net income up to 2000 EUR. In scope of health related habits, 67% of the respondents did not suffer from a serious disease. About risk behaviour, 49,5% do not smoke and 30,8% do not drink. In general, the respondents reveal favourable health status as 52,0% indicated a self-reported health status of "good" and 13,1% "very good". In relation to consumption behaviour towards medication, 44,9% indicated that they take medication at least once a week. In the specific case of the Aspirin brand, 54,5% usually buy this medicine.

Table 1. Sample description, health related habits and consumption behaviour towards medication (percentage)

Variable	Freq. (%)
Sociodemographic variables	
Gender	
Female	56,4%
Male	43,6%
Age	
Under 20 years old	7,2%
[20-40]	43,0%
[41-60]	33,3%
Over 60 years old	16,5%
Marital status	
Single	31,5%
Married	44,2%
Divorced	19,3%
Widow	5,0%
Schooling (complete)	
Elementary studies	11,8%
Secondary studies	30,2%
Superior (Degree, Master degree or PhD)	58,0%
Net monthly income	
Less than 1000 EUR	23,1%
[1001-2000]	43,9%

continues on following page

Table 1. Continued

Variable	Freq. (%)
[2001-3000]	21,8%
Over 3000 EUR	11,2%
Health Related Habits	
Do you suffer or have you ever suffered from any serious illness?	
Yes	33,0%
No	67,0%
Do you smoke?	
Yes	30,8%
No	49,5%
Occasionally	19,7%
Do you drink alcohol?	
Yes	29,9%
No	30,8%
Occasionally	39,3%
Self-reported health status	
Very good	13,1%
Good	52,0%
Reasonable	28,3%
Bad	5,3%
Very bad	1,3%
Consumption Behaviour Towards Medication	
How often do you take any medicine?	
Rarely/never	31,8%
1-2 per month	23,4%
1-2 per week	17,4%
5-6 per week	17,8%
6-7 per week	9,7%
Do you usually buy aspirin?	
Yes	54,5%
No	45,5%

Descriptive Statistics of the Scales

Table 2 shows the results of the level of agreement/disagreement of the respondents, in each statement of the three scales applied, using a five-point Likert scale (1 = "strongly disagree" and 5 = "strongly agree"). In the brand love scale the statements BL2-This brand makes me feel good and BL4-I like this brand present the highest mean. In turn, in the brand engagement scale, the items BE1 I have a special bond with the brands I like BE3-I usually feel a personal connection between the brands and BE6-I can identify with important brands in my life were enhanced.

Table 2. Brand Love and Brans Engagement, descriptive analysis

	Variables	SDIS (%)	DIS (%)	NAND (%)	AGR (%)	SAGR (%)	Mean	Standard Deviation
BL1	This is a wonderful brand	12,8	20,9	44,9	16,2	5,2	2,804	1,0287
BL2	This brand makes me feel good	10,6	22,4	36,4	25,9	4,7	2,916	1,0439
BL3	This brand makes me very happy	14,3	31,2	41,1	10,6	2,8	2,564	0,9568
BL4	I like this brand!	11,5	17,4	41,1	26,5	3,5	2,928	1,0176
BL5	I am in love with this brand	19,4	35,3	31,3	9,1	4,9	2,450	1,0582
BL6	I am very attached to this brand	17,8	29,9	32,4	15,9	4,0	2,586	1,0780
BE1	I have a special bond with the brands I like	11,2	20,2	24,6	32,4	11,6	3,13	1,193
BE2	I consider my favourite brands to be a part of myself	9,0	28,3	29,3	24,6	8,8	2,956	1,1144
BE3	I usually feel a personal connection between the brands and me	9,0	25,2	28,0	28,3	9,5	3,037	1,1285
BE4	Part of me is defined by important brands in my life	10,9	30,2	28,0	22,4	8,5	2,872	1,1344
BE5	I feel like I have a personal connection with my favourite brands	10,9	26,5	29,6	21,2	11,8	2,966	1,1787
BE6	I can identify with important brands in my life	10,0	23,4	29,3	29,0	8,3	3,025	1,1233
BE7	There are links between the brands I prefer and the way I see myself	10,6	30,8	31,8	19,6	7,2	2,819	1,0890
BE8	My favourite brands are an important indication of what I am	12,1	31,8	29,9	18,7	7,5	2,776	1,1150

Notes: SDIS = strongly disagree; DIS = disagree; NAND = neither agree nor disagree; AGR = agree; SAGR = strongly agree.

4. RESULTS AND DISCUSSION EXPLORATORY FACTOR ANALYSIS FOR THE BRAND LOVE AND BRAND ENGAGEMENT DIMENSIONS

An exploratory factor analysis was performed to verify the items that should remain in each of the scales used. We consider the items in which the communalities assume a value of less than 0,6. For the brand love scale of Carroll and Ahuvia (2006) three items retained explain 84,314% of the total data variance. For the brand engagement scale of Sprott et al. (2009) six items explain 79,338% of the data variance. For the two scales we verify that the Kaiser-Meyer-Olkin (KMO) test and the Bartlett's test give an indication that the correlations between variables are suitable for doing a factor analysis.

Econometric Model: Explanatory Factors of the Consumption of Aspirin

A logistic regression was performed to ascertain the effects of the sociodemographic characteristics of the respondents, health related habits, consumer behaviour towards medication consumption, and the dimensions of brand love and brand engagement on the likelihood that the respondent would buy Aspirin. We verify that only the self-reported health status and the two dimensions show a level of significance in the model. This result differs from others already obtained in the literature, as for example, higher education influences the decision to purchase OTC drugs (Cîrstea, Moldovan-Teselios & Iancu, 2017).

Table 3. The exploratory factor analysis of emotional factors

Variables	Brand Love	Brand Engagement
BL3-This brand makes me very happy	0,904	
BL5-I am passionate about this brand	0,942	
BL6-I am very attached to this brand	0,908	
BE2-I consider my favourite brands to be a part of myself		0,891
BE3-I often feel a personal connection between my brands and me		0,888
BE4-Part of me is defined by important brands in my life		0,905
BE5-I feel as if I have a close personal connection with the brands I most prefer		0,914
BE6-I can identify with important brands in my life		0,904
BE7-There are links between the brands that I prefer and how I view myself		0,839
Eigenvalues/Rotation Sums Squared Loadings	2,529	4,760
% Variance	84,314	79,338
Bartlett's test	646,597***	1835,339***
KMO' test	0,734	0,899

Notes: Significant at *** $p < 0.01$. *Extraction Method: Principal Component Analysis. Rotation Method: Varimax with Kaiser Normalization.

For the sake of simplicity, Table 6 presents the results considering these three independent variables. The logistic regression model was statistically significant, $X^2(8) = 44{,}815$, p <0,000. The model explained 30,7% (Nagelkerke R^2) of the variance in buying aspirin and correctly classified 75,3% of the cases. A respondent who reported a health status as "very bad" or "bad" have 4,237 and 3,556 times more likely to purchase an Aspirin than the respondent with a "very good" self-reported health status. Increasing the emotional factors related with the brand: brand love and self-brand engagement are associated with an increased likelihood of buying the Aspirin.

Table 6. Explanatory factors of the consumption of aspirin brand

	Odds ratio	(95% CI)
Self-reported health status		
Very good	-	-
Good	2,065	(1,33; 7,09)
Reasonable	1,124***	(0,09; 13,82)
Bad	4,237**	(1,74; 10,28)
Very bad	3,556**	(1,58; 7,99)
Brand Love	1,166***	(0,87; 1,66)
Brand Engagement	2,034***	(1,49; 2,77)
Constant	0,415**	
$X^2 = 44{,}815$***, df = 8, Nagelkerke R^2=0,307; Overall Percentage = 75,3		

Note: Significant at: * $p < 0.10$ level ;** $p < 0.05$ level; *** $p < 0.01$.

The results indicate that emotions (brand love and brand engagement) are what really drive the purchasing behaviours, and also, the decision making process in the case of the Aspirin brand. These results are in in accordance with the work of Rauchnabel and Ahuvia (2014), i. e., utilitarian attributes of functional brands can be considered as explanatory antecedents of consumer brand love. In the same vein, it can be concluded that the results confirm that the consumer brand usage duration may influence consumer brand engagement, as posit by Dwivedi (2015).

5. CONCLUSION AND IMPLICATIONS

Aspirin or simply Acetylsalicylic Acid (AAS), is one of the oldest and most widely used medicines in the world that can relieve pain and decrease inflammation (Farmácias Portuguesas, 2019). Currently, it is over 110 years old and continues to arouse the interest of the scientific world and is commonly used as an antipyretic (fever fighting), analgesic, anti-inflammatory as well as antiplatelet, contributing to reduce the risk of thrombus formation and the risk of stroke (Farmácias Portuguesas, 2019).

Aspirin falls into the category of OTC drugs. As it is well known, the pharmaceutical industry spends billions of dollars in marketing and advertising prescription medicines and OTC drugs. This research investigates the main explanatory factors of the consumption of the Aspirin brand. The contribution of the article is essentially distinguished by i) fill a gap in the literature that investigates consumers' purchasing patterns of OTC drugs; ii) this research does not only consider the sociodemographic characteristics of the respondents, the consumption habits, but it also included emotional factors related with the brand: self-brand engagement and brand love; iii) this research is pioneer in the scientific investigation for the Aspirin brand in Portugal.

Emotional factors, self-brand engagement and brand love, are the crucial determinants in the consumer decision-making of the Aspirin brand. This study offers useful implications for marketers, health professionals, and public policy makers concerning the determinants that influence the consumers and non-consumers of the Aspirin brand. First of all, in the marketing communication techniques the emotional factors have to be considered. Second, the importance of health professionals should not be forgotten because the consumption must be controlled and overconsumption should be avoided.

A new challenge faces marketers, health professionals, and public policy makers concerning the role of emotional factors in purchasing the Aspirin brand. Pharmaceutical companies should use emotional factors in their marketing communication tools to enable consumers to strengthen their brand connection. However, overconsumption should be avoided. Here, the pharmacists have an important role as consultants of OTC drugs and self-medication (Memisoglu, 2017).

Some limitations can be highlighted in this research. We do not take into account explanatory factors in the purchase decision process, such as the recommendation from experts (doctors and pharmacists), previous experience in brand consumption, prospect information, commercial factors such as price and promotions, among others. It was also not distinguished whether the consumer associates the medicine with the company that markets it. Furthermore, we are conscious of the widespread limitations of employing online surveys as a way to collect answers. There are the advantages of being able to reach a larger number of people, in a faster way, and without incurring costs. Due to the existence of advantages and inconvenience in the way of questionnaires are administered, several studies have been carried out in this area, and have found similar responses across the different modes of administration (Damschroder *et al.*, 2004; Dillman, 2009; Covey *et al.*, 2010; Mulhern *et al.*, 2013; Rowen *et al.*, 2016). Some of limitations could be overcome in the future research.

REFERENCES

Alba, J. W., & Hutchinson, J. (1987). Dimensions of consumer expertise. *The Journal of Consumer Research*, *13*(4), 411–454. doi:10.1086/209080

Albert, N., Merunka, D., & Valette-Florence, P. (2008). When consumers love their brands: Exploring the concept and its dimensions. *Journal of Business Research*, *61*(10), 1062–1075. doi:10.1016/j.jbusres.2007.09.014

Albert, N., Merunka, D., & Valette-Florence, P. (2009). The feeling of love toward a brand: Concept and measurement. *Advances in Consumer Research. Association for Consumer Research (U. S.)*, *36*, 300–307.

Bagozzi, R., & Yi, Y. (1988). On the evaluation of structural equation models. *Journal of the Academy of Marketing Science*, *16*(1), 74–94. doi:10.1007/BF02723327

Bagozzi, R., Batra, R., & Ahuvia, A. (2017). Brand love: Development and validation of a practical scale. *Marketing Letters*, *25*(2), 235–243. doi:10.100711002-016-9406-1

Bairrada, C., Coelho, F., & Coelho, A. (2018). Antecedents and outcomes of brand love: Utilitarian and symbolic brand qualities. *European Journal of Marketing*, *52*(3-4), 656–682. doi:10.1108/EJM-02-2016-0081

Batra, R., Ahuvia, A., & Bagozzi, R. (2012). Brand Love. *Journal of Marketing*, *76*(2), 1–16. doi:10.1509/jm.09.0339

Bauer, H. H., Heinrich, D., & Martin, I. (2004). How to Create High Emotional Consumer Brand Relationships? The Causalities of Brand Passion. *Psychological Review*, 2189–2198.

Belk, R. (1988). Possessions and the extended self. *The Journal of Consumer Research*, *15*(2), 139–168. doi:10.1086/209154

Bergkvist, L., & Bech-Larsen, T. (2010). Two studies of consequences and actionable antecedents of brand love. *Brand Management*, *7*(7), 504–518. doi:10.1057/bm.2010.6

Bowden, J. L. H. (2009). The process of customer engagement: A conceptual framework. *Journal of Marketing Theory and Practice*, *17*(1), 63–74. doi:10.2753/MTP1069-6679170105

Bowden, J., Conduit, J., Hollebeek, L., Luoma-aho, V., & Solem, B. (2017). Engagement valence duality and spillover effects in online Brand communities. *Journal of Service Theory and Practice*, *27*(4), 877–897. doi:10.1108/JSTP-04-2016-0072

Brandão, A., Pinho, E. & Rodrigues, P. (2019). Antecedents and consequences of luxury brand engagement in social media. *Spanish Journal of Marketing – ESIC*, *23*(2), 163-183.

Brodie, R. J., Hollebeek, I., Juric, B., & Ilic, A. (2011). Customer engagement: Conceptual domain, fundamental propositions and implications for research. *Journal of Service Research*, *14*(3), 1–20. doi:10.1177/1094670511411703

Carroll, B., & Ahuvia, A. C. (2006). Some antecedents and outcomes of brand love. *Marketing Letters*, *17*(2), 79–89. doi:10.100711002-006-4219-2

Cîrstea, S. D., Moldovan-Teselios, C., & Iancu, A. I. (2017). Analysis of Factors that Influence OTC Purchasing Behavior. *IFMBE Proceedings*, *59*, 303–308. doi:10.1007/978-3-319-52875-5_63

Covey, J., Robinson, A., Jones-Lee, M., & Loomes, G. (2010). Responsibility, scale and valuation of rail safety. *Journal of Risk and Uncertainty*, *40*(1), 85–108. doi:10.100711166-009-9082-0

Damschroder, L., Baron, J., Hershey, J., Asch, D. A., Jepson, C., & Ubel, P. A. (2004). The validity of person trade-off methods: Randomized trial of computer elicitation versus face-to-face interview. *Medical Decision Making*, *24*(2), 170–180. doi:10.1177/0272989X04263160 PMID:15090103

Dhar, R., & Wertenbroch, K. (2000). Consumer choice between hedonic and utilitarian goods. *JMR, Journal of Marketing Research*, *37*(1), 60–71. doi:10.1509/jmkr.37.1.60.18718

Delgado-Ballester, E., Palazón, M., & Pelaez-Muñoz, J. (2017). This anthropomorphized brand is so loveable: The role of self-brand integration. *Spanish Journal of Marketing – ESIC*, *21*(2), 89-101.

Dessart, L., Veloutsou, C., & Morgan-Thomas, A. (2016). Capturing consumer engagement: Duality, dimensionality and measurement. *Journal of Marketing Management*, *32*(5/6), 399–426. doi:10.1080/0267257X.2015.1130738

Dillman, D., Smith, J., & Christian, L. (2009). *Internet, Mail and Mixed-Mode Surveys. The Tailored Design Method* (3rd ed.). John Wiley & Sons.

Dodd, T. H., Laverie, D. A., Wilcox, J. F., & Duhan, D. F. (2005). Differential effects of experience, subjective knowledge, and objective knowledge on sources of information used in consumer wine purchasing. *Journal of Hospitality & Tourism Research (Washington, D.C.)*, *29*(1), 3–19. doi:10.1177/1096348004267518

Dwivedi, A. (2015). A higher-order model of consumer brand engagement and its impact on loyalty intentions. *Journal of Retailing and Consumer Services*, *24*, 100–109. doi:10.1016/j.jretconser.2015.02.007

Farmácias Portuguesas. (2019). *A história da Aspirina*. Disponível em: https://www.farmaciasportuguesas.pt/menu-principal/bem-estar/a-historia-da-aspirina-r.html

Fernandes, T., & Moreira, M. (2019). Consumer brand engagement, satisfaction and brand loyalty: A comparative study between functional and emotional brand relationships. *Journal of Product and Brand Management*, *28*(2), 274–286. doi:10.1108/JPBM-08-2017-1545

Fetscherin, M., & Heinrich, D. (2014). Consumer Brand relationships: A research landscape. *Journal of Brand Management*, *21*(5), 366–371. doi:10.1057/bm.2014.22

Fetscherin, M. (2014). What type of relationship do we have with loved brands? *Journal of Consumer Marketing*, *31*(6/7), 430–440. doi:10.1108/JCM-05-2014-0969

Fetscherin, M., & Conway Dato-on, M. (2012). Brand love: investigating two alternative love relationships. In *Consumer Brand Relationships: Theory and Practice*. Taylor and Francis.

Fornell, C., & Larcker, D. (1981). Structural equation models with unobservable variables and measurement error: Algebra and statistics. *JMR, Journal of Marketing Research*, *18*(3), 382–388. doi:10.1177/002224378101800313

Fournier, S. (1998). Consumers and their brands: Developing relationship theory in consumer research. *The Journal of Consumer Research*, *24*(4), 343–373. doi:10.1086/209515

Fournier, S. (2009). Lessons learned about consumers' relationship with their brands. In D. MacInnis, W. Park, & J. Priester (Eds.), *Handbook of Brand Relationships* (pp. 5–23). M.E. Sharpe.

Gambetti, R. C., & Graffigna, G. (2010). The concept of engagement: A systematic analysis of the ongoing marketing debate. *International Journal of Market Research*, *52*(6), 801–826. doi:10.2501/S147078531020166

Garg, R., Mukherjee, J., Biswas, S., & Kataria, A. (2015). An investigation of antecedents and consequences of Brand love in India. *Asia-Pacific Journal of Business Administration*, *7*(3), 174–196. doi:10.1108/APJBA-09-2014-0112

Grisaffe, D. B., & Nguyen, H. P. (2011). Antecedents of emotional attachment to brands. *Journal of Business Research*, *64*(10), 1052–1059. doi:10.1016/j.jbusres.2010.11.002

Hair, J., Black, W., & Babin, B. (2010). *Multivariate Data Analysis: A Global Perspective*. Pearson Education.

Heinrich, D., Albrecht, C.-M., & Bauer, H. H. (2012). Love actually? Measuring and exploring consumers' brand love. In S. Fournier, M. Breazeale, & M. Fetscherin (Eds.), *Consumer Brand Relationships* (pp. 137–150). Routledge. doi:10.1007/978-3-8349-3898-5

Holbrook, M. B., & Hirschman, E. C. (1982). The experiential aspects of consumption: Consumer fantasies, feelings, and fun. *The Journal of Consumer Research*, *9*(2), 132–140. doi:10.1086/208906

Hollebeek, L. D. (2011). Demystifying customer brand engagement: Exploring the loyalty nexus. *Journal of Marketing Management*, *27*(7/8), 785–807. doi:10.1080/0267257X.2010.500132

Hollebeek, L. D., Glynn, M. S., & Brodie, R. J. (2014). Consumer brand engagement in social media: Conceptualization, scale development and validation. *Journal of Interactive Marketing*, *28*(2), 149–165. doi:10.1016/j.intmar.2013.12.002

Huang, C.-C. (2017). The impacts of Brand experiences on Brand loyalty: Mediators of Brand love and trust. *Management Decision*, *55*(5), 915–934. doi:10.1108/MD-10-2015-0465

Hwang, J., & Kandampully, J. (2012). The role of emotional aspects in younger consumer-brand relationships. *Journal of Product and Brand Management*, *21*(2), 98–108. doi:10.1108/10610421211215517

Junaid, M., Hou, F., Hussain, K., & Kirmani, A. A. (2019). Brand love: The emotional bridge between experience and engagement, generation-M perspective. *Journal of Product and Brand Management*, *28*(2), 200–215. doi:10.1108/JPBM-04-2018-1852

Kamat, V., & Parulekar, A. A. (2007). Brand Love- the Precursor to Loyalty. *Advertising and Consumer Psychology Conference, New Frontiers in Branding: Attitudes, Attachments, and Relationships.*

Keller, K. (2012). Understanding the richness of Brand relationships: Research dialogue on brands as intentional agents. *Journal of Consumer Psychology*, *22*(2), 186–190. doi:10.1016/j.jcps.2011.11.011

Keh, H. T., Pang, J., & Peng, S. (2007). Understanding and Measuring Brand Love. In J. R. Priester, D. J. MacInnis, & C. Whan Park (Eds.), *Advertising and Consumer Psychology New Frontiers in Branding: Attitudes, Attachments, and Relationships*. Society for Consumer Psychology.

Kohli, E., & Buller, A. (2013). Factors Influencing Consumer Purchasing Patterns of Generic Versus Brand Name Over-the-Counter Drugs. *Southern Medical Journal*, *106*(2), 155–160. doi:10.1097/SMJ.0b013e3182804c58 PMID:23380752

Kwon, J., Seo, Y., & Ko, D. (2016). Effective luxury-brand advertising: The ES–IF matching (Entity–Symbolic versus Incremental–Functional) model. *Journal of Advertising*, *45*(4), 459–471. doi:10.1080/00913367.2016.1226995

Lau, G. T., & Lee, S. H. (1999). Consumers' trust in a brand and the link to brand loyalty. *Journal of Market Focused Management*, *4*(4), 341–370. doi:10.1023/A:1009886520142

Leckie, C., Nyadzayo, M., & Johnson, L. (2016). Antecedents of consumer Brand engagement and Brand loyalty. *Journal of Marketing Management*, *32*(5/6), 558–578. doi:10.1080/0267257X.2015.1131735

Malär, L., Nyffenegger, B., Krohmer, H., & Hoyer, W. D. (2012). Implementing an intended Brand personality: A dyadic perspective. *Journal of the Academy of Marketing Science*, *40*(5), 728–744. doi:10.100711747-011-0251-8

Mann, C. C., & Plummer, M. L. (1991). *The aspirin wars: money, medicine, and 100 years of rampant competition* (1st ed.). Knopf.

Memisoglu, M. (2017). Marketing communications for over-the-counter drugs and non-pharmaceutical products: The professionals' perspective. *International Journal of Healthcare Management*, 1–8. Advance online publication. doi:10.1080/20479700.2017.1417075

Mulhern, B., Longworth, L., Brazier, J., Rowen, D., Bansback, N., Devlin, N., & Tsuchiya, A. (2013). Binary choice health state valuation and mode of administration: Head to head comparison of online and CAPI. *Value in Health*, *16*(1), 104–113. doi:10.1016/j.jval.2012.09.001 PMID:23337221

Novak, T. P., & Hoffman, D. L. (2019). Relationship journeys in the internet of things: A new framework for understanding interaction between consumers and smart objects. *Journal of the Academy of Marketing Science*, *47*(2), 216–237. doi:10.100711747-018-0608-3

Patwardhan, H., & Balasubramanian, S. (2011). Brand romance: A complementary approach to explain emotional attachment toward brands. *Journal of Product and Brand Management*, *20*(4), 297–308. doi:10.1108/10610421111148315

Rauschnabel, P. A., & Ahuvia, A. C. (2014). You're so lovable: Anthropomorphism and Brand love. *Journal of Brand Management*, *21*(5), 372–395. doi:10.1057/bm.2014.14

Roberts, K. (2005). *Lovemarks: The Future beyond Brands*. Powerhouse Books.

Rodrigues, C., & Rodrigues, P. (2019). Brand love matters to Millennials: The relevance of mystery, sensuality and intimacy to neo-luxury brands. *Journal of Product and Brand Management, 28*(7), 830–848. Advance online publication. doi:10.1108/JPBM-04-2018-1842

Rosch, E. (1978). Principles of categorization. In E. Rosch & B. B. Lloyd (Eds.), *Cognition and Categorization* (pp. 27–48). Lawrence Erlbaum.

Shimp, T. A., & Madden, T. J. (1988). Consumer-object relations: a conceptual framework based analogously on Sternberg's triangular theory of love. In Advances in Consumer Research. Provo, UT: Association for Consumer Research.

Rowen, D., Brazier, J., Keetharuth, A., Tsuchiya, A., & Mukuria, C. (2016). Comparison of modes of administration and alternative formats for eliciting societal preferences for burden of illness. *Applied Health Economics and Health Policy, 14*(1), 89–104. doi:10.100740258-015-0197-y PMID:26445967

Sprott, D., Czellar, S., & Spangenberg, E. (2009). The importance of a general measure of brand engagement on market behavior: Development and validation of a scale. *JMR, Journal of Marketing Research, 46*(February), 92–104. doi:10.1509/jmkr.46.1.92

Sternberg, R. (1986). A triangular theory of love. *Psychological Review, 93*(2), 119–135. doi:10.1037/0033-295X.93.2.119

Ülkümen, G., Chakravarti, A., & Morwitz, V. G. (2010). Categories create mind-sets: The effect of exposure to broad versus narrow categorizations on subsequent, unrelated decisions. *JMR, Journal of Marketing Research, 47*(4), 659–671. doi:10.1509/jmkr.47.4.659

World Health Organization. (2019). World Health Organization model list of essential medicines: 21st list 2019. Geneva: World Health Organization.

Van Doorn, J., Lemon, K. N., Mittal, V., Nass, S., Pick, D., Pirner, P., & Verhoef, P. C. (2010). Customer engagement behavior: Theoretical foundations and research directions. *Journal of Service Research, 13*(3), 253–266. doi:10.1177/1094670510375599

Veloutsou, C. (2007). Identifying the dimensions of the product-brand and consumer relationship. *Journal of Marketing Management, 23*(1/2), 7–26. doi:10.1362/026725707X177892

Veloutsou, C., & Moutinho, L. (2009). Brand relationship through brand reputation and brand tribalismo. *Journal of Business Research, 62*(3), 314–322. doi:10.1016/j.jbusres.2008.05.010

Venkatesan, R., Petersen, J. A., & Guissoni, L. (2018). Measuring and managing customer engagement value through the customer journey. In R. Palmatier, V. Kumar, & C. Harmeling (Eds.), *Customer Engagement Marketing* (pp. 53–74). Palgrave Macmillan. doi:10.1007/978-3-319-61985-9_3

Vivek, S. D., Beatty, S. E., Dalela, V., & Morgan, R. M. (2014). A generalized multidimensional scale for measuring customer engagement. *Journal of Marketing Theory and Practice, 22*(4), 401–420. doi:10.2753/MTP1069-6679220404

Compilation of References

Aaker, D. A., & Equity, M. B. (1991). Capitalizing on the Value of a Brand Name. New York, 28, 35-37.

Aaker, D. (2010). *Building Strong Brands*. P. Book.

Aaker, D. A. (1996). Measuring brand equity across products and markets. *California Management Review*, *38*(3), 102–120. doi:10.2307/41165845

Aaker, D. A., & Joachimsthaler, E. (2007). *Como construir marcas líderes;* tradução: Daniel Grassi, Porto Alegre. *The Bookman*.

Aaker, D. A., & Mcloughin, D. (2010). *Strategic Market Management: Global Perspectives*. John Wiley & Sons Ltd.

Aaker, J. (1997). Dimensions of Brand Personality. *JMR, Journal of Marketing Research*, *34*(3), 347–356. doi:10.1177/002224379703400304

Abbaspour, F., Soltani, S., & Tham, A. (2020). *Medical tourism for COVID-19 post-crisis recovery?* Anatolia. doi:10.1080/13032917.2020.1815067

Abimbola, T. (2001). Branding as a Competitive Strategy for Demand Management in SMEs. *Journal of Research in Marketing and Entrepreneurship*, *3*(2), 97–106. doi:10.1108/14715200180001480

Abirami, A. M., & Askarunisa, A. (2017). Sentiment analysis model to emphasize the impact of online reviews in healthcare industry. *Online Information Review*, *41*(4), 471–486. doi:10.1108/OIR-08-2015-0289

Adair, R. F., & Holmgren, L. R. (2005). Do drug samples influence resident prescribing behavior? A randomized trial. *The American Journal of Medicine*, *118*(8), 881–884. doi:10.1016/j.amjmed.2005.02.031 PMID:16084181

Adaval, R. (2003). How good bets better and bad gets worse: Understanding the impact of affect on evaluations of known brands. *The Journal of Consumer Research*, *30*(December), 352–367. doi:10.1086/378614

Adjei, M., Noble, S., & Noble, C. (2010). The influence of C2C communications in online brand communities on customer purchase behavior. *Journal of the Academy of Marketing Science*, *38*(5), 634–653. doi:10.100711747-009-0178-5

Ahadzadeh, A. S., Pahlevan Sharif, S., & Sim Ong, F. (2018). Online health information seeking among women: The moderating role of health consciousness. *Online Information Review*, *42*(1), 58–72. doi:10.1108/OIR-02-2016-0066

Ahuvia, A. C. (2005). Beyond the extended self: Loved objects and consumers' identity narratives. *The Journal of Consumer Research*, *32*(1), 171–184. doi:10.1086/429607

Aknin, L. B., Wiwad, D., & Hanniball, K. (2018). *Buying well-being: spending behavior and happiness*. Academic Press.

Aknin, L. B., Norton, M., & Dunn, E. W. (2009). From wealth to well-being? Money matters, but less than people think. *The Journal of Positive Psychology*, *4*(6), 523–527. doi:10.1080/17439760903271421

Alba, J. W., & Hutchinson, J. (1987). Dimensions of consumer expertise. *The Journal of Consumer Research*, *13*(4), 411–454. doi:10.1086/209080

Albert, N., Merunka, D., & Valette-Florence, P. (2008). When consumers love their brands: Exploring the concept and its dimensions. *Journal of Business Research*, *61*(10), 1062–1075. doi:10.1016/j.jbusres.2007.09.014

Albert, N., Merunka, D., & Valette-Florence, P. (2009). The feeling of love toward a brand: Concept and measurement. *Advances in Consumer Research. Association for Consumer Research (U. S.)*, *36*, 300–307.

Albliwi, S., Antony, J., & Lim, A. H. (2014). Critical failure factors of Lean Six Sigma: A systematic literature review. *International Journal of Quality & Reliability Management*, *31*(9), 1012–1030. doi:10.1108/IJQRM-09-2013-0147

Alén, E., Domínguez, T., & Losada, N. (2002). New Opportunities for the Tourism Market : Senior Tourism and Accessible Tourism. In Visions for Global Tourism Industry-Creating and Sustaining Competitive Strategies (pp. 140–166). Academic Press.

Alén, E., Losada, N., & Domínguez, T. (2016). The impact of ageing on the tourism industry: An approach to the senior tourist profile. *Social Indicators Research*, *127*(1), 303–322. doi:10.100711205-015-0966-x

Alkhateeb, F. M., & Doucette, W. R. (2008). Electronic detailing (e-detailing) of pharmaceuticals to physicians: A review. *International Journal of Pharmaceutical and Healthcare Marketing*, *2*(3), 235–245. doi:10.1108/17506120810903999

Almeida, Á. S. (2017). The role of private non-profit healthcare organizations in NHS systems: Implications for the Portuguese hospital devolution program. *Health Policy (Amsterdam)*, *121*(6), 699–707. doi:10.1016/j.healthpol.2017.03.016 PMID:28433325

Ambitur. (2016). Obtido de Ambitur: http://www.ambitur.pt

American Academy of Cosmetic Dentistry (AACD). (2015). *Cosmetic dentistry state of the industry survey 2015*. Retrieved from http://www.aacd.com/proxy/files/Publications%20and%20Resources/AACD%20State%20of%20the%20Cosmetic%20Dentistry%20Industry%202015.pdf

American Society of Plastic Surgeons. (2016). *Plastic surgery statistics report (2015)*. Retrieved from https://www.plasticsurgery.org/Documents/news-resources/statistics/2015-statistics/2015-plastic-surgery-statistics-report.pdf

Anabila, P., & Awunyo-vitor, D. (2014). Assessing the role of branding in the marketing of pharmaceutical products in Ghana : A case of three pharmaceutical companies. doi:10.5897/AJBM2013.7297

Andaleeb, S. S., & Tallman, R. F. (1996). Relationships of physicians with pharmaceutical sales representatives and pharmaceutical companies: An exploratory study. *Health Marketing Quarterly*, *13*(4), 79–89. doi:10.1300/J026v13n04_07 PMID:10159647

Andersen, R. (1995). Revisiting the behavioral model and access to medical care: Does it matter? *Journal of Health and Social Behavior*, *36*(1), 1–10. doi:10.2307/2137284 PMID:7738325

Anderson, J., & Markides, C. (2007). Strategic Innovation at the Base of the Pyramid. MIT Sloan Management Review. Retrieved from: https://sloanreview.mit.edu/article/strategic-innovation-at-the-base-of-the-pyramid/

Anderson, E., & Oliver, R. L. (1987). Perspectives on Behavior-Based versus Outcome-Based Salesforce Control Systems. *Journal of Marketing*, *51*(4), 76–88. doi:10.1177/002224298705100407

Andreine, D., Pedeliento, G., Zarantonello, L., & Solero, C. (2019). Reprint of "A renaissance of brand experience: Advancing the concept through a multi-perspective analysis". *Journal of Business Research*, *96*, 355–365. doi:10.1016/j.jbusres.2018.05.047

Angell, M. (2006). The truth about the drug companies. *Trial (Boston, Mass.)*, *42*(7), 66.

Aravind Eye Care's Vision for India. (n.d.). Forbes. Retrieved from: https://www.forbes.com/global/2010/0315/companies-india-madurai-blindness-nam-familys-vision.html

Aravind. (n.d.). https://aravind.org

Asamoah, E. S. (2014). Customer based brand equity (CBBE) and the competitive performance of SMEs in Ghana. *Journal of Small Business and Enterprise Development*, *21*(1), 117–131. doi:10.1108/JSBED-10-2013-0154

Ascend2. (2013). *Marketing Strategy Report Social Media.* Available at: http://ascend2.com/home/wp-content/uploads/Social-Marketing-Strategy-Report-Ascend2-Edition.pdf

Asean. (2014). *Asean Member States.* Available in: https://www.asean.org/asean/asean-member-states

Auren Consultores & EOI. (2013). *Turismo de salud en España.* Secretaría de Estado de Turismo, Ministerio de Industria, Energía y Turismo.

Awareness Inc. (2011). *11 ways to create engagement.* Available at: https://www.academia.edu/7151949/1_Strategies_to_Increase_Engagement_11_Strategies_to_Increase_Engagement_from_Awareness_Inc_Creators_of_the_Social_Marketing_Hub

Babu, B. K., Lakshmaiah, K., Foundation, E., Lakshmaiah, K., Foundation, E., Pradesh, A., & Pradesh, A. (2018). *Pharmaceutical Branding Strategies and Communication.* Academic Press.

Backer, E. L., Lebsack, J. A., Van Tonder, R. J., & Crabtree, B. F. (2000). The value of pharmaceutical representative visits and medication samples in community-based family practices. *The Journal of Family Practice*, *49*(9), 811–811. PMID:11032205

Bagga, T., Vishnoi, S. K., Jain, S., & Sharma, R. (2020). Medical Tourism: Treatment, Therapy & Tourism. *International Journal Of Scientific & Technology Research*, *9*(3), 4447–4453.

Bagozzi, R. P., Batra, R., & Ahuvia, A. (2017). Brand love: Development and validation of a practical scale. *Marketing Letters*, *28*(1), 1–14. doi:10.100711002-016-9406-1

Bagozzi, R. P., & Dholakia, U. M. (2006). Antecedents and purchase consequences of customer participation in small group brand communities. *International Journal of Research in Marketing*, *23*(1), 45–61. doi:10.1016/j.ijresmar.2006.01.005

Bagozzi, R., & Yi, Y. (1988). On the evaluation of structural equation models. *Journal of the Academy of Marketing Science*, *16*(1), 74–94. doi:10.1007/BF02723327

Bairrada, C., Coelho, F., & Coelho, A. (2018). Antecedents and outcomes of brand love: Utilitarian and symbolic brand qualities. *European Journal of Marketing*, *52*(3-4), 656–682. doi:10.1108/EJM-02-2016-0081

Baker, M. J., & Balmer, J. M. T. (1997). Visual identity: Trappings or substance? *European Journal of Marketing*, *31*(5/6), 366–382. doi:10.1108/eb060637

Bakker, A. B., & Demerouti, E. (2007). The job demands-resources model: State of the art. *Journal of Managerial Psychology*, *22*(3), 309–328. doi:10.1108/02683940710733115

Ballester, E. D. (2004). Applicability of a brand trust scale across product categories. *European Journal of Marketing*, *38*(5/6), 573–592. doi:10.1108/03090560410529222

Ballester, E. D., & Alemán, J. L. M. (2001). Brand trust in the context of consumer loyalty. *European Journal of Marketing*, *35*(11/12), 1238–1258. doi:10.1108/EUM0000000006475

Balmer, J. T. (2013). The transformation of continuing medical education (CME) in the United States. *Advances in Medical Education and Practice*, *4*, 171–182. doi:10.2147/AMEP.S35087 PMID:24101887

Baloglu, S., Busser, J., & Cain, L. (2019). Impact of experience on emotional well-being and loyalty. *Journal of Hospitality Marketing & Management*, *28*(4), 427–445. doi:10.1080/19368623.2019.1527269

Banerjee, S. (2016). Logo Change : Little Image Touch up or Serious Overhaul! Imperatives and Scanning Parameters. *Journal of Marketing Communications*, *4*(1), 59–70.

Barnato, K. (2014). *Top destinations for health tourism*. CNBC. Available in: https://www.cnbc.com/id/101487998/page/10

Barros, P. P. (2010). As parcerias público-privadas na saúde em Portugal [Health PublicPrivate Partnerships in Portugal]. In J. Simões (Ed.), 30 Anos do Serviço Nacional de Saúde – Um percurso comentado [30 Years of National Health Service – A commented pathway] (pp. 519–560). Almedina.

Barros, P. P. (2016). Public-private partnerships. In R. M. Scheffler (Ed.), *World Scientific handbook of global health economics and public policy*. World Scientific. doi:10.1142/9789813140530_0009

Barros, P. P., Machado, S., & Simões, J. (2011). Portugal: Health system review. *Health Systems in Transition*, *13*(4), 1–156. PMID:22222781

Barsky, A. (2008). Understanding the Ethical Cost of Organizational Goal-Setting: A Review and Theory Development. *Journal of Business Ethics*, *81*(1), 63–81. doi:10.100710551-007-9481-6

Bastos, D. H., Moura, L. R. C., & Christino, J. M. M. (2015). Measurement, testing and confidence validation in brand. *Revista Capital Científico-Eletrônica, 13*.

Bastos, D. H., Rodrigo, L., Moura, C., Maria, J., & Christino, M. (2015). Measurement, testing and confidence validation in brand. *Revista Capital Científico-Eletrônica, 13*.

Batra, R., Ahuvia, A., & Bagozzi, R. P. (2012). Brand Love. *Journal of Marketing*, *76*(2), 1–16. doi:10.1509/jm.09.0339

Bauer, H. H., Heinrich, D., & Martin, I. (2004). How to Create High Emotional Consumer Brand Relationships? The Causalities of Brand Passion. *Psychological Review*, 2189–2198.

Baumgarth, C. (2010). "Living the brand": Brand orientation in the business-to-business sector. *European Journal of Marketing*, *44*(5), 653–671. doi:10.1108/03090561011032315

Baumöl, U., Hollebeek, L., & Jung, R. (2016). Dynamics of customer interaction on social media platforms. *Electronic Markets*, *26*(3), 199–202. doi:10.100712525-016-0227-0

BCSD. (2019). Tendencias uma questão de velocidade. BCSD Conselho Empresarial para o Desenvolvimento Sustentável, 1-4.

Becker, G. S. (1962). Investment in human capital: A theoretical analysis. *Journal of Political Economy*, *70*(5), 9–49. doi:10.1086/258724

Beladi, H., Chao, C. C., Ee, M. S., & Hollas, D. (2019). Does medical tourism promote economic growth? A cross-country analysis. *Journal of Travel Research, 58*(1), 121–135. doi:10.1177/0047287517735909

Belk, R. (1988). Possessions and the extended self. *The Journal of Consumer Research, 15*(2), 139–168. doi:10.1086/209154

Bendror, Y. (2013). *Which Social Media Channels Should I Use For My Business?* Available at: https://smallbusiness.yahoo.com/advisor/social-media-channels-business-223554094.html

Benetoli, A., Chen, T. F., & Aslani, P. (2017). Consumer health-related activities on social media: Exploratory study. *Journal of Medical Internet Research, 19*(10), e352. doi:10.2196/jmir.7656

Berg. (2008). *Health tourism and Wellness tourism*. Munchen: Oldenbourg Publisher.

Bergkvist, L., & Bech-Larsen, T. (2010). Two studies of consequences and actionable antecedents of brand love. *Brand Management, 7*(7), 504–518. doi:10.1057/bm.2010.6

Berthon, P., Ewing, M. T., & Napoli, J. (2008). Brand Management in small to medium-sized enterprises. *Journal of Small Business Management, 46*(1), 27–45. doi:10.1111/j.1540-627X.2007.00229.x

Bhattacharjee, A., & Mogilner, C. (2014). Happiness from ordinary and extraordinary experiences. *The Journal of Consumer Research, 41*(1), 1–17. doi:10.1086/674724

Bilro, R. G., & Loureiro, S. M. C. (2020). *A consumer engagement systematic review: Synthesis and research agenda*. Spanish Journal of Marketing – ESIC. doi:10.1108/SJME-01-2020-0021

BioMedTrends. (2016). *Dental business trends & latest market research*. Retrieved from http://www.biomedtrends.com/GetDetails.asp?CatName=Dental

Biricik, A. (2006). *The role of logo design in creating brand emotion: a semiotic comparison of the Apple and IBM logos*. School of Engineering and Sciences of İzmir Institute of Technology.

Blackett, T., & Harrison, T. (2001). *Brand medicine : Use and future potential of branding in pharmaceutical markets*. Academic Press.

Blau, P. M. (1964). *Exchange and power in social life*. Transaction Publishers.

Bloom, D. E., Canning, D., & Fink, G. (2010). Implications of population ageing for economic growth. *Oxford Review of Economic Policy, 26*(4), 583–612. doi:10.1093/oxrep/grq038

BMJ. (2020). Will medical tourism survive covid-19? *BMJ, 370*. doi:10.1136/bmj.m2677

Boell, S. K., & Cecez-Kecmanovic, D. (2015). On being 'systematic' in literature reviews. In L. P. Willcocks, C. Sauer, & M. C. Lacity (Eds.), *Formulating Research Methods for Information Systems* (Vol. 2, pp. 48–78). Palgrave Macmillan UK. doi:10.1057/9781137509888_3

Böhnke, P., & Kohler, U. (2010). Well-being and inequality. In S. Immerfall, & G. Therborn (Eds.), Handbook of European societies (pp. 629–666). Berlin: Springer Science + Business Media. doi:10.1007/978-0-387-88199-7_20

Bonfada, P. L. B., Bonfada, M. R. H., González, M. E. A., & Gândara, J. M. G. (2011). El turismo de salud y el uso terapéutico del agua. *Estudios y Perspectivas en Turismo, 20*(2), 462–477.

Booth, A., Sutton, A., & Papaioannou, D. (2016). Systematic approaches to a successful literature review. *Sage (Atlanta, Ga.)*.

Bowden, J. L. H. (2009). The process of customer engagement: A conceptual framework. *Journal of Marketing Theory and Practice*, *17*(1), 63–74. doi:10.2753/MTP1069-6679170105

Bowden, J., Conduit, J., Hollebeek, L., Luoma-aho, V., & Solem, B. (2017). Engagement valence duality and spillover effects in online Brand communities. *Journal of Service Theory and Practice*, *27*(4), 877–897. doi:10.1108/JSTP-04-2016-0072

Bower, J. L., Leonard, H. B., & Paine, L. S. (2011). *Capitalism at Risk: Rethinking the Role of Business*. Harvard Business Review Press.

Boyett, J. H., & Boyett, J. T. (2003). The Guru Guide to Marketing: A Concise Guide to the Best Ideas from Today's Top Marketers (1a Edição). John Wiley & Sons, Inc.

Brakus, J. J., Schmitt, B. H., & Zarantonello, L. (2009). Brand experience: What is it? How is it Measured? Does it affect Loyalty. *Journal of Marketing*, *73*(3), 52–68. doi:10.1509/jmkg.73.3.052

Bramão, M. P., & Costa, A. (2003). *Código da publicidade: Anotado e comentado*. Vida Económica.

Brandão, A., Pinho, E. & Rodrigues, P. (2019). Antecedents and consequences of luxury brand engagement in social media. *Spanish Journal of Marketing – ESIC*, *23*(2), 163-183.

Bravo, P., Carlos, C., & Anette, S. (2013). Assessing determinants of organic food consumption using data from the German National Nutrition Survey II. *Food Quality and Preference*, *28*(1), 60–70. doi:10.1016/j.foodqual.2012.08.010

Bresciani, S., & Eppler, M. J. (2010). Brand new ventures? Insights on start-ups'" branding practices. *Journal of Product and Brand Management*, *19*(5), 356–366. doi:10.1108/10610421011068595

Bristow, R. S., & Yang, W. T. (2015). Sea, sun, sand and…. Selecting surgery: An exploration of health, medical and wellness tourist's mobility. *Human Geographies*, *9*(2), 117–129. doi:10.5719/hgeo.2015.92.1

Brodie, R. J., Hollebeek, L. D., Juric´, B., & Ilic´, A. (2011). Customer engagement conceptual domain, fundamental propositions, and implications for research. *Journal of Service Research*, *14*(3), 252–271. doi:10.1177/1094670511411703

Brodie, R. J., Ilic, A., Juric, B., & Hollebeek, L. (2013). Consumer engagement in a virtual brand community: An exploratory analysis. *Journal of Business Research*, *66*(1), 105–114. doi:10.1016/j.jbusres.2011.07.029

Büyüközkan, G., & Çifçi, G. (2012). A combined fuzzy AHP and fuzzy TOPSIS based strategic analysis of electronic service quality in healthcare industry. *Expert Systems with Applications*, *39*(3), 2341–2354. doi:10.1016/j.eswa.2011.08.061

Campbell, E. G., Gruen, R. L., Mountford, J., Miller, L. G., Cleary, P. D., & Blumenthal, D. (2007). A National Survey of Physician–Industry Relationships. *The New England Journal of Medicine*, *356*(17), 1742–1750. doi:10.1056/NEJMsa064508 PMID:17460228

Capella, M. L., Taylor, C. R., Campbell, R. C., & Longwell, L. S. (2009). Do Pharmaceutical Marketing Activities Raise Prices? Evidence from Five Major Therapeutic Classes. *Journal of Public Policy & Marketing*, *28*(2), 146–161. doi:10.1509/jppm.28.2.146

Caprariello, P., & Reis, H. T. (2013). To do, to have or to share? Valuing experiences over material possessions depends on the involvement of others. *Journal of Personality and Social Psychology*, *104*(2), 199–215. doi:10.1037/a0030953 PMID:23276272

Carrera, P., & Lunt, N. (2010). A European perspective on medical tourism: The need for a knowledge base. *International Journal of Health Services*, *40*(3), 469–484. doi:10.2190/HS.40.3.e PMID:20799671

Carroll, B. A., & Ahuvia, A. C. (2006). Some antecedents and outcomes of brand love. *Marketing Letters*, *17*(2), 79–89. doi:10.100711002-006-4219-2

Carter, T. J., & Gilovich, T. (2012). I am what I do, not what I have: The differential centrality of experiential and material and purchases to the self. *Journal of Personality and Social Psychology*, *98*(1), 1304–1317. doi:10.1037/a0027407 PMID:22369046

Casaló, L. V., Flavián, C., & Guinalíu, M. (2010). Relationship quality, community promotion and brand loyalty in virtual communities: Evidence from free software communities. *International Journal of Information Management*, *30*(4), 357–367. doi:10.1016/j.ijinfomgt.2010.01.004

Central Administration of the Health System. (2016). *Circular Normativa n.º 8/2016. Alteração do regulamento de aplicação de Taxas Moderadoras* [Normative Circular No. 8/2016. Changes in application rules for user charges]. Central Administration of the Health System. http://www.acss. min-saude.pt/circulares/Circular_Normativa/2016/Circular_Normativa_8_2016.pdf

Chahal, H., & Bala, M. (2012). Significant components of service brand equity in healthcare sector. *International Journal of Health Care Quality Assurance*, *25*(4), 343–362. doi:10.1108/09526861211221518 PMID:22755484

Chambers, D., & McIntosh, B. (2008). Using authenticity to achieve competitive advantage in medical tourism in the English-speaking Caribbean. *Third World Quarterly*, *29*(5), 919–937. doi:10.1080/01436590802106056

Cham, T. H., Lim, Y. M., Sia, B. C., Cheah, J. H., & Ting, H. (2020). Medical tourism destination image and its relationship with the intention to revisit: A study of Chinese medical tourists in Malaysia. *Journal of China Tourism Research*, 1–29. doi:10.1080/19388160.2020.1734514

Chauhan, K., & Pillai, A. (2013). Role of content strategy in social media brand communities: A case of higher education institutes in India. *Journal of Product and Brand Management*, *22*(1), 40–51. doi:10.1108/10610421311298687

Chaves, R. M. (2005). *Regime jurídico da publicidade*. Almedina.

Chen, C.-H., Wu, M.-H., & Cheng, J.-S. (2013). Service Demand of Senior for Spa on Wellness Tourism: An Explorative Study. *International Proceedings of Economics Development and Research*, *67*(6), 178–183. doi:10.7763/IPEDR

Cheng, A. C. L., Gursoy, D., & Lu, C. Y. (2015). Authenticity perceptions, brand equity and brand choice intention: The case of ethnic restaurants. *International Journal of Hospitality Management*, *50*, 36–45. doi:10.1016/j.ijhm.2015.07.008

Chen, Y.-K., & Hsieh, T. (2010). A study of the relationship among experiential marketing, experiential value and customer satisfaction. *Journal of Statistics and Management Systems*, *13*(6), 1283–1303. doi:10.1080/09720510.2010.10701534

Chew, Y. T., & Darmasaputra, A. (2015). 12 Identifying research gaps in medical tourism. *Destination Marketing: An international perspective*, 119.

Chew, L. D., O'Young, T. S., Hazlet, T. K., Bradley, K. A., Maynard, C., & Lessler, D. S. (2000). A physician survey of the effect of drug sample availability on physicians' behavior. *Journal of General Internal Medicine*, *15*(7), 478–483. doi:10.1046/j.1525-1497.2000.08014.x PMID:10940134

Chiu, Y. C., & Hsieh, Y. L. (2013). Communication online with fellow cancer patients: Writing to be remembered, gain strength, and find survivors. *Journal of Health Psychology*, *18*(12), 1572–1581. doi:10.1177/1359105312465915

Choo, E. K., Ranney, M. L., Chan, T. M., Trueger, N. S., Walsh, A. E., Tegtmeyer, K., McNamara, S. O., Choi, R. Y., & Carroll, C. L. (2015). Twitter as a tool for communication and knowledge exchange in academic medicine: A guide for skeptics and novices. *Medical Teacher*, *37*(5), 411–416. doi:10.3109/0142159X.2014.993371

Cîrstea, S. D., Moldovan-Teselios, C., & Iancu, A. I. (2017). Analysis of Factors that Influence OTC Purchasing Behavior. *IFMBE Proceedings*, *59*, 303–308. doi:10.1007/978-3-319-52875-5_63

Cleff, T., & Rennings, K. (2012). Are there any first-mover advantages for pioneering firms? *European Journal of Innovation Management*, *15*(4), 491–513. doi:10.1108/14601061211272394

Cone, J., & Gilovich, T. (2010). Understand money limits: People's beliefs about the income-happiness correlation. *The Journal of Positive Psychology*, *5*(4), 294–301. doi:10.1080/17439760.2010.498620

Conference, H. T. I. (2020). *Tourism post-Covid19 – What got you here, won't get you there!* Academic Press.

Connell, J. (2006). Medical tourism: Sea, sun, sand and ... surgery. *Tourism Management*, *27*(6), 1093–1100. doi:10.1016/j.tourman.2005.11.005

Content Marketing Institute and MarketingProfs. (2015a). *B2B Small Business Content Marketing: 2015 Benchmarks, Budgets and Trends North-America*. Available at: https://www.slideshare.net/CMI/b2b-small-business-content-marketing-2015-benchmarks-budgets-and-trends-north-america?qid=de17404c-06e7-49ba-a457-078fdb7ac8e9&v=qf1&b=&from_search=11

Content Marketing Institute and MarketingProfs. (2015b). *B2C Content Marketing Benchmarks, Budgets, and Trends North-America*. Available at: https://www.slideshare.net/mprofs/b2c-content-marketing-2014-benchmarks-budgets-and-trendsnorth-america?qid=d4bc6ef8-b24b-4a23-8566-57e0f4bf0328&v=default&b=&from_search=1

Content Marketing Institute. (2013). *The CMI Content Marketing Framework: 7 building blocks to success*. Available at: https://contentmarketinginstitute.com/wp-content/uploads/2013/03/CMI_Framework.pdf

Costea, D., Bend, S., Chou, S., & King, A. (n.d.). Is Advertising Effective or Not ? Evidence from the Pharmaceutical Market. Academic Press.

Covey, J., Robinson, A., Jones-Lee, M., & Loomes, G. (2010). Responsibility, scale and valuation of rail safety. *Journal of Risk and Uncertainty*, *40*(1), 85–108. doi:10.100711166-009-9082-0

Cretchley, J., Gallois, C., Chenery, H., & Smith, A. (2010). Conversations between carers and people with schizophrenia: A qualitative analysis using Leximancer. *Qualitative Health Research*, *20*(12), 1611–1628. doi:10.1177/1049732310378297 PMID:20675536

Crofts, K., & Bisman, J. (2010). Interrogating accountability: An illustration of the use of Leximancer software for qualitative data analysis. *Qualitative Research in Accounting & Management*, *7*(2), 180–207. doi:10.1108/11766091011050859

Cropanzano, R., & Mitchell, M. S. (2005). Social exchange theory: An interdisciplinary review. *Journal of Management*, *31*(6), 874–900. doi:10.1177/0149206305279602

Crow, H., Gage, H., Hampson, S., Hart, J., Kimber, A., Storey, L., & Thomas, H. (2002). Measurement of satisfaction with health care: Implications for practice from a systematic review of the literature. *Health Technology Assessment*, *6*(32). Advance online publication. doi:10.3310/hta6320

Cubanacan. (2014). *Cubanacan Turismo y Salud*. Available in: http://www.cubanacan.cu/index.php/es/component/content/article/118-cubanacan-turismo-y-salud

Cunha, L. (2006). *Turismo de Saude - Conceito e mercados*. Revista Lusófona de Humanidades e Tecnologias.

Cvijikj, I. P., & Michahelles, F. (2013). Online Engagement Factors on Facebook Brand Pages. *Social Network Analysis and Mining*, *3*(4), 843–861. doi:10.100713278-013-0098-8

Daly, A., & Moloney, D. (2004). Managing Corporate Rebranding. *Irish Marketing Review*, *17*, 30–36.

Damschroder, L., Baron, J., Hershey, J., Asch, D. A., Jepson, C., & Ubel, P. A. (2004). The validity of person trade-off methods: Randomized trial of computer elicitation versus face-to-face interview. *Medical Decision Making*, *24*(2), 170–180. doi:10.1177/0272989X04263160 PMID:15090103

Dana, J., & Loewenstein, G. (2003). A social science perspective on gifts to physicians from industry. *Journal of the American Medical Association*, *290*(2), 252–255. doi:10.1001/jama.290.2.252 PMID:12851281

Dang, H. S., Nguyen, T. M. T., Wang, C. N., Day, J. D., & Dang, T. M. H. (2020). Grey System Theory in the Study of Medical Tourism Industry and Its Economic Impact. *International Journal of Environmental Research and Public Health*, *17*(3), 961. doi:10.3390/ijerph17030961 PMID:32033177

Datta, P. T. (2016). Medical rep's suicide raises concern over sales pressure. *The Hindu Business Line*.

Datta, A., & Dave, D. (2017). Effects of Physician-directed Pharmaceutical Promotion on Prescription Behaviors: Longitudinal Evidence. *Health Economics*, *26*(4), 450–468. doi:10.1002/hec.3323 PMID:26893065

Day, G. S. (1994). The of Market-Drive Capabilities Organizations. *Journal of Marketing*, *58*(4), 37–52. doi:10.1177/002224299405800404

de Chernatony, L. (1999). Brand Management Through Narrowing the Gap Between Brand Identity and Brand Reputation. *Journal of Marketing Management*, *15*(1-3), 157–179. doi:10.1362/026725799784870432

de Chernatony, L. (2010). *From Brand Vision to Evaluation* (3rd ed.). Butterworth-Heinemann.

De Chernatony, L., Drury, S., & Segal-Horn, S. (2004). Identifying and sustaining services brands' values. *Journal of Marketing Communications*, *10*(2), 73–93. doi:10.1080/13527260410001693785

De la Hoz-Correa, A., Muñoz-Leiva, F., & Bakucz, M. (2018). Past themes and future trends in medical tourism research: A co-word analysis. *Tourism Management*, *65*, 200–211. doi:10.1016/j.tourman.2017.10.001

de la Puente Pacheco, M. A. (2017). Turismo médico comparado en Colombia y Singapur: Estudio sectorial y perspectivas de desarrollo. *Revista de derecho. División de Ciencias Jurídicas de la Universidad del Norte*, (47), 290–309.

De la Rosa, R. (2012). *Turismo de Salud*. México: Asociación Mexicana de Turismo de Salud. Disponible en: https://turespacio.com/blogs/turismo-de-salud/

de Lencastre, P. (1999). A marca: O sinal, a missão e a imagem. *Revista Portuguesa de Marketing*, (June), 23–71.

De Martino, I., D'Apolito, R., McLawhorn, A. S., Fehring, K. A., Sculco, P. K., & Gasparini, G. (2017). Social media for patients: Benefits and drawbacks. *Current Reviews in Musculoskeletal Medicine*, *10*(1), 141–145. doi:10.100712178-017-9394-7

De Silva, D., Ranasinghe, W., Bandaragoda, T., Adikari, A., Mills, N., Iddamalgoda, L., ... Gray, R. (2018). Machine learning to support social media empowered patients in cancer care and cancer treatment decisions. *PLoS One*, *13*(10), e0205855. doi:10.1371/journal.pone.0205855

de Toni, D., & Mazzon, J. A. (2014). Teste de um modelo teórico sobre o valor percebido do preço de um produto. *Revista ADM*, *49*(3), 549–565. doi:10.5700/rausp1167

Deci, E., & Ryan, R. (2008). Self-determination theory: Macrotheory of human motivation development and health. *Canadian Psychology*, *49*(3), 182–185. doi:10.1037/a0012801

Defibaugh, S. (2019). Discourse, Context & Media "I talked to my doctor": Constructing the neoliberal patient-consumer in direct-to-consumer pharmaceutical advertising. *Discourse*, Context & Media, 28, 1–7. doi:10.1016/j.dcm.2018.12.001

Delgado-Ballester, E., Palazón, M., & Pelaez-Muñoz, J. (2017). This anthropomorphized brand is so loveable: The role of self-brand integration. *Spanish Journal of Marketing – ESIC*, *21*(2), 89-101.

Deloitte. (2014). *Global health care outlook: Shared challenges, shared opportunities*. Retrieved from https://www2.deloitte.com/content/dam/Deloitte/global/Documents/Life-Sciences-Health-Care/dttl-lshc-2014-global-health-care-sector-report.pdf

Deloitte. (2015). *Global health care outlook: Common goals, competing priorities*. Retrieved from https://www2.deloitte.com/content/dam/Deloitte/global/Documents/Life-Sciences-Health-Care/gx-lshc-2015-health-care-outlook-global.pdf

DeMicco, F. J. (2016). A Disney strategic approach to patient/guest services in Hospitality Bridging Healthcare (H2H) and medical tourism and wellness. The Routledge Handbook of Health Tourism, 261.

DeMicco, F. J. (2017a). A Disney Approach to Medical Tourism and Wellness. In *Medical Tourism and Wellness* (pp. 135–142). Apple Academic Press. doi:10.1201/9781315365671-5

DeMicco, F. J. (Ed.). (2017). *Medical Tourism and Wellness: Hospitality Bridging Healthcare (H2H)*. CRC Press. doi:10.1201/9781315365671

DeMicco, F. J., & Reid, R. D. (1988). Older workers: A hiring resource for the hospitality industry. *The Cornell Hotel and Restaurant Administration Quarterly*, *29*(1), 56–61. doi:10.1177/001088048802900116

Dessart, L., Aldás-Manzano, J., & Veloutsou, C. (2019). Unveiling heterogeneous engagement-based loyalty in brand communities. *European Journal of Marketing*, *53*(9), 1854–1881. doi:10.1108/EJM-11-2017-0818

Dessart, L., Veloutsou, C., & Morgan-Thomas, A. (2015). Consumer engagement in online brand communities: A social media perspective. *Journal of Product and Brand Management*, *24*(1), 28–42. doi:10.1108/JPBM-06-2014-0635

Dessart, L., Veloutsou, C., & Morgan-Thomas, A. (2016). Capturing consumer engagement: Duality, dimensionality and measurement. *Journal of Marketing Management*, *32*(5–6), 399–426. doi:10.1080/0267257X.2015.1130738

DeVoe, S., & House, J. (2012). Time, money and happiness: How does putting a price on time affect our ability to smell the roses? *Journal of Experimental Psychology*, *48*(2), 466–467.

Dhar, R., & Wertenbroch, K. (2000). Consumer choice between hedonic and utilitarian goods. *JMR, Journal of Marketing Research*, *37*(1), 60–71. doi:10.1509/jmkr.37.1.60.18718

Diariocritico. (2012). Cifras del 'turismo sanitario': España facturó en un sólo año 441 millones a los países europeos, frente a los 46 que pagó por los gastos de españoles en el extranjero. *Diario Crítico*. Available in: https://www.diariocritico.com/economia/sanidad/tribunal-de-cuentas/extranjeros/410713

Dilip, R., & Banerjee, S. (2012). Strategic branding roadmap for SMEs operating in business-to-business sector. *Journal of Research in Marketing and Entrepreneurship*, *14*(2), 142–163. doi:10.1108/14715201211271384

Dillman, D., Smith, J., & Christian, L. (2009). *Internet, Mail and Mixed-Mode Surveys. The Tailored Design Method* (3rd ed.). John Wiley & Sons.

Dixon, A. (1999). *Health Care Systems in Transition—Portugal*. European Observatory on Health Care Systems.

Dodd, T. H., Laverie, D. A., Wilcox, J. F., & Duhan, D. F. (2005). Differential effects of experience, subjective knowledge, and objective knowledge on sources of information used in consumer wine purchasing. *Journal of Hospitality & Tourism Research (Washington, D.C.)*, *29*(1), 3–19. doi:10.1177/1096348004267518

Domingues, M. E. (2019). *40 Anos do SNS*. Ministerio da Saúde.

Dong, X., Li, M., & Xie, Y. (2013). Understanding Sample Usage and Sampling as a Promotion Tool: State of Industry Practice and Current Research. In M. Ding, J. Eliashberg, & S. Stremersch (Eds.), *Innovation and Marketing in the Pharmaceutical Industry: Emerging Practices, Research, and Policies* (Vol. 20, pp. 507–530). Springer Science & Business Media. doi:10.1007/978-1-4614-7801-0_17

Donnally, C. J. III, Li, D. J., Maguire, J. A. Jr, Roth, E. S., Barker, G. P., McCormick, J. R., Rush, A. J. III, & Lebwohl, N. H. (2018). How social media, training, and demographics influence online reviews across three leading review websites for spine surgeons. *The Spine Journal*, *18*(11), 2081–2090. doi:10.1016/j.spinee.2018.04.023

Donohue, J. M., & Berndt, E. R. (2004). Effects of direct-to-consumer advertising on medication choice: The case of antidepressants. *Journal of Public Policy & Marketing*, *23*(2), 115–127. doi:10.1509/jppm.23.2.115.51395

Dryglasa, D., & Salamaga, M. (2017). Applying destination attribute segmentation to health tourists: A case study of Polish spa resorts. *Journal of Travel & Tourism Marketing*, *34*(4), 503–514. doi:10.1080/10548408.2016.1193102

Dwivedi, A. (2015). A higher-order model of consumer brand engagement and its impact on loyalty intentions. *Journal of Retailing and Consumer Services*, *24*, 100–109. doi:10.1016/j.jretconser.2015.02.007

Dyer, G. Jr, & Wilkins, A. (1991). Better stories, not better constructs to generate better theory: A rejoinder to Eisenhardt. *Academy of Management Review*, *16*(3), 613–619. doi:10.5465/amr.1991.4279492

Earley, P. (2009). Work, learning and professional practice: The role of leadership apprenticeships. *School Leadership & Management: Formerly School Organisation*, *29*(3), 307–320. doi:10.1080/13632430902793718

Edmonds, A. (2011, Winter). Almost Invisible Scars. *Medical Tourism to Brazil*, *36*(2), 297–302. PMID:21114074

Ehrbeck, T., Guevara, C., & Mango, P. D. (2008). Mapping the market for medical travel. *The McKinsey Quarterly*, *11*. https://www.researchgate.net/publication/265184262_Mapping_the_market_for_medical_travel

Elling, M. E., Fogle, H. J., McKhann, C. S., & Simon, C. (2002). Making more of pharma's sales force: Pharmaceutical companies have lost their focus on doctors. The key to higher sales is regaining it. *The McKinsey Quarterly*, *3*, 86 95.

Erbay, E., & Esatoglu, A. (2017). Reputation Management in Healthcare. In Developments in Health Sciences (pp. 591–610). St. Kliment Ohridski University Press.

Erdogan, S., & Yilmaz, E. (2012). Medical Tourism: an assessment on Turkey. In *International Joint Conference of 10th, International Conference on Knowledge, Economy and Management; 11th International Conference of the ASIA Chapter of the AHRD & 2nd International Conference of the MENA Chapter of the AHRD. Proceedings*. Istanbul Medeniyet Üniversitesi.

Escuela de Organización Industrial. (2013). *El turismo de Salud en España*. Gobierno de España.

Espanha, R., & Ávila, P. (2016). Health Literacy Survey Portugal: A Contribution for the Knowledge on Health and Communications. *Procedia Computer Science*, *100*, 1033–1041. doi:10.1016/j.procs.2016.09.277

Estar, A. d. (2013). *Associação de Turismo e Bem Estar*. Academic Press.

Estevão, H. F. (2016). *O Turismo de Experiencia no âmbito da Saúde e Bem-Estar; Orientação à Turismoterapia*. Dissertação - Instituto Politecnico de Tomar.

Euromonitor – Country Report Portugal. (2014). *Internet Retailing in Portugal*. Available at: www.euromonitor.com/internet-retailing-in-portugal/report

European Commission. (2014). *Population ageing in Europe*. Retrieved from https://ec.europa.eu/research/social-sciences/pdf/policy_reviews/kina26426enc.pdf

European Commission. (2015). *Competition among health care providers: Investigating policy options in the European Union*. Publications Office. https://data.europa.eu/doi/10.2875/867590

Evolution, B. (2010). *The Changing Roles of Brand Management*. Academic Press.

Executive, R. P., & Vol, D. (1999). *Rx branding : A brand new culture*. Academic Press.

Eysenbach, G. (2008). Medicine 2.0: Social networking, collaboration, participation, apomediation, and openness. *Journal of Medical Internet Research*, *10*(3), e22. doi:10.2196/jmir.1030

Farber, B. A., & Nitzburg, G. C. (2016). Young adult self-disclosures in psychotherapy and on Facebook. *Counselling Psychology Quarterly*, *29*(1), 76–89. doi:10.1080/09515070.2015.1078286

Farhana, M. (2014). Implication of Brand Identity Facets on Marketing Communication of Lifestyle Magazine: Case Study of A Swedish Brand. *Journal of Applied Economics & Business Research*, *4*(1), 23–41. http://search.ebscohost.com/login.aspx?direct=true&db=buh&AN=94709306&site=ehost-live

Farmácias Portuguesas. (2019). *A história da Aspirina*. Disponível em: https://www.farmaciasportuguesas.pt/menu-principal/bem-estar/a-historia-da-aspirina-r.html

Farrow, S., Gillgrass, D., Pearlstone, A., Torr, J., & Pozniak, E. (2012). Setting CME standards in Europe: Guiding principles for medical education. *Current Medical Research and Opinion*, *28*(11), 1861–1871. doi:10.1185/03007995.2012.738191 PMID:23043468

Fernandes, T., & Moreira, M. (2019). Consumer brand engagement, satisfaction and brand loyalty: A comparative study between functional and emotional brand relationships. *Journal of Product and Brand Management*, *28*(2), 274–286. doi:10.1108/JPBM-08-2017-1545

Ferreira, J., & Sousa, B. (2020). Experiential Marketing as Leverage for Growth of Creative Tourism: A Co-creative Process. In Advances in Tourism, Technology and Smart Systems. Smart Innovation, Systems and Technologies, (vol. 171, pp. 567-577). Springer. doi:10.1007/978-981-15-2024-2_49

Ferreira, S., & Vieira, T. (2016). *Termas Norte de Portugal*. Academic Press.

Fetscherin, M., & Conway Dato-on, M. (2012). Brand love: investigating two alternative love relationships. In *Consumer Brand Relationships: Theory and Practice*. Taylor and Francis.

Fetscherin, M. (2014). What type of relationship do we have with loved brands? *Journal of Consumer Marketing*, *31*(6/7), 430–440. doi:10.1108/JCM-05-2014-0969

Fetscherin, M., & Heinrich, D. (2014). Consumer Brand relationships: A research landscape. *Journal of Brand Management*, *21*(5), 366–371. doi:10.1057/bm.2014.22

Fingerman, K. L., & Perlmutter, M. (1995). Future time perspective and life events across adulthood. *The Journal of General Psychology*, *122*(1), 95–111. doi:10.1080/00221309.1995.9921225 PMID:7714506

Fischer, E., & Reuber, A. R. (2011). Social interaction via new social media: (How) can interactions on Twitter affect effectual thinking and behavior? *Journal of Business Venturing*, *26*(1), 1–18. doi:10.1016/j.jbusvent.2010.09.002

Five paradoxes of Indian Healthcare. (2018, July 27). The Economic Times.

Flores, L. (2013). *Un mercado muy sano*. CNEExpansion. Available in: http://www.cnnexpansion.com/economia/2013/06/26/un-mercado-muy-sano

Fornell, C., & Larcker, D. (1981). Structural equation models with unobservable variables and measurement error: Algebra and statistics. *JMR, Journal of Marketing Research*, *18*(3), 382–388. doi:10.1177/002224378101800313

Fournier, S. (1998). Consumers and their brands: Developing relationship theory in consumer research. *The Journal of Consumer Research*, *24*(4), 343–373. doi:10.1086/209515

Fournier, S. (2009). Lessons learned about consumers' relationship with their brands. In D. MacInnis, W. Park, & J. Priester (Eds.), *Handbook of Brand Relationships* (pp. 5–23). M.E. Sharpe.

Frost, J., Okun, S., Vaughan, T., Heywood, J., & Wicks, P. (2011). Patient-reported outcomes as a source of evidence in off-label prescribing: Analysis of data from PatientsLikeMe. *Journal of Medical Internet Research*, *13*(1), e6. doi:10.2196/jmir.1643

Fugh-Berman, A., & Ahari, S. (2007). Following the Script: How Drug Reps Make Friends and Influence Doctors. *PLoS Medicine*, *4*(4), e150. doi:10.1371/journal.pmed.0040150 PMID:17455991

Fuller, J., Jawecki, G., & Muhlbacher, H. (2007). Innovation creation by online basket- ball communities. *Journal of Business Research*, *60*(1), 60–71. doi:10.1016/j.jbusres.2006.09.019

Gagnon, M.-A., & Lexchin, J. (2008). The cost of pushing pills: A new estimate of pharmaceutical promotion expenditures in the United States. *PLoS Medicine*, *5*(1), e1. doi:10.1371/journal.pmed.0050001 PMID:18177202

Gaines, J., & Lee, C. V. (2019). Medical tourism. In *Travel Medicine* (pp. 371–375). Elsevier. doi:10.1016/B978-0-323-54696-6.00039-2

Gambetti, R. C., & Graffigna, G. (2010). The concept of engagement: A systematic analysis of the ongoing marketing debate. *International Journal of Market Research*, *52*(6), 801–826. doi:10.2501/S147078531020166

Gambetti, R. C., Graffigna, G., & Biraghi, S. (2012). The grounded theory approach to consumer-brand engagement: The practitioner's standpoint. *International Journal of Market Research*, *54*(5), 659–687. doi:10.2501/IJMR-54-5-659-687

Ganguli, S., & Ebrahim, A. H. (2017). A qualitative analysis of Singapore's medical tourism competitiveness. *Tourism Management Perspectives*, *21*, 74–84. doi:10.1016/j.tmp.2016.12.002

Ganley, D., & Lampe, C. (2009). The ties that bind: Social network principles in online communities. *Decision Support Systems*, *47*(3), 266–274. doi:10.1016/j.dss.2009.02.013

Garg, R., Mukherjee, J., Biswas, S., & Kataria, A. (2015). An investigation of antecedents and consequences of Brand love in India. *Asia-Pacific Journal of Business Administration*, *7*(3), 174–196. doi:10.1108/APJBA-09-2014-0112

Gensler, S., Völckner, F., Liu-Thompkins, Y., & Wiertz, C. (2013). Managing Brands in the Social Media Environment. *Journal of Interactive Marketing*, *27*(4), 242–256. doi:10.1016/j.intmar.2013.09.004

Gentile, C., Spiller, N., & Noci, G. (2007). How to Sustain the Customer Experience: An Overview of Experience Components that Co-create Value with the Customer. *European Management Journal*, *25*(5), 395–410. doi:10.1016/j.emj.2007.08.005

Gerdtham, U. G., & Johannesson, M. (2001). The relationship between happiness, health, and socio-economic factors: Results based on Swedish microdata. *Journal of Socio-Economics*, *30*(6), 553–557. doi:10.1016/S1053-5357(01)00118-4

Germany.travel. (2013). *Hospitals in Germany*. Available in: https://www.germany.travel/es/viajes-tematicos/turismo-medicinal/hospitals/clinicas.html (09.05.2017).

Germany.travel. (2014). *German National Tourist Board. Incoming-Tourism. Germany Facts and Figures 2013, Germany, the travel destination.* Alemania. Available in: https://www.germany.travel/media/pdf/dzt_marktforschung/GNTB-Incoming-Tourism-Germany-2014.pdf

Getz, D. (2012). *Event Studies. Theory, Research and Policy for Planned Events.* Routledge.

Geuens, M., Weijters, B., & De Wulf, K. (2009). A new measure of brand personality. *International Journal of Research in Marketing*, *26*(2), 97–107. doi:10.1016/j.ijresmar.2008.12.002

Ghaseminezhad, M. (2016). Investigating the impact of rebranded experience on purchase intention and rebranded evaluation. *International Journal of Humanities and Cultural Studies.*

Ghosh, T., & Mandal, S. (2019). Medical tourism experience: Conceptualization, scale development, and validation. *Journal of Travel Research*, *58*(8), 1288–1301. doi:10.1177/0047287518813469

Gielens, K., & Steenkamp, J. E. M. (2019). Branding in the era of digital (dis) intermediation. International Journal of Research in Marketing, 1–18. doi:10.1016/j.ijresmar.2019.01.005

Gilbert, D. T. (2006). *Stumbling on Happiness.* Knof.

Gilbody, S., Wilson, P., & Watt, I. (2005). Benefits and harms of direct to consumer advertising: A systematic review. *Quality & Safety in Health Care*, *14*(4), 246–250. doi:10.1136/qshc.2004.012781 PMID:16076787

Gill, L., & White, L. (2009). A critical review of patient satisfaction. *Leadership in Health Services*, *22*(1), 8–19. doi:10.1108/17511870910927994

Gilovich, T., Kumar, A., & Jampol, L. (2015). A Wonderful Life: Experiential Consumption and the Pursuit of Happiness. *Journal of Consumer Psychology*, *25*(1), 152–165. doi:10.1016/j.jcps.2014.08.004

Glass, H. E., & Rosenthal, B. (2004). Demographics, practices, and prescribing characteristics of physicians who are early adopters of new drugs. *P&T*, *29*, 699–708.

Gobé, M. (2002). *A emoção das marcas: conectando marcas às pessoas.* Campus.

Goffee, Rob, & Nicholson, N. (1994). Career development in male and female managers–convergence or collapse. *Women in management: Current research issues*, 80-92.

Goi, C., & Goi, M. (2011). Review on Models and Reasons of Rebranding. *International Conference on Social Science and Humanity*, *5*, 445–449.

Gómez-Zúñiga, B., Fernandez-Luque, L., Pousada, M., Hernández-Encuentra, E., & Armayones, M. (2012). ePatients on YouTube: analysis of four experiences from the patients' perspective. Medicine 2.0, 1(1).

Gönül, F. F., Carter, F., Petrova, E., & Srinivasan, K. (2001). Promotion of prescription drugs and its impact on physicians' choice behavior. *Journal of Marketing*, *65*(3), 79–90. doi:10.1509/jmkg.65.3.79.18329

Gönül, F. F., & Jr, F. J. (2012). Estimation of promotional strategies for newer vs older drugs based on physician prescribing data. *International Journal of Pharmaceutical and Healthcare Marketing*, *6*(1), 39–54. doi:10.1108/17506121211216897

Good, D. J., & Schwepker, C. H. (2012). Sales Quotas: Unintended Consequences on Trust in Organization, Customer-Oriented Selling, and Sales Performance. *Journal of Marketing Theory and Practice*, *20*(4), 437–452. doi:10.2753/MTP1069-6679200406

Goodman, R. A., Bunnell, R., & Posner, S. F. (2014). What is "community health"? Examining the meaning of an evolving field in public health. *Preventive Medicine*, *67*, 28–61. doi:10.1016/j.ypmed.2014.07.028 PMID:25069043

Govindarajan & Ramamurti. (2013, November). Delivering World-Class Health Care, Affordably. *Harvard Business Review*.

Grande, D., Shea, J. A., & Armstrong, K. (2012). Pharmaceutical Industry Gifts to Physicians: Patient Beliefs and Trust in Physicians and the Health Care System. *Journal of General Internal Medicine*, *27*(3), 274–279. doi:10.100711606-011-1760-3 PMID:21671130

Gray, H. H., & Poland, S. C. (2008). Medical tourism: Crossing borders to access health care. *Kennedy Institute of Ethics Journal*, *18*(2), 193–201. doi:10.1353/ken.0.0006 PMID:18610785

Grinder, B., Pascal, J. V., & Schwartz, G. R. (2010). Entrepreneurship and the early American clock industry. *Journal of Research in Marketing and Entrepreneurship*, *12*(1), 54–70. doi:10.1108/14715201011060885

Grisaffe, D. B., & Nguyen, H. P. (2011). Antecedents of emotional attachment to brands. *Journal of Business Research*, *64*(10), 1052–1059. doi:10.1016/j.jbusres.2010.11.002

Groot, W., & Van Den Brink, H. M. (2007). The health effects of education. *Economics of Education Review*, *26*(2), 186–200. doi:10.1016/j.econedurev.2005.09.002

Group, Health Strategies. (1999). *Access to high prescribers: the world of doorknob details*. Author.

Grytten, J., & Sorensen, R. (2000). Competition and dental services. *Health Economics*, *9*(5), 447–461. doi:10.1002/1099-1050(200007)9:5<447::AID-HEC529>3.0.CO;2-A PMID:10903544

Guerra, R. J. (2016). *Turismo de Saude e Bem-Estar - estratégia de desenvolvimento local para as Caldas da Cavaca*. Tese de Doutoramento da Universidade de Coimbra.

Gültüvin, E., & Cengiz, E. (2013). Health Tourism in Turkey: Opportunities and Threats. *Mediterranean Journal of Social Sciences*, *4*(10).

Gummerus, J., Liljander, V., Weman, E., & Pihlström, M. (2012). Customer engagement in a Facebook brand community. *Management Research Review*, *35*(9), 857–877. doi:10.1108/01409171211256578

Hair, J., Black, W., & Babin, B. (2010). *Multivariate Data Analysis: A Global Perspective*. Pearson Education.

Hall, C. M. (2011). Health and medical tourism: Kill or cure for global public health? *Tourism Review*, *66*(1/2), 4–15. doi:10.1108/16605371111127198

Hanefeld, J., Horsfall, D., Lunt, N., & Smith, R. (2013). Medical Tourism: A Cost or Benefit to the NHS? *PLoS One*, *8*(10).

Han, H. (2013). The healthcare hotel: Distinctive attributes for international medical travelers. *Tourism Management*, *36*, 257–268. doi:10.1016/j.tourman.2012.11.016

Han, H., & Hyun, S. S. (2015, February). Customer retention in the medical tourism industry: Impact of quality, satisfaction, trust, and price reasonableness. *Tourism Management*, *46*, 20–29. doi:10.1016/j.tourman.2014.06.003

Hanzel, T., Richards, J., Schwitters, P., Smith, K., Wendland, K., Martin, J., & Keltgen, J. (2018). # DocsOnTwitter: How Physicians use Social Media to Build Social Capital. *Hospital Topics*, *96*(1), 9–17. doi:10.1080/00185868.2017.1354558

Harindranath, R. M., & Jacob, J. (2017). Promotional support: A formative scale development. *International Journal of Pharmaceutical and Healthcare Marketing*, *11*(1), 97–110. doi:10.1108/IJPHM-04-2016-0023

Harindranath, R. M., & Sivakumaran, B. (2020). Perceived Impact of Promotional Support: Issues and Scale. *Journal of Promotion Management*.

Harindranath, R. M., Sivakumaran, B., & Jacob, J. (2019). The moderating role of sales experience in adaptive selling, customer orientation and job satisfaction in a unionized setting. *Journal of Business and Industrial Marketing*, *34*(8), 1724–1735. doi:10.1108/JBIM-08-2018-0233

Harrigan, P., Evers, U., Miles, M., & Daly, T. (2017). Customer engagement with tourism social media brands. *Tourism Management*, *59*, 597–609. doi:10.1016/j.tourman.2016.09.015

Harrison, V. (2013). *GSK to scrap targets for sales reps*. Retrieved 31-05-2019, from https://money.cnn.com/2013/12/17/news/companies/gsk-sales-targets/index.html

Haug, J. D. (1997). Physicians' preferences for information sources: A meta-analytic study. *Bulletin of the Medical Library Association*, *85*(3), 223–232. PMID:9285121

Health Regulation Authority. (2017). *Literacia em direitos dos utentes de cuidados de saúde* [Literacy on patients' rights in health care]. Health Regulation Authority. https://www.ers.pt/pages/171?news_id=1688

Heding, T., Knudtzen, C. F., & Bjerre, M. (2009). *Brand management: Research, theory and practice*. Routledge.

Heinrich, D., Albrecht, C.-M., & Bauer, H. H. (2012). Love actually? Measuring and exploring consumers' brand love. In S. Fournier, M. Breazeale, & M. Fetscherin (Eds.), *Consumer Brand Relationships* (pp. 137–150). Routledge. doi:10.1007/978-3-8349-3898-5

Hettler, B. (1980). Wellness promotion on a university campus. *Family & Community Health*, *3*(1), 77–95. doi:10.1097/00003727-198005000-00008 PMID:10246133

Heung, V. C., Kucukusta, D., & Song, H. (2011). Medical tourism development in Hong Kong: An assessment of the barriers. *Tourism Management*, *32*(5), 995–1005. doi:10.1016/j.tourman.2010.08.012

Heun, R., Bonsignore, M., Barkow, K., & Jessen, F. (2001). Validity of the five-item WHO Well-Being Index (WHO-5) in an elderly population. *European Archives of Psychiatry and Clinical Neuroscience*, *251*(2), 27–31. doi:10.1007/BF03035123 PMID:11824831

Heun, R., Burkart, M., Maier, W., & Bech, P. (1999). Internal and external validity of the WHO Well-Being Scale in the elderly general population. *Acta Psychiatrica Scandinavica*, *99*(3), 171–178. doi:10.1111/j.1600-0447.1999.tb00973.x PMID:10100911

Hobfoll, S. E. (1989). Conservation of resources: A new attempt at conceptualizing stress. *The American Psychologist*, *44*(3), 513–524. doi:10.1037/0003-066X.44.3.513 PMID:2648906

Hoeffler, S., & Keller, K. L. (2002). Building brand equity through corporate societal marketing. *Journal of Public Policy & Marketing*, *21*(1), 78–89. doi:10.1509/jppm.21.1.78.17600

Hoffman, D., & Fodor, M. (2010). Can you measure the ROI of your social media marketing? *MIT Sloan Management Review*, *52*(1), 40–49.

Holbrook, M. B., & Hirschman, E. C. (1982). The experiential aspects of consumption: Consumer fantasies, feelings, and fun. *The Journal of Consumer Research*, *9*(September), 132–140. doi:10.1086/208906

Hollebeek, L. (2011). Exploring customer brand engagement: Definition and themes. *Journal of Strategic Marketing*, *19*(7), 555–573. doi:10.1080/0965254X.2011.599493

Hollebeek, L. D. (2011). Demystifying customer brand engagement: Exploring the loyalty nexus. *Journal of Marketing Management*, *27*(7/8), 785–807. doi:10.1080/0267257X.2010.500132

Hollebeek, L. D., Glynn, M. S., & Brodie, R. J. (2014). Consumer Brand Engagement in Social Media: Conceptualization, Scale Development and Validation. *Journal of Interactive Marketing*, *28*(2), 149–165. doi:10.1016/j.intmar.2013.12.002

Holliday, R., Bell, D., Jones, M., Hardy, K., Hunter, E., Probyn, E., & Taylor, J. S. (2013). *Beautiful face, beautiful place: relational geographies and gender in cosmetic surgery tourism websites. Gender, Place & Culture*. Taylor & Francis., doi:10.1080/0966369X.2013.832655

Holliman, G., & Rowley, J. (2014). Business to business digital content marketing: Marketers' perceptions of best practice. *Journal of Research in Interactive Marketing*, *8*(4), 269–293. doi:10.1108/JRIM-02-2014-0013

Househ, M., Borycki, E., & Kushniruk, A. (2014). Empowering patients through social media: The benefits and challenges. *Health Informatics Journal*, *20*(1), 50–58. doi:10.1177/1460458213476969

Hoy, M. (2011). Building pathways to working with collections: Can internships and student work experience help? *Australian Academic and Research Libraries*, *42*(1), 29–42. doi:10.1080/00048623.2011.10722202

Huang, C.-C. (2017). The impacts of Brand experiences on Brand loyalty: Mediators of Brand love and trust. *Management Decision*, *55*(5), 915–934. doi:10.1108/MD-10-2015-0465

Hudson, S., & Li, X. (2012). Domestic medical tourism: A neglected dimension of medical tourism research. *Journal of Hospitality Marketing & Management*, *21*(3), 227–246. doi:10.1080/19368623.2011.615018

Hudson, S., & Shephard, G. W. (1998). Measuring service quality at tourist destinations: An application of importance-performance analysis to an alpine ski resort. *Journal of Travel & Tourism Marketing*, *7*(3), 61–77. doi:10.1300/J073v07n03_04

Hungarian Tourism. (2014). *Medical Tourism in Hungary, Spa Hungary*. Hungría. Available in: http://spa.gotohungary.com/en_GB/about-medical-tourism1

Hunter, W. C. (2007). Medical tourism: A new global niche. *International Journal of Tourism Science*, *7*(1), 129–140. doi:10.1080/15980634.2007.11434599

Hurwitz, M. A., & Caves, R. E. (1988). Persuasion or Information? Promotion and the Shares of Brand Name and Generic Pharmaceuticals. *The Journal of Law & Economics*, *31*(2), 299–320. doi:10.1086/467158

Husemann, K., Eckhardt, G., Grohs, R., & Saceanu, R. (2016). The dynamic interplay between structure, anastructure and antistructure in extraordinary experiences. *Journal of Business Research*, *69*(9), 3361–3370. doi:10.1016/j.jbusres.2016.02.008

Hwang, J., & Kandampully, J. (2012). The role of emotional aspects in younger consumer-brand relationships. *Journal of Product and Brand Management*, *21*(2), 98–108. doi:10.1108/10610421211215517

Idealista. (2013). Obtido de Idealista: http://www.idealista.pt

IMTD. (2012). *Industry Overview*. India Medical Tourism and Wellness Destination (IMTD). India. Available in: http://www.imtd.in/industry-overview/

IMTJ. (2013). Hungary: Hungarian Tourism promotes medical tourism. *International Medical Travel Journal*. Available in: https://www.imtj.com/news/?entryid82=416494

Indulska, M., Hovorka, D. S., & Recker, J. (2011). Quantitative approaches to content analysis: Identifying conceptual drift across publication outlets. *European Journal of Information Systems*, *21*(1), 49–69. https://www.hticonference.com/medical-tourism-post-covid19-what-got-you-here-wont-get-you-there/Medical

INFOSALUS. (2013). *Alemania.- El turismo médico crece un 20 por ciento cada año a pesar de ser un todavía "un mercado sin explotar"*. Available in: https://www.infosalus.com/actualidad/noticia-alemania-turismo-medico-crece-20-ciento-cada-ano-pesar-ser-todavia-mercado-explotar-20130307143011.html

Institute, G. W. (2018). *Empowering Wellness Worldwide*. Author.

Instituto de Estudios Turísticos. (2012). Informe anual 2012. Movimientos turísticos de los españoles (FAMILITUR). Madrid: Instituto de Turismo de España, Ministerio de Industria, Energía y Turismo.

International Trade Centre. (2014). *Medical and Wellness Tourism: Lessons From Asia*. Author.

Isen, A. M. (2003). *Positive Affect as a Source of Human Strength. In A Psychology of Human Strengths*. American Psychological Associations.

Jack, A., & Neville, S. (2013). More medical tourists leave UK than come to country, says study. *The Financial Times*. Available in: http://www.ft.com/cms/s/0/6e27935e-3cc0-11e3-86ef-00144feab7de.html#axzz36NzrUhlx

Jacob, N. T. (2018). Drug promotion practices: A review. *British Journal of Clinical Pharmacology*, *84*(8), 1659–1667. doi:10.1111/bcp.13513 PMID:29349812

Jafari, J., & Aaser, D. (1988). Tourism as the subject of doctoral dissertations. *Annals of Tourism Research*, *15*(3), 407–429. doi:10.1016/0160-7383(88)90030-8

Jami Pour, M., & Jafari, S. M. (2019). Toward a maturity model for the application of social media in healthcare: The health 2.0 roadmap. *Online Information Review*, *43*(3), 404–425. doi:10.1108/OIR-02-2018-0038

Jang, H., Olfman, L., Ko, I., Koh, J., & Kim, K. (2008). The influence of on-line brand community characteristics on community commitment and brand loyalty. *International Journal of Electronic Commerce*, *12*(3), 57–80. doi:10.2753/JEC1086-4415120304

Jankovic, M. (2012). Integrated marketing communications and brand identity development. *Management*, *17*(63), 91–100. doi:10.7595/management.fon.2012.0015

Jantsch, J. (2009). *Let's Talk: Social Media for Small Business – Version 2*. Available at: https://www.ducttapemarketing.com/socialmediaforbusiness.pdf

Jarvis, L. (2001). Productivity of big pharma falls after consolidation. *Chemical Market Reporter, 259*(5).

Joachimsthaler, E., & Aaker, D. A. (1997, January). Building brands without mass media. *Harvard Business Review*.

Jones, M. A., Reynolds, K. E., Mothersbaugh, D. L., & Beatty, S. E. (2007). The positive and negative effects of switching costs on relational outcomes. *Journal of Service Research*, *9*(4), 335–355. doi:10.1177/1094670507299382

Junaid, M., Hou, F., Hussain, K., & Kirmani, A. A. (2019). Brand love: The emotional bridge between experience and engagement, generation-M perspective. *Journal of Product and Brand Management*, *28*(2), 200–215. doi:10.1108/JPBM-04-2018-1852

Juntunen, M., Saraniemi, S., & Jussila, R. (2009). Corporate re-branding as a process. *Proceedings of the 5th Thought Leaders International Conference on Brand Management*, (April), 6–7.

Jurgens, M., Berthon, P., Edelman, L., & Pitt, L. (2016). Social media revolutions: The influence of secondary stakeholders. *Business Horizons*, *59*(2), 129–136. doi:10.1016/j.bushor.2015.11.010

Kaltcheva, D. V., Patino, A., Michael, V., Dennis, L., Pitta, A., & Imparato, N. (2014). Customers' relational models as determinants of customer engagement value. *Journal of Product and Brand Management*, *23*(1), 55–61. doi:10.1108/JPBM-07-2013-0353

Kamat, V., & Parulekar, A. A. (2007). Brand Love- the Precursor to Loyalty. *Advertising and Consumer Psychology Conference, New Frontiers in Branding: Attitudes, Attachments, and Relationships*.

Kandampully, J., Zhang, T., & Bilgihan, A. (2015). Customer loyalty: A review and future directions with a special focus on the hospitality industry. *International Journal of Contemporary Hospitality Management*, *27*(3), 379–414. doi:10.1108/IJCHM-03-2014-0151

Kapferer, J. N. (2012). *The new strategic brand management: Advanced insights and strategic thinking*. Kogan Page Publishers.

Kapferer, J. N. (1997). *Strategic Brand Management: Creating and Sustaining Brand Equity Long Term*. P. Konga.

Kapferer, J.-N. (1992). *Stractegic brand management, new approaches to creating and evaluating brand equity*. Free Press.

Kapferer, J.-N. (2008). *The New Strategic Brand Management: Creating and sustaining brand equity long term*. Kogan Page.

Kapferer, J.-N. (2012). *The New Strategic Brand Management Advanced Insights and Strategic Thinking*. K. Page.

Kaplan, A. M., & Haenlein, M. (2010). Users of the world, unite! The challenges and opportunities of Social Media. *Business Horizons*, *53*(1), 59–68. doi:10.1016/j.bushor.2009.09.003

Keh, H. T., Pang, J., & Peng, S. (2007). Understanding and Measuring Brand Love. In J. R. Priester, D. J. MacInnis, & C. Whan Park (Eds.), *Advertising and Consumer Psychology New Frontiers in Branding: Attitudes, Attachments, and Relationships*. Society for Consumer Psychology.

Keller, K. (2012). Understanding the richness of Brand relationships: Research dialogue on brands as intentional agents. *Journal of Consumer Psychology*, *22*(2), 186–190. doi:10.1016/j.jcps.2011.11.011

Keller, K. L. (1993). Conceptualizing, measuring and managing customer-based brand equity. *Journal of Marketing*, *57*(1), 1–22. doi:10.1177/002224299305700101

Keller, K. L. (1998). *Strategic brand management*. Prentice-Hall.

Keller, K. L. (1998). *Strategic Brand Management*. Prentice-Hall.

Keller, K. L. (2003). *Strategic Brand Management: Building, Measuring and Managing Brand Equity*. Prentice Hall.

Keller, K. L., & Lehmann, D. R. (2006). Brands and Branding: Research Finding and Future Priorities. *Journal of Marine Science*, *25*(6), 551–765.

Keller, K. L., & Machado, M. (2006). *Gestão estratégica de Marcas*. Pearson.

Kelley, E., & Lunt, N. (2013). *Medical tourism*. WTO Patient Safety Programme.

Kemp, E., Jillapalli, R., & Becerra, E. (2014). Healthcare branding: Developing emotionally based consumer brand relationships. *Journal of Services Marketing*, *28*(2), 126–137. doi:10.1108/JSM-08-2012-0157

Kerin, R. A., Jain, A., & Howard, D. (2002). Store shopping experience and consumer price-quality-value perceptions. *Journal of Retailing*, *68*(4), 376–397.

Kho, N. D. (2014). The State of Content Marketing. *EContent (Wilton, Conn.)*, *37*(1), 14–15.

Kim, A., & Ko, E. (2011). Do social media marketing activities enhance customer equity? An empirical study of luxury fashion brand. *Journal of Business Research*, *65*(10), 1480–1486. doi:10.1016/j.jbusres.2011.10.014

Kim, H., Park, K., & Schwarz, N. (2010). Will this trip really be exciting? The role of incidental emotions in product evaluation. *The Journal of Consumer Research*, *36*(6), 983–991. doi:10.1086/644763

Kim, J.-H. (2010). Determining the factors affecting the memorable nature of travel experiences. *Journal of Travel & Tourism Marketing*, *36*(April), 780–796. doi:10.1080/10548408.2010.526897

Kim, J.-H., & Ritchie, B. (2014). Cross Cultural validation of a memorable tourism experience scale. *Journal of Travel Research*, *53*(3), 323–335. doi:10.1177/0047287513496468

Kirsten, K. (2012). Content creation (Core Concepts/Content Marketing). *Marketing News*, *46*(2).

Knowledge@Wharton. (n.d.). Narayana Hrudayalaya: A Model for Accessible, Affordable Health Care? Retrieved from: https://knowledge.wharton.upenn.edu/article/narayana-hrudayalaya-a-model-for-accessible-affordable-health-care/

Kohli, E., & Buller, A. (2013). Factors Influencing Consumer Purchasing Patterns of Generic Versus Brand Name Over-the-Counter Drugs. *Southern Medical Journal*, *106*(2), 155–160. doi:10.1097/SMJ.0b013e3182804c58 PMID:23380752

Koporcic, N. (2020). Interactive Network Branding: Demonstrating the importance of firm representatives for small and medium-sized enterprises in emerging markets. *Journal of Business and Industrial Marketing*, *35*(7), 1179–1189. doi:10.1108/JBIM-10-2018-0301

Kordzadeh, N. (2016). Social media in health care. In *Contemporary Consumer Health Informatics* (pp. 101–123). Springer., . doi:10.1007/978-3-319-25973-4_6

Kotler, P., & Keller, K. (2013). Administração de Marketing (10aEdição). São Paulo: Academic Press.

Kotler, P., & Armstrong, G. (2007). *Princípios de Marketing*. Pearson Prentice Hall.

Kotler, P., & Keller, K. (2006). Administração de Marketing. São Paulo: Pearson.

Kotler, P., & Keller, K. L. (2011). *Marketing Management* (13th ed.). Prentice Hall.

Kotler, P., & Pfoertsch, W. (2006). *B2B Brand Managemet*. Springer-Verlag Berlin Heidelberg.

Krake, B. G. J. M. F. (2005). Successful brand management in SMEs: A new theory and practical hints. *Journal of Product and Brand Management*, *14*(4), 228–239. doi:10.1108/10610420510609230

Kremer, S., Bijmolt, T. H. A., Leeflang, P. S. H., & Wieringa, J. E. (2008). Generalizations on the effectiveness of pharmaceutical promotional expenditures. *International Journal of Research in Marketing*, *25*(4), 234–246. doi:10.1016/j.ijresmar.2008.08.001

Kuchler, H., Verbitsky, N., Jennings, T., & Connaire, S. (2020). Opioid executive admits to 'no morals' ahead of prison term. *Financial Times*. Retrieved from https://www.ft.com/insys

Kucukusta, D., & Guillet, B. D. (2014). Measuring spa-goers' preferences: A conjoint analysis approach. *International Journal of Hospitality Management*, *41*, 115–124. doi:10.1016/j.ijhm.2014.05.008

Kucukusta, D., Mak, A., & Chan, X. (2013). Corporate social responsibility practices in four and five-star hotels: Perspectives from Hong Kong visitors. *International Journal of Hospitality Management*, *34*, 19–30. doi:10.1016/j.ijhm.2013.01.010

Kucukusta, D., Pang, L., & Chui, S. (2013). Inbound travelers' selection criteria for hotel spas in Hong Kong. *Journal of Travel & Tourism Marketing*, *30*(6), 557–576. doi:10.1080/10548408.2013.810995

Kumar, D., & Gupta, P. (2019). Ethical Branding Best Practices. In Ethical Branding: Best Practice Cases and Lessons from the World's Most Ethical and Unethical Companies. Routledge (Taylor & Francis). doi:10.4324/9780429442520-8

Kumar, D., & Gupta, P. (2017). Rural Marketing. *Sage (Atlanta, Ga.)*.

Kwon, J., Seo, Y., & Ko, D. (2016). Effective luxury-brand advertising: The ES–IF matching (Entity–Symbolic versus Incremental–Functional) model. *Journal of Advertising*, *45*(4), 459–471. doi:10.1080/00913367.2016.1226995

Labonté, R., Runnels, V., Packer, C., & Deonandan, R. (Eds.). (2013). *Travelling Well: Essays in Medical Tourism. Transdisciplinary Studies in Population Health Series* (p. 20). Institute of Population Health, University of Ottawa.

Labroo, A. A., & Patrick, V. M. (2009). Providing a moment of respite: Why a positive mood helps seeing the big picture. *The Journal of Consumer Research*, *35*(5), 800–809. doi:10.1086/593683

Laesser, C. (2011). Health travel motivation and activities: Insights from a mature market – Switzerland. *Tourism Review*, *66*(1/2), 83–89. doi:10.1108/16605371111127251

Lakatos, E. M., & Marconi, M. A. (2007). *Técnicas de pesquisa: Planejamento e execução de pesquisas, amostragens e técnicas de pesquisa, elaboração, análise e interpretação de dados* (6th ed.). Atlas.

Lamiraud, K. (2014). Switching Costs in Competitive Health Insurance Markets. In *Encyclopedia of Health Economics* (pp. 375–381). Elsevier. doi:10.1016/B978-0-12-375678-7.01312-2

Lang, B., & Hyde, K. F. (2013). Word of Mouth: What We Know and What We Have Yet To Learn. *Journal of Consumer Satisfaction, Dissatisfaction & Complaining Behavior*, *26*, 1–18.

Larsen, J. (2003). Tourism Mobilities and the Travel Glance:Experiences of Being on the Move. *Scandinavian Journal of Hospitality and Tourism*, *1*(2), 81–98.

Lau, G. T., & Lee, S. H. (1999). Consumers' trust in a brand and the link to brand loyalty. *Journal of Market Focused Management*, *4*(4), 341–370. doi:10.1023/A:1009886520142

Layard, R. (2005). *Hppiness: Lessons from a new science*. Penguin.

Leckie, C., Nyadzayo, M., & Johnson, L. (2016). Antecedents of consumer Brand engagement and Brand loyalty. *Journal of Marketing Management*, *32*(5/6), 558–578. doi:10.1080/0267257X.2015.1131735

Lee, D., & Begley, C. E. (2016). Physician report of industry gifts and quality of care. *Health Care Management Review*, *41*(3), 275–283. doi:10.1097/HMR.0000000000000042 PMID:25427138

Leek, S., Canning, L., & Houghton, D. (2016). Revisiting the Task Media Fit Model in the era of Web 2.0: Twitter use and interaction in the healthcare sector. *Industrial Marketing Management*, *54*, 25–32. doi:10.1016/j.indmarman.2015.12.007

Leffler, K. B. (1981). Persuasion or information-the economics of prescription drug advertising. *The Journal of Law & Economics*, *24*(1), 45–74. doi:10.1086/466973

Leung, D., Law, R., van Hoof, H., & Buhalis, D. (2013). Social Media in Tourism and Hospitality: A Literature Review. *Journal of Travel & Tourism Marketing*, *30*(1–2), 3–22. doi:10.1080/10548408.2013.750919

Lewis, S. (2013). *Consumer Engagement Relationships in Social Media Campaigns*. Available at: https://www.american.edu/soc/communication/upload/Shani-Lewis-capstone.pdf

Leximancer Pty Ltd. (2016). *Leximancer User Guide, Release 4.5*. Author.

Leximancer. (2013). *Leximancer: From words to meaning*. Retrieved from http://www.leximancer.com/ cms/

Lien, C. H., Wen, M. J., Huang, L. C., & Wu, K. L. (2015). Online hotel booking: The effects of brand image, price, trust and value on purchase intentions. Elsevier.

Lim, C. W., & Kirikoshi, T. (2008). Understanding the effects of pharmaceutical promotion: a neural network approach guided by genetic algorithm-partial least squares. *Health Care Management Science, 11*(4), 359-372. doi:10.100710729-008-9053-z

Lima, M. (2016). *Saude e Bem Estar como Tendencia - o futuro do aperfeiçoamento (The Future of Betterman).* Academic Press.

Lim, W. M. (2016). Social media in medical and health care: Opportunities and challenges. *Marketing Intelligence & Planning*, *34*(7), 964–976. doi:10.1108/MIP-06-2015-0120

Liu, K. (2013). Happiness and tourism. *International Journal of Business and Social Science*, *4*(15). https://ijbssnet.com/journals/Vol_4_No_15_Special_Issue_November_2013/8.pdf

Li, Y., & Wang, X. (2017). Online social networking sites continuance intention: A model comparison approach. *Journal of Computer Information Systems*, *57*(2), 160–168. doi:10.1080/08874417.2016.1183448

Li, Y., Wang, X., Lin, X., & Hajli, M. (2018). Seeking and sharing health information on social media: A net valence model and cross-cultural comparison. *Technological Forecasting and Social Change*, *126*, 28–40. doi:10.1016/j.techfore.2016.07.021

Locker, D., Clarke, M., & Payne, B. (2000). Self-perceived oral health status, psychological well-being, and life satisfaction in an older adult population. *Journal of Dental Research*, *79*(4), 970–975. doi:10.1177/00220345000790041301 PMID:10831100

Lomax, W., Mador, M., & Fitzhenry, A. (2002). *Corporate Rebranding : Learning from Experience*. Kingston University.

Lunt, N. T., Mannion, R., & Exworthy, M. (2013). A framework for exploring the policy implications of UK medical tourism and international patient flows. *Social Policy and Administration*, *47*(1), 1–25. doi:10.1111/j.1467-9515.2011.00833.x

Lunt, N., & Carrera, P. (2010). Medical tourism : Assessing the evidence on treatment abroad. *Maturitas*, *66*(1), 27–32. doi:10.1016/j.maturitas.2010.01.017 PMID:20185254

Lunt, N., & Carrera, P. (2011). Systematic review of web sites for prospective medical tourists. *Tourism Review*, *66*(1/2), 57–67. doi:10.1108/16605371111127224

Lunt, N., Horsfall, D., & Hanefeld, J. (2016). Medical tourism: A snapshot of evidence on treatment abroad. *Maturitas*, *88*, 37–44. doi:10.1016/j.maturitas.2016.03.001 PMID:27105695

Lunt, N., Horsfall, D., Smith, R., Exworthy, M., Hanefeld, J., & Mannion, R. (2014). Market size, market share and market strategy: Three myths of medical tourism. *Policy and Politics*, *42*(4), 597–614. doi:10.1332/030557312X655918

Lu, W., & Stepchenkova, S. (2015). User-Generated Content as a Research Mode in Tourism and Hospitality Applications: Topics, Methods, and Software. *Journal of Hospitality Marketing & Management*, *24*(2), 119–154. doi:10.1080/19368623.2014.907758

Luxury Magazine. (2016). Obtido de Fluxury Magazine: http://www.fluxurymagazine.com

Lyubomirsky, S., Seldon, K., & Schkade, D. (2005). Pursuing happiness: The architecture of sustainable change. *Review of General Psychology*, *9*(2), 111–131. doi:10.1037/1089-2680.9.2.111

M'zungu, S., Merrilees, B., & Miller, D. (2019). Strategic and Operational Perspectives of SME Brand Management: A Typology. *Journal of Small Business Management*, *57*(3), 943–965. doi:10.1111/jsbm.12387

Macik-Frey, M. (2013). The age wave crests during economic crisis: New challenges for older workers. *Journal of Management and Marketing Research*, *12*, 1. http://www.aabri.com/manuscripts/121295.pdf

Macrae, C. (1996). *The brand chartering handbook : how brand organizations learn "living scripts."* Addison-Wesley.

Madhavan, S., Amonkar, M. M., Elliott, D., Burke, K., & Gore, P. (1997). The gift relationship between pharmaceutical companies and physicians: An exploratory survey of physicians. *Journal of Clinical Pharmacy and Therapeutics*, *22*(3), 207–218. doi:10.1046/j.1365-2710.1997.94975949.x PMID:9447476

Magnusson Maria, K. (2001). Attitudes towards organic foods among Swedish consumers. *British Food Journal*, *103*(3), 209–227. doi:10.1108/00070700110386755

Ma, L. S. H. (2008). A medical tourism primer for US physicians. The Journal of medical practice management. *MPM*, *23*(5), 291. PMID:18472606

Malär, L., Nyffenegger, B., Krohmer, H., & Hoyer, W. D. (2012). Implementing an intended Brand personality: A dyadic perspective. *Journal of the Academy of Marketing Science*, *40*(5), 728–744. doi:10.100711747-011-0251-8

Malhotra, A., Malhotra, C. K., & See, A. (2013). How to create brand engagement on Facebook. *MIT Sloan Management Review*, *54*(2), 18–20.

Malthouse, E. C., Haenlein, M., Skiera, B., Wege, E., & Zhang, M. (2013). Managing customer relationships in the social media era: Introducing the social CRM house. *Journal of Interactive Marketing*, *27*(4), 270–280. doi:10.1016/j.intmar.2013.09.008

Mann, C. C., & Plummer, M. L. (1991). *The aspirin wars: money, medicine, and 100 years of rampant competition* (1st ed.). Knopf.

Marketeer. (2016). Obtido de Marketeer: http://marketeer.pt

Marple, B. F., Fornadley, J. A., Patel, A. A., Fineman, S. M., Fromer, L., Krouse, J. H., Lanier, B. Q., & Penna, P.American Academy of Otolaryngic Allergy Working Group on Allergic Rhinitis. (2007). Keys to successful management of patients with allergic rhinitis: Focus on patient confidence, compliance, and satisfaction. *Otolaryngology Head and Neck Surgery*, *136*(6), S107–S124. doi:10.1016/j.otohns.2007.02.031 PMID:17512862

Mathijsen, A. (2019). Home, sweet home? Understanding diasporic medical tourism behaviour. Exploratory research of Polish immigrants in Belgium. *Tourism Management*, *72*, 373–385. doi:10.1016/j.tourman.2018.12.009

McAlexander, J. H., Schouten, J. W., & Koening, H. F. (2002). Building Brand Community. *Journal of Marketing*, *66*(1), 38–54. doi:10.1509/jmkg.66.1.38.18451

McHattie, L. S., Cumming, G., & French, T. (2014). Transforming patient experience: health web science meets medicine 2.0. Medicine 2.0, 3(1).

Medical Tourism Resource Guide. (2011). *India Medical Tourism. India*. Available in: https://www.medicaltourismresourceguide.com/india-medical-tourism

Medicaltourism. (2013a). *United States Medical Tourism. United States Medical Tourism offers the latest and best technology, as well as the best medical schools, teaching hospitals and research centers*. Medical Tourism Association. Available in: https://www.medicaltourism.com/en/destination/united-states.html

Medicaltourism. (2013b). *Singapore Medical Tourism*. Available in: https://www.medicaltourism.com/en/destination/singapore.html

Mellahi, K., & Johnson, M. (2000). Does it pay to be a first mover in e.commerce? The case of Amazon.com. *Management Decision*, *38*(7), 445–452. doi:10.1108/00251740010373458

Memisoglu, M. (2017). Marketing communications for over-the-counter drugs and non-pharmaceutical products: The professionals' perspective. *International Journal of Healthcare Management*, 1–8. Advance online publication. doi:10.1080/20479700.2017.1417075

Mendes. (2013). *O cluster da Saude e Bem-Estar: uma aposta de futuro.* Lisboa: CCP-Confederação de Comercio e Serviços de Portugal.

Merrilees, B. (2007). A theory of brand-led SME new venture development. *Qualitative Market Research*, *10*(4), 403–415. doi:10.1108/13522750710819739

Metz, D., & Underwood, M. (2005). *Older, richer, fitter: Identifying the consumer needs of Britain's ageing population.* Age Concern England.

Michaelidou, N., Micevshi, M., & Cadogan, J. W. (2015). An evaluation of nonprofit brand image: Towards a better conceptualization and measurement. *Journal of Business Research*, *68*(8), 43. doi:10.1016/j.jbusres.2015.03.024

Michalkó, G., Rátz, T., & Hinel, M. (2012). Spatial differences in Hungarian medical tourism supply based on service providers' online presence. *Hungarian Geographical Bulleton*, *61*(1), 31–47.

Milan, G. S., De Toni, D., de Lima, V. Z., Eberle, L., Milan, G. S., De Toni, D., ... Eberle, L. (2017). Papel Moderador da Marca e Mediação do Valor Percebido na Intenção de Recompra. *Revista de Administração Contemporânea*, *21*(3), 347–372. doi:10.1590/1982-7849rac2017160062

Miller, D., Merrilees, B., & Yakimova, R. (2014). Corporate Rebranding. *An Integrative Review of Major Enablers and Barriers to the Rebranding Process*, *16*(3), 265–289. doi:10.1111/ijmr.12020

Mittal, V., Ross, W. T. Jr, & Baldasare, P. M. (1998). The Asymmetric Impact of Negative and Positive Attribute-Level Performance on Overall Satisfaction and Repurchase Intentions. *Journal of Marketing*, *62*(1), 33–47. doi:10.1177/002224299806200104

Mizik, N., & Jacobson, R. (2004). Are physicians "easy marks"? Quantifying the effects of detailing and sampling on new prescriptions. *Management Science*, *50*(12), 1704–1715. doi:10.1287/mnsc.1040.0281

Moghavvemi, S., Ormond, M., Musa, G., Isa, C. R. M., Thirumoorthi, T., Mustapha, M. Z. B., & Chandy, J. J. C. (2017). Connecting with prospective medical tourists online: A cross-sectional analysis of private hospital websites promoting medical tourism in India, Malaysia and Thailand. *Tourism Management*, *58*, 154–163. doi:10.1016/j.tourman.2016.10.010

Mogilner, C., Kamvar, D., & Aaker, J. (2011). The shifting meaning of happiness. *Social Psychological & Personality Science*, *2*(4), 395–402. doi:10.1177/1948550610393987

Mogilner, C., Kamvar, S., & Aaker, J. (2012). How happiness affects choice. *The Journal of Consumer Research*, *39*(2), 429–443. doi:10.1086/663774

Mollerup, P. (1999). *Marks of Excelence- The history and taxonomy of trademarks.* Phaidon.

Morton, F. M. S. (2000). *Barriers to entry, brand advertising, and generic entry in the US pharmaceutical industry.* Academic Press.

Moss, G. D., Moss, G. D., & Bouleaux, A. (2007). What can the pharmaceutical world learn from consumer branding practice? Consumer and Pharmaceutical, 7(4), 315–320. doi:10.1057/palgrave.jmm.5050102

Mossberg, L. (2007). A marketing approach to the tourist experience. *Scandinavian Journal of Hospitality and Tourism*, *7*(1), 59–74. doi:10.1080/15022250701231915

Moss, G. D. (2016). *Pharmaceuticals-Where's the Brand Logic? Branding Lessons and Strategy*. CRC Press. doi:10.1201/b14470

Most private hospitals overcharging. (2019, Apr. 6). Bangkok Post. Retrieved from: https://www.bangkokpost.com/business/1657444/most-private-hospitals-overcharging

Mota, F. (2014). *Como otimizar o modelo de compra na gestão de stocks com base num método de avaliação da quantidade económica de compra: O caso da Sonae MC*. Relatório de Estágio do Mestrado em Economia da Faculdade de Economia do Porto.

Mulhern, B., Longworth, L., Brazier, J., Rowen, D., Bansback, N., Devlin, N., & Tsuchiya, A. (2013). Binary choice health state valuation and mode of administration: Head to head comparison of online and CAPI. *Value in Health*, *16*(1), 104–113. doi:10.1016/j.jval.2012.09.001 PMID:23337221

Muniz, A. M. Jr, & Schau, H. J. (2005). Religiosity in the abandoned Apple Newton brand community. *The Journal of Consumer Research*, *31*(4), 737–747. doi:10.1086/426607

Muniz, A. Jr, & O'Guinn, T. (2001). Brand Community. *The Journal of Consumer Research*, *27*(4), 412–436. doi:10.1086/319618

Muntinga, D., Moorman, M., & Smit, E. G. (2011). Introducing COBRA: Exploring Motivations for Brand-Related Social Media Use. *International Journal of Advertising*, *30*(1), 13–46. doi:10.2501/IJA-30-1-013-046

Muzellec, L., Doogan, M., & Lambkin, M. (2003). Corporate rebranding-an exploratory review. *Irish Marketing Review*, *16*, 31.

Muzellec, L., & Lambkin, M. (2006). Corporate rebranding: Destroying, transferring or creating brand equity? *European Journal of Marketing*, *40*(7/8), 803–824. doi:10.1108/03090560610670007

Myers, C., Kudsi, Y., & Ghaaferi, A. (2017). Surgeons Are Using Social Media to Share and Learn New Skills. Retrieved from https://hbr.org/2017/10/surgeons-are-using-social-media-to-share-and-learn-new-skills

Mymedholiday.com. (2013). *Thailand's medical tourism statistics: a look at the international patient numbers*. Tailandia. Available in: http://www.mymedholiday.com/blog/2013/10/793/thailands-medical-tourism-statistics-a-look-at-the-international-patient-numbers/

Namkung, Y., & Jang, S. (2013). Effects of restaurant green practices on brand equity formation: Do green practices really matter? *International Journal of Hospitality Management*, *33*, 11. doi:10.1016/j.ijhm.2012.06.006

NaRanong, A., & NaRanong, V. (2011). The effects of medical tourism: Thailand's experience. Bulletin of the World Health Organization, *89*, 336-344.

Narayana Health. (n.d.). https://www.narayanahealth.org/

Nemec, M., Kolar, T., & Rusjan, B. (2018). Online communities as a new source of exploring patient dissatisfaction. *Journal of Health Organization and Management*, *32*(8), 962–979. doi:10.1108/JHOM-03-2018-0104

Ngai, E. W., Tao, S. S., & Moon, K. K. (2015). Social media research: Theories, constructs, and conceptual frameworks. *International Journal of Information Management*, *35*(1), 33–44. doi:10.1016/j.ijinfomgt.2014.09.004

Ngamvichaikit, A., & Beise-Zee, R. (2014). Communication needs of medical tourists: An exploratory study in Thailand. *International Journal of Pharmaceutical and Healthcare Marketing*, *8*(1), 98–117. doi:10.1108/IJPHM-10-2012-0010

NHS England. (2020). *NHS Identity Guidelines*. https://www.england.nhs.uk/nhsidentity/

Norman, W. C., Daniels, M. J., McGuire, F., & Norman, C. A. (2001). Wither the mature market: An empirical examination of the travel motivations of neo-mature and veteran-mature markets. *Journal of Hospitality & Leisure Marketing*, *8*(3/4), 113–130. doi:10.1300/J150v08n03_08

Novak, T. P., & Hoffman, D. L. (2019). Relationship journeys in the internet of things: A new framework for understanding interaction between consumers and smart objects. *Journal of the Academy of Marketing Science*, *47*(2), 216–237. doi:10.100711747-018-0608-3

Nunes, A. M., & Ferreira, D. C. (2019). Reforms in the Portuguese health care sector: Challenges and proposals. *The International Journal of Health Planning and Management*, *34*(1), e21–e33. doi:10.1002/hpm.2695 PMID:30370564

O'Bannon, G. (2001). Managing our future: The generation X factor. *Public Personnel Management*, *30*(1), 95–110. doi:10.1177/009102600103000109

Odoom, R., Narteh, B., & Boateng, R. (2017). Branding in small- and medium-sized enterprises (SMEs): Current issues and research avenues. *Qualitative Market Research*, *20*(1), 68–89. doi:10.1108/QMR-12-2015-0091

OECD. (1998). *OECD Economic Surveys: Portugal 1998*. OECD. https://www.oecd-ilibrary.org/economics/oecd-economic-surveys-portugal-1998_eco_surveys-prt-1998-en

OECD. (2013). *Waiting Time Policies in the Health Sector: What Works?* (L. Siciliani, M. Borowitz, & V. Moran, Eds.). OECD. https://www.oecd-ilibrary.org/social-issues-migration-health/waiting-times-for-elective-surgery-what-works_9789264179080-en

Oh, H., Fiore, A., & Jeoung, M. (2007). Measuring experience economy concepts: Tourism applications. *Journal of Travel Research*, *46*(2), 119–132. doi:10.1177/0047287507304039

Ojasalo, J., Nätti, S., & Olkkonen, R. (2008). Brand building in software SMEs: An empirical chapter. *Journal of Product and Brand Management*, *17*(2), 92–107. doi:10.1108/10610420810864702

Okoli, C., & Schabram, K. (2010). *A guide to conducting a systematic literature review of information systems research*. Academic Press.

Oliveira, C., Brochado, A., & Correia, A. (2018). Seniors in international residential tourism: Looking for quality of life. *Anatolia*, *29*(1), 11–23. doi:10.1080/13032917.2017.1358189

Oliver, P., Marwell, G., & Teixeira, R. (1985). A Theory of the Critical Mass. I. Interdependence, Group Heterogeneity, and the Production of Collective Action. *American Journal of Sociology*, *91*(3), 522–556. doi:10.1086/228313

Oliver, R. L. (1997). *Satisfaction: A Behavioral Perspective on the Consumer*. McGraw-Hill.

Oliver, R. L. (2010). *Satisfaction: A behavioral perspective on the consumer* (2nd ed.). M.E. Sharpe.

Osinga, E. C., Leeflang, P. S. H., Srinivasan, S., & Wieringa, J. E. (2011). Why Do Firms Invest in Consumer Advertising with Limited Sales Response? A Shareholder Perspective. *Journal of Marketing*, *75*(1), 109–124. doi:10.1509/jm.75.1.109

Ouwersloot, H., & Odekerken-Schröder, G. (2008). Who's who in brand communities—And why? *European Journal of Marketing*, *42*(5/6), 571–585. doi:10.1108/03090560810862516

Pandey, N., & Shinde, S. (2019). V-Xpress: B2B marketing in the logistics industry. *Emerald Emerging Markets Case Studies*, *9*(1), 1–23. doi:10.1108/EEMCS-05-2018-0079

Pandey, N., & Gudipudi, B. (2019). Understanding 'what is privacy'for millennials on Facebook in India. *Journal of Data Protection & Privacy*, *2*(3), 224–233.

Pandey, N., Jha, S., & Singh, G. (2019). (in press). Promotion of green products on Facebook: Insights from Millennials. *International Journal of Management Practice.*

Pandey, N., Nayal, P., & Rathore, A. S. (2020). Digital marketing for B2B organizations: Structured literature review and future research directions. *Journal of Business and Industrial Marketing*, *35*(7), 1191–1204. Advance online publication. doi:10.1108/JBIM-06-2019-0283

Pandey, N., & Singh, G. (2012). *Marketing issues in SMEs: cases from India.* Pearson Education India.

Panigyrakis, G. G. (1999). *Brand managers in the pharmaceutical industry : are they any different.* Academic Press.

Park, H., & Kim, Y. K. (2014). The role of social network websites in the consumer–brand relationship. *Journal of Retailing and Consumer Services*, *21*(4), 460–467. doi:10.1016/j.jretconser.2014.03.011

Pasamontes, J. C. (2013). *España multiplicará por 40 el negocio del turismo de salud.* 02b.com. Available in: http://www.02b.com/es/notices/2013/09/espana_multiplicara_por_40_el_negocio_del_turismo_de_salud_7345.php

Patel, S. (2015). How businesses should be using social media in 2015. Forbes/Entrepreneurs. Retrieved from http://www.forbes.com/sites/sujanpatel/2015/06/24/how-businesses-should- be-using-social-media-in-2015/#577081854a5b

Patterson, I., & Pegg, S. (2009). Marketing the Leisure Experience to Baby Boomers and Older Tourists. *Journal of Hospitality Marketing & Management*, *18*(2–3), 254–272. doi:10.1080/19368620802594136

Patterson, M., & O'Malley, L. (2006). Brands, Consumers and Relationships: A Review. *Irish Marketing Review*, *18*(1/2), 10–20.

Patwardhan, A. A., Pandey, N., & Dhume, S. M. (2014). Analysis of physicians technology acceptance literature in changing indian pharmaceutical marketing context: A markus and robeys causal structure approach. *International Journal of Marketing & Business Communication*, *3*(2), 33–45.

Patwardhan, A. A., Pandey, N., & Dhume, S. M. (2017). Integrated model for understanding Indian physicians' internet usage pattern: An empirical approach. *International Journal of Healthcare Management*, *10*(1), 19–33. doi:10.1080/20479700.2016.1270385

Patwardhan, H., & Balasubramanian, S. (2011). Brand romance: A complementary approach to explain emotional attachment toward brands. *Journal of Product and Brand Management*, *20*(4), 297–308. doi:10.1108/10610421111148315

Pedro, A. R., Amaral, O., & Escoval, A. (2016). Literacia em saúde, dos dados à ação: Tradução, validação e aplicação do European Health Literacy Survey em Portugal. *Revista Portuguesa de Saude Publica*, *34*(3), 259–275. doi:10.1016/j.rpsp.2016.07.002

Peneda de Oliveira, C., & Sousa, B. M. (2019). Green Consumer Behavior and Its Implications on Brand Marketing Strategy. In V. Naidoo & R. Verma (Eds.), *Green Marketing as a Positive Driver Toward Business Sustainability* (pp. 69–95). IGI Global. doi:10.4018/978-1-5225-9558-8.ch004

Pentescu, A., Cetină, I., & Orzan, G. (2015). Social media's impact on healthcare services. *Procedia Economics and Finance*, *27*, 646–651. doi:10.1016/S2212-5671(15)01044-8

Peppers, D., & Rogers, M. (2011). *Managing Customer Relationships: A Strategic Framework* (2nd ed.). Wiley.

Pershad, Y., Hangge, P., Albadawi, H., & Oklu, R. (2018). Social medicine: Twitter in healthcare. *Journal of Clinical Medicine*, *7*(6), 121. doi:10.3390/jcm7060121

Petouhoff, N. (2013). *The Social Engagement Report: Competitive Brand Performance*. Available at: http://www.infinigraph.com/webinar/The_Social_Engagement_Report_2013.pdf

Phillips-Salimi, C. R., Haase, J. E., & Kooken, W. C. (2012). Connectedness in the context of patient-provider relationships: A concept analysis: Connectedness. *Journal of Advanced Nursing*, *68*(1), 230–245. doi:10.1111/j.1365-2648.2011.05763.x PMID:21771040

Piece of Moments. (2016). Obtido de Piece of Moments: http://piece-of-moments.webnode.pt

Pine, B., & Gilmore, J. (2011). The experience economy. Boston: Harvard Business Review Press.

Pine, B., & Gilmore, J. H. (1998). Welcome to the experience economy. *Harvard Business Review*, 97–105. PMID:10181589

Pinho-Costa, L., Yakubu, K., Hoedebecke, K., Laranjo, L., Reichel, C. P., Colon-Gonzalez, M. D. C., Neves, A. L., & Errami, H. (2016). Healthcare hashtag index development: Identifying global impact in social media. *Journal of Biomedical Informatics*, *63*, 390–399. doi:10.1016/j.jbi.2016.09.010

Pinho, M., & Borges, A. (2015). Bedside healthcare rationing dilemmas: A survey from Portugal. *International Journal of Human Rights in Healthcare*, *8*(4), 233–246. doi:10.1108/IJHRH-03-2015-0008

Pinho, M., Borges, A. P., & Zahariev, B. (2017). Bedsides healthcare rationing dilemmas: A survey from Bulgaria and comparison with Portugal. *Social Theory & Health*, *15*(3), 285–301. doi:10.105741285-017-0029-2

Pinho, M., & Pinto Borges, A. (2019). The views of health care professionals and laypersons concerning the relevance of health-related behaviors in prioritizing patients. *Health Education & Behavior*, *46*(5), 728–736. doi:10.1177/1090198119853604 PMID:31204850

PORDATA. (2018). *Fundação Francisco Manuel dos Santos*. http://www.pordata.pt/en/Portugal

Porter, C., Donthu, N., MacElroy, W. H., & Wydra, D. (2011). How to foster and sustain engagement in virtual communities. *California Management Review*, *53*(4), 80–110. doi:10.1525/cmr.2011.53.4.80

Porter, M. E., & Kramer, M. R. (1999, November). Philanthropy's New Agenda: Creating Value. *Harvard Business Review*.

Portugal, T. d. (2006). *Saúde e Bem-Estar*. Trismo de Portugal.

Portuguese Health Regulation Authority (ERS). (2014). *Gestão da Lista de Inscritos para Cirurgia no SNS* [Management system of the waiting list for surgery in the NHS]. Portuguese Health Regulation Authority.

Portuguese Health Regulation Authority. (2006). *Avaliação do Modelo de Celebração de Convenções pelo SNS* [Assessment of the NHS contracting model]. Portuguese Health Regulation Authority.

Portuguese Health Regulation Authority. (2008). *Estudo sobre as Convenções em 2008* [Study on NHS coventions in 2008]. Portuguese Health Regulation Authority.

Portuguese Health Regulation Authority. (2009a). *ERS/005/2009*. https://www.ers.pt/uploads/writer_file/document/273/Deliberacao_ERS-005-09_-Hosp_Misericordia_de_Paredes.pdf

Portuguese Health Regulation Authority. (2009b). *ERS/092/2009*. https://www.ers.pt/uploads/writer_file/document/244/ERS_092_09.pdf

Portuguese Health Regulation Authority. (2009c). *ERS/101/2009*. https://www.ers.pt/uploads/writer_file/document/235/ERS_101_09.pdf

Portuguese Health Regulation Authority. (2010). *ERS/052/2010*. https://www.ers.pt/uploads/writer_file/document/234/ERS_052_10.pdf

Portuguese Health Regulation Authority. (2011). *ERS/123/2011*. https://www.ers.pt/pages/484?news_id=674

Portuguese Health Regulation Authority. (2012). *ERS/034/2012*. https://www.ers.pt/uploads/writer_file/document/821/ERS_034_12.pdf

Portuguese Health Regulation Authority. (2013a). *Acesso, Concorrência e Qualidade no Sector Convencionado com o SNS: Análises Clínicas, Diálise, Medicina Física e Reabilitação e Radiologia* [Access, competition and quality issues in the provision of services by private providers to the National Health Service: Clinical Pathology, Dialysis, Physical Medicine and Rehabilitation and Radiology]. Portuguese Health Regulation Authority.

Portuguese Health Regulation Authority. (2013b). *ERS/036/2013*. https://www.ers.pt/uploads/writer_file/document/1044/ERS_36_13.pdf

Portuguese Health Regulation Authority. (2013c). *ERS/083/2013*. https://www.ers.pt/uploads/writer_file/document/1040/ERS_083_13.pdf

Portuguese Health Regulation Authority. (2013d). *ERS/091/2013*. https://www.ers.pt/uploads/writer_file/document/989/ERS_091_13__TM__.pdf

Portuguese Health Regulation Authority. (2013e). *O novo regime jurídico das Taxas Moderadoras* [The New Legal Framework of Moderating Fees]. Author.

Portuguese Health Regulation Authority. (2014a). *ERS/009/2014*. https://www.ers.pt/uploads/writer_file/document/1583/Publica__o_-_vers_o_n_o_confidencial_-_ERS_009_14.pdf

Portuguese Health Regulation Authority. (2014b). *ERS/021/2014*. https://www.ers.pt/uploads/writer_file/document/1454/Publica__o_-_vers_o_n_o_confidencial_-_ERS_021_14.pdf

Portuguese Health Regulation Authority. (2014c). *ERS/051/2014*. https://www.ers.pt/uploads/writer_file/document/1575/Publica__o_-_vers_o_n_o_confidencial_-_ERS_051_14.pdf

Portuguese Health Regulation Authority. (2014d). *ERS/052/2014*. https://www.ers.pt/uploads/document/file/8794/Publica__o_-_vers_o_n_o_confidencial_-_ERS_052_14.pdf

Portuguese Health Regulation Authority. (2014e, September 16). *Recomendação n.º 1/2014—Recomendação da ERS relativa a práticas publicitárias dos prestadores de cuidados de saúde*. https://www.ers.pt/pt/regula%C3%A7%C3%A3o/recomenda%C3%A7%C3%B5es/hist%C3%B3rico/hist%C3%B3rico/recomendacao-n%C2%BA-12014-recomendacao-da-ers-relativa-a-praticas-publicitarias-dos-prestadores-de-cuidados-de-saude/

Portuguese Health Regulation Authority. (2015a). *ERS/001/2015*. https://www.ers.pt/uploads/writer_file/document/1459/Publica__o_-_vers_o_n_o_confidencial_-_ERS_001_15.pdf

Portuguese Health Regulation Authority. (2015b). *ERS/014/2015*. https://www.ers.pt/uploads/writer_file/document/1585/Publica__o_-_vers_o_n_o_confidencial_-_ERS_014_15.pdf

Portuguese Health Regulation Authority. (2015c). *ERS/021/2015*. https://www.ers.pt/uploads/document/file/8797/Publica__o_-_vers_o_n_o_confidencial_-_ERS_021_15.pdf

Portuguese Health Regulation Authority. (2015d). *ERS/039/2015*. https://www.ers.pt/uploads/document/file/8798/Publica__o_-_vers_o_n_o_confidencial_-_ERS_039_15.pdf

Portuguese Health Regulation Authority. (2015e). *ERS/042/2015*. https://www.ers.pt/uploads/document/file/8793/Publica__o_-_vers_o_n_o_confidencial_-_ERS_042_15.pdf

Portuguese Health Regulation Authority. (2015f). *ERS/043/2015*. https://www.ers.pt/uploads/document/file/9243/Vers_oPublica__o_ERS-43-2015.pdf

Portuguese Health Regulation Authority. (2015g). *ERS/067/2015*. https://www.ers.pt/uploads/document/file/9245/Vers_oPublica__o_ERS-67-2015.pdf

Portuguese Health Regulation Authority. (2016a). *Estudo de avaliação das parcerias público-privadas na saúde* [Assessment of public-private partnerships in the health sector]. Portuguese Health Regulation Authority.

Portuguese Health Regulation Authority. (2016b). *PCO/114/2016*. https://www.ers.pt/pages/123?news_id=1647

Portuguese Health Regulation Authority. (2016c). *Relatório do Sistema de Gestão de Reclamações—Síntese descritiva de 2015*. Health Regulation Authority. https://www.ers.pt/uploads/writer_file/document/1794/Relat_rio_RECS_2015.pdf

Portuguese Health Regulation Authority. (2017). *PCO/160/2017*. https://www.ers.pt/pages/123?news_id=2307

Portuguese Health Regulation Authority. (2018a). *PCO/204/2018*. https://www.ers.pt/pages/123?news_id=2307

Portuguese Health Regulation Authority. (2018b). *PCO/428/2018*. https://www.ers.pt/pages/123?news_id=2329

Portuguese Ministry of Health. (2017). *Acesso a cuidados de saúde nos estabelecimentos do SNS e entidades convencionadas*. Author.

Powpaka, S. (1996). Factors Affecting the Doctor's Adoption of a New Pharmaceutical Product: An Empirical Investigation. *Journal of Pharmaceutical Marketing & Management*, *11*(2), 67–97. doi:10.3109/J058v11n02_05

Private hospitals fleece patients, overcharge up to 1737%. (2018, Feb. 21). DNA India. Retrieved from: https://www.dnaindia.com/delhi/report-private-hospitals-fleece-patients-overcharge-up-to-1737-2586945

PRWEB. (2013). *HealthcareAbroad.com Launches Medical Tourism Directory*. Author.

Publituris. (2016). Obtido de Publituris: http://www.publituris.pt

Quan, S., & Wang, N. (2004). Towards a structural model of the tourist experience: An illustration from food experiences in tourism. *Tourism Management*, *25*(3), 297–305. doi:10.1016/S0261-5177(03)00130-4

Rahman, M. K. (2019). Medical tourism: Tourists' perceived services and satisfaction lessons from Malaysian hospitals. *Tourism Review*, *74*(3), 739–758. doi:10.1108/TR-01-2018-0006

Rajala, R., & Westerlund, M. (2004). *Business models and networks: assets and capabilities in software business*. Paper presented at the 20th Industrial Marketing and Purchasing Conference, Copenhagen.

Rauschnabel, P. A., & Ahuvia, A. C. (2014). You're so lovable: Anthropomorphism and Brand love. *Journal of Brand Management*, *21*(5), 372–395. doi:10.1057/bm.2014.14

Reicheld, F., & Sasser, W. E. (1990). Zero defections: Quality comes to services. *Harvard Business Review*, 105-111.

Reicheld, F. (1996). *The loyalty effect: The hidden force behind growth, profits and lasting value*. Harvard Business Review School Press.

Reich, R. B. (2016). *Saving Capitalism: For the Many, Not the Few*. Icon Books.

Relman, A. S. (2001). Separating continuing medical education from pharmaceutical marketing. *Journal of the American Medical Association*, *285*(15), 2009–2012. doi:10.1001/jama.285.15.2009 PMID:11308441

Rentz, J. O., Shepherd, C. D., Tashchian, A., Dabholkar, P. A., & Ladd, R. T. (2002). A Measure of Selling Skill: Scale Development and Validation. *Journal of Personal Selling & Sales Management*, *22*(1), 13–21. doi:10.1080/08853134.2002.10754289

Reynolds, P. D. (1971). *A Primer in Theory Construction*. MacMillan Publishing Co.

Rezai, Teng, Phuah, Zainalabidin, & Shamsudin. (2014). Structural Equation Modeling of Consumer Purchase Intention Toward Synthetic Functional Foods. *Journal of Food Products Marketing, 20*(sup1), 13-34. doi:10.1080/10454446.2014.921868

Rizzo, J. A. (1999). Advertising and competition in the ethical pharmaceutical industry: The case of antihypertensive drugs. *The Journal of Law & Economics*, *42*(1), 89–116. doi:10.1086/467419

Robert, R. (2014). Content Marketing Forecast. *EContent (Wilton, Conn.)*, *37*(9), 28–28.

Roberts, C., & Alpert, F. (2010). Total customer engagement: Designing and aligning key strategic elements to achieve growth. *Journal of Product and Brand Management*, *19*(3), 198–209. doi:10.1108/10610421011046175

Roberts, K. (2005). *Lovemarks: The Future beyond Brands*. Powerhouse Books.

Rodrigues, P., Real, E., Vitorino, F., & Cantista, I. (2011, January). The importance of corporate social responsibility in the brand image. In *10th International Marketing Trends Congress, Paris, France* (pp. 21-23). Academic Press.

Rodrigues, C., & Rodrigues, P. (2019). Brand love matters to Millennials: The relevance of mystery, sensuality and intimacy to neo-luxury brands. *Journal of Product and Brand Management*, *28*(7), 830–848. Advance online publication. doi:10.1108/JPBM-04-2018-1842

Rodrigues, H., Brochado, A., & Troilo, M. (2019). Listening to the murmur of water: Essential satisfaction and dissatisfaction attributes of thermal and mineral spas. *Journal of Travel & Tourism Marketing*, *24*, 16–25. doi:10.1080/10548408.2019.1633986

Rodrigues, H., Brochado, A., Troilo, M., & Mohsin, A. (2017). Mirror, mirror on the wall, who's the fairest of the mall? A critical content analysis on medical tourism. *Tourism Management Perspectives*, *24*, 16–25. doi:10.1016/j.tmp.2017.07.004

Rodrigues, P., & Borges, A. P. (2015). Corporate social responsibility and its impact in consumer decision-making. *Social Responsibility Journal*, *11*(4), 690–701. doi:10.1108/SRJ-02-2014-0026

Rogers, W. A., Mansfield, P. R., Braunack-Mayer, A. J., & Jureidini, J. N. (2004). The ethics of pharmaceutical industry relationships with medical students. *The Medical Journal of Australia*, *180*(8), 411–414. doi:10.5694/j.1326-5377.2004.tb05995.x PMID:15089733

Roof Magazine. (2016). Obtido de Roof Magazine: http://roof-magazine.com

Rosch, E. (1978). Principles of categorization. In E. Rosch & B. B. Lloyd (Eds.), *Cognition and Categorization* (pp. 27–48). Lawrence Erlbaum.

Rosenthal Meredith, B., Berndt Ernst, R., Donohue Julie, M., Epstein Arnold, M., & Frank Richard, G. (2003). Demand Effects of Recent Changes in Prescription Drug Promotion. *Forum for Health Economics & Policy*, *6*(1). Advance online publication. doi:10.2202/1558-9544.1044

Rowen, D., Brazier, J., Keetharuth, A., Tsuchiya, A., & Mukuria, C. (2016). Comparison of modes of administration and alternative formats for eliciting societal preferences for burden of illness. *Applied Health Economics and Health Policy*, *14*(1), 89–104. doi:10.100740258-015-0197-y PMID:26445967

Rowley, J. (2008). Understanding digital content marketing. *Journal of Marketing Management, 24*(5/6), 517–540. doi:10.1362/026725708X325977

Ryan, R., & Deci, E. (2000). Self-determination theory and facilitation of intrinsic motivation, social development and well-being. *The American Psychologist, 55*(1), 68–78. doi:10.1037/0003-066X.55.1.68 PMID:11392867

Sackett, D. L. (1989). Rules of evidence and clinical recommendations on the use of antithrombotic agents. *CHEST Journal, 95*(2, Supplement), 2S–4S. doi:10.1378/chest.95.2_Supplement.2S PMID:2914516

Sadacharan, C. M. (2016). Vertical and horizontal facial proportions of Indian American men. *Anatomy & Cell Biology, 49*(2), 125–131. doi:10.5115/acb.2016.49.2.125 PMID:27382514

Sáenz, G. (2010). *Colombia como destino de turismo médico*. Conexión Colombia. Available in: https://www.conexioncolombia.com/colombia-como-destino-de-turismo-medico

Salehahmadi, Z., & Rafie, S. R. (2012). Factors Affecting Patients Undergoing Cosmetic Surgery in Bushehr, Southern Iran. *World Journal of Plastic Surgery, 1*(2), 99–106. PMID:25734051

Sanyal, N., & Shamindra, D. S. (2013). Conceptualisation of branding: Strategy based on the Indian pharma sector. *International Journal of Pharmaceutical and Healthcare Marketing, 7*(2), 175–198. doi:10.1108/IJPHM-04-2013-0013

Sashi, C. M. (2012). Customer engagement, buyer-seller relationships, and social media. *Management Decision, 50*(2), 253–272. doi:10.1108/00251741211203551

Saxe, R., & Weitz, B. A. (1982). The SOCO scale: A measure of the customer orientation of salespeople. *JMR, Journal of Marketing Research, 19*(3), 343–351. doi:10.1177/002224378201900307

Schau, H. J., & Gilly, M. C. (2003). We are what we post? Self-presentation in personal web space. *The Journal of Consumer Research, 30*(3), 385–404. doi:10.1086/378616

Schmitt, B. (1999). Experiential marketing. *Journal of Marketing Management, 15*(1–3), 53–67. doi:10.1362/026725799784870496

Schmitt, B. H., Brakus, J., & Zarantonello, L. (2014). The current state and future of brand experience. *Journal of Brand Management, 21*(9), 727–733. doi:10.1057/bm.2014.34

Schmitt, B., & Simonson, A. (1997). *Marketing aesthetics: the strategic management of brands, identity, and image*. The Free Press.

Schuiling, I., & Moss, G. (2004). *How different are branding strategies in the pharmaceutical industry and the fast-moving consumer goods sector*. Academic Press.

Schuiling, I., & Moss, G. (2004). How different are branding strategies in the pharmaceutical industry and the fast-moving consumer goods sector? *Journal of Brand Management, 11*(5), 366–380. doi:10.1057/palgrave.bm.2540182

Schwarz, N., & Clore, G. L. (1983). Mood, misattribution and judgments of well-being: Informative and directive functions of affective states. *Journal of Personality and Social Psychology, 45*(3), 512–523. doi:10.1037/0022-3514.45.3.513

Sciences, L. (2020). *Pharma 2020 : Marketing the future Which path will you take*. Academic Press.

SECTUR. (2013). *Impulso al turismo médico*. Presidencia de la República. Available in: http://www.presidencia.gob.mx/impulso-al-turismo-medico/

Seetanah, B. (2011). Assessing the dynamic economic impact of tourism for island economies. *Annals of Tourism Research, 38*(1), 291–308. doi:10.1016/j.annals.2010.08.009

Seiler, S. (2013). The impact of search costs on consumer behavior: A dynamic approach. *Quantitative Marketing and Economics*, *11*(2), 155–203. doi:10.100711129-012-9126-7

Şencan, I., Aydin, D., Constantinides, C., Mike, C., Yilmaz, C., Genç, A. & Lanyi, A. (2012). Definitions and Descriptions regarding Heatlh Tourism. Turquía: General Directorate of Health Services, Department of Health Tourism, Ministry of Health.

Seow, A. N., Choong, Y. O., Moorthy, K., & Choong, C. K. (2020). Predicting medical tourism behavioural intention using social cognition models. *Tourism Review*. Advance online publication. doi:10.1108/TR-06-2019-0267

Servimedcuba. (2012). *Quienes somos*. http://www.servimedcuba.com/index.php?option=com_content&view=article&id=72&Itemid=30 (20.05.2018).

Shapiro, B. T. (2018). Informational Shocks, Off-Label Prescribing, and the Effects of Physician Detailing. *Management Science*, *64*(12), 5925–5945. doi:10.1287/mnsc.2017.2899

Sheth, J. N. (2011). Impact of Emerging Markets on Marketing: Rethinking Existing Perspectives and Practices. *Journal of Marketing*, *75*(4), 166–182. doi:10.1509/jmkg.75.4.166

Shimp, T. A., & Madden, T. J. (1988). Consumer-object relations: a conceptual framework based analogously on Sternberg's triangular theory of love. In Advances in Consumer Research. Provo, UT: Association for Consumer Research.

Simões, J. (2010). *30 anos do Serviço Nacional de Saúde: Um percurso comentado*. Almedina.

Simon, F., & Tossan, V. (2018). Does brand-consumer social sharing matter? A relational framework of customer engagement to brand-hosted social media. *Journal of Business Research*, *85*, 175–184. doi:10.1016/j.jbusres.2017.12.050

Sinha, M. S., Kesselheim, A. S., & Darrow, J. J. (2018). Pharmaceutical Advertising in Medical Journals: Revisiting a Long-Standing Relationship. *Chest*, *153*(1), 9–11. doi:10.1016/j.chest.2017.09.048 PMID:29307432

Sirdeshmukh, D., Singh, J., & Sabol, B. (2002). Consumer Trust, Value, and Loyalty in Relational Exchanges. *Journal of Marketing*, *66*(1), 15–37. doi:10.1509/jmkg.66.1.15.18449

Smailhodzic, E., Hooijsma, W., Boonstra, A., & Langley, D. J. (2016). Social media use in healthcare: A systematic review of effects on patients and on their relationship with healthcare professionals. *BMC Health Services Research*, *16*(1), 442. doi:10.118612913-016-1691-0

Smaldone, F., Ippolito, A., & Ruberto, M. (2019). The shadows know me: Exploring the dark side of social media in the healthcare field. *European Management Journal*.

Smith, A. E., & Humphreys, M. S. (2006). Evaluation of unsupervised semantic mapping of natural language with Leximancer concept mapping. *Behavior Research Methods*, *38*(2), 262–279. doi:10.3758/BF03192778 PMID:16956103

Smith, K. T., Blazovich, J., & Smith, L. M. (2015). Social media adoption by corporations: An examination by platform, industry, size, and financial performance. *Academy of Marketing Studies Journal*, *19*(2), 127–143.

Smith, M. K., & Puckzo, L. (2009). *Health and Wellness tourism*. Butterworth-Heinemann.

Smith, P. C., & Forgione, D. A. (2007). Global outsourcing of healthcare: A medical tourism decision model. *Journal of Information Technology Case and Application Research*, *9*(3), 19–30. doi:10.1080/15228053.2007.10856117

Sousa, B. B., & Magalhães, F. C. (2019). An Approach on Attachment in Public Marketing and Higher Education Management Contexts. In C. Machado & J. Davim (Eds.), *Higher Education and the Evolution of Management, Applied Sciences, and Engineering Curricula* (pp. 151–171). IGI Global. doi:10.4018/978-1-5225-7259-6.ch006

Sousa, B., & Alves, G. (2019). The role of relationship marketing in behavioural intentions of medical tourism services and guest experiences. *Journal of Hospitality and Tourism Insights*, *2*(3), 224–240. doi:10.1108/JHTI-05-2018-0032

Sousa, B., & Rocha, A. T. (2019). The role of attachment in public management and place marketing contexts: A case study applied to Vila de Montalegre (Portugal). *International Journal of Public Sector Performance Management*, *5*(2), 189–205. doi:10.1504/IJPSPM.2019.099094

Sousa, B., & Silva, J. (2015). The Brand Management: A perspective applied in the context of sports media. *International Journal of Marketing. Communication and New Media*, *4*(3), 118–133.

Spence, M., & Essoussi, L. H. (2010). SME brand building and management: An exploratory chapter. *European Journal of Marketing*, *44*(7/8), 1037–1054. doi:10.1108/03090561011047517

Speziale, G. (2015). Strategic management of a healthcare organization: engagement, behavioural indicators, and clinical performance. European Heart Journal Supplements, 17(A). doi:10.1093/eurheartjuv003

Spiller, L. D., & Wymer, W. W. Jr. (2001). Physicians' Perceptions and Uses of Commercial Drug Information Sources. *Health Marketing Quarterly*, *19*(1), 91–106. doi:10.1300/J026v19n01_07 PMID:11727295

Spiro, R. L., & Weitz, B. A. (1990). Adaptive selling: Conceptualization, measurement, and nomological validity. *JMR, Journal of Marketing Research*, *27*(1), 61–69. doi:10.1177/002224379002700106

Sprott, D., Czellar, S., & Spangenberg, E. (2009). The importance of a general measure of brand engagement on market behavior: Development and validation of a scale. *JMR, Journal of Marketing Research*, *46*(February), 92–104. doi:10.1509/jmkr.46.1.92

Srivastava, N. V., & Mookerjee, A. (2004). Determinants of brand equity for banking business application software products. *International Journal of Technology Management*, *28*(1), 128–138. doi:10.1504/IJTM.2004.005057

Srivastava, R. K., Fahey, L., & Christensen, H. K. (2001). The resource-based view and marketing: The role of market-based assets in gaining competitive advantage. *Journal of Management*, *27*(6), 777–802. doi:10.1177/014920630102700610

Steele, S. R., Arshad, S., Bush, R., Dasani, S., Cologne, K., Bleier, J. I., Raphaeli, T., & Kelz, R. R. (2015). Social media is a necessary component of surgery practice. *Surgery*, *158*(3), 857–862. doi:10.1016/j.surg.2015.06.002

Stelzner, M. A. (2014). *2014 Social Media Report*. Social Media Examiner. Available at: https://www.socialmediaexaminer.com/SocialMediaMarketingIndustryReport2014.pdf

Steptoe, A., Deaton, A., & Stone, A. A. (2015). Subjective wellbeing, health, and ageing. *Lancet*, *385*(9968), 640–648. doi:10.1016/S0140-6736(13)61489-0 PMID:25468152

Sternberg, R. (1986). A triangular theory of love. *Psychological Review*, *93*(2), 119–135. doi:10.1037/0033-295X.93.2.119

Stevenson, R., & Moore, D. E. Jr. (2018). Ascent to the Summit of the CME PyramidDefining Outcomes for CME ActivityDefining Outcomes for CME Activity. *Journal of the American Medical Association*, *319*(6), 543–544. doi:10.1001/jama.2017.19791 PMID:29356817

Stremersch, S. (2008). Health and marketing: The emergence of a new field of research. *International Journal of Research in Marketing*, *25*(4), 229–233. doi:10.1016/j.ijresmar.2008.09.002

Strombom, B. A., Buchmueller, T. C., & Feldstein, P. J. (2002). Switching costs, price sensitivity and health plan choice. *Journal of Health Economics*, *21*(1), 89–116. doi:10.1016/S0167-6296(01)00124-2 PMID:11845927

Stros, M., & Lee, N. (2015). Marketing dimensions in the prescription pharmaceutical industry: A systematic literature review. *Journal of Strategic Marketing*, *23*(4), 318–336. doi:10.1080/0965254X.2014.931878

Stuart, H., & Muzellec, L. (2004). Corporate makeovers : Can a hyena be rebranded? *Journal of Brand Management, 11*(July), 472–482. Advance online publication. doi:10.1057/palgrave.bm.2540193

Sudovar, B. (1992). Branding in the Pharmaceutical Industry. In J. M. Murphy (Ed.), *Branding: A Key Marketing Tool* (pp. 130–137). Palgrave Macmillan UK. doi:10.1007/978-1-349-12628-6_13

Suess, C., Baloglu, S., & Busser, J. A. (2018). Perceived impacts of medical tourism development on community wellbeing. *Tourism Management, 69*, 232–245. doi:10.1016/j.tourman.2018.06.006

Superbock Group. (n.d.). Obtido de https://www.superbockgroup.com/detalhe/about-the-group/

Szabó, A. (n.d.). Hungary the leading elite in Medical tourism. Medical tourism and spas in Hungary. *Hungarian Tourism Plc.*

T&L. (2013). *Plan de negocios para el subsector de Turismo de Bienestar en Colombia.* T&L Tourism Leisure and Sports, Europraxis, Grupo Aviatur.

Targis, P. W. (2001). *The role of advertising in branding pharmaceuticals.* Academic Press.

Tat news. (2013). *World Travel Market (WTM) 2012.* Tailandia: Tourism Authority of Thailand Newsroom. Available in: https://www.tatnews.org/world-travel-market-wtm-2012/

Tevi, A. C., & Otubanjo, O. (2013). Understanding Corporate Rebranding. *An Evolution Theory Perspective, 5*(3), 87–93. doi:10.5539/ijms.v5n3p87

Thailand Med Tourism. (2013). *Thailand's Medical Tourism Statistics: A Look at the International Patient Numbers.* Available in: http://www.thailandmedtourism.com/NewsArticleDetail/108/8856/Thailands-Medical-Tourism-Statistics-A-Look-at-the-International-Patient-Numbers

The future of medicine. (2012, June 2). The Economist.

Thom, D. H., Kravitz, R. L., Bell, R. A., Krupat, E., & Azari, R. (2002). Patient trust in the physician: Relationship to patient requests. *Family Practice, 19*(5), 476–483. doi:10.1093/fampra/19.5.476 PMID:12356698

Thomke, S. (2019). *The magic that makes customer experiences stick.* MIT- Management Review.

Time Out. (2016). Obtido de Time Out: http://timeout.pt

Tota, I., & Shehu, H. (2012). The Dilemma of Business Ethics. *Procedia Economics and Finance, 3*, 555–559. doi:10.1016/S2212-5671(12)00195-5

Tranfield, D., Denyer, D., & Smart, P. (2003). Towards a methodology for developing evidence-informed management knowledge by means of systematic review. *British Journal of Management, 14*(3), 207–222. doi:10.1111/1467-8551.00375

Treatmentabroad. (2014). *The healthcare system and hospital facilities in the USA.* Treatmentabroad. Available in: http://www.treatmentabroad.com/destinations/usa/travel-and-accommodation-0

Treatmentabroad. (n.d.). Why consider Spain for medical tourism? Spain: TreatmenAbroad.com Available in: http://www.treatmentabroad.com/destinations/spain/why-choose-spain (10.05.2018).

Tresidder, R. (2011). 19 Health and Medical Tourism. *Research Themes f or Tourism*, 266.

Trong Tuan, L. (2014). Clinical governance, corporate social responsibility, health service quality, and brand equity. *Clinical Governance: An International Journal, 19*(3), 215–234. doi:10.1108/CGIJ-02-2014-0007

Trucco, M. Y., & Amirkhanova, S. (2006). *Transforming Pharmaceutical Marketing Through e-detailing: Case Studies and Recommendations.* Paper presented at the 8th IEEE International Conference on E-Commerce Technology and the 3rd IEEE International Conference on Enterprise Computing, E-Commerce, and E-Services (CEC/EEE'06).

Tsakiridou, E., Boutsouki, C., Zotos, Y., & Mattas, K. (2008). Attitudes and behaviour towards organic products: An exploratory study. *International Journal of Retail & Distribution Management*, *36*(2), 158–175. doi:10.1108/09590550810853093

Tsimonis, G., & Dimitriadis, S. (2014). Brand strategies in social media. *Marketing Intelligence & Planning*, *32*(3), 328–344. doi:10.1108/MIP-04-2013-0056

Tumbat, G., & Belk, R. (2011). Marketplace tensions in extraordinary experiences. *The Journal of Consumer Research*, *38*(1), 42–61. doi:10.1086/658220

Turismo Argentina. (2014). *Turismo Salud, Productos Turísticos*. http://www.turismo.gov.ar/

Turkeyhealthguide. (2011). *You're invited to Turkey for medical tourism.* turkeyhealthguide.com. Available in: http://www.turkeyhealthguide.com/you_are_invited_to_turkey_for_medical_tourism.asp (09.05.18).

Ukoha, C., & Stranieri, A. (2019). Criteria to Measure Social Media Value in Health Care Settings: Narrative Literature Review. *Journal of Medical Internet Research*, *21*(12), e14684. doi:10.2196/14684

Ülkümen, G., Chakravarti, A., & Morwitz, V. G. (2010). Categories create mind-sets: The effect of exposure to broad versus narrow categorizations on subsequent, unrelated decisions. *JMR, Journal of Marketing Research*, *47*(4), 659–671. doi:10.1509/jmkr.47.4.659

Ulkuniemi, P. K., & Helander, N. M. (2005). *Marketing challenges in the software component business.* Paper presented at the 21st Industrial Marketing and Purchasing Conference, Rotterdam.

Upshaw, L. B. (1995). *Building Brand Identity: A Strategy for Success in a Hostile Marketplace*. Wiley.

Value, I., & Prescribing, F. I. (n.d.). Its Value and Role as One of Many. Academic Press.

Van Boven, L., & Gilovich, T. (2003). To do or to have? That is the question. *Journal of Personality and Social Psychology*, *85*(6), 1193–1202. doi:10.1037/0022-3514.85.6.1193 PMID:14674824

Van Doorn, J., Lemon, K. N., Mittal, V., Nass, S., Pick, D., Pirner, P., & Verhoef, P. C. (2010). Customer engagement behavior: Theoretical foundations and research directions. *Journal of Service Research*, *13*(3), 253–266. doi:10.1177/1094670510375599

Van Niekerk, M. (2014). The role of the public sector in tourism destination management from a network relationship approach. *Tourism Analysis*, *19*(6), 701–718. doi:10.3727/108354214X14146846679402

VanNieuwenborg, L., Goossens, M., De Lepeleire, J., & Schoenmakers, B. (2016). Continuing medical education for general practitioners: A practice format. *Postgraduate Medical Journal*, *92*(1086), 217–222. doi:10.1136/postgradmedj-2015-133662 PMID:26850504

Veerasoontorn, R., Beise-Zee, R., & Sivayathorn, A. (2011). Service quality as a key driver of medical tourism: The case of Bumrungrad International Hospital in Thailand. *International Journal of Leisure and Tourism Marketing*, *2*(2), 140–158. doi:10.1504/IJLTM.2011.038886

Veloutsou, C. (2007). Identifying the dimensions of the product-brand and consumer relationship. *Journal of Marketing Management*, *23*(1/2), 7–26. doi:10.1362/026725707X177892

Veloutsou, C., & Moutinho, L. (2009). Brand relationship through brand reputation and brand tribalismo. *Journal of Business Research*, *62*(3), 314–322. doi:10.1016/j.jbusres.2008.05.010

Venkatesan, R., Petersen, J. A., & Guissoni, L. (2018). Measuring and managing customer engagement value through the customer journey. In R. Palmatier, V. Kumar, & C. Harmeling (Eds.), *Customer Engagement Marketing* (pp. 53–74). Palgrave Macmillan. doi:10.1007/978-3-319-61985-9_3

Ventola, C. L. (2014). Social media and health care professionals: Benefits, risks, and best practices. *P&T*, *39*(7), 491.

Ver Portugal. (2015). Obtido de Ver Portugal: http://www.verportugal.net

Verbeke, W., Dietz, B., & Verwaal, E. (2011). Drivers of sales performance: A contemporary meta-analysis. Have salespeople become knowledge brokers? *Journal of the Academy of Marketing Science*, *39*(3), 407–428. doi:10.100711747-010-0211-8

Vickers, M. (2015). Is your CRM system social media friendly? *CRM Magazine*, *19*(6), 7.

Vidago Palace. (n.d.). Obtido de https://www.vidagopalace.com/pt/

Vivek, S. D., Beatty, S. E., Dalela, V., & Morgan, R. M. (2014). A generalized multidimensional scale for measuring customer engagement. *Journal of Marketing Theory and Practice*, *22*(4), 401–420. doi:10.2753/MTP1069-6679220404

Vukasovic, T. (2013). *Brand Developing Relationships Through Social Media.* Available on: http://www.toknowpress.net/ISBN/978-961-6914-02-4/papers/ML13-228.pdf

Waheed, K. A., Jaleel, M., & Laeequddin, M. (2011). Prescription loyalty behavior of physicians: An empirical study in India. *International Journal of Pharmaceutical and Healthcare Marketing*, *5*(4), 279–298. doi:10.1108/17506121111190112

Wallace, E., Buil, I., & de Chernatony, L. (2014). Consumer engagement with self-expressive brands: Brand love and WOM outcomes. *Journal of Product and Brand Management*, *23*(1), 33–42. doi:10.1108/JPBM-06-2013-0326

Walmsley, A., Thomas, R., & Jameson, S. (2012). Internships in SMEs and career intentions. *Journal of Education and Work*, *25*(2), 185–204. doi:10.1080/13639080.2011.573774

Wang, T., Huang, Z., & Gan, C. (2016). On mining latent topics from healthcare chat logs. *Journal of Biomedical Informatics*, *61*, 247–259. doi:10.1016/j.jbi.2016.04.008

Wang, Y., Rod, M., Ji, S., & Deng, Q. (2017). Social media capability in B2B marketing: Toward a definition and a research model. *Journal of Business and Industrial Marketing*, *32*(8), 1125–1135. doi:10.1108/JBIM-10-2016-0250

Wazana, A. (2000). Physicians and the pharmaceutical industry: Is a gift ever just a gift? *Journal of the American Medical Association*, *283*(3), 373–380. doi:10.1001/jama.283.3.373 PMID:10647801

What Companies are for. (2019, Aug. 22). The Economist.

Wheeler, A. (2009). Designing Brand Identity- an essential guide for the entire branding team (3aEdição). John Wiley & Sons, Inc.

Whillans, A., Dunn, E., Smeets, P., Bekkers, R., & Norton, M. (2012). Bying the time promotes happiness. *Proceedings of the National Academy of Sciences.*

WHO. (2018). *Health System Review—Portugal. Phase 1 Final Report.* WHO.

Wieringa, J. E., & Leeflang, P. S. H. (2012). Modelling the effects of promotion expenditures on sales of pharmaceuticals. *Applied Economics*, *45*(24), 3389–3399. doi:10.1080/00036846.2012.711940

Williams, J. (2006). *The Art of Rebranding*. Retrieved January 4, 2018, from https://www.entrepreneur.com/article/159470

Wind, J., Mahajan, V., & Bayless, J.L. (1990). *The role of new product models in supporting and improving the new product development process: Some preliminary results.* Cambridge, MA: The Marketing Science Institute.

Wirtz, J., den Ambtman, A., Bloemer, J., Horváth, C., Ramaseshan, B., van de Klundert, J., Canli, Z. G., & Kandampully, J. (2013). Managing brands and customer engagement in online brand communities. *Journal of Service Management, 24*(3), 223–244. doi:10.1108/09564231311326978

Wocher, J. (2009). *Japan lags behind.* Retrieved from http:/ /www.imtj.com/articles/2008/japan-lags-behind

Wong, A., & Sohal, A. (2002). An examination of the relationship between trust, commitment and relationship quality. *International Journal of Retail & Distribution Management, 30*(1), 34–50. doi:10.1108/09590550210415248

Wong, H. Y., & Merrilees, B. (2005). A brand orientation typology for SMEs: A case research approach. *Journal of Product and Brand Management, 14*(3), 155–162. doi:10.1108/10610420510601021

Woodman, J. (2010). *The Top 10 Medical Travel Destinations.* Internationalliving. Available in: https://internationalliving.com/2010/06/the-top-10-medical-travel-destinations/

World Health Organization. (2011). *Global health and aging.* Retrieved from https://www.who.int/ageing/publications/global_health.pdf

World Health Organization. (2015). *World Report on Ageing and Health.* WHO.

World Health Organization. (2019). World Health Organization model list of essential medicines: 21st list 2019. Geneva: World Health Organization.

Wu, S., & Fang, W. (2010). The effect of consumer-to-consumer interactions on idea generation in virtual brand community relationships. *Technovation, 30*(4), 238–248. doi:10.1016/j.technovation.2010.07.005

Yakar, F., Jacobs, R., & Agarwal, N. (2019). The current usage of Instagram in neurosurgery. *Interdisciplinary Neurosurgery: Advanced Techniques and Case Management, 19*, 100553. doi:10.1016/j.inat.2019.100553

Yin, R. K. (2009). *Case Chapter Research: Design and Methods* (4th ed.). Sage Publications.

Yoo, B., & Donthu, N. (2001). Developing and validating a multi-dimensional consumer based brand equity scale. *Journal of Business Research, 10*(1), 61–67. doi:10.1016/S0148-2963(99)00098-3

Yoo, B., Donthu, N., & Lee, S. (2000). An Examination of Seiected Marketing Mix ELements and Brand Equity. *Journal of the Academy of Marketing Science, 28*(2), 195–211. doi:10.1177/0092070300282002

You, X., & O'leary, J. T. (1999). Destination behaviour of older UK travellers. *Tourism Recreation Research, 1*(24), 23–34. doi:10.1080/02508281.1999.11014854

Zaglia, M. E. (2013). Brand communities embedded in social networks. *Journal of Business Research, 66*(2), 216–223. doi:10.1016/j.jbusres.2012.07.015 PMID:23564989

Zauberman, G., Rebecca, K. R., & Kim, K. B. (2009). Memories as assets: Strategic memory protection in choice over time. *The Journal of Consumer Research, 35*(5), 715–728. doi:10.1086/592943

Zeithaml, V. A. (1988). Consumer Perceptions of Price, Quality and Value: A Means-End Model Synthesis of Evidence. *Journal of Marketing, 52*(July), 2–22. doi:10.1177/002224298805200302

Zeithaml, V. A., Berry, L. L., & Parasuraman, A. (1996). The Behavioral Consequences of Stroke. *The Behavioral Consequences of Serviece Quality, 60*(April), 31–46. doi:10.1007/978-1-4614-7672-6

Zhang, M., Guo, L., Hu, M., & Liu, W. (2017). Influence of customer engagement with company social networks on stickiness: Mediating effect of customer value creation. *International Journal of Information Management*, *37*(3), 229–240. doi:10.1016/j.ijinfomgt.2016.04.010

Zhong, Y. Y., Busser, J., & Baloglu, S. (2017). A model of memorable tourism experience: The effects on satisfaction, affective commitment, and storytelling. *Tourism Analysis*, *22*(2), 201–217. doi:10.3727/108354217X14888192562366

Ziegler, M. G., Lew, P., & Singer, B. C. (1995). The Accuracy of Drug Information From Pharmaceutical Sales Representatives. *Journal of the American Medical Association*, *273*(16), 1296–1298. doi:10.1001/jama.1995.03520400066047 PMID:7715044

Zielke, S. (2011). Integrating Emotions in the Analysis of Retail Price Images. *Psychology & Marketing*, *28*(4), 330–359. doi:10.1002/mar

Zielke, S. (2010). How price image dimensions influence shopping intentions for different store formats. *European Journal of Marketing*, *44*(6), 748–770. doi:10.1108/03090561011032702

About the Contributors

Ana Pinto Borges has a PhD in Economics, Faculty of Economics, University of Porto. Economic Degree in Lusíada University - North. Coordinating Professor at ISAG - European Business School (ISAG) since 2010, President of the Pedagogical Council since 2015 and has been the Executive Coordinator of the ISAG Research Center (NIDISAG) since 2014. She is the author of more than 30 publications in scientific journals with peer review and indexed in the various international databases (Web of Science - Clarivate Analytics, Scopus, among others). Participation in presentations in various national and international congresses and member of the Scientific Commissions and Organizing Committees in academic events. Editor and one of the founding members of the academic journal European Journal of Applied Business and Management (EJABM). She was consultant at Accenture in the financial area. Economist at the Portuguese Healthcare Regulation Authority since 2010. More information available at: https://sites.google.com/site/anapintoborges/.

Paula Rodrigues holds a Ph.D. in Management, in Faculty of Economics at the University of Porto, Portugal. She is an Associate Professor in Brand Management at the School of Economics and Management, Lusíada University - North, Portugal. Since 1995, she teaches Brand Management, Consumer Behaviour, Econometrics, Statistic, and Quantitative Methods at the Lusíada University - North. She has published several scientific papers, chapters, and books. Her on-going research projects concern consumer-brand relationships in the field of luxury, tourism, and hospitality, and consumer goods.

* * *

Gisela Maria Maia Alves was Master in Marketing and Strategic Management and PhD in Marketing and Strategy at the School of Economics and Management at the University of Minho (EEG) and professor and researcher in the Marketing area. Gisela Alves participated in several annual EMAB conferences with the presentation of research topics, having won in 2018 the best paper. In 2019, he suffered from prolonged illness and his projects and his promising career were tragically interrupted.

Amélia Brandão is graduated in Enterprises Management from the Universidade Portucalense Infante D. Henrique, Porto, in 1995. She holds a Master degree in Finance from the Universidade Portucalense Infante D. Henrique, 2003. She has a Ph.D. graduation at the Faculdade de Economia do Porto (FEP) in the Brand Management valuation. Presently she is lecturer of Marketing and Brand Management subjects at FEP, since 2004. Additionally she is teaching Managerial Communication, Strategy Communication and Marketing at Faculdade de Letras da Universidade do Porto, since 2008 until present. She is invited teacher at Porto Business School (PBS) in Integrated Communication of Marketing subjects in Post-graduate courses since 2006 until present. Scientific Committee member of the International Journal of Marketing, Communication and New Media. Her previous work experience was in brand communication consultancy at Associação Nacional de Jovens Empresários (ANJE), Associação Empresarial de Portugal (AEP), Markamos and XZ Consultores. She was coordinator and trainer for various projects and was senior consultant in micro enterprises (Formação e Ação em Micro Empresas -Fame project). She was Supervisor of Work Placements and Assistant Teacher at Universidade Portucalense Infante D. Henrique, 1995-2005, in undergraduate course, of Managerial Communication, Marketing Research, Brand Management and Marketing Management subjects. From 2000 to 2004 she was Visiting Assistant Teacher at Faculdad de Ciencias Economicas y Empresariales, Universidad de Sevilla, in Marketing Undergraduate course.

Ana Brochado is a professor of management at the ISCTE-IUL-Instituto Universitário de Lisboa - Lisbon University Institute and a researcher at DINAMIA'CET-Centre for Socioeconomic and Territorial Studies. She served as the Vice Dean for administrative affairs and Vice Dean for faculty for five years and coordinated the Ph.D. in Tourism Management. She worked for more than one decade as Senior Economist for the Portuguese Competition Authority and the Securities Commission. She joined the Strategic Board of Compete2020. She has a Bachelor of Science in Economics, a Master of Science in Quantitative Methods, and a Doctor of Management. Her main research interests are market research, hospitality and tourism management, Fintech, sustainability management, and innovation. She has authored or co-authored over 50 publications in top international journals in these fields, wrote over 40 book chapters, and presented over 200 talks in international conferences. Her research received over 1000 citations.

Jose Antonio Fraiz is a professor and researcher at the University of Vigo. Director of the Master's Degree in Management and Planning of Interior and Health Tourism. Director of the EMITUR Research Group (Marketing and Tourism).

Punam Gupta is Principal of Career College, Bhopal. She worked as Associate Professor for over 35 years at Dev Samaj College for Women, Chandigarh. She is a scholar in English literature and linguistics, and was awarded the gold medal during her BA Hons (English) and again for obtaining the first position in Panjab University in MA (English). She has written several papers and has published books on English as well as co-authored a book on Rural Marketing.

Dinesh Kumar (PhD) is Associate Professor at Jagran Lakecity University, Bhopal. He has corporate experience for over 15 years after which he switched to teaching in 1995. He has taught at leading business schools in India. He has travelled widely and has published and presented many papers. He is the author of four major books on Marketing, including Marketing Channels (2012) and Consumer Behavior (2015), both published by Oxford University Press, `The Connected Consumer published by Business Expert Press, New York, and Rural Marketing, which has been published by Sage (2017).

André Lopes is a master's student of the Faculty of Economics at the University of Porto.

Preeti Nayal is a Fellow (Ph.D.) student at NITIE Mumbai. Her research interests are Digital Marketing and Marketing Analytics.

Neeraj Pandey is Associate Professor of Marketing at NITIE Mumbai. He did his Post-Doc at Johns Hopkins University, USA in the area of healthcare pricing. He has authored two Books besides publications in reputed international journals. His research and teaching interests are Pricing, Digital Marketing and B2B Marketing.

Ajit Parulekar has nineteen years of experience in academics and as a brand manager in the pharmaceuticals sector. He has consulted with the Government of Goa, IndiaPost, UNDP and many private sector organisations. He has published books, chapters, cases and journal articles. He is visiting faculty at S.P. Jain, Mumbai and Antwerp Management School, Belgium. His areas of interest are Branding, Consumer Behaviour, Marketing Strategy and Healthcare Financing.

Harindranath R. M. received his PhD. in Management from Anna University, Chennai in 2017. Currently, he is employed in Great Lakes Institute of Management, Chennai. His research interest are personal selling, construct development & structural equation modelling. He has published in International journal of Pharmaceutical and Healthcare marketing, Journal of Business and Industrial Marketing, Journal of Promotion Management, and Management Research and Review. He worked in marketing function with Schering AG pharmaceutical for over 15 years.

Ana Maria Reis is an Assistant Professor of Economics at the ISAG – European Business School and a researcher of the Research Center in Business Sciences and Tourism (CICET – FCVC). She received her PhD in Economics from the Faculty of Economics, University of Coimbra, in 2017. Author of papers and book chapters published in indexed international scientific journals. Work has a peer reviewer in several journals. Her areas of interest include tourism management, tourism economics, health economics, health management, public health and health policy. Economist at the Portuguese Healthcare Regulation Authority since 2011.

Helena Rodrigues holds a PhD in Management-Specialization in Marketing at ISCTE-IUL, Lisbon, Portugal. She received the B.Sc. and M.Sc. degrees in Marketing from ISLA-Lisboa and Laureate. She has worked for global Asset Management Banks and in the Marketing Department for a Global Pharmaceutical Company. She is the Director of the Bachelor Degree in Marketing- IPAM the Marketing School and lecturers as an Invited Assistant Professor in ISCTE-IUL and an Integrated Researcher in BRU-IUL. Her main publications are in the area of Service Quality, Medical Tourism, Wellness and Thermal and Mineral Spas, Higher Education.

Paula Rodrigues holds a PhD in Management, in the Faculty of Economics at the University of Porto, Portugal. She is an Associate Professor in Brand Management at the School of Economics and Management, Lusíada University - North, Portugal. Since 1995, she teaches Brand Management, Consumer Behaviour, Econometrics, statistics, and Quantitative Methods at the Lusíada University - North. She has published several scientific papers, chapters, and books. Her on-going research projects concern consumer-brand relationships in the field of luxury, tourism and hospitality, and consumer goods.

Bharadhwaj Sivakumaran holds a PhD in Marketing from the University of Maryland, College Park and is currently Dr Bala V and Vasantha Balachandran Chair Professor of Marketing at the Great Lakes Institute of Management, Chennai, India. His work appears in leading journals such as the Journal of Academy of Marketing Science, Journal of Business Research, Journal of Advertising, European Journal of Marketing, Journal of Marketing Management, Journal of Retailing and Consumer Services, and Marketing Intelligence and Planning.

Bárbara Soares has a Degree in Law by Faculty of Law University of Porto, received in 2008, and postgraduate studies in Public Law by Faculty of Law University of Porto received in 2019. Her main areas of expertise include public law, health law, competition law and regulation. Jurist at the Portuguese Healthcare Regulation Authority since 2015.

Bruno Sousa is a Professor in Polytechnic Institute of Cavado and Ave (IPCA, Portugal) Head of Master Program - Tourism Management - PhD Marketing and Strategy. He was Market Analist at Sonae Distribuição – Modelo e Continente, S.A. (2006 to 2009) and he was Marketing Assistant - Jornal O Jogo at Controlinveste (2005) - Teaching Award of the School of Economics and Management of the University of Minho 2015/2016 - Best Thesis in Tourism Award - ICIEMC 2015 - Management Graduation, University of Minho Award - Best performance (2006) - Merit Scholarship for Students in Public Higher Education Awards of Merit Scholarship by University of Minho in 2001/02 - 2002/03 - 2003/04 Rresearch centre: CiTUR and Applied Management Research Unit (UNIAG). He is author or co-author of several papers and her research interests include tourism management, marketing and strategy. Editorial board member of several peer reviewed scientific journals and ad-hoc reviewer of several peer-reviewed scientific journals. Member of the scientific committee of several national and international congresses and conferences.

Nafisa Vaz is a faculty of Healthcare Marketing at Goa Institute of Management with an interest in Branding and Service Marketing.She has an experience of over 10 years in the area of healthcare. Her rich corporate experience is concentrated in the area of Operations and Healthcare Branding.

Noelia Araújo Vila is PhD in Tourism Management and Planning and Bachelor in Business Administration and Management. Since 2007 she collaborates in the coordination tasks of the University Master in Tourism Management and Planning and teaches as professor in the Departments of Business Organization and Marketing and Financial Economics and Accounting (University of Vigo). She participates in various research projects linked to the tourism and business sector. She is a member of the research group of the University of Vigo Emitur (Marketing and Tourism). She holds a Master in Management and Management of SMEs with a prize for the best business project.

Index

U

V

W

www.ingramcontent.com/pod-product-compliance
Lightning Source LLC
LaVergne TN
LVHW062156300926
849161LV00010B/2678

* 9 7 8 1 7 9 9 8 3 0 3 4 4 *